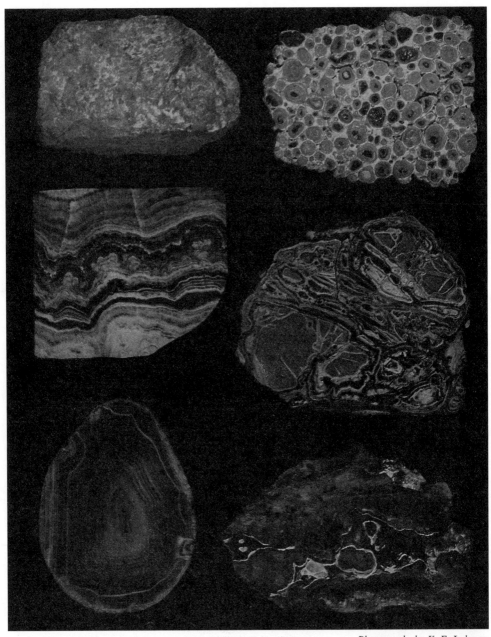

*This illustration is shown in color on the inner back cover of the book. See pp. xiii-xiv for descriptions.*

# THE ROCK BOOK

## CARROLL LANE FENTON

AND

## MILDRED ADAMS FENTON

*With an Introduction and*
*Two Supplementary Chapters by*

THOMAS H. RICH
Museum of Victoria
Melbourne, Victoria
Australia

*and*

PATRICIA VICKERS-RICH
Earth Sciences Dept. and Monash Science Centre
Monash University
Clayton, Victoria
Australia

DOVER PUBLICATIONS, INC.
MINEOLA, NEW YORK

*Bibliographical Note*

This Dover edition, first published in 2003, is an unabridged republication of the text and illustrations from the work originally published in 1940 by Doubleday & Company, Inc., Garden City, New York. The Dover edition includes, as Appendix 1 and Appendix 2, chapters II and III from *The Fossil Book: A Record of Prehistoric Life,* by Patricia Vickers-Rich, Thomas Hewitt Rich, Mildred Adams Fenton, and Carroll Lane Fenton. The color plates from the first edition of *The Rock Book* are reproduced on the outside and inside covers of the Dover edition; except for the frontispiece (shown in black and white), they are not reproduced on the book pages, but their identifying captions are listed on pages xiii–xiv. The black-and-white photographs, with full captions, are reproduced as an insert between pages 144 and 145 of the Dover edition.

*International Standard Book Number: 0-486-42267-4*

Manufactured in the United States of America
Dover Publications, Inc., 31 East 2nd Street, Mineola, N.Y. 11501

# Acknowledgments

A BOOK of this type necessarily goes far beyond the authors' own researches, which have been limited to the fields treated in Chapters XIV, XVI and part of Chapter XII. We therefore have made free use of information in technical articles and reports, as well as in standard text and reference books. Only a few of these are listed in Chapter XX, but we acknowledge our debt to many authors whose work cannot be mentioned.

Ranchmen, guides, rangers, miners and tourists, as well as geologists, have helped us to find and examine rocks in many parts of the United States and Canada. Our descriptions and discussions are based largely on the questions asked by persons who wanted to know more about the rocks to which they called our attention. The queries of teachers and students also have helped us to decide what should be told—and how.

Most of our chapters were read in manuscript by specialists in the appropriate fields. The men who thus took time from research to give this assistance are W. H. Bradley, L. W. Currier, T. A. Hendricks, W. D. Johnston, Jr, C. S. Ross, W. W. Rubey and P. D. Trask. To them we give special thanks.

Illustrations also have brought us into debt. The U.S. Geological Survey and the Bureau of Mines provided photographs used in many plates; the former is indicated by the name of the

# ACKNOWLEDGMENTS

scientist photographer and the initials U.S.G.S. Several photographs came from the National Park Service, while Dr K. E. Lohman made those for the frontispiece. Authorities of the U.S. National Museum allowed us to photograph rocks and minerals, including stones shaped and used by early man. Mr J. H. Benn, of the Museum staff, gave special assistance in selecting specimens. Without his aid many interesting things would not have come to light.

The four color plates of rocks and minerals were prepared by Mr Dmitri Kessel, staff photographer of *Life*. Used by courtesy of that magazine, these plates were received too late to be mentioned in the text and index, but are listed on page xiii.

CARROLL LANE FENTON
MILDRED ADAMS FENTON

*July, 1940*

PUBLISHER'S NOTE TO DOVER EDITION

The color illustrations appear on the outer and inner covers of the Dover edition. They are identified on pages xiii–xiv.

Carroll Lane Fenton (left) and
Mildred Adams Fenton

## INTRODUCTION TO THE DOVER EDITION

Mildred Adams Fenton and Carroll Lane Fenton spent their lives opening the eyes of millions of people—young and old—to the wonders of rocks, fossils, and all manner of natural phenomena. We became close friends of Mildred when we extensively revised *The Fossil Book* with her to bring that book up to date and internationalize it after more than thirty years of new ideas had built up in paleontology. We spent more than three years working on that book, which covered a discipline in which we were practitioners.

Mildred died on the third of December 1995, active to the last, in both mind and body, at the age of 96. Prior to her death Mildred had asked that we see to the republication of as many of the Fenton and Fenton books as we

[VII]

could—all had been very useful references for so many for so long. Tom and I both grew up relishing *The Fossil Book*.

The reissue of *The Rock Book* thus is in accord with Mildred's wish—but in this case we have not attempted to revise as we did in *The Fossil Book*. Instead, we have left the text as Mildred and Carroll wrote it, to preserve it as the historical and useful book it always has been.

Much has happened in the field of geology since the original issue of *The Rock Book*. In 1940 the concept of moving continents was supported by only a few geologists, while plate tectonics, encompassing the idea that the upper part of the Earth's crust was divided into a number of thin plates that changed shape depending on what went on along their edges, had not even been thought of. It was only in the 1960s that Vine and Matthews and Tuzo Wilson, along with many others, proposed such ideas, which would have been radical at the time when *The Rock Book* first was published. Those ideas had great impact on our understanding of where and under what conditions rocks and minerals form. For this reason, we have incorporated in the new edition of *The Rock Book* two chapters that were written for *The Fossil Book,* to explain not only the concepts of mobile continents but also something about the major groups of rocks and something about how rocks are dated. Otherwise, we have not tried to revise *The Rock Book* extensively. It is a classic in its own right.

Had there been more time for revising and more space in *The Rock Book* we would have pointed out in detail how certain kinds of minerals and mineral suites, as well as rock types, form in particular places on Earth. These places are related to where on those great crustal plates such rocks and minerals formed. Serpentinite, for example, forms along the great crustal slabs that are being thrust beneath other crustal slabs, such as in the Franciscan sequence along the west coast of California, where the Pacific Plate is underthrusting the North American continent. The active volcanoes, like Mount St. Helens and the great mountain of Japan, Fuji, with their particular suite of rocks and minerals, form as parts of the sinking slab heat up as it moves beneath North America or the Archipelago of Japan.

Excellent books on these topics abound, and two that give extensive further references are one by Kenneth Hamblin (*The Earth's Dynamic Systems: A Textbook in Geology,* published by Macmillan Publishing Company in several editions, our favorite being the 5th edition, 1985) and a more recent work by Philip Kearey and Frederick J. Vine (*Global Tectonics,* 1996, Blackwell Science). Another very comprehensive and readable book on rocks and minerals, including where and how they form, which is lavishly illustrated, is Lin Sutherland's *Gemstones of the Southern Continents,* published by Reed (Sydney, Australia), in 1991. This book discusses rocks and minerals of the great southern land, Gondwana, unlike most books on rocks and minerals, which have a Northern Hemisphere bias. Also interesting is, *The Geology and Origin of Australia's Mineral Deposits,* by Solomon and Groves, published by the University of Western Australia in Perth, 1996.

Besides the information in such publications, much is available on the Internet by using one of the common search engines and inputting the name of the rock or mineral of interest. Even with all that has happened since the 1940s and the ready access to information in cyberspace, *The Rock Book* still stands as an excellent starting point for getting to know the rocks and minerals that make up this great ball of rocks on which we live, the Earth.

Patricia Vickers-Rich
Thomas H. Rich
July 4, 2001

# Contents

# CONTENTS

PUBLISHER'S NOTE TO DOVER EDITION

Between pages 144 and 145 are 48 numbered plates with 109 captioned reproductions of photographs of rocks and minerals. Reference is made to these plates frequently throughout the text, and the plate numbers are given in the index under the names of the minerals shown in the photographs.

The names of many countries and areas of the world have changed since *The Rock Book* was published in 1940. For example, in the book are found references to locations in Ceylon (now Sri Lanka) and Rhodesia (Northern Rhodesia now is Zambia; Southern Rhodesia now is Zimbabwe).

**List of Color Illustrations***

Except as otherwise noted, the original color
photographs are by Dmitri Kessel.

1   LIMONITE. This mineral is chemically the same as iron rust. The botryoidal (kidney-shaped) mass is iridescent. Shasta County, California. (*back cover, left*)

2.  CALCITE WITH RHODONITE. Cleavage blocks of white calcite with crystals of rhodonite, a pink mineral containing manganese. Both are gangue (see page 320) in the zinc deposits at Franklin, New Jersey. (*back cover, center*)

3.  PYRITE. Crystals of pyrite, or "fool's gold," have a pale, brassy color and are harder than gold. Bingham County, Utah. (*back cover, right*)

4.  ANTHRACITE. A film on the surface of this anthracite makes it iridescent; this is the source of its common name, "peacock coal." Notice the layers and the conchoidal fracture. Carbondale, Pennsylvania. (*inside front cover, illustration 4*)

5.  ASBESTOS. Asbestos filling a vein in serpentine rock. Mineralogically, asbestos is chrysotile, a variety of serpentine. (*inside front cover, illustration 5*)

6.  MICROCLINE. Richly colored crystals of green microcline, or Amazon stone, from Pike's Peak, Colorado. (Compare the specimens shown in black and white on Plate 8.) (*inside front cover, illustration 6*)

7.  NATIVE COPPER. A nugget of native copper from Houghton County, Michigan. Such copper was mined by ancient Indians. (*inside front cover, illustration 7*)

8.  VELVET MALACHITE. "Velvet" malachite consists of needle-shape crystals arranged in clusters and mats. The mineral looks like velvet. Bisbee, Arizona. (*inside front cover, illustration 8*)

9.  AZURITE AND MALACHITE. Crystals of azurite (blue) and crusts of malachite (green) on limonite. The first two minerals are important copper ores. Bisbee, Arizona. (*inside front cover, illustration 9*)

10. NEPHELITE SYENITE. This nephelite syenite contains blue sodalite and a related yellow mineral. Nephelite syenite sometimes is called princess marble. Litchfield, Maine. (*inside front cover, illustration 10*)

* See covers of book

[XIII]

11. WULFENITE. The red crystals of the mineral wulfenite are on a partly crystalline mass of the same material. A comparison of this with the yellow specimen of wulfenite (illustration 2, shown on the outer front cover, upper right) indicates how much one mineral can vary in color. Yuma County, Arizona. (*inside front cover, illustration 11*)

12. CINNABAR OR MERCURY ORE, Nevada. (*inside back cover, illustration 12*; also shown in black and white as part of the frontispiece; original color photograph by K. E. Lohman)

13. CAVE ONYX, Mexico. (*inside back cover, illustration 13*; also shown in black and white as part of the frontispiece; original color photograph by K. E. Lohman)

14. BANDED AGATE, Germany. (*inside back cover, illustration 14*; also shown in black and white as part of the frontispiece; original color photo by K. E. Lohman)

15. PISOLITES OF HEMATITE AND LIMONITE, Australia. (*inside back cover, illustration 15*; also shown in black and white as part of the frontispiece; original color photograph by K. E. Lohman)

16. NODULE OF VARISCITE AND OTHER MINERALS, Nevada. (*inside back cover, illustration 16*; also shown in black and white as part of the frontispiece; original color photograph by K. E. Lohman)

17. AZURITE AND PYROLUSITE, Arizona. (*inside back cover, illustration 17*; also shown in black and white as part of the frontispiece; original color photograph by K. E. Lohman)

# Line Illustrations

# LINE ILLUSTRATIONS

PUBLISHER'S NOTE TO DOVER EDITION

In Appendix 1 and Appendix 2 are 22 additional line illustrations. They originally
were published in Chapters II and III of the first edition of *The Fossil Book* (1958).

CHAPTER I

# Rocks in Our World

MAN does not live by bread alone; he exists on, by and because of rocks. The planet earth, which is his home, is nothing more than a huge, bulging ball of rock, partly covered by water and surrounded by a mixture of gases known as the atmosphere. We human beings inhabit continents and islands, where rocks form a solid surface. We also use a great number of substances from that surface, as we shall see further on in this chapter and especially in Chapter XIX.

But, you may say, this does not prove that we live because of rocks. After all, we need water and air in order to exist, food in order to grow. Yet that food contains materials which ultimately came from rocks, and some of these rock materials are essential to both life and growth. As for air and water: both are parts of our planet and were partly derived from volcanic eruptions. They also would fly away into space if the rocky part of the earth did not hold them where they are.

## ROCKS HAVE IMPORTANT QUALITIES

Their power to hold things, called attraction, is one very important property of rocks. If we use its familiar name of gravity, we recognize it as the force that makes organized ex-

istence of any sort possible. It makes the earth follow the sun
as it travels among the other stars at the rate of 13 miles per
second. It keeps our special system of stars in place amid systems
of star clouds and clusters which pass us with speeds that reach
1200 miles per minute. At the other extreme, it keeps us right
side up and on land while our footing whirls round and round
in the endless cycle of day and night. It also pulls chips of rocks
from cliffs, forces dust to settle after high winds and makes sand
grains sink in quiet water. In doing so it produces new rocks
of the type described in Chapters X and XI.

Another quality of rocks—at least of most rocks—is stiffness,
or rigidity. Without it our planet could not keep its shape and
could have neither the high places which are land nor the low
ones under oceans. An earth built of sand would fly into pieces;
a planet composed of clay would soon spread out into a biscuit-
shaped lump with a thin rim at the equator. But the great
majority of rocks are neither loose sand nor soft clay; some,
indeed, are as rigid as steel. Thanks to this, our planet keeps its
almost spherical shape, with the irregularities that produce
continents, islands and oceans.

In fact, rigidity does much more than this. It allows the hard
rocks to break and hold their shape while they are being pushed
upward into mountains like the Tetons, the Sierra Nevada and
many ranges of the Southwestern deserts. Rigidity also enables
rocks to hold their shape when they are worn into "needles"
(PLATE 19) or overhanging canyon walls like those shown on
PLATE 27.

Though they are hard, rocks can be squeezed and bent: a
third quality that means a great deal in the earth's development.
A planet whose crust could neither squeeze nor bend would
have to break whenever stress became intense. It therefore
would have a great many earthquakes and mountains like the
Tetons, but it would have none resembling the Appalachians,
the Coast Ranges of California or the Alps. There also would
be little, if any, of the slow sinking that has let seas spread across

land many times in the past and is allowing our Atlantic coast to sink today, so that salt water floods the valleys of such rivers as the Potomac, the Delaware and the Hudson.

Quite as important is the fact that rock melts, especially when it contains water, forming the fluid we generally call lava but which should be called magma. Some magmas work their way to the surface, where they make volcanoes or lava flows. Other magmas do not quite come to the surface, but they do rise high enough to push up some mountains and fill the cores of others. A great deal of North America and some of its highest mountains consist of magma that worked upward from great depths but cooled before it could erupt. Earth movements raised these masses still higher long after they became hard.

Rocks break, bend, melt and harden; they also go to pieces and dissolve. Because they do so, hills are worn down and mountains crumble, while the stony mesas of deserts slowly turn into sand. All this changes the earth's surface; it also provides vast quantities of rubbish which are carried here and there, are dropped and turn into new rocks. Clays, shales, sandstones and conglomerates are formed by this rubbish from older rocks; so, for the most part, are soils. Chert, limestone and much iron ore, however, consist of material that was dissolved and deposited again—often in roundabout ways. Even lavas may contain a good deal of made-over rock which became part of the molten stone as it worked its way toward the surface. Had that rock not been remade, or had it been a different sort of rock, the lava would not look as it does nor contain the same minerals.

## ROCKS CONTROL LIVING THINGS

Rocks decide what shape the earth shall have, how its outer part shall shift and what its surface shall look like. They also determine what plants and animals shall do on this planet, telling where, when and how they may live.

Does this seem to be an exaggeration? Then recall that every

[ 3 ]

living thing must have water, which fills holes, channels or basins in rocks. Plants can turn water into food, but they also need minerals that come from dissolved, broken rocks. Animals, which feed upon plants, get most of their mineral foods already prepared; but this does not mean that they can do without them. Even the lion, which eats only meat, depends on substances that zebras or antelopes get by eating plants and that plants, in their turn, can prepare only by getting water and dissolved minerals from the broken, decayed rock known as soil.

Homes are almost as important as food, and they also are formed by rocks of varying sizes and kinds. Some seaweeds must live on sandy bottoms which are formed by millions of small grains. Others fasten themselves to boulders along the shore, among snails, shelled worms and other animals that would die if they tried to exist on sand. Land animals also need special kinds of ground. Thus the prairie dog must burrow in loose earth, but the pika would soon fall prey to hawks without large broken stones among which to hide. Mountain goats would be almost helpless on prairies of the Middle West, but they get along very well among the northern mountains where rocks form ledges on which they can rest and where high valleys provide places to graze.

Land plants depend on their homes even more closely. In Iowa and Illinois melting glaciers piled up long ridges of clay that formed the shores of ancient lakes. Winds then heaped hillocks, or dunes of sand on the ridges. Today the lakes are gone, but elms and maples grow on the clay, while cacti of the type called prickly pear live among the sand hills. Seldom does an elm stand on the dunes, and never does a cactus grow on the compact, bouldery clay. In the Sand Hills of Nebraska there are cacti, Russian thistles and yuccas, but where the sand ends we find grassy prairie with "bottoms" where box elders and wild plums grow. Equally great contrasts may be seen in other parts of the country and even on single hillsides whose rocks vary from bottom to top.

## ROCKS IN OUR WORLD

In short, about the only living things that do not depend on the rock beneath them are those that swim or float in the open sea. Even they use minerals that have been dissolved from the land and carried out to sea by rivers.

## MAN'S THREE AGES OF STONE

Plants and animals depend on rocks, and we share their dependence. It is true that we are not limited to sand, limestone or granite for our homes nor are we helpless in places where stones are very large, very small or arranged in some inconvenient way. On the other hand, we use more kinds of rocks and get more substances from them than do any other living things. In fact, we have reached such a state that our civilization would go to pieces if we could not find a constant supply of rocks and minerals that meant little or nothing to the first-known human beings. Viewed from this angle, human progress becomes a story of increasing dependence on rocks and substances that are found in them.

Let us sketch this story very briefly. The first human being— still unknown—probably lived in a cave or under a fallen tree. He ate fruit and small animals that he was able to catch with his hands. Sometimes he used a sharp stick instead, or a broken piece of stone that he found on a gravel bank. When his prey was killed he dropped the stone and promptly forgot about it.

His descendants were more observant. They noticed that some stones were better than others, the best being those that were hard and that had very sharp edges. Soon these men began to break lumps of flint or quartzite, saving the sharpest pieces and those of convenient size. Thus the Eolithic, or "Dawn-Stone," Age began. Unfortunately for our knowledge of it, the broken stones (eoliths) were so much like those produced when rivers pound cobbles together that the two seldom can be distinguished.

As centuries—hundreds of centuries—passed, men learned to chip stone into axes, spears, knives and other useful things

[5]

that distinguished the Paleolithic, or Old Stone, Age. Still
later, artistic individuals found that pictures could be scratched
on slabs of shale or painted on the limestone walls of caverns
in which they lived. Those pictures still decorate the caves,
while tools and weapons of flint are buried in the clay that
settled on the cavern floors.

Even in paleolithic times, which ended about 10,000 years
ago, a few little statues were carved from soapstone, shale or
ivory and were smoothed or polished. In the Neolithic Age
workmen began to polish knives, daggers, axes and even ornaments of stone, though they also made tools by the old method
of chipping. Thus the old-time Indians polished pipes, ornaments, ceremonial knives, awls and even hammers, while they
were quite content to chip arrow and spear heads, everyday
knives and the crude hoes with which their wives worked in the
gardens.

As knowledge of chipping, carving and polishing grew,
more and more kinds of stone were used. Eolithic man had been
satisfied with chips of quartzite or flint. Neolithic man used
both of these, as well as basalt, sandstone, hard shale, limestone,
soapstone, volcanic glass, granite, jade and a variety of other
substances. Specially desirable materials sometimes were traded
from tribe to tribe; more often Stone Age man traveled long
distances to get what he wanted or needed. Thus Mound Builders of Ohio went to the Yellowstone country for obsidian, while
soapstone was carried many miles from places where it was
quarried. On the other hand, Indians of central Arkansas made
arrow and spear heads of novaculite, which was found in the
hills where they lived. The stone which they found suitable
for spears is now quarried for high-grade oilstones that are
shipped throughout the world.

For many years it was supposed that pottery was not invented
until late in the Neolithic, or New Stone, Age; but discoveries
made in Egypt seem to prove that paleolithic men shaped clay
into pottery and baked it 14,000 to 15,000 years ago. In 1925

some burned clay statuettes were found with chipped stone weapons in southern Moravia. This is a region where tribes that lived in skin tents hunted mammoths and wild horses not long after the end of the Ice Age. If the statuettes are as old as they seem, they show that men knew how to mold and harden clay long before they learned to polish stone. Yet clay was not much used before 5700 B.C., when the Chaldeans made both brick and tile.

## COPPER, BRONZE AND IRON

Copper is the only metal that is common in the pure, or "native," state, and it was the first one to be used. Green glazed beads and powdered malachite, a green copper mineral, have been found with the Egyptian tools and pottery which are 14,000 to 15,000 years old. The use of copper from nuggets probably began a few centuries later. By 4800 B.C. Egyptians were working copper mines on the Sinai Peninsula, east of the Gulf of Suez. Slag dumps show that smelting was carried on. Mines in this region continued to be a source of copper until the time of Rameses III (1200 B.C.), when they apparently were abandoned. Copper was used in Babylon before 3000 B.C. and in China about 2500 B.C.

Copper is more easily shaped than stone, but it is soft and will not hold a sharp edge. About a hundred years after the Sinai mines were opened an unknown Egyptian metalworker found that by mixing tin with copper he could make the harder, more durable alloy which we know as bronze. But tin was extremely rare in Egypt and in most other parts of the ancient world. Bronze therefore did not become plentiful until about 1000 B.C., when the Phoenicians began to get tin from Britain and take it to the Mediterranean countries. Bronze made with British tin was used in swords, knives, daggers, spear points, hammers, dishes, statues and many other things. In Europe the Bronze Age lasted until about 800 B.C., but Indians of Mexico and Peru still made utensils and weapons of bronze when they were conquered by the Spaniards.

The next step, of course, was the use of iron, which also had its beginnings in remote antiquity. Iron beads, made from meteorites, have been found in neolithic graves near Cairo; iron was discovered in pyramids at Gizeh, which date from 4700 B.C. By 1000 B.C., when the Bronze Age was only well under way, many nations were skilled in ironworking. Long before Caesar invaded Gaul and Britain the Iron Age was firmly established in many parts of Asia, Africa and Europe.

As new metals were added, old ones were kept and rocks also were used. Richard the Lionhearted (1157–1199 A.D.) was a warrior of the Iron Age who knew nothing of chipped stone weapons and tools and who would have scorned a polished jade dagger. His home was a castle and his weapons were steel, which was better than flint or jade. Yet the castle walls were built of limestone, while the steel was an alloy of iron made from rocks that had settled in an ancient sea. What Richard's men could not make he bought with silver or gold secured from still other ores. He also used brass and bronze, whose tin had come from the same mines that had supplied the Phoenicians 2000 years before.

## MODERN MAN USES STONE

Modern men have kept all that Richard had and have added many other substances. During the eighteenth century coal became a dominant fuel—the crusading king and his henchmen had been happy with wood. Oil became a fuel about 1900, though it had been used for lighting since 1858 and still is important in regions which are not served by electricity or gas. Natural gas was used as fuel at Fredonia, New York, in 1821; it now is piped hundreds of miles and used for heating, cooking and industrial purposes. We still quarry granite, marble and limestone for building, but much greater amounts of limestone and shale are turned into cement for frameworks, founda-

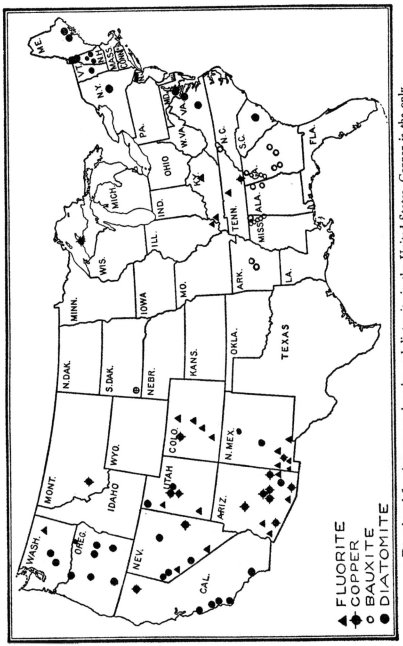

Deposits of fluorite, copper, bauxite and diatomite in the United States. Copper is the only one of these minerals and rocks that was used by ancient Indians.

tions, floors, pavements and sidewalks. Rock wool insulation, gypsum board and asbestos shingles illustrate a few of the new uses for stone materials. On the other hand, we buy newspapers with bronze coins and use 1,700,000 tons of copper per year in power lines, electric motors, plumbing fixtures and hundreds of other things. Aluminum, secured from clay, is equally important, and our lives would be difficult without mica, glass, talc, tungsten and many other rock or mineral products of which Richard the Lionhearted knew nothing. When pavements, brake linings, windows, roofs, perfumes, drugs, dyes, face powders and even food flavors are made from rocks or minerals in them, we surely cannot look down on the cave man because he, crude fellow, depended on stones!

## KNOWING ROCKS IS IMPORTANT

Rocks decide the make-up of our world and provide many of the things we need. Neither of these facts, however, means that we think a great deal about stones and related substances. Like electricity, daylight or the sky, rocks are so common that we rarely think much about them. Since they are with us always, we take them for granted; why worry about things that never are scarce? And what difference does it make whether the rocks in a hill are limestone, dolomite, quartzite or granite—whether they are shattered or are undisturbed?

What difference? A great deal, if you have bought stock in a mine that is to be dug through that hill. A great deal more, perhaps, if you want to open a quarry and crush rock for concrete work, for fertilizer on "sour" fields or for flux in steel-making. Quite as much, perhaps, if you neither run a quarry nor have money to speculate in mines. For then you may want to enjoy the earth by knowing it. For that enjoyment nothing is more essential than an adequate acquaintance with rocks in hills, on coasts and under valleys.

If you doubt that, recall the trip you took during last summer's vacation. You started from a railway station or your own garage, followed roads across prairies and among valleys to mountains, North Woods or the seashore. You enjoyed the shifting, varied scenes, but unless you knew the rocks that made them, you realized only part of their story. What spread bouldery soil across the prairie or covered some deserts with loose sand? How did the coal of Illinois form, and what were the rusty-looking ledges in cliffs that you passed in central Wyoming? Do Yosemite Falls plunge over granite? And what are the queer stones that look like columns packed on end, along roads in Yellowstone National Park? Are they anything like the "trap" of New Jersey and New England?

Such questions arise every hour as one motors across the country; their answers add much to the pleasure of every vacation trip. A knowledge of rocks also can give a sense of adventure in parks, on streets and in vacant lots. Just across the street from our apartment is a bank of clay and gravel, beyond which a path leads through woods. That bank looks commonplace, but it tells a story of streams that flowed across Maryland and Virginia some 125,000,000 years ago, while dinosaurs roamed through swamps of the West. Following the path, we come to a slope of dark, glistening rock called schist, which is ages older than the gravel. Its composition shows that this schist once was sea mud, but its thin layers and gleaming mica prove that it was tipped, crumpled and squeezed into mountains, which then were worn down to lowlands on which the clay and gravel settled.

In some places molten rock worked its way upward while the marine beds were being crumpled and changed. This molten rock hardened in narrow bands that now make ridges across the weathered slope. Other ridges consist of quartz, which was deposited along cracks by hot waters that also came up from below. Indians once used that quartz for arrowheads, while rock gardeners now seek clear white pieces to put in terraces or the borders of flower beds.

[ *11* ]

Thus a walk across vacant city lots takes us through ancient stream valleys to ancient mountains and a still more ancient sea. It traces a story of sinking, uplift and earthquakes; of molten rock that was forced upward; of rivers that overflowed as they crossed an old, degraded land. It is a story of ages, told in twenty minutes on a summer evening.

Knowledge of rocks is practical, but it also discovers adventure around the corner from anyone's home.

CHAPTER II

# Atoms to Minerals

THE SOLID PART of our earth is known as the *lithosphere*. This may seem to be a useless technical name, but it has two real virtues. First, it is a name: the only one we have for the firm part of our planet. Second, it tells what this firm part is. Lithosphere, directly translated, means a "ball of rock."

Perhaps we should say "ball of *rocks*," for the stuff that forms the lithosphere belongs to many different kinds, each with its own qualities and name. By discovering those qualities we may divide a boulder, a hill or a continent into the rock kinds, or species, of which it is composed. Such division is the first step in deciphering its story.

## ROCKS CONSIST OF MINERALS

Rocks, then, are not just rocks; they belong to different kinds, with different origins. And as everyone who has looked at granite knows, even one sort of rock may consist of several things. Thus some grains in a piece of granite are light and some are dark; some have satiny surfaces, while others resemble bits of broken glass. By trying to scratch them with a knife we learn that some are harder than others. They also show differences in color, which determine the appearance of the rock.

[ *13* ]

These substances are *minerals,* with such names as quartz, mica, feldspar and hornblende. Other minerals form still other rocks: calcite, for instance, makes up most marbles, while hematite forms much iron ore. In short, instead of dividing the lithosphere into rock species, we have carried the process one step further and have resolved it into minerals.

## ELEMENTS FORM MINERALS

May we stop with this? We may not, for minerals themselves consist of simpler substances known as elements. A few years ago an element was said to be a substance that could not be divided into anything simpler. Even then, however, it was known that such elements as uranium and radium could turn themselves into other things by shooting out some of their electrons. Man is now learning how to duplicate this achievement and someday may be able to produce elements as he wants them, as well as vast amounts of energy that are now unavailable. Thus every uranium atom that is "split" releases 175,000,000 electron volts of energy. The uranium itself can be turned into barium, antimony, iodine and about a dozen other elements. Their production, however, requires special methods and apparatus that is available in only a few laboratories. For this reason we still may say that an element is a substance that cannot be broken up into simpler materials by any practical method.

Some elements exist alone, forming such minerals as graphite, diamond and copper. The great bulk of minerals, however, contain two, three or more elements that are joined to each other in compounds. Although there are hundreds of mineral compounds (and thousands of compounds which are not minerals), they are produced by ninety-odd known elements. Some of these are very rare, while others occur in such small amounts that they mean little in the earth's make-up. Indeed, only fifteen elements constitute 99.75 per cent of the earth's outer portion, including the seas and the atmosphere. This leaves only one fourth of one per cent for all the others, which include such familiar and valuable metals as gold, silver, copper, lead and tin.

What are the common elements and how do they rank? Thousands of mineral samples have been collected from mountains, mine shafts and deep wells. Each sample has been analyzed, and the analyses have been turned into tables which tell the percentage of each element in the lithosphere's outer part, or "crust." Though the tables do not agree in details, they do show that eight of the fifteen "common" elements are much more abundant than the others. Here are the rankings of these eight, as they were determined by two leading earth chemists, Clarke and Washington:

## THE COMMON ELEMENTS

| | PER CENT |
|---|---|
| 1. Oxygen | 46.71 |
| 2. Silicon | 27.69 |
| 3. Aluminum | 8.07 |
| 4. Iron | 5.05 |
| 5. Calcium | 3.65 |
| 6. Sodium | 2.75 |
| 7. Potassium | 2.58 |
| 8. Magnesium | 2.08 |
| | 98.58 |

We have said that the fifteen principal elements form 99.75 per cent of the earth's outer part, or *crust*. Since eight of these fifteen total 98.58 per cent, only 1.17 per cent are left for the remaining seven. Figures for them are not important, but we should know their relative abundance, which is:

| 9. Titanium | 12. Hydrogen |
|---|---|
| 10. Phosphorus | 13. Manganese |
| 11. Carbon | 14. Sulphur |
| | 15. Chlorine |

Three of these fifteen elements are gases: oxygen, hydrogen and chlorine. Neither they nor the twelve solids are heavy—at least not if we compare them with such things as radium, lead or platinum. They explain why the crust of the lithosphere is comparatively light. The "core" is much heavier and denser and doubtless contains most of the earth's iron, nickel and heavier elements. Thus, while the crust contains 5.05 per cent of iron (which is 7.86 times as heavy as water), this element amounts to 39.76 per cent of the earth's core. The corresponding figures for nickel, which is heavier than iron, are 0.019 and 3.16 per cent—almost 170 times as much in the core as there is in the crust. It would be useless to compute the amounts of lead, silver, gold and platinum in the earth's core, but in the crust they amount to only 0.0008, 0.000004, 0.0000001 and 0.000000008 per cent. Although these heavy elements are important in our civilization, it is plain that they form a very small part of rocks that lie within the reach of man.

## COMMON ELEMENTS COMBINE

There are other features, aside from lightness of weight, in which the common elements resemble each other. Five—the gases, carbon and sulphur—exist alone as well as in compounds. In nature the others always are compounds. Even those which can be independent join other elements readily and so add to the ranks of the compounds. Much of earth's hydrogen is in water; oxygen is in water and solids; carbon is familiar in limestone and oil. We encounter chlorine most often in salt, while sulphur is present in compounds that form impurities in coal and marble.

We see how much this power to combine means if we glance at the formulae of a few important minerals. In these formulae each element is represented by a capital letter, or a capital and one small letter, while numerals show the number of atoms, if there are more than one. Thus the formula $SiO_2$ means that one atom of silica has joined two of oxygen; $CaCO_3$ indicates that one calcium, one carbon and three oxygen atoms have united. Though such compounds seem simple, they actually may be the results of several combinations and exchanges. We can do little more than guess at the steps involved in the production of minerals such as epidote, with the formula $H_2O.4CaO.3(Al, Fe)_2O_3.6SiO_2$, or augite, whose formula reads $CaMgSi_2O_6$ with $(Mg,Fe)$ $(Al, Fe)_2SiO_6$.

Those commas between Al and Fe and between Mg and Fe mean that either or both of these elements may be present and in variable proportions. Thus some epidotes contain much iron and less aluminum and others have much aluminum, while augite has variable amounts of magnesium, iron and aluminum in its molecules.

In spite of these differences and their many elements, minerals are not mere jumbles of atoms, just put together hit-or-miss. The fact that the chemical make-up of a mineral can be put into even a provisional formula means that the mineral has a fairly definite composition. Thus anhydrite contains one atom of calcium, one of sulphur and four atoms of oxygen, all arranged in a special way. Spodumene, sometimes found in the coarsest granites, contains one atom of lithium, one of aluminum, two atoms of silicon and six of oxygen. Take any of these away or add new atoms and the substance no longer will be spodumene. This also is true of most of the very complex minerals, whose molecules contain six to eight elements and large numbers of atoms.

In short, a mineral is a definite substance, usually with uniform chemical composition. It also is something found in non-living nature—something not produced by the skill of man nor the bodies of animals and plants. Quartz glass, carborundum and "synthetic" rubies are not regarded as minerals, for they are manufactured. Coal is ruled out on two counts: it has no definite chemical make-up, and it was formed by the partial decay of dead plants. Natural deposits of paraffin and asphalt meet similar objections, though we do not eliminate fossils in which mineral matter has replaced bones, shells or wood. We also include some minerals that began as shells or hard deposits made by simple plants. The reason is that these substances do have definite chemical composition and never actually were alive, even though they were made by living things.

From these limitations and allowances we at last frame a definition: *A mineral is a natural, lifeless (or inorganic) substance that has essentially one nature throughout and a chemical make-up which commonly is so definite that it can be stated in a formula.*

## CRYSTALS ARE FORMED BY MOLECULES

"But," you may say, "this definition is not complete. The minerals which I know are crystals: regularly shaped things with smooth sides that meet in edges and points. These crystals have different forms and colors, according to their different kinds. Don't they belong in our definition?"

The answer is both yes and no. It is true that most familiar minerals form crystals, which we see in museum exhibits or on curio stands near mines. But it is equally true that some minerals never crystallize, while others which form beautiful crystals are much more abundant as earthy or granular masses. The most we can say, therefore, is that under proper conditions many minerals do take on the regular internal structure that produces crystals.

This internal structure depends on molecules, which are the smallest units of mineral matter. We already have seen that most of these molecules are compounds, produced when atoms of different elements unite. But even in such minerals as gold and silver, which are elements, atoms join in molecules. These, in turn, form crystals, grains or irregular masses.

So much for the chemical side of the picture; let us now look at its physics. Here we find that minerals, like all other solids, are not as dense as they seem. To begin with, atoms themselves are not much more than sections of space, given shape by electrons that whirl around a nucleus. There is more space between the atoms in a molecule and still more between the molecules that make up a mineral. They remind us of the up-rights and crossbeams in a fire tower or an oil well derrick.

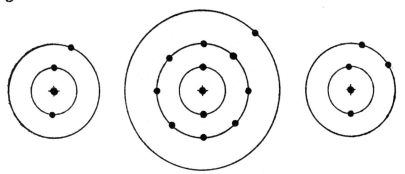

The structure of lithium, sodium and beryllium atoms, all common in minerals. Dots with crosses indicate the nuclei, which contain several particles. Dots represent electrons, which revolve in the paths marked by circles. Most of each atom is space.

From a distance they seem to make a solid structure. Seen at close range, they merely form a framework that is rigid because its parts are tightly fastened to each other.

Molecules are not always tightly fastened. When minerals are molten or dissolved, molecules can roll or slip past each other. But when molten rock becomes solid, or dissolved minerals settle from water, molecules are crowded together until they make a rigid mass. If they do this in hit-or-miss fashion, they produce grains and shapeless lumps. If they have a chance to settle down in definite order, they produce crystals. Even if orderly molecules are so crowded that they cannot take on their proper crystal outlines, they assume crystalline arrangement within the space into which they are squeezed.

We can see the gradations between crystals and these crystalline grains in a magnified section of granite. Hornblende molecules settled down first, developing perfect crystals that are

[ 19 ]

marked by thin lines in our section. Feldspar (thick lines) crystallized next; some of its crystals had room to grow, but others had to develop between and partly around the hornblende. Quartz (dotted) solidified last. Its molecules had to settle down in spaces that were too small and too irregular for crystals to develop. The quartz therefore formed irregular

Thin section of granite, magnified. Hornblende (thin lines) crystallized first, feldspar (thick lines) second, and quartz (dots) last. Its grains do not have crystal shape.

grains, yet its molecules arranged themselves in typical crystalline structure.

But, you may ask, how do we know that orderly molecules make crystals? It must be admitted that we don't know it—at least not as we know that quartz is silicon dioxide or that cemented grains of sand form sandstone. Yet there are facts that give all but final proof. One of these facts is the regularity of the crystal sides, or faces, which are as smooth as if they had been cut and polished. Second, these faces meet in sharp angles that are constant in crystal after crystal, indicating regular structure. With these qualities goes the way in which most crystals split, or cleave, in special directions. Finally, crystals have definite effects on light that passes through them, while X-ray photographs show that they consist of particles which have an orderly arrangement. Though they are too large to be molecules, these particles are very tiny. Since they have formed in regular order, it is very likely that molecules are arranged in the same way.

Molecules give crystals their shapes; this conclusion may be accepted, though it is not proved. We also feel sure that molecules and their arrangement determine other characteristics of minerals. They also decide the nature of rocks, most of which are mixtures of minerals.

## PHYSICAL PROPERTIES OF MINERALS

There are about 1500 known minerals, but only a few are so common that they form rocks or decide what they shall look like. These abundant, or rock-forming, minerals may be studied by the most detailed methods, using chemical analyses and special microscopes. They also may be studied very simply, with attention to six qualities which the textbooks label *physical properties*. Because they are simple, these properties enable us to recognize common minerals even though we may know little about them.

*Hardness* is determined by the ability of a smooth surface to resist scratching or cutting. Though no two minerals have exactly the same resistance, many are so nearly alike that we can group them together in classes or *degrees*. We generally recognize ten such degrees of hardness. Here they are, with one example of each:

1. Easily scratched by the fingernail; the mineral itself feels soft and greasy. (Talc)
2. Just scratched by the fingernail; not greasy or soft. (Gypsum)
3. Very easily scratched by a knife; just scratched by a sharp edge of copper, such as that of a new penny. (Calcite)
4. Easily scratched by a knife but not hard enough to scratch glass. (Fluorite)
5. Scratched by a knife but just scratches ordinary glass. (Apatite)

6. Not scratched by a knife and scratches common window or bottle glass easily. (Orthoclase feldspar)
7. Scratches both a knife and hard glass easily; harder than any other common substance. (Quartz)
8. Scratches quartz easily and much harder than *any* common substance. (Topaz)
9. Scratches topaz and compares with the manufactured product called carborundum, though it is very different chemically. (Corundum)
10. Scratches topaz and corundum easily; is the hardest substance known. (Diamond)

A knife and some small pieces of gypsum, calcite, apatite, orthoclase, glass and quartz are enough for most hardness determinations. Topaz will not be necessary, for minerals harder than quartz are not common enough to be rock builders.

*Color* is easily seen, but it does not sort minerals into classes quite so simply as does hardness. Many minerals, such as pure quartz, calcite, gypsum and salt (halite), are either colorless or white. Others have definite tints of their own: galena always is steel gray, pyrite is pale, brassy yellow, malachite is green and magnetite is black. Minerals such as orthoclase and apatite show varying tones of pink, green and other colors. Tourmaline is pink, red, black, green or brown. We also find that amethyst, which is purple, and rose quartz, which is pink, are colored by impurities. The amount of impurity determines the shade, which therefore is of little use in determining the mineral.

*Luster* has been defined as the appearance of a mineral, aside from its color. It depends upon the mineral's surface and the way in which it reflects light. About the only way to describe lusters is to compare them with familiar things. Thus we say that some lusters are brilliant or glassy, while others are metallic, waxy, pearly and so on.

*Transparency* and *translucency* are obvious. A mineral is transparent if you can see objects clearly through it. If you can see objects only as hazy shadows, or merely can get light to pass

through without showing shapes at all, the mineral is translucent. One that lets no light pass through it is opaque. Many
opaque and translucent minerals are light-colored while many
transparent ones are dark.

*Streak* is the mark made when a mineral is rubbed across a
piece of white unglazed porcelain, such as a "streak plate" or
the under side of a bathroom tile. The rough surface turns a
part of the mineral into very fine powder, whose color may be
different from that of the mineral itself and much more characteristic. Thus the color of hematite ranges from black to dull
red, but even the shiny black crystals give dark red streaks.
Limonite, which may be yellow, brown or black, gives a
yellowish brown streak and so helps us to tell what it is. Some
hard minerals must be powdered by pounding them with a
hammer.

*Specific gravity* is the weight of a substance in proportion
to the weight of its own volume of water. A few minerals weigh
less than water, but others are much heavier; their average
weight is about 2.6 times as much as water. Leaving out the last
five words, we say that their specific gravity is 2.6. Even though
we do not determine actual specific gravities, we may distinguish some minerals by mere differences in weight. Thus barite,
which often looks like calcite, weighs almost twice as much,
while pyrite, which some people mistake for gold, weighs less
than that precious mineral.

*Cleavage* is the tendency of a mineral to split in definite directions, apparently because its molecules are arranged in layers.
Such cleavage generally produces smooth surfaces that are
parallel to faces of the crystals themselves. In such minerals as
mica cleavage is nearly perfect; in calcite it is good; in quartz it
is poor or undeveloped. There also is a difference in the number
of cleavage directions, for mica has only one, calcite three and
fluorite four. Some minerals, however, have very poor or
irregular cleavage.

*Fracture* is developed when minerals break without cleavage or across it. There are several types of fracture: fibrous, irregular, jagged (hackly) and so on. If the broken surface suggests a clam shell, it is conchoidal; this character also is shown by such rocks as flint and glassy lava (PLATE 22). Though fracture is less useful than other properties, it helps us recognize a few important minerals.

## VARIETIES OF MINERAL STRUCTURE

We already have seen that some minerals form *crystals,* which are solid bodies bounded by smooth surfaces called faces, that meet in definite angles. Both faces and angles are determined by the crystal's internal structure—the arrangement of its molecules. Minerals that have crystal structure, but not shape, are *crystalline.* Quartz in granite and calcite in marble are the most familiar examples of crystalline structure without crystal shape.

Examine a piece of marble closely. Especially if it is weathered, you will notice that it consists of grains, so that the structure is granular. Granular marble from Baltimore is shown on PLATE 47 and granular magnetite on PLATE 48. Many minerals that form beautiful crystals are much more plentiful and important as granular deposits.

In contrast to marble, the calcite of lithographic limestone (PLATE 34) consists of microscopic grains packed closely together, thus showing *compact* structure. Some hematite, or red iron ore, is compact, but much of it is coarse, soft and *earthy.* It differs greatly from the *fibrous* structure of asbestos and the platy (*foliated*) structure of graphite. Platy structure in which thin sheets of a mineral can be peeled off is so characteristic of mica that it is called *micaceous.*

# CHAPTER III

# Important Minerals

W E NOW COME to the rock-making minerals them-
selves, as well as some others of importance or general interest.
We might arrange them in the order of their physical or
chemical make-up: feldspars, ferromagnesians and so on. Since
this chapter is primarily for reference, however, it seems best
that we arrange the minerals and even some of their varieties
alphabetically, thereby saving a great deal of index thumbing.
A few varieties must be sought in brief descriptions under
principal kinds, or "species." More detailed discussions, and
accounts of minerals not mentioned here, will be found in some
of the books listed in Chapter XX.

**Agate** (FRONTISPIECE) is a variegated form of quartz, be-
longing largely to the variety chalcedony but including jasper,
smoky quartz and even amethyst. The most familiar agates are
banded and are deposited in cavities, especially in ancient lavas,
though a few are found in veins. The latter commonly consist
of angular fragments of banded agate cemented by crystalline
quartz. Other agates are clouded; those that contain dendrites
(Chapter XVI) of dark minerals are known as *moss agates*.

*Banded agates* consist of layers that reach a quarter inch in
thickness, though some are extremely thin, numbering as many
as 17,000 to the inch. In spite of their thinness and hardness,

these layers are porous, so that water was able to seep through them and deposit still more layers until the cavity was filled. Rather commonly, the last deposits consist of quartz crystals. Since agates generally are more resistant than the lavas or other rocks in which they develop, they weather into nodules or pebbles that are found in glacial drift, gravel banks and the beds of streams.

Natural agates range from grayish white to dull green or brown in color and rarely are bright. Most commercial agates are colored artificially by being placed in solutions of various sorts, by being exposed to bright sun or by being heated. The agate of the frontispiece contained a brown iron mineral (limonite) in many of its layers; when heated, this mineral turned red. Dark brown or black bands are produced by soaking agates in a sugar solution and then in sulphuric acid.

Agates are used for many ornamental purposes, for small mortars and pestles used in chemical work and for the edges on which high-grade balances swing. Most commercial agates come from weathered lavas of Brazil and Uruguay and are cut in Germany. Agates also are plentiful in ancient lavas of the Lake Superior region, in New South Wales and in South Africa. Worn pebbles of agate are found in ancient beach deposits (conglomerates) of England.

**Amphiboles** (PLATE 3) are complex minerals that always contain silica and magnesium and usually calcium and other metals, such as iron and manganese. The crystals are usually long and bladed and may appear as needles whose prism faces are scarcely discernible, even with a lens. The ends of the crystals commonly are imperfect. Cleavages, which are perfect and parallel to the prism faces, meet at angles of approximately 55 and 125 degrees. As is shown in the drawing, these angles distinguish amphibole from pyroxene. The color varies from white, gray green, dark green and brown to black, according to the amount of iron present. The luster is glassy, pearly, horny or silky. The hardness varies from 5 to 6 and the specific gravity from 2.9 to 3.5; the streak grades from white to brown and is paler than the color of the mineral.

Amphiboles are among the commonest rock-forming minerals; they occur in both igneous and metamorphic rocks.

**Anhydrite** is white, gray or pale blue and generally forms granular, compact or fibrous masses; crystals are rare. Cleavage

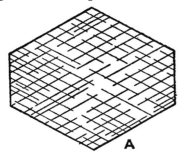 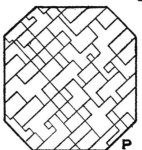

Cross sections of amphibole (A) and pyroxene (P) crystals, showing the different angles at which cleavages meet.

is in three directions, each at right angles to the others; it may produce cubelike forms in coarsely crystalline material. The cleavage faces have a pearly to glassy luster. The hardness is 3 to 3.5, though the mineral is easily cut by a knife. Anhydrite ($CaSO_4$) resembles gypsum in appearance but differs from it in having no water; cleavage in three directions is also a distinguishing character.

Anhydrite forms strata among sandstones, limestones and shales; such strata are usually large enough to be classed as rocks (Chapter XIII). Many beds of anhydrite have been turned into gypsum by the absorption of water.

**Apatite** (PLATE 3) is a combination of phosphorous, oxygen, calcium and fluorine or chlorine whose crystals are six-sided prisms. The prisms may be capped at each end by pyramids or truncated pyramids, as are those shown in the photograph, or they may be rounded. Apatite is scratched by a knife (hardness 5) and has a specific gravity of 3.2. It is brittle, has a glassy luster and is white, green or brown in color. Small crystals are transparent; large ones are opaque. Cleavage is imperfect, the

[ 27 ]

fracture is conchoidal, and the streak is white. Very large crystals are common in pegmatite dikes, but very tiny ones are present in almost all igneous and many metamorphic rocks.

Though it generally makes up less than one three hundredth of any rock, apatite is very important to life. When formations containing it are weathered and broken down into soil, apatite provides the phosphorous needed by both animals and plants.

**Aragonite** (PLATE 4) is a combination of calcium, carbon and oxygen, having the same composition as calcite. It occurs as stalactites, as transparent spire-shaped crystals which sometimes coat stalactites and frequently as coarse fibrous or columnar masses. Aragonite has a hardness of 3.5 to 4; its specific gravity is 2.9. The mineral effervesces freely when touched with cold dilute hydrochloric acid. It has no cleavage, a character which distinguishes it from calcite. Aragonite occurs in England, Sicily and the Pyrenees Mountains; in the United States it is found in Mammoth and other caves and in the mountainous Western states.

**Asbestus** (PLATE 4) is a fibrous variety of amphibole. Its fibers reach lengths of 18 inches or more, but they are less flexible than those of commercial asbestos, which is described under serpentine. Asbestus occurs in Idaho, Georgia and a few other Southern states.

**Azurite** (FRONTISPIECE) is a carbonate of copper and is an ore of copper. It has a characteristic blue color, though it may vary from light to dark blue or even black. The crystals are very beautiful and complex, with a glassy or dull luster. The fracture is conchoidal in crystals and imperfect in other forms. The hardness is 3.5 to 4 and the specific gravity is 3.77 to 3.89. Azurite also occurs as crusts, compact masses and earthy lumps. Very fine specimens are found at Bisbee, Arizona, Chessy, France and Tsumeb, South-West Africa.

**Barite** (PLATE 5), or "heavy spar," is characterized by its weight, which is nearly twice that of calcite and gypsum. It forms crystals of several different shapes and has three cleavages,

two of which are perfect. These produce cleavage rhombs somewhat like those of calcite (PLATE 4) but with different angles.
Barite may be colorless, white, yellow, blue, red or green. Its
luster is glassy, its streak white, its hardness from 2.5 to 3.5 and
specific gravity 4.5.

Barite is a widely distributed mineral, occurring as bedded
deposits, as veins in limestone, as nodules in sandstone and shale
and as residual deposits. It is used in the refining of sugar, as
pigment in paints, as filler in paper, cloth and linoleum, in
surfacing Bristol board and in making glazes and enamels.
Barite occurs in many states, but the principal producers are
Missouri, Georgia, Tennessee, California and Nevada.

**Beryl** (PLATE 5) is a combination of beryllium, aluminum,
silicon and oxygen that usually occurs as simple hexagonal
prisms with flat ends. It is brittle and has a hardness of 7.5 to 8,
which readily distinguishes it from apatite. Cleavage is poor,
the fracture is uneven, and the specific gravity is 2.7. The streak
is white, but because of the hardness it can be determined only
by powdering the mineral. The luster is glassy to greasy. *Common beryl* is light green, white or colorless. Gem varieties are
determined by color, *aquamarine* being bluish green or greenish
blue, *emeralds* deep, rich green, *golden beryl* yellow and *mor-
ganite* pink.

Beryl occurs mainly in pegmatite veins and cavities in granite,
though it may also occur in mica schist. Enormous crystals of
common beryl have been found in Maine; one measuring 14
by 4 feet weighed 18 tons. It is the only important mineral containing beryllium, most of which is used to make hard, tough
alloys of copper. These alloys are employed in tools and in
springs of electrical devices, where long life is desirable. Beryl
is obtained as a by-product in the mining of quartz, mica and
feldspar in the Black Hills of South Dakota, Maine, New
Hampshire, Massachusetts, Connecticut and North Carolina.
Beryl occurs also in Colorado and Idaho. India is the leading
foreign producer.

Gem beryl is obtained as a by-product in some places, but in others veins are worked for the gem minerals alone. Golden beryl has been produced near Milford, Connecticut, and aquamarine near East Hampton, Connecticut. Emeralds, the most valuable of all gems, come mainly from Russia, Africa and Colombia; a few have been found in Alexander County, North Carolina, one crystal being 9 inches long.

**Calcite** (PLATE 4) is a combination of calcium, carbon and oxygen which takes a number of crystal forms. It has three almost perfect cleavages that produce rhombohedrons with angles of 102 and 78 degrees. Calcite is white or colorless when pure, but impurities produce shades of pink, yellow or even brown. It is transparent to opaque and produces a white or gray streak. The hardness is 3 and the specific gravity 2.72. Calcite bubbles strongly when touched with cold dilute hydrochloric acid or strong vinegar. Lines or letters seen through a piece of transparent calcite (*Iceland spar*) appear double; this feature is called double refraction.

Calcite is one of the commonest minerals. It is found in igneous rocks and often forms a white surface coating weathered lavas. It cements many sandstones, occurs in dolomite, forms limestones and marbles and is present in most clays and shales.

*Sand-calcite crystals* (PLATE 4) were produced where water containing dissolved calcite seeped through beds of sand. By depositing molecules between grains it finally produced calcite crystals that surrounded and included the sand. When such crystals are broken they show typical cleavage. Sand-calcite crystals are found in only a few places in the world, and those on Rattlesnake Butte in the Badlands of South Dakota are unusually perfect.

**Cassiterite** (PLATE 3) is tin oxide and the main ore of tin. It is usually black or brown, with a glassy or dull luster. Since its hardness is 6 to 7, the mineral must be powdered to determine the pale brown or white streak. The specific gravity is 6.8 to 7.1.

Cassiterite has been mined for hundreds of years at Cornwall, England; the Malay Peninsula now leads the world in production. No important deposits occur in the United States, though small ones are found in Alaska, Nevada, the Black Hills, South Dakota, Washington, North and South Carolina, Texas and California.

**Chalcocite** sometimes is called copper glance; when pure it is 79.8 per cent copper and 21.2 per cent sulphur. The mineral is dark lead gray with a black streak; the hardness is 2.5 to 3 and its specific gravity about 5.7. Chalcocite usually occurs in fine-grained masses, crystals being rare and complex. It yields most of the copper produced in the United States and is abundant in Alaska, Utah, Arizona, Montana and New Mexico.

**Chalcopyrite** (PLATE 48), a sulphide of copper and iron, is sometimes called copper pyrites; it is an important ore of copper and contains 34.5 per cent of that metal. Chalcopyrite is brassy yellow, though tarnished crystals are dark and display rainbow hues. It has a metallic luster and greenish black streak, a hardness of 3.5 to 4 and a specific gravity of about 4.2. Chalcopyrite is brittle, a character that distinguishes it from gold, which also is much heavier.

Though fine groups of crystals occur in relatively few regions, such as Missouri, Japan and Pennsylvania, large quantities of the massive mineral are found in most copper mines. It is most abundant at Butte, Montana; Bisbee, Arizona; Bingham, Utah; and Ducktown, Tennessee.

**Chlorites** (PLATE 6), whose name comes from the Greek word for green, are a group of soft, light green to dark green minerals that look like mica. They have excellent cleavage in one direction, but the split plates do not spring back into shape when bent. The streak is pale green to white, and the luster of the cleavage faces is rather pearly. Chlorites have a hardness of 2 to 2.5 and are just scratched by the fingernail; their specific gravity is 2.7. They commonly occur in irregular grains or plates that form masses, fans or rosettes.

Chlorites, of which clinochlore is the most familiar, are found in many igneous and metamorphic rocks, forming entire mountains in western New England. In Pennsylvania chlorites are mined, crushed and used in the manufacture of green roofing.

Cinnabar (FRONTISPIECE) is a sulphide and the principal ore of mercury, containing 86.2 per cent of that metal. Its color varies from scarlet to brownish red and may fade to dull gray; a scarlet streak is its most distinctive character. Crystals, which are very rare, have a deep, rich, almost ruby-red color. The hardness is 2 to 2.5 and the specific gravity is about 8.1, making this one of the heaviest minerals. It is mined in California, Oregon, Texas and Arkansas.

Copper (PLATE 3) is the only metal that occurs abundantly in nature. It has a hardness of 2.5 and is both malleable and ductile; fresh surfaces show metallic luster and the familiar red color. Copper occurs as sheets, crystals, grains and irregular masses that fill cracks or pores in rocks. One mass weighing 420 tons was found in the Lake Superior region in 1857. Some native copper occurs in most regions where other copper ores are mined.

Corundum (PLATE 6) is an oxide of aluminum; though it contains 53 per cent of that element, it is not used as an ore. Corundum is of special interest because of its hardness (9) which is exceeded only by that of diamond. Crystals are barrel-shaped or long prisms; colors range from white through gray, brown and black. Red produces the variety *ruby* and blue the *sapphire,* both of which are valuable gems. *Emery* is a granular variety colored black or gray by magnetite or hematite. Corundum has a parting, or pseudocleavage, shown by the cross section on PLATE 6. The specific gravity is 4.

Rubies and sapphires come mainly from Ceylon, Siam and Burma, though Montana has produced some excellent sapphires. Ordinary corundum occurs in Canada, Georgia, Montana, North Carolina and the Transvaal, South Africa. Emery comes mainly from Turkey and Greece, though there are deposits of it in Montana, Massachusetts and North Carolina.

Corundum is used as an abrasive, though it is being supplanted by carborundum, a combination of carbon and silicon prepared in electric furnaces.

**Dolomite** (PLATE 4) is a mineral that looks like calcite but is slightly harder (3.5) and does not have such perfect cleavage. Chemically it contains magnesium as well as calcium, carbon and oxygen, the elements found in calcite. Dolomite will not effervesce unless it is powdered or the acid dropped upon it is hot. Perfect crystals are hexagonal, though the faces are commonly curved. Their color ranges from white to yellow or delicate pink, and their luster is glassy or pearly.

Dolomite is found in some of the metamorphic rocks called *schists* and in beds of gypsum. It also forms thick beds of rock that look almost like limestone. It commonly is mixed with calcite, so that there are all stages between pure dolomite and pure limestone.

**Epidote** (PLATE 3) is a complex silicate of calcium, aluminum and iron with water. It typically is yellowish green but ranges to olive or dark green and brownish black. Crystals are long prisms, needles or blades with one good cleavage across the prism face. The ends of the prisms are usually rounded. Epidote occurs in angular or spherical grains, in aggregates of these or in crystals. It has a glassy luster and is transparent to opaque. The streak is white, the hardness 6 to 7, and the specific gravity is 3.2 to 3.5.

Epidote is found in almost all sorts of rocks. It is formed during the metamorphism of igneous rocks and impure limestone. In the latter epidote may occur in large solid masses.

**Feldspar** is the name of a group of minerals that are light in color, with satiny or glassy luster and perfect cleavage in two directions at right angles, or almost right angles, to one another. Impurities may stain feldspars pink, red, brown or gray, but their streak is white. The hardness is about 6. They are found most abundantly in igneous rocks but occur in the other classes; there is more feldspar in the world than there is of any other *one* mineral, for the group as a whole makes up about 60 per cent of all rocks. Orthoclase and plagioclase are among the most important feldspars and are described separately.

**Fluorite** (PLATES 5, 11), sometimes called "fluorspar," is calcium fluoride. When pure it contains 48.9 per cent fluorine and 51.1 per cent calcium. It occurs in very beautiful cubical crystals which may be twinned; less commonly as octahedrons and abundantly as massive or coarsely granular material. Fluorite may be green, purple, yellow, pink, blue, brown, gray or colorless. It is transparent to translucent and has a glassy luster. It has good cleavage in four directions (PLATE 5). Its hardness is 4 and specific gravity 3.0 to 3.2.

Fluorite occurs as veins in limestone and igneous rocks in many parts of the world. Fine specimens come from England, Switzerland and New Hampshire. Unusually large ones have come from Jefferson County, New York, where one 12-inch cube was found. Illinois, Kentucky, Colorado, Nevada and New Mexico produce most of the fluorite used commercially.

About 82 per cent of the fluorite that is mined is used as a flux in open-hearth furnaces. Very pure material is used to make hydrofluoric acid for etching glass. Fluorite also is used in making colored glass, enamels and as a binder in emery wheels.

**Franklinite** (PLATE 6) is a complex compound of iron, zinc, manganese and oxygen that is a valuable ore of zinc. Its crystals generally have eight or twelve sides and resemble magnetite; cubes are rare. Franklinite is iron black, metallic or dull and has parting but no true cleavage. The streak is brown or black, the hardness 5.5 to 6.5 and the specific gravity about 5.2. Crystals are brittle.

Franklinite is found chiefly at Franklin and Ogdensburg, New Jersey, northwest of New York City, where the greatest zinc mines in the United States are located. Franklinite is mixed with another rich zinc mineral in coarsely granular ore and also is found imbedded in calcite.

Galena (PLATE 3), a compound of lead and sulphur, is the commonest lead mineral. It is lead gray with a bright metallic luster on freshly broken surfaces. Crystals are usually cubes, very perfect and sometimes very large; a crystal 6¼ inches wide was found in the Mississippi Valley and one measuring 9¾ inches on the Isle of Man. Galena also occurs in granular or very fine-grained compact masses which, like the crystals, show well-developed cubical cleavage. The hardness is about 2.5, and the streak, which is lead gray, is easily obtained. Galena is quite heavy, having a specific gravity of 7.5.

Galena occurs in many different kinds of rock in many parts of the world. It is mined as lead ore in Missouri, Kansas, Oklahoma, Idaho, Colorado, Utah, Germany, England, Mexico and Chile. Gold and silver are found in some galena.

Garnets (PLATE 6) are a group of minerals whose crystals are dodecahedrons, trapezohedrons or a combination of these forms. The luster is glassy, and the hardness ranges from 6.5 to 7.5. Colors are red to brown, black and even green, though some garnets are colorless; red and brown are the most familiar. The streak, varying with each special kind of garnet, is light-colored and of little importance in determining the mineral. The specific gravity is 3.4 to 4.3.

*Almandite* probably is the commonest variety and the one most often encountered on collecting trips and in jewelry. It is deep red to purplish red or brownish black. Almandite occurs in many parts of the world; a crystal weighing 14½ pounds was found near Salida, Colorado, and fine ones are mined near Fort Wrangel, Alaska.

*Pyrope* is the deep red "precious garnet." It occurs in Colorado, Arizona, New Mexico and Kentucky, as well as in South Africa and various parts of Europe. Most garnet jewelry set with pyrope is made in Bohemia.

Garnets are most plentiful in metamorphosed rocks, espe-

THE ROCK BOOK

cially in schists that contain a great deal of mica. Common garnets are mined in New York, New Hampshire and North Carolina for use in making sandpaper.

**Gold** (PLATE 48) is deep yellow; light yellow if it is combined with silver in the alloy electrum. Gold's distinguishing characters are its great weight—specific gravity 19.3—and its golden yellow streak. It is quite soft (hardness 2.5 to 3) and is very malleable and ductile. It has a rough fracture and no cleavage. Crystals, usually octahedrons, are rare and highly prized by collectors. Gold mainly occurs in a massive form as grains, nuggets, wires or sheets. It is associated with such minerals as pyrite, galena and sphalerite and especially with vein quartz. Small amounts of gold are found in igneous, sedimentary and metamorphic rocks in many parts of the world; it also is dissolved in some fresh water and all sea water. There is approximately one grain of gold (about seven cents' worth) in a ton of sea water. Much gold has been mined from "placers" in stream gravels. Ores of the famous Mother Lode of California are in quartz veins that cut through slates.

**Graphite** (PLATE 6) occurs as imperfect six-sided plates and scales with perfect cleavage parallel to their surfaces. Cleavage flakes are flexible but not elastic. The color is steel gray to iron black; the luster is metallic or dull and earthy, and lumps of graphite feel greasy. The hardness is 1 to 2. Graphite is pure carbon and therefore is chemically identical with diamond, from which it differs in hardness, color and crystal form. It is found as separate flakes and irregular masses in such crystalline rocks as gneiss, schist and marble, as well as in pegmatite dikes. Graphite is widely distributed and is produced commercially in Russia, Germany, Austria, Ceylon and Madagascar. The most important deposits in the United States are in Montana, California, Nevada, New York, Alabama, Colorado and a few other states. There is little graphite produced in this country.

Graphite is used in crucibles, foundry facings, paints and

[ 36 ]

lubricants. For "lead" pencils it is mixed with a binder of clay and compressed to the desired hardness.

Gypsum (PLATE 5) is a hydrous calcium sulphate ($CaSO_4$.$2H_2O$) and is the material of common school "chalk." As a rock-forming mineral it usually is massive, granular or fibrous and ranges in color from white to buff or pink. There are three cleavages, though only one is perfect; the cleavage plates may be bent but are not elastic. The hardness is 1.5 to 2, the luster is glassy, pearly or dull, and the streak is white. Gypsum commonly occurs as clear and rather complex crystals, some of which are curved; these crystals form the variety *selenite*.

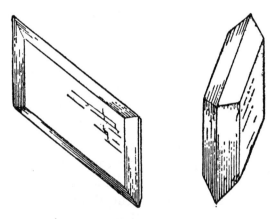

Two common forms of selenite.

Gypsum forms thick beds of rock described in Chapter XIII. When heated it loses some of its water, becoming plaster of Paris, a white powder. When water is added the plaster "sets" or hardens quickly, becoming gypsum again.

Halite (PLATE 6) is more familiar as salt, whose crystals usually are transparent colorless cubes, though masses may be white or stained gray, yellow or red by impurities. There are three good cleavages at right angles to each other and parallel to the crystal faces. The hardness is 2.5 and the specific gravity 2.16.

Salt always can be distinguished by its taste. It is common in sedimentary rocks of all ages and in some places forms thick beds. At others it appears in brine that seems to be part of the water from ancient vanished seas. This water was held in muds or sands after they settled; when they were covered by new sediments it had no chance to escape. In other rocks we find casts of salt crystals (PLATE 40) which formed when ancient muds or sands dried.

**Hematite** (PLATES 7, 29) is a compound of oxygen and iron ($Fe_2O_3$) that is called *red ocher* when it is earthy and mixed with clay. Common hematite is noncrystalline and massive or granular; it may occur in stalactitic or botryoidal forms. The color and streak are dark brick red; there is no luster, and the mineral is opaque. The hardness is about 6. Hematite has a specific gravity of 5, being heavier than most minerals.

*Specular hematite* forms masses and plates. It is steel gray to black with a red streak. The luster is metallic: dull in some pieces and very bright in others. There is no cleavage, and the fracture is not smooth enough to be conchoidal. The hardness is 6.5 and the specific gravity is 5.2.

*Micaceous hematite,* really one form of specular hematite, consists of thin flakes that look a little like flakes of mica and may be so thin as to be translucent, though deep red in color. The luster is metallic, even polished in appearance.

Specular and micaceous hematite are found in both igneous and metamorphic rocks, especially schists. Common hematite occurs in both metamorphic rocks and sediments. Its tiny grains may be scattered through the rock, or it may make up thick beds that contain little else. Deposits of the latter type are described in Chapter XIII as Lake Superior iron ores.

**Hornblende** (PLATE 7) is one of the group of minerals called amphiboles. Hornblende is a dark green, brown or black mineral whose chemical composition varies. Its crystals usually are short prisms in volcanic rocks but are bladed in metamorphic rocks. The cleavage is perfect and parallel to the prism faces (see the illustration accompanying the description of amphibole). The fracture is uneven, the luster glassy, the hardness 5 to 6 and the specific gravity 2.9 to 3.4.

Hornblende is common in granite and other intrusive rocks but is rare in basalts and dark "trap" rocks. It also is common in metamorphic rocks. Unfortunately, it is very hard to tell hornblende from pyroxene without microscopic study or careful examination of the cleavage angles.

**Kaolin, or Kaolinite** (PLATES 28, 32)', is one of the clay minerals. It crystallizes into thin plates or scales that commonly have hexagonal shapes but are too small to be seen without a good microscope. These scales generally form masses that are white, buff, brown or gray, the dark colors being made by impurities. When rubbed between the fingers kaolin has a smooth, greasy feel; touched with the tongue, it seems unusually dry.

Kaolin is produced by the weathering of feldspar. Water and carbon dioxide force feldspar molecules to recombine, producing kaolin, potassium carbonate and the ever-present mineral, quartz. This process is important in the development of many soils. Uses and distribution of kaolin are discussed in Chapter XII.

**Kyanite** (PLATE 11) is an aluminum silicate which may be white, colorless or green but usually is sky blue. It occurs in bladed crystals that are pearly and have a hardness of 5 on their flat faces, though the edges are glassy and have a hardness of 7. Gems resembling sapphire can be cut from transparent blue crystals.

Though rather expensive as yet, kyanite is used in making electrical porcelain and a number of other things. Mixed with silica and other minerals, it makes tough glass. Its ability to expand on heating is being utilized in ceramics to offset the shrinking of clays. Kyanite occurs in metamorphic rocks of Georgia, New Mexico, Arizona, Wyoming and Virginia but is mined mainly in Yancey County, North Carolina, Cherokee

County, South Carolina and Imperial County, California.

**Limonite** (FRONTISPIECE, PLATE 29) is a compound of iron, oxygen and water. It is formed by the alteration of other iron minerals and is never crystalline. It may form a brown, yellow or even black coating on other minerals and rocks, it may be concretionary or it may be a powder very much like rust. It is opaque, has a hardness of about 5 and a yellowish brown streak that distinguishes it from other iron ores.

Limonite gives color to most brown rocks and soils and often is called brown ocher or yellow ocher. It also is an important iron ore, especially in Europe. The loose or porous form is called *bog iron ore* because it often is found in swamps. Limonite sometimes forms stalactites in caves and in the tunnels of mines.

**Magnetite** (PLATES 6, 48) is called black ore or magnetic iron ore. Its molecules have three atoms of iron and four of oxygen ($Fe_3O_4$) instead of the two and three found in hematite; 100 pounds of pure magnetite contain 72.4 pounds of iron. Magnetite is dark gray to iron black, with metallic luster, black streak, hardness of 5.5 to 6.5 and specific gravity of 5.18. Crystals generally are octahedrons; less commonly dodecahedrons with striated faces. Magnetite has octahedral parting but no true cleavage; the fracture is uneven. As the name suggests, the mineral is strongly attracted by a magnet, while some pieces are magnets themselves and so are called "lodestones" (PLATE 48). Magnetite is an important iron ore, especially in New York, Pennsylvania, Europe and Brazil. There is only one mineral with which it is easily confused and that one is very much less common, as well as nonmagnetic.

Magnetite is found in all sorts of igneous rocks, generally in small grains. It also occurs in rocks that have been changed by contact igneous metamorphism and in crystalline schists.

**Malachite** (PLATE 9) is a carbonate of copper with a rich green color. It occurs in kidney-shaped masses with a fibrous structure, as crusts or as radiating tufts with a velvety texture.

The streak is blue, the hardness 3.5 to 4 and the specific gravity 3.9 to 4.03.

Malachite, like azurite, is developed by the action of carbon dioxide on native copper or copper-bearing minerals. Azurite, with 5.2 per cent of water, usually forms first and then changes into malachite, which has 8.2 per cent water. By this change in the percentage of water a totally different mineral is produced.

Malachite is an important ore of copper at Bisbee, Arizona, and Bingham Canyon, Utah. Beautiful specimens come from Arizona, Belgian Congo and Russia.

**Marcasite** (PLATE 9) is a pale, brassy sulphide of iron whose crystals are thin and flat. They commonly combine, or "twin," in the shape of a spearhead. The streak is grayish or brownish black. Marcasite is common in the chalk beds of Dover, England, and in the Joplin mining district of Missouri, Kansas and Oklahoma. Disks, or "marcasite rosettes," such as the one illustrated, are especially well developed in Randolph County, Illinois.

**Micas** (PLATE 7) are a group of minerals that have one perfect cleavage, splitting into thin, tough layers which may be bent but spring back into shape again. Micas crystallize into six-sided flat plates whose sides generally are rough, while their flat faces are bright and shiny. Very often, however, they form irregular flakes and slivers that may even be bent or curled. The luster is glassy, the streak white, and the hardness generally is 2 to 3.

*Muscovite,* or white mica, is also called isinglass. It is transparent and is colorless, white, greenish or even brown. It is common in granite and pegmatite, gneiss and mica schist, but is rare in volcanic rocks. Crystals as much as 10 feet wide have been found in pegmatite, which supplies all muscovite of commercial value. The most important mines in the United States are in North Carolina, Virginia and the Black Hills; most of the muscovite used in industry is imported from India. The mineral is used for electrical insulation and in roofing, wallpaper and lubricants. Movie "snow" is ground-up muscovite.

*Biotite,* or black mica, is colored by iron. It ranges from brown or deep green to black and in thin sheets is translucent. It is very common in granite, syenites, gabbros and some lavas, as well as in gneiss and schists. Excellent crystals are found in the lavas of Vesuvius and very large ones in Canada. Biotite has little commercial value.

*Phlogopite,* or brown mica, contains little iron; it therefore is not very dark and may be the hue of amber. It occurs chiefly in crystalline limestones and serpentine. Large crystals are found in eastern Canada and at Franklin, New Jersey. Phlogopite is more desirable than muscovite for electrical equipment.

*Lepidolite* is a very complex mica that contains lithium. It usually is lavender but may be pink, gray or yellow. Most commonly it forms masses made up of scales which may be so small that they are visible only with a lens. Lepidolite generally is found in pegmatite, associated with spodumene and tourmaline. Most museums exhibit pale lavender masses that are mined near San Diego, California.

**Nephelite** is a mineral related to the feldspars. It crystallizes in short, thick, six-sided blocks or prisms, but crystals rarely show in masses of rock. Nephelite generally forms grains and shapeless lumps or masses resembling quartz. Colors are white, gray, pale yellow or brick red, gray being commonest. The mineral is translucent; when freshly broken it has a greasy luster. It is brittle, has no good cleavage and a poor conchoidal fracture. The hardness is 6. Nephelite dissolves in dilute hydrochloric acid. It is important in a few igneous rocks, especially one called nephelite syenite. Small crystals occur in the lavas of Mount Vesuvius; large ones in Renfrew County, Ontario.

*Sodalite* often is associated with nephelite; it has a glassy luster and commonly is deep blue. Sodalite rock from Bancroft, Ontario, is sold as "Princess Marble." Most of it is used in England.

**Olivine** generally is olive to yellowish green in color, though other shades are common. It is transparent to translucent. The streak is colorless, white or yellowish and must be obtained by powdering. The luster is glassy, the hardness about 7 and the fracture conchoidal; cleavage is indistinct. Olivine rarely forms crystals. Transparent olivine-green masses sometimes are cut and polished to make the gem called peridot by jewelers.

Olivine is common in igneous rocks that contain large amounts of magnesium and iron. It occurs in peridotite, basalt and a rock colled dunite, which is almost pure olivine. Diamonds and platinum are found in olivine-bearing rocks, and the mineral is plentiful in stony-iron meteorites.

**Orthoclase** is a well-known feldspar which is a silicate of aluminum and potassium. When pure it is colorless, but such substances as iron oxide generally stain it buff, pink or red. The luster is glassy or pearly, cleavage faces commonly being pearly; crystals generally reflect light from their entire surface. There is good cleavage in two directions; cleavage faces meet at an angle of 90 degrees, so that the mineral generally breaks into plates or blocks. The fracture is uneven and somewhat conchoidal in directions that differ from cleavage. Crystals are variable, being thick and stout, tabular or columnar; many of them are double, or "twinned." Hardness is 6 to 6.5, which means that orthoclase cannot be scratched by most knives. Specific gravity is 2.54 to 2.58.

*Microcline* (PLATE 8) is so closely related to orthoclase that most collectors cannot distinguish them unless the microcline is bluish green, when it is called Amazon stone. This is the feldspar that occurs in large masses in pegmatite, though it often is called orthoclase. It is abundant at Amelia Court House, Virginia; Bedford, New York; in the Pikes Peak region of Colorado and in Delaware County, Pennsylvania; also in Maine, eastern Canada, North Carolina and the Black Hills. Orthoclase is common in porphyry and felsite; a variety called *sanidine* is found in some lavas, such as trachyte. Both orthoclase and microcline are used in making glass, in glazing pottery, in making enamel, or "granite," ware and in electrical insulators.

**Plagioclase** feldspars are distinguished from orthoclase by the fact that their two good cleavages are not at right angles, though this character may be hard to determine. Another important character is the striations, which commonly show on the best cleavage faces.

*Albite* (PLATE 8) is typically white, but it may be pale green, gray or red. It is a silicate of sodium and aluminum with prominent striations; large masses may be made up of so many tabular crystals that they seem to consist of layers. Albite is found in many granites, pegmatites, gneisses and other rocks in many parts of the world. Potters prefer it to other feldspars because it fuses easily and makes a smooth glaze.

*Anorthite* is a glassy feldspar found in such igneous rocks as diorite and basalt. Crystals come from Vesuvius and Japan.

*Labradorite* (PLATE 20) usually is dark gray; it is the principal mineral in anorthosites of the Adirondacks in New York. It also is prominent in dolerite porphyries of Massachusetts. Large masses show iridescence and have been made into table tops, paperweights and ornaments.

**Pyrite** (PLATE 9) is a compound of iron and sulphur, $FeS_2$. It generally forms cubic or eight-sided crystals whose faces are smooth or crossed by fine, straight, generally parallel lines. Pyrite has no good cleavage, an uneven or conchoidal fracture and a hardness of 6 to 6.5; the specific gravity is about 5. It is opaque, with a brassy yellow color, metallic luster and greenish black streak. The color is darker than that of marcasite, and the mineral does not crumble so readily.

The common name of pyrite is "fool's gold." Many inexperienced prospectors have mistaken it for real gold, which is much softer and darker than pyrite, does not crystallize in cubes and has a yellow streak.

Pyrite is found in igneous rocks, in metamorphosed formations and in sediments. In the last it commonly replaces fossils and seems to have been produced by reactions of sulphur in dead animals or plants with iron in the rocks covering them. Almost the only use of pyrite is in making sulphuric acid, but this is declining as sulphur becomes cheaper. Virginia has been our greatest producer of pyrite, though there are workable deposits in many other states, as well as in Europe and Japan.

**Pyrolusite** (FRONTISPIECE) is manganese dioxide. In its commonest form it is a soft black mineral that is an important manganese ore; it also was used as a paint by Stone Age artists of Europe, whose pictures still are preserved in caves. Dendrites (PLATE 40) may be pyrolusite. Crystals are black and metallic, with bluish black streak and a hardness not greater than 2.5. Pyrolusite is found in Minnesota, California, Arizona, Virginia and other states, but American deposits are not important.

**Pyroxene** (PLATE 9) are a group of minerals which are complex silicates of magnesium and calcium; they commonly contain iron and sometimes other metals. The most abundant pyroxenes are blackish green, black, brown or white; several kinds look much alike. Their luster ranges from glassy or resinous to dull, while their streak is white to grayish green. There is good cleavage in two directions, almost at right angles, and the minerals are brittle. All pyroxenes are hard (5 to 6) and their specific gravity is 3.2 to 3.6.

*Augite* (PLATE 9) is one of the most abundant minerals in basaltic lavas; it is common in other dark igneous rocks and occurs in marble. It is black or very dark green and is opaque. The crystals are short prisms, commonly with their pyramidal faces imperfectly developed. The mineral also forms grains and irregular masses.

*Diopside* is much less common than augite, being most plentiful in marbles but rare in lavas and granites. It is whitish, gray or light green and commonly forms eight-sided prisms that break along cross partings that suggest cleavage. Transparent crystals found at De Kalb, New York, and in Italy, are used for gems.

Quartz (PLATES 10, 11) is composed of silicon and oxygen: one atom of the former and two of the latter in each molecule. Quartz is transparent to translucent and is colorless when pure; impurities stain it brown, rose, violet and other hues. Crystals consist of prisms with pyramids at one end or both ends, but the mineral commonly forms masses or grains. There is no cleavage or a very poor one; the fracture is conchoidal and the hardness is 7. The streak is white or very pale and therefore is not diagnostic.

Quartz characteristically shows horizontal lines that cross the prism faces (PLATE 11); these distinguish even very irregular crystals. Some crystals enclose needles of tourmaline or other minerals; one of these also is shown on PLATE 11.

*Rock crystal* is colorless, glassy quartz. Fine specimens come from Herkimer County, New York, and from Arkansas, North Carolina and California. Most of the rock crystal used in optical glass, jewelry and quartz glass comes from Brazil.

*Amethyst* is rock crystal colored purple or violet, probably by manganese. *Smoky quartz* (PLATE 11) is colored by a carbon compound; when cut into gems it is called cairngorm from a locality in Scotland. *Citrine* is a yellow quartz colored by another carbon compound; it often is sold as Spanish topaz. Most of it comes from Brazil and Madagascar.

*Rose quartz* (PLATE 10) is colored by compounds of titanium or manganese. It almost never occurs as crystals but forms thick veins in New York, the Black Hills and elsewhere. Pieces that are not fractured can be cut into gems.

*Milky quartz* is very common in massive veins and may form crystals. Much gold-bearing quartz belongs to this variety.

*Chalcedony* (PLATE 10) is quartz that has a waxy luster; it never is crystalline but forms layers, stalactites or grapelike masses. Colors range from white to yellow, brown or green. *Carnelian* is red chalcedony, and agate, which is separately described, is another variety.

*Opal* resembles chalcedony but contains water; it probably

was deposited as a jelly that hardened into a noncrystalline layer or mass. Opal also is deposited by sponges, diatoms and other living things. Its hardness is 6.

**Selenite** (PLATE 5) is a variety of gypsum and is described under that heading.

**Serpentine** (PLATES 9, 10) is a compound of magnesium, silicon, hydrogen and oxygen. In masses its color ranges from yellowish green to dark green; fibrous forms range from yellowish brown to pale brown or even white. It is translucent to opaque, has a white streak and a waxy or silky luster. There is no cleavage, and the fracture is conchoidal or splintery. When it is fibrous the fibers are fine and flexible. The hardness is 2.5 to 3.

Serpentine is a common mineral in both igneous and metamorphic rocks; it is produced when olivine, amphibole or pyroxene is altered by heat, pressure and hot water or vapors. Serpentine also forms veins or large masses of rock. The massive type can be sawed into slabs and polished; a great deal of the green "marble" used in buildings and soda fountains is serpentine from quarries in Georgia. The fibrous sort, whose mineral name is *chrysotile* though we generally call it *asbestos,* is found in veins which cut through massive serpentine. It is mined in Quebec and Arizona, as well as in Rhodesia and South Africa.

**Silver** (PLATE 48) in its native state generally is rough and tarnished, in which case its color ranges from yellow to bronze or black. If untarnished, it is white with a metallic luster. It is highly malleable and ductile; its hardness is 2.5 to 3 and its specific gravity is 10.5. Crystals are rare, but wire silver is frequently found. Silver is widely distributed, though it is less important in ores than are several compounds. Norway, the Lake Superior region, Cobalt, Ontario, and Aspen, Colorado, have produced much native silver. One mass found in Colorado weighed 1842 pounds.

**Sphalerite** (PLATE 11), or zinc blende, is zinc sulphide. Pure varieties are almost colorless; others are yellow, brown, green and red or black, brown being commonest. Almost perfect cleavage divides sphalerite into twelve-sided blocks. The luster is resinous to glassy, the mineral is transparent to translucent, and the streak is brown, pale yellow or almost white. The fracture is conchoidal, the hardness 3.5 to 4 and the specific gravity about 4. Granular and cleavable masses are abundant, and crystals are common. Sphalerite is distinguished most readily by its cleavage, the angles between adjoining faces being 120 degrees.

Sphalerite is the most important ore of zinc and is common in veins. The principal American deposits are in the Tri-State mining district about Joplin, Missouri.

**Spodumene** (PLATE 10) is a white, yellowish or brown mineral that looks like feldspar. It has two good cleavages, a hardness of 6.5 to 7 and a specific gravity of 3.2. It forms rough, elongate crystals which reach their greatest size in pegmatites, one crystal being 47 feet long. Spodumene is mined in Connecticut and the Black Hills; a lilac variety (*kunzite*) is found in California.

**Staurolite** (PLATE 11) crystals are six-sided prisms that are characteristically twinned in the form of a cross. The mineral is translucent to opaque and dark reddish brown to black. The fracture is poorly conchoidal; the hardness is 7 to 7.5 and the specific gravity is 3.75. The streak is white to gray.

Staurolite is a product of metamorphism and therefore may be found in mica schist, or even slate. It is commonly associated with garnet and kyanite and may be confused with garnet because of the similarity of color.

**Stibnite** (PLATE 11) is a sulphide of antimony, bluish gray in color, with a metallic luster that is brilliant on fresh surfaces. The hardness is 2 and the specific gravity about 4.6. The mineral generally forms bladed masses, though clusters of long crystals are fairly common. There is perfect cleavage parallel to one vertical face of the crystal. Stibnite is the commonest and most important ore mineral of antimony, being found in Utah, Idaho, Mexico, Central Europe, Japan and China. China is the greatest producer and Mexico is second.

**Sulphur** (PLATE 9) is a mineral formed of one element. Crystals are transparent or translucent, have a resinous luster and are bright yellow. They are generally pyramidal but may be spheroidal or tabular. Hardness is 1 to 2; cleavage is imperfect and specific gravity is 1.9 to 2.1.

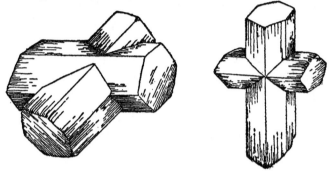

Twinned staurolite crystals. One pair forms a symmetrical cross.

Sulphur is widely distributed, both in the free state as well as in combination. Impure sulphur beds 125 feet thick underlie parts of Texas and Louisiana and produce about 2,000,000 tons per year.

**Talc** (PLATE 47) is a green, gray or yellow mineral having a pearly to greasy luster and a white streak. It is translucent to opaque and rarely forms crystals. It occurs in masses which are sometimes foliated or consist of scales that may be arranged in rosettes. The cleavage is perfect in one direction so that the mineral splits into thin, wavy, flexible but not elastic flakes. The hardness is 1; talc can be cut with a knife or scratched with the fingernail.

Talc is a secondary mineral and therefore is generally found in metamorphic rocks where water charged with carbon dioxide has decomposed minerals rich in magnesium. Where a great deal of mineral matter has been changed, talc forms masses of rock called steatite or soapstone. Crushed and ground into powder, it is used to fill some sorts of paper and as talcum powder. There are important deposits in Virginia, North Carolina, New York and Rhode Island.

Tourmaline (PLATE 11) is a very complex mineral always containing boron, aluminum and water, with other minerals in varying amounts. The commonest variety of tourmaline is black, though pink, green, red and other forms occur, their colors depending on chemical composition. The black form, called *schorl*, is opaque, has a glassy luster, no cleavage, irregular fracture and a colorless streak. Prisms are in threes or multiples of three, commonly having a striated or channeled appearance. The hardness is 7 to 7.5.

Tourmaline is common in granite and pegmatite and frequently occurs in ore deposits. When tourmaline is found in gneiss, schist or marble it indicates that at least part of the metamorphism of these rocks was accomplished by mineral-laden water from igneous masses. Because of tourmaline's resistance to weathering it is frequently found in sands, clays and marls.

Vesuvianite (PLATE 8) is a complex silicate of lime and aluminum, originally found in blocks of marble thrown out of Monte Somma, Italy. It generally forms crystals with four or eight sides; the crystals are transparent to translucent, have a glassy luster and are brown, green or even blue. The specific gravity is 3.4 and the hardness 6.5. Vesuvianite is typical of marble produced by igneous metamorphism; it also is found in serpentines, chlorite schists and gneisses. It is widely distributed; good specimens come from Norway, Italy, Siberia, Maine and other regions.

Wollastonite (PLATE 10) is a compound of calcium, silicon and oxygen that belongs to the pyroxene group. It usually is white and is either compact or fibrous masses of interwoven crystals. Its hardness is 4 to 5 and its specific gravity is about 2.8. Wollastonite is characteristic of rocks that have been changed by igneous metamorphism, and crystals have been found in limestone blocks thrown out of Monte Somma, the ancient Vesuvius. A large deposit in Mexico contains gold ore. Wollastonite also has been found in Norway, Hungary, Ontario, New York, California and other regions.

CHAPTER IV

# Rocks, Minerals and Ages

IN CHAPTER I we said that rocks form the solid part of the earth, make homes for plants and animals and provide many of the materials used by modern as well as ancient man. We then proceeded to take rocks to pieces, describing the principal minerals that form them. Yet we did all this without telling what rocks themselves are. To define them is the first task that awaits us in this chapter.

## ROCKS ARE MANY THINGS

To most of us the word *rock* has the same meaning as *stone*. Rocks are boulders, cobblestones or massive blocks in monuments or public buildings. They are granites, quartzites or ledges of limestone that rise in quarry walls. The least firm among them can stand alone, while the most resistant ones form high mountains or have endured wear by waves, ice or rivers for thousands upon thousands of years.

Such are the rocks of everyday language; but it tells only part of the story. By putting emphasis on hardness, solidity and resistance to wear, it wrongly rules out many things that are rocks even though they are not stones. Among these are clay, which may be cut with a spade; dust, which is scattered by breezes;

"scree." or talus, which slides and rolls down mountain slopes (PLATE 24). There also are sand banks, silts which settle upon flood plains and beds of shifting shingle along shores. All make up parts of the earth's outer portion. Since they are neither gases nor liquids, they demand recognition as rocks.

Perhaps we try to mend matters by saying that rocks are all natural combinations of mineral matter, whether they are compact or loose. Here, again, we encounter difficulties. As we have seen in Chapter II, a mineral is a natural inorganic substance of one nature throughout, its make-up generally being so definite that it can be expressed in a chemical formula. Granite consists of minerals and so does limestone, clay or dust. But soil is a mixture of mineral and rock grains with decayed plant material. Coal, which forms stony beds, is made almost wholly from plants and has no definite chemical composition. The same is true of asphalt, which is not stony but which occurs in such large deposits that it deserves the name of rock.

At the other extreme, we find stones that do not consist of minerals. Volcanic glass forms cliffs in the West; it is lava which cooled and hardened without forming minerals. Pumice and volcanic ash are essentially like volcanic glass, except that one is blown into a stony froth by gas, while the other is exploded into little grains. When ash falls it is not solid, though later changes may turn it into firm stone.

Finally, many mineral deposits are too small to be called rocks. In this group belong the *veins* of calcite (PLATE 40), quartz and other minerals which water often deposits in cracks. Geodes and concretions (PLATE 41) belong here, for they also are too small to be rocks, even though they are interesting structures in both loose and stony deposits.

Here, then, are our problems. Any satisfactory definition of rocks must include stones, as well as loose deposits which consist of mineral grains. It also must include stony and loose-grained masses of glass, as well as coal and other deposits that came from living things; yet it must rule out crystals, veins, geodes and other bodies of small size. These requirements sound complex indeed, yet we may meet them with two simple statements:

*Rocks are any large natural masses of mineral or mineral-like matter, including glass. They also include massive organic deposits, such as asphalt and coal.* The word *natural* rules out such artificial substances as concrete and slag. Though stony, they are made by man and so may not rank as rocks.

## MINERALS AND MIXTURES

At its simplest, the difference between rocks and minerals amounts to nothing more than size. A crystal of calcite is a mineral; so is the calcite vein that runs like a white line across a piece of marble. The marble may be pure calcite, too, with grains of that mineral showing in its broken or polished face; but it forms a large block or slab which was cut from a still larger bed exposed in a hillside quarry. Other marble beds are exposed there as well; together they make a series of rocks that perhaps underlie a thousand square miles of country.

The same distinction applies to a few other substances. Silica is a mineral; it also forms pure sand, sandstone and quartzite, all of which rank as rocks. The best china clays are pure kaolin, and some soapstones contain little else than talc. Very rich iron ores consist of hematite or magnetite, both of which are minerals produced when iron and oxygen combine. Common salt, or halite, makes beds or strata so thick that mine tunnels and rooms have been cut in them. Gypsum, also, is both mineral and rock, its massive beds underlying thousands of square miles of country from Nova Scotia to the Southwest.

In most cases, however, very large masses of mineral matter are "impure," which means they are mixed with other minerals. All except the purest marbles contain some compounds of iron, a little clay and some graphite, while brightly colored ones hold abundant impurities. Limestone is likely to contain clay as well

[ 54 ]

as calcite, plus some silica in the form of sand. Sand is discolored by iron or contains grains of feldspar as well as quartz. Sandstone may be cemented with lime or hematite, while the great hematite beds themselves contain sand and clay. Most clays have so much hematite, limonite, alumina and silica that they cannot be used for china.

Many combinations of this sort are made by water. Seeping underground, it dissolves minerals and drops, or precipitates, them elsewhere. It leaves lime among grains of sand, cementing them into sandstone. It dissolves silica (quartz) from some of those grains, takes some iron oxide at another place and deposits both as colored nodules of chert or agate among otherwise pure limestones. Waters of another sort rise from underground masses of molten rock, making their way to holes and cracks near the surface. There the waters deposit quartz, lead, zinc, silver and other minerals which they have brought in solution. The result may be a mere crevice-filling or vein, or it may be a change in the character of great thicknesses of rock.

Most mixtures, however, have not come by addition; they were made when the rocks themselves were formed. Gravel, for instance, is a mixture of pebbles, each containing several minerals and all deposited by streams or dropped by melting glacial ice. Smaller particles make up sand; those worn until they are microscopic form clays and shales or add their bit to impurities in muds which will become limestones. An even greater variety of material may be found in wind-blown dust deposits or in clays dropped by melting ice or by streams.

Another type of mixture is found in granite and most other rocks that once were molten. Here several minerals existed together in a hot fluid mass. When it cooled and hardened they crystallized, each mineral separating from its neighbors and forming crystals or grains. Almost any polished piece of granite will show three kinds of minerals and may show five or six.

## ROCK CLASSIFICATION

We have said that rocks have no definite composition that can be put into chemical formulae. We seldom even can set percentages for the minerals in them or divide them according to their crystals. In spite of this we can name rocks and classify them. Indeed, we already have done so, on several different plans. We have grouped them into hard rocks, or stones, and rocks that are unconsolidated, or loose. We have separated pure from impure deposits and coarse ones from those whose grains are tiny. We also have distinguished organic rocks, such as coal, from inorganic ones, whose material did not come from plants or animals.

Each of these groupings is useful. Each includes a great many rocks and gives a hint of their origin. To frame a really adequate classification, however, we must emphasize origin still more. Doing this, we find that all the rocks that are known can be placed into three great groups:

*Igneous rocks* are those that once were hot and liquid, or molten, whether they came to the surface in that condition or not. Many did so and were erupted as volcanic ash and lava. Many hardened far underground and are granites or similar rocks.

*Sedimentary rocks* are those that were deposited by gravity, wind, water or ice, or were built up by plants and animals. Directly or indirectly, most of their material came from older rocks which were worn, broken or dissolved before sediments could form. Most sedimentary rocks form layers or beds: sandstone, limestone and shale are familiar examples.

*Metamorphic rocks* are those which have been changed by heat, pressure, mineral-bearing water or a combination of these agents. This change is known as metamorphism. In some places it has destroyed all trace of the rock's original nature, so that we cannot tell a metamorphosed granite from a metamorphosed conglomerate. In other places the original nature of the rock can be distinguished. Slate and schist are familiar members of this group.

Each of these divisions may be divided again, but that may be left to later chapters which describe rocks as well as classify them.

## ROCKS HAVE FORMED AT VARIED TIMES

We now come to three familiar questions. How old are the different kinds of rocks? What geologic periods do they distinguish? What do they tell of the earth's age—not in indefinite epochs and eras, but in our own calendar years?

The first of these questions has no answer, for rock groups cannot be divided by age. According to one theory, there was a time when all rocks of the earth's crust were igneous: products of terrific eruptions that followed the era in which our planet was built. That, however, was very long ago. Even if the theory is correct, those primeval rocks have been so deeply buried by eruptions, upheavals and later deposits that no mine or well can reach them.

For at least 1,500,000,000 years, and probably for a much longer time, rocks of our three main groups have been forming *during the same periods.* Choose almost any period you wish; its record will include granites, basalts, ash beds and other igneous rocks whose appearance tells little about their age. There also will be sandstones, limestones and shales, all very much like similar rocks that are both younger and more ancient. Limestones, for instance, are forming today; they also formed during the Cretaceous, Carboniferous, Devonian and several Pre-Cambrian ages. Fossil plants and animals in these various deposits enable us to tell them apart, but limestone itself persists through the record of more than 1,250,000,000 years.

Rocks form where materials and conditions are right for them, not at special times. This becomes obvious if we select a few conspicuous kinds and note some of the ages in which they were produced:

| Group | Rock | Some Ages in Which the Rock Formed* |
|---|---|---|
| IGNEOUS | Basalt<br>Obsidian<br>Ash, Tuff | Keeweenawan, Carboniferous, Tertiary, Quaternary<br>Devonian, Tertiary, Quaternary<br>Ordovician, Silurian, Jurassic, Tertiary, Quaternary |
| SEDIMEN-TARY | Coal<br>Tillite<br>Gypsum | Devonian, Carboniferous, Permian, Cretaceous, Tertiary<br>Huronian, Keweenawan, Permian, Tertiary, Quaternary<br>Silurian, Permian, Jurassic, Tertiary |
| METAMOR-PHIC | Slate*<br>Schist*<br>Marble* | Late Huronian, Permian, Tertiary<br>Keewatin, Temiskaming, Jurassic, Tertiary<br>Archeozoic (?), Late Keweenawan, Permian, Jurassic, Tertiary |

*In this table the ages given for metamorphic rocks are those in which the original formations were changed, not those in which they were deposited.

## EVENTS, NOT ROCKS, DIVIDE AGES

We must not conclude, however, that the rock formations, or *systems,* of all ages are exactly alike. A geologic period is distinguished because it was a time when conditions on earth differed from those which prevailed both earlier and later. One age, for example, was a time when long narrow seas invaded the West while lavas filled the basin that now holds Lake Superior. Another was a period of moist climates and swamps where trees and rushes grew in such abundance that they formed thick beds of muck. A third age was marked by wide valleys and deltas at the edge of high, perhaps desert, lands.

Many different rocks were produced during each of these ages, but some were so much more plentiful than others that they do help to set the period off from its neighbors in the geologic column. Thus we may speak of the Keweenawan as the age of copper-bearing lavas, the Carboniferous as the Coal Age and the Permian as the time of great red beds. The Cretaceous also does very well as the Chalk Age, even though deposits of chalk formed during other periods and are forming in some places today. But if we try to select an age of limestone, we find that at least five periods deserve this honor. There also were several periods of basaltic lava flows and great granite intrusions, as well as of sandstone formations and shale.

No, rocks alone are not enough to divide geologic time. Things happened to the earth, changing lands, shifting seas or building mountains. These changes then were recorded in rocks which might or might not be different from those formed at other times. Some parts of the story were told by new deposits, some by changes in old formations, some by plants and animals whose remains were buried and became fossils. A brief summary of this record is given in the geologic time chart at the end of this chapter. It mentions some rocks formed during each age, those which are specially distinctive being marked by asterisks.

## TIMETABLES IN ROCK

We now come to the third question. What do rocks tell of the earth's age—and its ages—in terms of ordinary years?

Rocks themselves tell almost nothing, except that our planet is very old. It is true that some clays and shales consist of thin layers that formed at the rate of two per year. By counting the number of these layers we learn how long some lakes have been in existence or when the last great glaciers melted from New York or northern Europe. Such seasonally banded shales (PLATE 39) show that a lake which covered part of Wyoming during Eocene times lasted some 6,500,000 years and that glaciers melted from the southern tip of Sweden about 13,500 years ago. Yet the first figure does not tell us when the Eocene epoch ended, while the second gives no hint as to when the Ice Age began. As for the age of the earth as a whole: these figures and others like them tell so little that they mean virtually nothing.

But can we not tell how fast rocks settle *on the average* and determine the earth's age from that? The first attempt in this direction was made by the Greek historian Herodotus, about 450 B.C., when he noticed that as the river Nile overflowed it spread a layer of mud in its valley. Realizing that the great river's delta had been built up by such deposits, Herodotus concluded that the delta's development had taken many thousands of years. His estimates were borne out when excavations showed that river deposits which were 40 feet thick at Memphis had gathered at the rate of 3.5 inches per century—a total of 13,700 years. Since these 40 feet are only the surface veneer of the delta, its age must be many times 13,700 years.

How many times? No one knows, just as no one knows the age of any really thick formation. Some rocks form quickly and others slowly; an inch of mud may settle in a month at one spot and may accumulate in 300 years at another. Lavas and magmas follow no rule. Great masses of them may indicate great age, but thickness alone has no meaning in years.

What thickness does not tell, minerals may. Dark minerals in many igneous rocks contain radioactive elements—queer substances that shoot out heat, alpha particles and electrons until they turn themselves into lead. Their behavior upset several well-established "laws" and formed the chief scientific wonder of the period from 1900 to the first World War.

There are several radioactive elements; radium is the most famous, but uranium and thorium mean most in deciphering the ages of rocks because they are found in formations of many different ages. Both these minerals are radioactive; each uranium atom, for example, shoots out a tiny amount of heat, six electrons and eight alpha particles. The heat is lost, while the alpha particles capture electrons and become atoms of helium, the nonburning gas used in airships. The remnant of the uranium atom is lead that weighs less than the ordinary kind and so can be recognized. The changes that produce this lightweight lead can neither be hastened nor delayed. In fact, many observations and experiments show that alpha particles and electrons are shot out just often enough to turn half the uranium into lead in about 5,000,000,000 years.

In theory the earth is not that old. It is significant, therefore, that no one has found a rock in which half the original uranium has been turned into lightweight lead. But in the Russian part of the Karelian Peninsula, near the Arctic Circle, igneous rocks contain minerals in which the ratio of uranium to lead is 0.36 to 1.00. This indicates that those rocks are 0.36 × 5,000,000,000, or 1,800,000,000 years old. On the same basis, igneous rocks on the shores of Lake Winnipeg, Manitoba, have an age of 1,700,000,000 years. Younger deposits of the Black Hills are 1,460,000,000 years old and still younger ones in Norway are 915,000,000.

Another method uses the helium formed when alpha particles capture electrons. This also occurs at a regular rate, and if the helium does not get away, it should give figures as good as those provided by lightweight lead. Unfortunately, there seem to be many ways in which helium does get out of rocks, so that figures based upon the amount that remains may be very much too low.

In spite of these difficulties and uncertainties, our geologic time chart includes dates—the best ones now available. They give at least a general idea of the length of each period or age, and that is much more important than precise numbers of years.

# A GEOLOGIC TIME CHART

| Eras | Periods (Ages) and Their Length | Important Events | Some Important Rocks | Years Ago (Beginning) |
|---|---|---|---|---|
| Quaternary / Cenozoic | Recent Epoch 15,000 to 25,000 yrs. | Glaciers melted; climates became warm again. Continents high. Several great deserts. | Coarse- to fine-grained clastic sediments are dominant. Lavas and ash beds still form. Peat in the North. | 15,000 in North to 25,000 in South |
| Quaternary / Cenozoic | Pleistocene, or Ice Age 2,000,000 (?) yrs. | Four great glacial advances in North America and Europe. Sierra Nevada and other mountains lifted again. | Glacial drift and outwash deposits. Residual soils in unglaciated regions. | 2,000,000 (?) |
| Tertiary / Cenozoic | Pliocene Epoch 10,000,000 yrs. | World-wide uplift and mountain building continued, affecting mountains of western North and South America. Great eruptions. Cooler. | Basalts, andesites, etc., continuing those of Miocene times. Conglomerates, soft sandstones and shales on coastal plains. | 12,000,000 |
| Tertiary / Cenozoic | Miocene Epoch 18,000,000 yrs. | Sierra Nevada and modern Rockies were lifted. Eruptions built the Cascades and Northwestern lava plains. Climates mild. | Diatomite in California and near Chesapeake Bay. Basalt and andesite in the Northwest and the Rockies. Laccoliths in the Black Hills region. | 30,000,000 |
| Tertiary / Cenozoic | Oligocene Epoch 10,000,000 yrs. | Lands became low; volcanoes erupted in the Rockies. Alps and Himalayas began to rise. Climates became mild and equable. | Basalt, andesite and tuff in the Rockies; soft clay* on the Great Plains (now best seen in badlands of South Dakota and Wyoming). | 40,000,000 |
| Tertiary / Cenozoic | Eocene Epoch 15,000,000 yrs. | Mountains were eroded, piling clastic sediment in valleys. Seas were narrow. | Conglomerates, sands, clays and some marine limestones. Agglomerates, lavas and oil shales* in the West. | 55,000,000 |
| Tertiary / Cenozoic | Paleocene Epoch 5,000,000 yrs. | Mountains were high; valleys sank or were eroded deeply. Seas were very narrow. | Conglomerates, sandstones, clays. Subbituminous coal* in Montana and Wyoming. | 60,000,000 |
| Mesozoic | Cretaceous, or Chalk Age 70,000,000 yrs. | Last great spread of seas, especially in the West. At the end of the period, uplift built the early Rockies. Climates became cool. | Chalk.* Bituminous and subbituminous coal in the West.* Greensand in New Jersey.* Extensive sandstones and dark shales of the Great Plains. Petroleum. | 130,000,000 |
| Mesozoic | Jurassic 38,000,000 yrs. | Continents were partly worn down. Shallow seas covered part of Europe and narrow basins in the West. | Sandstone, shale and marine limestone. Black shale in Europe; contains many fossils. Bituminous coal in Alaska.* Andesite in northern California. | 168,000,000 |
| Mesozoic | Triassic 32,000,000 yrs. | Continents were rather high; dry in many regions. Rivers were flooded by seasonal rains. Many eruptions in the East. | Red beds;* diabase (trap) flows and sills east of the Appalachians.* Sandstone, shale and tuff in Arizona. Many shales are light gray to purplish in color. | 200,000,000 |
| Paleozoic | Permian 35,000,000 yrs. | Continents were raised; Appalachian, Ouachita and Ural mountains were built. Climates cooled; deserts developed. Extensive glaciation in both hemispheres. | Red beds,* gypsum,* anhydrite,* especially in the Southwest. Thick tillites,* best known in Africa and Australia. Lava and tuff near the Pacific coast of North America. | 235,000,000 |

| Era | Period | Physical history | Rocks | Age (years) |
|---|---|---|---|---|
| PALAEOZOIC | Carboniferous 80,000,000 yrs. | Lands were low but became higher; seas spread and withdrew many times. Extensive coal swamps in many parts of the world. Climates equable; generally warm and moist. | Coal* and petroleum. Much limestone in the Mississippi basin and in parts of the West, especially in early part of the period. Shale and gypsum in eastern Canada. Shale, sandstone and limestone with coal deposits. | 315,000,000 |
| | Devonian 35,000,000 yrs. | Seas spread widely. Uplift in Appalachian region. Eruptions in New England, eastern Canada, Scotland. | Limestone, shale; sandstone late in the period. Lavas in New England; granite in Australia. | 350,000,000 |
| | Silurian 25,000,000 yrs. | Seas widespread; some deserts; climate warm and generally uniform except near end of the period. Deserts in northeastern United States. | Much limestone and dolomite; also shale. Clinton iron ore.* Gypsum in northeastern United States.* Great salt deposits from New York to Kansas.* | 375,000,000 |
| | Ordovician 70,000,000 yrs. | More than 60 per cent of North America covered by shifting seas. Deltas in western New York and Pennsylvania. Volcanoes in the East. | Much shale and limestone; deposits in East largely slate and marble. Ash beds (tuff) in the East. Thick tuffs and pillow lavas in Quebec and Newfoundland. | 445,000,000 |
| | Cambrian 105,000,000 yrs. | Seas covered much of North America three times. Climates apparently uniform and mild. No mountain building. | Extensive limestones, especially in the Rockies. Conglomerates (Great Smokies); sandstones in the upper Mississippi basin; quartzites in Minnesota and the Appalachians. | 550,000,000 |
| PROTEROZOIC | Keweenawan, or Belt 250,000,000 yrs. | Great eruptions of lava; also intrusions in Minnesota and Michigan. Mountains uplifted and worn down, and great glaciation at end of the period. | Copper-bearing diabase* in northern Michigan. Argillites* and mud-cracked, ripple-marked dolomite* in the northern Rockies. Tillites* in China and Australia. Conglomerate, sandstone and quartzite in various regions. | 800,000,000 |
| | Huronian 250,000,000 yrs. | Shallow seas were widespread. Glaciers covered much of eastern Canada. | World's greatest iron ores.* Tillite in Canada; also conglomerate, chert and granite in Canada. Many gold, silver and other ores. | 1,050,000,000 |
| | Temiskaming 150,000,000 yrs. | Seas widespread at first, followed by mountain building and great intrusions in eastern Canada. | Granites, greywacke, conglomerate and quartzite, chiefly in northern Canada. Some dolomite. | 1,200,000,000 |
| ARCHEOZOIC | Keewatin 800,000,000 yrs. | Great intrusions and extrusions, especially in Canada. Mountain building and metamorphism. | Granite, gneiss, marble, schist and other metamorphic rocks. Many granites are pegmatitic.* Iron ore.* | 2,000,000,000 |
| AZOIC | No periods recognized 1,000,000,000±yrs. | Solar system began; planets grew to almost their present size. Continents and ocean basins developed. Tremendous vulcanism. | Rocks unknown. | 3,000,000,000± |

Asterisk (*) indicates rocks that are specially characteristic.

CHAPTER V

# Up from the Depths

Each SUMMER thousands of tourists motor through the Black Hills of South Dakota. These travelers cross ridges of brown sandstone, wind through valleys cut in red shale and finally reach the gray granite mountains. Roads climb several of them, one threading the maze of tall pointed "needles" on one shoulder of Harney Peak.

The trip is beautiful and surprising, which is why most travelers take it. It also is a journey into the past. About 1,460,000,000 years ago those gray granites were a mass of intensely hot, almost fluid rock far down inside the earth. When the mass became soft enough it moved upward for thousands of feet before it crystallized and hardened. Then it stayed in one place for millions of years, only to be pushed upward again. In the end one of North America's oldest and most deeply buried formations stood thousands of feet higher than younger, different rocks of the plains.

## HOW DO MAGMAS RISE?

We have said that igneous rocks once were hot molten masses that came from depths within the earth. Those that managed to reach the surface often erupted amid explosions, steam clouds and flames. They justify the name *igneous,* which comes from the Latin word meaning fire.

Why say *molten masses* instead of *lavas?* Because most geologists use *lava* for hot rock that is erupted on land or under the sea. Hot, molten or plastic rock that does not erupt is *magma*—its name being the Greek word for "dough." Many lavas are offshoots of deep-seated magmas which, like the granites of the Black Hills, hardened long before they reached the surface. Such magmas produced more hard rock than did all the lavas in existence. This entitles them to our first attention, even though they were very slow about coming into view.

Though everyone agrees that magmas moved, no one knows just how they did so. In days when every geologist felt sure that the earth was a ball of molten rock whose surface had cooled and hardened into a "crust," the process seemed obvious and simple. A magma was merely a part of the central molten mass that was forced outward into "pockets" that honeycombed the interior of the crust. There it encountered cracks which were opened as the crust cooled and shrank. If the molten material worked its way through several miles of these, it burst forth in eruptions and became lava. If none of the molten stuff got through, it remained magma. Its movements might be accompanied by upheavals of the crust and tremendous earthquakes, but the magma hardened as an *intrusion* of granite or related stone.

This theory was simple, but it was not correct. First, physicists showed that the center of the earth was neither syrupy nor fluid but was almost as rigid as steel. Petrographers found that igneous rocks varied too much to come from a single great storehouse of magma located at the earth's center or any other place. Records proved that eruptions took place independently, even though the volcanoes that produced them might stand side by side. Geologists piled up evidence that magmas were of several sorts and came from various depths that ranged from 5 to 15

[*65*]

miles. Many of them, moreover, did not penetrate cracks. Some actually seemed to have made the spaces into which they moved.

## THE EARTH HAS SEVERAL SHELLS

From these data came a new theory—indeed, a group of theories. We can understand them best if we first examine modern ideas of the earth's structure.

These ideas are summarized in the accompanying drawing. It shows a central core of nickel and iron, more than 4000 miles in diameter and almost four times as dense as granite. Around this core is a shell 435 miles thick, in which iron, nickel, olivine and a few other substances are mixed; it is three times as dense as granite, with an average specific gravity of 8. A second shell, of about the same thickness, has a specific gravity of 6. It contains pyroxene and more olivine in proportion to its iron and nickel.

The third shell is more than 900 miles thick; it contains olivine, magnetite, pyroxene and labradorite, with metals in separate masses, or pockets. The outermost 600 miles of this shell are essentially like the igneous rock described in Chapter VI as peridotite. Temperatures probably reach 800 to 1100 degrees centigrade, in contrast to those of the nickel-iron core, which have been estimated at 8000 to 10,000 degrees.

The *crust* is the surface shell of the earth, ranging from 35 to 40 miles in thickness, with an average of 37 miles. Its innermost 25 miles (the *subcrust*) apparently resemble basalt or gabbro and have a specific gravity of 3.2. The outermost 12 to 15 miles (the *true crust*) have much the composition of granite. A mixture of dark rocks, however, makes it somewhat heavier than granite.

We have represented these parts of the earth as shells, sharply separated. Actually they probably are very irregular and grade from one into another. Much of this intergradation was brought about by magmas that moved from shell to shell. A series of these moving magmas is represented in the drawing, with their size so much exaggerated that they show clearly.

Even in the true crust rocks become very hot. Records from mines and deep wells show an average rise in temperature of

Crust
Subcrust
Peridotite shell

Pyroxene-olivine shell
Nickel-iron-olivine shell

Nickel-iron core

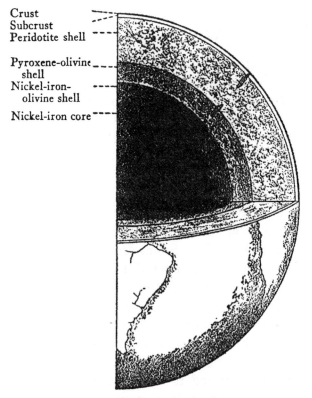

The earth's core and shells shown diagrammatically as distinct parts of the planet. Magmas are moving from shell to shell.

one degree Fahrenheit with every 60 feet in depth. At this rate, rocks 15 miles below the surface have temperatures of 1320 degrees Fahrenheit, or 733 degrees centigrade. Under 37 miles of crust the temperature would be about 1830 degrees centigrade.

It would be—if the increase continued at a uniform rate. Actually the rate begins to diminish below depths of a few miles. Pressure, however, steadily increases. At depths of 25 to 35 miles it apparently is great enough to keep rocks from becoming fluid, even if they were hot enough to melt. Intense pressure certainly has this effect at still greater depths.

## MAGMAS WERE FORCED UPWARD

This is a modern picture of the earth. Though it is frankly theoretical, it fits the facts much better than did old ideas of a seething, molten core that was ready to break through the crust.

But how—and why—did magmas rise? Here, again, we encounter theories. To make them as clear as possible, let us fit them to a special intrusion such as Little Sundance Hill (PLATE 12), in Wyoming, a few miles west of the Black Hills. Another good place to test them is the Henry Mountains of Utah. Unfortunately, the Henry Mountains are so far from motor roads that few people except Indians and sheepherders ever see them. Therefore we choose Little Sundance Hill, which rises near a paved highway and is small enough to be seen as a whole.

Our story starts when the hill was a mass of hot rock 5 or 10 miles below what then was the land surface. For some reason this rock became even hotter; perhaps it lay above a pocket of uranium or radium whose radiations increased the temperature. Probably, too, this special mass of rock contained more water than did the rocks around it. This water helped the hot mass become fluid, thus turning into magma. When this happened the molten rock began to work its way upward. In other words, *the magma moved.*

It moved, but theories that tell why are conflicting. One says that pressure around the magma squeezed it upward, much as pressure forces water through weak spots in the ice of a pond. Another theory says that water in the magma turned into steam, which was under such tremendous pressure that it forced the magma through the hard crust. Believers in this theory point to intrusions in southern Germany and South Africa, where magmas were driven upward through thousands of feet of strata, making holes that are almost as sharp as those cut by a punch forced through a pile of paper. What else than steam, they ask, could provide the motive force for such intrusions? To which still other geologists reply that the magma may have melted, or dissolved, rocks above it, thus "eating" its way through them as acid eats through iron or zinc.

Be that as it may, there came a time when the magma approached the surface and could lift rocks instead of breaking through them. Lifting produced a dome-shaped blister under which the molten stuff could spread out. As it spread, the magma began to cool, for heat could radiate through the cover of the blister. Steam also escaped through cracks and pores, removing still more heat.

Loss of steam, however, meant more than cooling. Water had helped the magma become liquid, forcing rocks to soften at temperatures below those which could have caused simple melting. We know by experiment that rocks which will not melt below 2500 degrees Fahrenheit in a dry furnace become fluid at 750 degrees when water is present. Water in the magma worked like water in this experiment; it was helped by carbon dioxide, hydrochloric acid and at least two other substances. When all these began to escape from the blister, the magma stiffened, or became viscous. This change was hastened by cooling, whose causes we already have seen.

Stiffening reduced movement—especially upward movement. The magma crowded into the blister, arching the rocks above it more and more steeply and tilting them along its sides. Soon the viscous mass began to harden and crystallize. In the end it became the solid dome-shaped affair which now forms the core of Little Sundance Hill. Even after millions of years of erosion it still is covered by bent, tilted strata. Bear Butte (PLATE 12), two hours' drive eastward in South Dakota, has suffered much more wear. Its hardened magma is now a barren peak whose cover of stratified rocks has been carried away. The tilted remnants form a series of ridges, or *hogbacks,* around the conical butte.

## MANY MAGMAS FILLED FOLDS

In the Sierras, the Canadian Coast Ranges and many parts of the Rockies events were more complicated. Instead of pushing rocks upward, enormous magmas were able to fill folds which were almost ready-made. Even before those magmas moved upward, earth movements squeezed great thicknesses of rock until they became mountain ranges consisting of arches or folds. While pressure to lift them was gathering, it heated the rocks far beneath. As soon as the upper rocks began to rise, pressure on those far below was lessened. Heat and dissolved gas began their work—work that soon produced magmas and sent them upward toward the folds. There they spread out in vast, elongate cores, worked their way along cracks and wedged themselves between strata. At their very edges they dissolved much rock or broke off sharp fragments that were heated, changed and yet preserved in the hardening magma. We find them today among granites or wedged among offshoots leading from the great intrusions.

## EROSION UNCOVERS HARDENED MAGMAS

But how, you ask, do we know of these rocks if they cooled and hardened underground?

The answer is that "ground" is no fixed thing. It falls or rises with earth movements; it is added to and worn away. Ground, or rock forming the land surface, was pushed upward by rising magma as Little Sundance Hill formed. Even before the hill stopped rising, wind, rain and streams began to wear it away. Though they have not yet removed the cover of bent rocks, they have dug most of the way through it in several deep ravines. On near-by buttes and mountains they have done much more, leaving the upturned beds as ringlike ridges around domes or cones of igneous rock from which all strata have been removed. We already have traced the results of such wear in the rocks around Bear Butte.

If erosion alone does not expose hardened magmas, uplift may help it out. It may even repeat the process of exposure. Granites in the Black Hills were laid bare by erosion once and

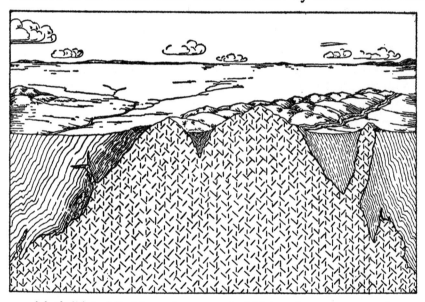

A batholith in folded formations, part of which have been worn away. At the right is a stock, forming an isolated hill.

then were covered by deposits of seas during several later ages. Perhaps 1,000,000 years ago the whole mass was pushed upward into a new dome, from which water and frost have cut the Needles as well as larger peaks.

In the Beartooth Mountains (which are crossed by the Red Lodge road to Yellowstone National Park) a block of equally ancient rocks has been broken and pushed upward more than 4000 feet. Motorists cross the main break as they enter the mountains and then climb for miles to reach the top of the ancient worn block. Then they come upon a mountain of marine strata, a remnant of material that covered the igneous block before it was uplifted.

## INTRUSIVE ROCK MASSES

Let us now leave the processes of intrusion and look at the things that are formed when masses of magma harden. Though few of these are small enough to show in individual rocks, they are important as the sources from which specimens and boulders come. For this reason, as well as because of general interest, we ask: What do magmas look like when they harden in cracks? What shape do they have when they are cores of mountains? What name shall we give intrusions like those of Little Sundance Hill? Let us answer the last question first and then go on to igneous masses that were formed in other ways.

### Laccoliths
(PLATE 12)

A laccolith is a dome-shaped mass of igneous rock that has been forced between older formations, most of which lie in layers or beds. The rising magma bent the rocks above it but spread across rocks below in a surface which may be almost flat. In some large laccoliths, however, the floor sags toward the center, as if its support had been weakened when the lava spread out above it. In other cases the floor of a laccolith is tilted or crumpled, with the hardened magma fitting its irregularities.

Magmas that built laccoliths were stiff and doughy, even while they were very hot. This explains why they were able to lift and bend strata into domes under which the magmas spread out in biscuit-shaped masses whose thicknesses range from a few hundred feet to a mile and whose diameters vary from 50 rods to several miles. Some laccoliths show the necks through which the hot rock moved upward, while many show that the magma spread out between beds or cut across them, producing structures of two other types which we shall call dikes and sills.

Laccoliths were discovered by a geologist named Gilbert when he worked in the Henry Mountains which, as we already have said, are in the deserts of southeastern Utah. Laccoliths of the Henry Mountains are oval domes one half to 4 miles in diameter and one seventh as high as they are wide. Laccoliths near the Black Hills are easily seen; the one now called Bear Butte (Sioux Indians named it Sits-with-its-young-one) is

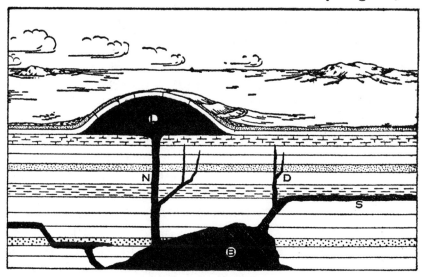

Several types of intrusions. The deepest and largest is a batholith (B), from which a neck (N) leads to a laccolith (L). Dikes (D) and sills (S) extend from the batholith.

very high for its width and from a distance suggests a volcanic cone. Little Sundance Hill, whose origin has been discussed, is unusual in having most of its cover still preserved.

## Bysmaliths

The name bysmalith comes from two Greek words meaning "plug" and "rock." It is used for a variety of laccolith whose magma either moved upward with great force or encountered very brittle strata. At least it arched its cover moderately and then broke it away from the country rock, forming a stony plug.

The magma then pushed this plug upward through the strata around it. Such intrusions are not common.

## Batholiths

This name also is spelled *bathyliths* and *batholites*. Batholiths are huge masses of rock intruded into formations that already were folded and uplifted. Though no one knows just why great masses of magma should lie beneath rocks that are being folded, some geologists have suggested that folding released so much pressure that the magmas could become fluid and rise. Thus they were able to move into the folds, melt or dissolve parts of them, and so build igneous cores inside mountains that were ready-made. Other batholiths cut across folded formations, but even they were related to crumpling and uplift.

Batholiths consist of granite and other coarsely crystalline rocks. A Mesozoic batholith in Idaho covers 16,000 square miles; that of the Sierra Nevada, in California, is 400 miles long and as much as 80 miles wide; the batholith of the Canadian Coast Range has an area of about 100,000 square miles. There are large batholiths of late Paleozoic age in the eastern United States, and Pre-Cambrian batholiths form about 2,000,000 square miles of northeastern Canada and Greenland. They must represent thousands of separate intrusions, for most of those that have been measured are 10 to 50 miles in width. Many geologists think that deep-seated batholiths have sent up extensions which formed laccoliths, but connections between them are hard to find.

As we shall see in Chapter XIX, hot watery solutions coming from batholiths have produced many valuable ores by depositing minerals in the surrounding rocks. They did this more effectively than solutions from laccoliths or stocks because they were more abundant and contained more dissolved material. Pegmatites, described in Chapter VI, also were produced by such solutions.

## Dikes and Veins
### (PLATES 13, 18)

A dike (also spelled *dyke*) is an upright or steeply inclined wall of igneous rock formed by magma that was forced into a break or crevice. Dikes range from a few yards to 100 miles in length, while their width may be several inches or 400 to 500 feet. Although dikes like those shown on PLATE 13 are dark, others (especially those to be described as pegmatite dikes) are light-colored. The dark basaltic dikes range from fine-grained to glassy, depending on the size of each dike, its material, its depth and the rate at which it cooled. Light-colored dikes, as a rule, are coarse-grained, and some contain the largest crystals of any rock masses known.

Small dikes, called igneous veins, probably did no more than fill cracks, through which they commonly bend and branch. Large dikes, however, must have done more than that. Few cracks in the earth are 5 feet wide, but dikes 20, 30 or even 50 feet wide are common. Evidence of chilling shows that their outer parts cooled very quickly, while traces of solution are rare. It seems, therefore, that magma was pushed upward with such great pressure that it acted like a huge wedge, pushing the older rocks apart. Indeed, many dikes are shaped like huge wedges, thinning toward the surface.

Dikes have not lifted strata nor did they rise above the ground when formed; but because their rocks generally are resistant, weathering and erosion may leave them as upright or slanting walls across slopes of weaker rocks. In some places the reverse is true, however, so that dikes are eroded into clefts or troughs while the rocks around them stand out boldly.

Dikes are found in both the East and West but are rare in the Central States and Prairie Provinces of Canada. They are abundant in Maine, at Cape Ann, Massachusetts, near the Spanish Peaks of Colorado, in the Crazy Mountains of Montana (north of Yellowstone National Park) and in many other regions.

## Sills

Sills are sheets of igneous rock that, while viscous, were forced between strata. Some merely lifted the rocks above them, wedging their way into the space so made. A few dissolved some of the rocks between which they moved. Many sills followed oblique joints, cutting across several beds only to spread out between others. Many sills are connected with dikes which brought magma from laccoliths or batholiths.

Sills vary greatly in size. Some of those on Mount Royal, in Montreal, are 2 to 4 inches thick and barely 6 feet wide. Visitors to Glacier National Park, Montana, see sills that once extended under at least 2000 square miles but which rarely are more than 100 feet thick. They cut across beds and spread from dikes, but there is no trace of the large igneous mass with which they probably are connected. The Palisades of the Hudson are made by a sill 70 miles long and 300 to 850 feet thick; another, 5000 feet thick, is known in Ontario. Sills are common in southern New England, New Jersey and southern New York.

Most sills consist of dark coarse-grained rocks such as diorite and grainy diabase, which were viscous even when they were hot. Thus they were able to force their way between strata with only a little melting and solution. This means that they formed near the surface, for even viscous lava was not able to lift very great thicknesses of rock. The sills of Glacier National Park apparently spread out only a few hundred feet below the bottom of a sea.

In small exposures, sills and lava flows may look much alike. Here are five ways to tell them apart.

1. Sills change, or metamorphose, beds above as well as below them. Lava flows can metamorphose only rocks below them, for they spread out upon the surface.

2. Sills cut sharply across beds, which lava flows rarely do.

The only way in which a lava flow can cut across strata is to roll down a hill, tumble over a cliff or spread across tilted rocks. In any of these cases the weathered and eroded surface is almost sure to show.

3. Sills do not show *aa* or *pahoehoe* structure; most lavas do.

4. Sills may contain fragments broken from the rocks above them; lavas can contain fragments only from those below.

5. Sills usually show the same sort of rock from top to bottom. Many lava flows are glassy or slaglike at the top and fine-grained at the bottom.

## Stocks and Bosses

A stock is a large mass of intrusive rock that worked its way close to the surface before solidifying. Most stocks are round to oval in cross section and are high in proportion to their width. Their sides are steep and irregular, and they cut across strata instead of bending them upward. Stocks range in diameter from 50 or 60 yards to several miles. When the rocks around them are worn away they form steep hills called *bosses*. Many stocks consist of diorite, gabbro or granite; they form most of the granite hills in New England, Scotland and other regions where old mountains have been worn away. Great Snake and Little Snake hills on the marshes near Newark, New Jersey, are familiar bosses, and Stone Mountain, in Georgia, is another. The New Jersey bosses or stocks were formed by magma rising from the great sill of the Palisades.

## Necks
### (PLATE 12)

Most necks are columns of hardened magma leading to volcanoes, though some lead to laccoliths. When a laccolith or volcanic cone is worn away erosion allows the solidified magma (which generally is more resistant than hardened lava) to stand out as a small stock among remnants of the cone or above the rocks on which it was formed. Volcanic necks are round or oval in ground plan and range from a few hundred feet to a mile in diameter. The rocks around them generally are cut by dikes and crossed by deep cracks; if they are stratified, they contain small sills.

Volcanic necks are found where old volcanoes have been worn away. The name also may be used for the columns of igneous rock left as magmas worked their way upward to form laccoliths. Large necks of this sort are not common, for few laccoliths have been completely worn away. Even if they were, their columns of magma might be confused with stocks.

## Inclusions
### (PLATE 45)

Inclusions, also called xenoliths, are pieces of older and generally very different rocks embedded in igneous dikes, sills, batholiths or laccoliths. Many are angular in shape, showing clearly that they were broken from pre-existing rocks through which the magma passed. Others are rounded from partial melting in the hot rock that tore them loose and often carried them upward as well. They may consist of almost any kind of rock, though the sediments generally are changed by heat, pressure and solutions from the magma.

Inclusions also are found in lavas. Chunks of once-soft mud lie in many flows, especially those that spread out under water. Such pieces range from a few inches to many feet in thickness and may be twisted and cracked by movement.

## GREAT AND SMALL ERUPTIONS

We have said that magma which reaches the earth's surface while molten is called *lava*. But we have said nothing about the ways in which lava actually emerges upon the earth or the things it makes when it gets there.

The simplest way in which magma can become lava is to work its way through a crack and spread out in a *fissure flow*.

In the Columbia River Valley of the northwestern United States there are 200,000 square miles in which lavas are as much as 4000 feet thick, covering mountains 2000 to 2500 feet high and filling deep valleys. These lavas were poured out by hundreds, even thousands, of eruptions in which the lava welled out of fissures with none of the explosions, steam clouds or earthquakes of which we sometimes read. The hot rock moved very much as syrup flows when it is poured on a plate. Sometimes it flowed until a ridge stopped it, as the raised edge of a plate stops the spread of syrup. Where there was no ridge the lava kept on spreading until it cooled and became too stiff to move.

Fissure flows also are found in Utah, Arizona and California and form many of the dark "trap" rocks of New England and New Jersey. Another famous region of fissure flows is the Deccan Plateau of India, in which the lavas cover more than 200,000 square miles and reach 6000 feet in thickness.

In many places lavas flowed—and still flow—quietly from volcanoes. Rising to the top, they spill over the edge of the crater or break through cracks in its sides and stream slowly down the slopes. Most of the lava streams find low places or valleys, where they may flow 30 to 50 miles before they harden and stop. Others reach level plains, where they spread out in sheets that resemble small fissure flows. Some roll down slopes so irregular and steep that they form falls and rapids of lava that persist even when they harden.

We may trace such quiet volcanic eruptions in many lava flows of the Northwest, Hawaii and New Mexico. At the Craters of the Moon, in Idaho, we see something very different. There the ground is covered with ashes, cinders and large stones that were thrown out by violent explosions. The volcanoes themselves were built up chiefly by fragments also exploded from within the earth.

We can guess what happened from the rocks. Magmas came to the surface at many times, through many tubes and cracks. On the way, the molten rock cooled enough to become viscous, while much of its water turned into steam. For a time—perhaps for several years—the thick magmas kept this steam from escaping, but steam pressure at last overcame the resistance of the molten rock. Both came out together in explosive eruptions that tore the sticky lava into chunks and threw them high into the air.

The most violent eruption of this sort that has been seen came from Mount Pelée, on the island of Martinique in the West Indies. For fifty-one years this volcano did not erupt, building up a tremendous steam pressure in its underground channels. On the morning of May 8, 1902, an enormous cloud of this steam escaped, carrying with it countless particles of hot lava. This mixture formed a black cloud that shot out horizontally from the side of the volcano, rushing down its slopes to the sea at a speed of more than a mile per minute. When this cloud reached the town of St Pierre it killed 30,000 people in a few seconds. For several months explosions of this sort occurred. The one shown in our sketch formed a cloud 13 miles high when it reached the foot of the volcano.

Perhaps the greatest of all explosive eruptions took place some 10,000 years ago at Crater Lake, Oregon. Before that time the site of the lake was a volcano about as large as Mount Shasta. It also must have been quiet for years, after which came eruptions that sent out vast amounts of pumice (PLATE 21). The last eruptions probably produced clouds like those of Mount Pelée but much larger, killing everything for miles around. After this the top of the volcano collapsed into the partly emptied magma reservoir, forming a bowl 5 miles wide and 4000 feet deep, now occupied by Crater Lake. Other pits, or *calderas,* as much as 3 miles in diameter were produced by explosions that blew the tops of volcanoes to pieces.

Many violent eruptions produced greater, though less spectacular, results. In the Yellowstone region explosions shattered billions of tons of lava and hurled them into the air. A large part of the Absaroka Mountains was built by these fragments as

A cloud from Mount Pelée reaching the sea. This mixture of steam and
rock fragments was 13,000 feet high.

they fell to earth and mingled with lava material lying on the surface.

Volcanic eruptions differ in intensity; they also differ in their lavas. Stromboli, in the Lipari Islands of Italy, erupts dark basalt while Vulcano, 25 miles away, produces light-colored rhyolite. The lava erupted by Vesuvius today is very different from that of the ancient volcano, known as Monte Somma. The San Francisco Mountains, which are Tertiary volcanoes near Flagstaff, Arizona, contain four kinds of lava that erupted at different times. Even if the first one (basalt) is called a fissure flow, it still is unlike the others.

Why should there be such differences? There seems to be no doubt that the magma under the San Francisco peaks began as

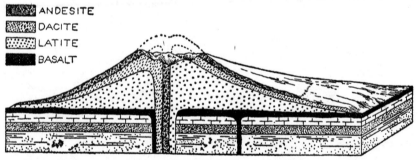

ANDESITE
DACITE
LATITE
BASALT

Four kinds of lava in the San Francisco Mountains near Flagstaff, Arizona. Each kind represents changes in the magma from which the lavas came.

one kind of molten rock. But as centuries passed, this magma changed. At first it was dark, with a plentiful mixture of pyroxene, olivine and magnetite, as well as plagioclase. When some of this material broke through cracks, it hardened into basalt.

Then came a period of quiet, when lava did not erupt and a crust filled the fissure. Below this crust the dark, heavy minerals were able to crystallize and sink to the bottom of the magma. When eruptions began again, the uncrystallized material came out in viscous flows of latite, which is not so dark as basalt and contains fewer heavy minerals. Still later came dacite and andesite, the latter somewhat more like basalt. Had eruptions continued long enough, they might have brought out the crystallized dark minerals in the form of a basalt porphyry.

A similar sorting of minerals may explain why Stromboli erupts dark lava though that of Vulcano is light. But here the sorting took place in a large, deeply buried magma, from which smaller magmas separated and moved outward from the crust. The one that feeds Stromboli came early; it, therefore, is basalt. The magma of Vulcano separated much later; it contains quartz and orthoclase and so is very much like granite. A bomb of this material, from the Lipari Islands, is shown on PLATE 16; it is bluish gray in color.

The heat of lavas, like that of magmas, long has been a puzzle. Some of it may be left over from the days, more than 2,000,000,000 years ago, when our planet was built. Much of it may come from pockets of radioactive minerals at depths of 10, 15 or 20 miles, for we already know that such elements as uranium and thorium produce heat as they turn into lead. If this heat is concentrated in special places (as it would be by "pockets" of radioactive minerals), it should explain the high temperatures that make some rocks molten while those around them remain hard.

## EXTRUSIVE, OR ERUPTIVE, MASSES

Lavas form three kinds of rock masses: volcanic cones, flows, and layers made when fragments settle. The last of these is considered in Chapter VII; only the first two are discussed here.

### Volcanic Cones

*Lava cones,* better called *shield volcanoes,* were built by quiet eruptions of fluid lava that spread widely before it hardened and so formed almost horizontal sheets. Instead of building true cones, these flows piled up in dome-shaped masses whose slopes are no steeper than many good roads. Mauna Loa, the world's largest volcano, is a dome 200 miles wide and 13,675 feet high. The slope near its base averages 2 degrees, increasing to 10 degrees at about 9000 feet and becoming more gentle above 10,000 feet. Mount Etna, in Sicily, is another shield volcano, with a steep cone 1000 feet high at its top. This cone shows that the nature of Etna's eruptions has changed with the last few centuries.

*Plug domes* are built by lavas that are too stiff to flow very far and so pile up in steep domes, hardening at the surface. When more lava rises to the interior of a dome the hardened surface breaks into blocks, which form piles of coarse rubbish, or talus. Mount Lassen, in California, is a large dome of this sort, and there are a dozen smaller ones within a few miles.

*Cinder cones* include most of the small volcanoes in the western and southwestern United States. They were built by eruptions of lapilli, ash and other small fragments. Most of this material fell near the vent, or hole through which the fragments were erupted; being sharp and irregular, the pieces lay in steep slopes and so built cones. These often appear to be cut off at the top because later eruptions blew ashes away and so kept the craters open.

There also are cones formed by fragments too large to be called ash (PLATE 12). Such cones have rough sides and narrow rims. They never are very large, and they may stand on lava flows.

*Compound cones* include most high, steep-sided volcanoes and are mixtures of cinders and lava. The cinders first built a cone; then lavas poured out and settled upon them. After this came more cinders and lavas, until the cone became thousands of feet high. Such active volcanoes as Vesuvius and most of those in the South Pacific were built in this way, as were Mounts Shasta, Rainier and many other "dead" volcanoes of North America. Really large volcanoes generally have small cones or vents on their sides, from which both lava and cinders erupt.

*Spatter cones* and *chimneys* are small structures built around unimportant vents. Explosions throw lumps of sticky lava a few feet into the air; falling, they build cones or domes. Some

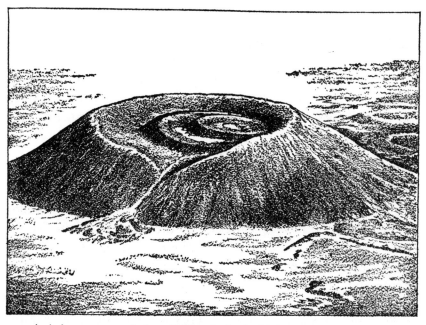

A cinder cone near Amboy, California, in the Mohave Desert. Two small craters in the large one represent late eruptions.

spatter cones form on top of lava flows, where gas gathers in pockets and makes tiny explosions.

## Lava Flows

*Sheets,* or *extrusive sheets,* are hardened lava flows that spread widely, most commonly from cracks or fissures. If the lava was fluid and flowed easily, it made sheets that were thin and smooth. If the lava was very stiff, or viscous, it built thick sheets that often hardened as they moved, forming steep, broken piles. Moderately fluid lavas sometimes made sheets so thick that vesicular, or bubbly, rocks formed on their surface, glassy rocks at lower levels and grainy ones at the bottom.

There seems to be no good word for hardened lava "streams" such as those that once flowed along valleys in the Southwest or those that now flow down the slopes of Mauna Loa.

*Block lava* (PLATE 14), better known by its Hawaiian name of *aa(ah-ah)*, is lava that was very viscous. Its inner part continued to flow while the upper portion hardened and broke into sharp, irregular chunks that tumbled over each other as they were carried forward. Such flows are extremely rough and hard to cross; in the Southwest, where they are plentiful, ranchmen and prospectors call them *malpais,* the Spanish term meaning "bad country."

*Pahoehoe* (PLATE 14) is lava that spread smoothly and hardened into twisted, ropy structures. The name, pronounced pah-hoay-hoay, also is Hawaiian and refers to the glistening surfaces of such flows. Specially fine pahoehoe may be seen among the explosive cones and ash beds of the Craters of the Moon, Idaho. Although the youngest of these flows are several hundred years old, they still glow with iridescent tones of blue, purple and bronze.

Pahoehoe lavas show a variety of other structures that depend on fluidity. In some places the lava worked its way through cracks or trickled over the broken edges of older flows. The result is lava "stalactites" or "icicles," produced as the molten rock hardened (PLATE 16). In other places lava dripped and fell into lumps, like the mass of lava drip also shown on PLATE 16.

*Pillow lavas* (PLATE 15) are flows that spread out in seas or lakes, where they stiffened and rolled into roundish masses. Many of these underwater lavas tore up chunks of the muddy bottom, rolled and twisted them, baked them and then hardened around them. These inclusions look very differently from muds that filled cracks and pits in pillow lavas after they hardened. Vast amounts of pillow lava must have formed under the Mediterranean Sea and the Pacific Ocean during historic times, and Tertiary flows of this type are found in California. Ancient pillow lavas are exposed along the Continental Divide in the northern part of Glacier National Park, Montana, where early prospectors mistook them for copper ore. These lavas, which are about 600,000,000 years old, also contain small pahoehoe structures, such as the one shown on PLATE 14.

*Lava tunnels* are long, narrow, winding caves formed in lava streams as they flow. At first the lava streams are soft, fluid affairs that roll along the ground with speeds of 4 to 6 miles per hour. Then the upper surface begins to harden, but the rolling mass breaks it into pieces which it carries toward the bottom of the flow. At last there comes a time when the crust becomes hard and does not break, while patches of hardened lava reach to the bottom of the flow. Then, if conditions are right, lavas which still are soft drain away, leaving tunnels 20 to 50 feet wide and a few hundred to thousands of feet long. Some of these tunnels have smooth sides and floors, but others are rough. One tunnel in the Craters of the Moon National Monument, Idaho, shows where fluid lava flowed through it, hardening, cracking and eddying as it went. In another tunnel near Flagstaff, Arizona, large pieces of rock fell from the roof and settled in the soft lava of the floor. The finest lava tunnels are found in Hawaii and Iceland.

## STRUCTURES OF IGNEOUS ROCKS

Before we begin the descriptions of igneous rocks let us glance at structures found in them. Some of these are large— so large that they can be seen only in quarries, hills or mountains where masses of rocks occur—while others are comparatively small and may be found in boulders or even pebbles.

*Jointing* (PLATE 19) is the result of the shrinking of a magma as it cools and crystallizes. Unlike a drying apple, molten rock cannot shrink toward the center and wrinkle to take up loose

[ *87* ]

outer parts. Shrinking in a magma means pulls in many directions, at many places and through long periods of time. Under
these strains the rock starts to crack, and the cracks grow larger
until they bring relief. As a result, the lava is crossed by many
fractures, or *joints,* which divide it into blocks and slabs even
when they receive no help from twisting or other outside forces.

Joints differ in different rocks. In granite they cut across
each other at high angles, dividing the stone into blocks. Some
of these are rude cubes; others are thin and curved, looking
almost like irregular strata. In the dark rocks of dikes and sills
joints may form upright sheets or they may curve so greatly that
weathering will split them in melon-shaped masses made up of
layer upon layer.

Jointing is helped by movements which bend, compress or
shake rocks. A single earthquake may make many joints; the
uplift of a mountain makes many more, while rising and sinking of continents have produced far too many joints for estimate.
So far as we can tell, however, most of the joints in igneous
rocks were started by cooling and shrinking.

*Columnar structure* (PLATE 19) is a special kind of jointing
which divides igneous rock into long blocks or columns with
flat sides that meet in angles. Such columns develop when fluid
rock cools, hardens and contracts. Instead of dividing the rock
into blocks, joints start at the top or sides and work inward.
Generally three cracks run out from one center; since there are
many of these centers, the cracks running from them soon meet.
If they were perfectly regular, they would make six-sided
figures and by deepening would make six-sided columns. Since
the shrinking is not regular, some centers are close together and
some are far apart, while some cracks spread rapidly and others
do not. The result is that they meet in various ways and split
off columns that may have as few sides as three or as many
as eight.

Columnar structure appears best in hardened lavas, which
cooled and shrank very quickly. It also is found in dikes, sills

and some laccoliths. Though the columns generally are upright or slanting, some are curved and others lie horizontally. In "trap" rocks of New Jersey and the Devil's Post Pile of California the vertical cracks have many curves. These give the columns cross wrinkles or flutings. Other famous localities where columns show are the canyon of the Yellowstone River near Tower Falls, the canyon of the Columbia River, Fingal's Cave in Scotland and the Giant's Causeway of Ireland's north coast. Sills in the Palisades of the Hudson show columns, some of which are 100 feet high.

*Flow structure* (PLATE 22) is any sort of banding produced as liquid rocks move. In some cases minerals are sorted into different layers which show crumpling produced as the rock flowed. In other deposits mineral grains merely are aligned in bands, or the rock may consist of layers and stringers of glassy and grainy material. Though flow structure generally is applied only to lavas, some authors also use it for bands of mica, hornblende and other minerals in foliated granite, described in Chapter VI.

*Vesicles* (PLATE 21) are made by the expansion of gases in lavas as they come from the ground, giving lava a spongy (vesicular) appearance. If the bubbles are very small, producing a glass-froth texture, the structure is *pumiceous;* if the bubbles are larger, the structure is *scoriaceous.* Pumice is very light and will float until its cavities are filled by water; scoria, though it also is light in weight, will not float.

*Amygdules* (PLATE 21) are whitish, round or almond-shaped bodies filling the vesicular structures commonly found in basalt. The material forming the crystals was carried through the spongy lava by heated, mineral-charged water. The crystals, usually quartz (sometimes the variety amethyst), epidote, calcite and zeolites, completely fill small cavities or line large ones. *Amygdules* is derived from the Greek word meaning almond, which these structures resemble.

*Miarolites* are cavities in intrusive igneous rocks. They were

[ *89* ]

formed when the minerals crystallized, thus taking up less space than the molten magma. *Pores,* which permit rocks to absorb water, are developed by the shrinking of the magma during crystallization.

Miarolitic cavities are usually quite small—an inch or two in diameter—but they may reach dimensions of several feet. In general they are more common in coarse-grained rocks than in those which are fine-grained.

CLASSIFICATION OF THE PRINCIPAL IGNEOUS ROCKS

| | GENERALLY LIGHT-COLORED (Few iron-magnesian minerals) | | | | | | GENERALLY DARK-COLORED (Iron-magnesian minerals abundant) | |
|---|---|---|---|---|---|---|---|---|
| | Orthoclase Dominant | | Orthoclase and Plagioclase about Equal | | Plagioclase Dominant | | Plagioclase | No Plagioclase |
| | Quartz | No Quartz | Quartz | No Quartz | Quartz | No Quartz | | |
| Coarse-Grained; most minerals recognizable by eye or lens. Intrusive. — **Not Porphyritic** | Granite, Pegmatite | Syenite, Nephelite Syenite | Quartz Monzonite, Granodiorite | Monzonite | Quartz Diorite | Diorite, Anorthosite, Dolerite | Gabbro; Diabase | Peridotite, Cortlandite, Dunite (No volcanic equivalents) |
| **Porphyritic** | Granite Porphyry | Syenite Porphyry | Quartz Monzonite Porphyry, Granodiorite Porphyry | Monzonite Porphyry | Quartz Diorite Porphyry | Diorite Porphyry | Gabbro Porphyry | |
| Dense or Very Fine-Grained; few minerals recognizable. Extrusive or intrusive near surface. — **Porphyritic** | Rhyolite | Trachyte Phonolite | Latite | Latite | Dacite | Andesite Porphyry | Basalt Porphyry | |
| **Not Porphyritic** | Felsite | Felsite | Felsite | Felsite | | Andesite | Basalt | |
| Glass, wholly or in part. Extrusive. — **Not Porphyritic** | Obsidian (dark), Pitchstone, Perlite, Pumice, etc. | | | | | | Tachylite | |
| **Porphyritic** | Vitrophyre (=Obsidian Porphyry and Pitchstone Porphyry) | | | | | | | |
| Fragmental; may form layers. Extrusive. | Volcanic Ash, Tuff, Agglomerate, Breccia, etc. | | | | | | | |

CHAPTER VI

# Coarse-Grained Igneous Rocks

AS WE HAVE SEEN, igneous rocks vary in their texture and in the depths at which they hardened. The coarse-grained group is dominated by rocks that hardened far underground; those of the fine-grained group became solid at or very near the surface. The third group, which is glassy or almost grainless, generally hardened at the surfaces of lava flows. Last come fragmental rocks, which were thrown out by violent eruptions. Many of them include glassy fragments.

Coarse-grained igneous rocks are those whose minerals, both in crystals and rough grains, can be seen without a lens. Some crystals are very large, but the majority compare with those of ordinary building granite. Coarse-grained rocks are found in all large igneous masses as well as in stocks, deep-seated dikes and thick sills.

### Granite
(PLATES 13, 17, 18, 19)

The name granite originally meant any coarsely crystalline igneous rock, and in popular language it keeps that meaning to this day. In scientific work, however, coarsely crystalline rocks are now called *phanerites,* leaving granite for rocks which are wholly composed of quartz and feldspar or which have mica and a few other minerals as well. The texture is evenly granular and is usually uniform throughout the rock. The color ranges from white to dark gray and from pale pink to deep brownish red. Some granites even are yellow, and others are green.

Feldspars are the commonest minerals in granite, orthoclase and microcline being dominant. Plagioclase may be present in smaller amounts; it generally is white, pale green or yellow, other feldspars being white or pink. Both have pearly luster and smooth faces. A hand lens may show fine parallel lines, or striations, on cleavage faces of the plagioclase.

Quartz ranks second to feldspar. As shown in the drawing on page 20, it fills the spaces between other minerals and therefore forms irregular grains. It may be recognized by its glassy luster and conchoidal fracture. Quartz may be colorless, white to dark gray, red (from included hematite) or rarely blue.

Micas appear as flakes of biotite (black) or muscovite (white). Either or both may be present, though muscovite rarely occurs alone. Hornblende forms dark green or black grains or long prisms. Like biotite, it adds dark color to the granite. Magnetite, appearing as metallic grains, is found in some coarse granites.

The specific gravity of granites varies with their mineral composition, ranging from 2.61 to 2.75. It is greater in granites which contain dark minerals, such as biotite and hornblende.

VARIETIES.—Granites were formed by cooling of magmas that contained a great deal of silica, alumina, potash and soda but held rather little lime, iron and magnesia. Because the proportions of minerals and rates of cooling varied, many kinds and colors of granite were formed. Some, such as *tourmaline* and *muscovite granites,* are named for their prominent minerals, but a few have other designations.

*Pink granite* contains pink or reddish feldspars. The quartz is light gray or white and there is not much hornblende. In *gray granite* the feldspar is white or gray, allowing the dark minerals

[ *93* ]

that are present to show plainly. The rock is not as dark as *hornblende granite,* which is deep greenish gray.

*Aplite,* or *binary granite* (PLATE 17), has no iron-bearing minerals. It resembles loaf sugar in texture, while its color is usually light: white, flesh or pale yellow, gray or brown. The chief minerals are feldspar and quartz, generally with small quantities of muscovite. Small specks of biotite, hornblende or black tourmaline may be present. This variety of granite occurs as dikes from a fraction of an inch to several feet in thickness. They generally cut granite masses. The larger ones may grade into pegmatite dikes.

*Graphic granite* (PLATE 17) is composed chiefly of feldspar (mainly orthoclase or its variety microcline) and quartz, though albite also may be present. Cleavage faces—which are those of the feldspar, since quartz does not have cleavage—show irregular crystals of quartz that resemble the characters of Arabic writing and so give the rock its name.

These crystals are unusual in appearance; their structure is equally surprising. Each one contains many openings and holes, which are filled by parts of a feldspar crystal. It also has open spaces, which are filled by quartz. In other words, the two crystals fill one another's cavities and actually intertwine. Such an arrangement may show that both minerals crystallized at the same time, or it may mean that quartz replaced part of the feldspar.

Graphic granites occur in pegmatite dikes that cut masses of more typical granite as well as in "offshoot" dikes which extend into the rocks surrounding the granites. In either place their materials came from the main granite magma but hardened at a later time.

*Orbicular granite* (PLATE 18) has mineral grains arranged in unusual manners, such as round or egg-shaped clusters. One variety, the "pudding" granite of Vermont, is filled with lumps of black mica. Commonly the nodules contain the same minerals as the rock mass, arranged shell fashion around a nucleus.

These structures suggest pebbles, but a study of the minerals shows that they crystallized while the granite magma cooled and hardened. Though orbicular granites are not common, they occur in Rhode Island and Vermont, Canada, Sweden and several other places.

*Foliated granite* looks like the metamorphic rock called gneiss and often cannot be told from it. It contains twisted, irregular bands which differ in color and mineral composition. These bands apparently formed because the granite magma was squeezed and forced to flow while it hardened. As it flowed, the minerals which crystallized first, such as biotite and some feldspars, came together in irregular bands. Rocks of this type sometimes are called "primary gneisses," meaning gneisses that formed directly from magmas; yet they actually are igneous. In the last twenty years petrologists have found that many ancient "gneisses" are foliated granites which have not been metamorphosed.

*Porphyritic granite* is a term applied by many petrographers to a granite having large crystals, called *phenocrysts,* of orthoclase scattered through it. The phenocrysts may be two or three inches in diameter and the groundmass of average grain. Such granites occur principally in the Sierra Nevadas, Colorado and New Hampshire.

*Granite porphyry,* as used by some petrographers, is a rock containing phenocrysts of quartz and feldspar in a groundmass composed of the same minerals whose grains are distinguishable. It may also be a rock in which the phenocrysts of quartz and feldspar occur in a groundmass of material whose grains cannot be distinguished. Biotite and hornblende may be present separately or together, either in the groundmass or as phenocrysts. As phenocrysts they usually are much smaller than either the quartz or feldspar. Orthoclase is the predominating feldspar.

Granite porphyries are widely distributed in regions where old crystalline rocks are now exposed, especially in the Rocky Mountains.

FIELD APPEARANCE.—Jointing in three directions is character
istic of granite. One set of joints is horizontal and the other two,
which are at right angles to one another, are approximately
vertical. These joints divide the rock mass into cubes or rhombs
and may produce large or small blocks which are of great importance in tunneling, excavating or quarrying. If the horizontal joints (PLATE 19) are more numerous than the per-
pendicular ones, granite may break or weather into slabs and
blocks whose appearance suggests the beds, or strata, of
sedimentary rocks.

Erosional forms of granite may be determined by the jointing, which helps frost, seeping water and other agents of weathering to produce such features as the "Needles" (PLATE 19) in
the Black Hills of South Dakota. Another form is the dome
produced by the scaling off of curved slabs—a result of sudden
changes of temperature combined with strains inside the rock.
On the tops of old mountains, and especially in glaciated regions, the domelike masses have gentle slopes and broad valleys.

Weathering breaks granite down into gravel, sand and soil.
In this process potash, silica, alumina, magnesia and lime are
made available to plants, which use them in building stems,
leaves and other structures. Since animals eat plants, these minerals ultimately reach all living things in the world.

ORIGINS.—For many years granite has been regarded as the
most typical of intrusive rocks, formed when magmas solidified
in batholiths, laccoliths, stocks and other large masses which
originally lay at considerable depths. Extensions from these
masses produced dikes and other minor intrusive bodies.

There is a growing tendency, however, to consider granites
such as those of Barre, Vermont, and several other parts of New
England as rocks that were metamorphosed by solutions from
granite magmas. Thus the Chelmsford granite, which is
quarried 6 miles west of Lowell, Massachusetts, apparently
began as shale or some other dark sediment that was squeezed,
heated and changed until it became schist, which is described

in Chapter XVIII. Water from a magma worked its way through pores and cracks in this schist, dissolving some materials and depositing others, such as feldspars of several kinds. In the last stages of this process quartz, apatite and epidote were deposited in the onetime schist that already had become a granite in which only a few dark bands and streaks remained.

Granite of similar origin is shown on PLATE 13; it forms parallel bands between layers of schist, most of which are bent or crumpled. Many rocks in Vermont show still earlier stages in the change from schist to granite.

OCCURRENCE.—Granite is found in all parts of the earth and in intrusive formations of many ages. It forms a great deal of the continental masses; as laccoliths and batholiths it makes the cores of many mountain ranges. Where the land has been pushed, broken and bent into mountains many times, and those mountains have been worn away, ancient granites are specially common rocks. Vast amounts of them are found in eastern Canada, New England and in regions east of the Appalachians, from New Jersey to Georgia. Huge intrusions of granite occur in the Rocky Mountains, the Coast Ranges of Canada and other mountains of the West. Deep borings show that there are granites under the stratified rocks of the Mississippi Valley and the High Plains.

USES.—Granite is a very strong, durable rock. When a series of granite blocks from Wisconsin were tested, they endured pressures of 15,000 to 40,000 pounds per cubic inch; the average was about 20,000 pounds. Granite also may be cut into pieces of almost any shape and given a high polish. It therefore is used in many monuments, buildings, ornamental columns and railings. Because of its strength, granite also is used in bridge piers, sea walls and foundations of buildings. Its chief defect lies in the fact that when it is heated and chilled the quartz and feldspar grains expand or contract at different rates, sometimes making the rock surface crumble or "peel." In some granites the quartz grains also contain very tiny bubbles filled with

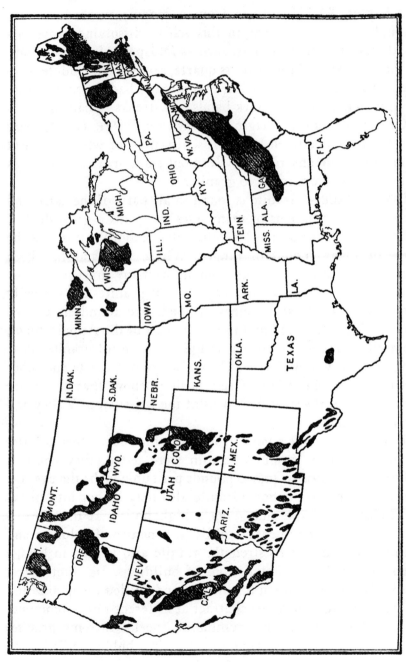

The principal outcrops of granite and related crystalline rocks in the United States. (*Merrill*)

water or liquid carbon dioxide. If a building of such granite burns, the bubbles expand until they break the crystals and so crumble or crack the stone. Yet the bubbles are so tiny that they can be seen only when thinly ground sections are examined under a high-power microscope.

## Pegmatite
### (PLATES 18, 43)

Pegmatite, or giant granite, is a variety of granite whose coarse texture, special origin and importance in mining entitle it to a separate place. So does the fact that it occurs only in dikes, some of which are very large.

Pegmatite contains minerals that are common in the granite around it as well as others which are scarce or lacking. The list of pegmatite minerals includes feldspar, quartz, micas (muscovite and lepidolite), tourmaline, topaz, garnet, fluorite, beryl, spodumene and many others. Crystals commonly are perfect and very large, some being the giants of the mineral world. Feldspars, for instance, commonly reach lengths of a foot or more and may be much larger; some of those in Maine are 18 to 20 feet across, and two carloads of feldspar were mined from one crystal near Spruce Pine, North Carolina. Many mica plates are 12 to 15 inches wide, while one crystal 14 feet wide and 30 feet long weighed 90 tons. Apatite crystals are as much as 3 feet high, while beryl crystals 14 feet long and 4 feet thick have been found in Maine. Mines in the Black Hills have reached spodumene crystals 30 to 42 feet in length and 3 to 5 feet in thickness. Such great sizes are not the rule, of course, but they emphasize the fact that crystals in pegmatites are large. They also may be loosely arranged, so that the rock is not solid. Indeed, it commonly contains holes so large that a man can stand up in them.

ORIGIN.—Many pegmatites fill cracks in the crumpled, changed rocks (mostly schists) surrounding granite intrusions, but others are in the granites themselves. In either position the pegmatites apparently formed after the outer parts of the intrusions crystallized and shrank. Shrinking opened cracks that widened and sometimes worked their way inward. More often they extended outward, either breaking the surrounding rocks or joining cracks already in them.

Things were happening, meanwhile, down in the magma. As some minerals crystallized, water was left over. This made part of the remaining molten material more fluid, so that it worked its way into the cracks. There it cooled and crystallized into microcline, perhaps with a small amount of quartz and few or no other minerals.

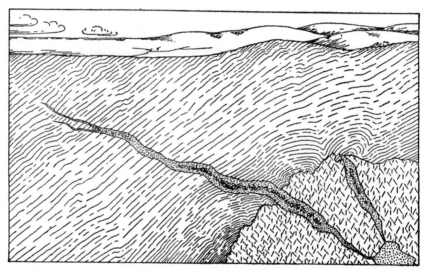

The origin of pegmatite dikes from a batholith whose liquid-gaseous core is marked by dots. One dike is mostly in the granite of the batholith; another extends far out from it, ending in two quartz veins.

This ended the story of many pegmatites, but others continued to develop and to receive new minerals. They did so because the magma continued to crystallize, forcing more and more water into its molten part, which finally became little more than a hot, watery solution. This solution was forced out through the centers of the crack fillings, or dikes. As it moved, the solution dissolved minerals and carried them away, at the same time depositing others. Thus microcline was replaced by beryl, quartz or mica, the original quartz was replaced by albite, and so on. Drawings show such replacement, as does a picture on PLATE 43, in which a lump of albite is partly replaced by apatite.

These changes occurred again and again, as more and more

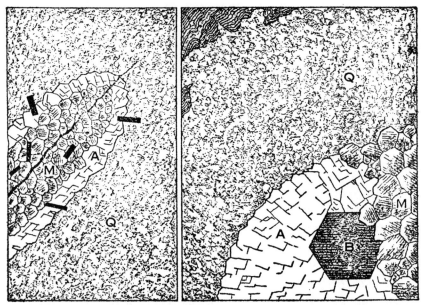

Replacement in a pegmatite dike. At the left, quartz (Q) was replaced by albite (A), which was replaced by mica (M). All these have been partly replaced by the black mineral. At the right, quartz was replaced by mica, which was replaced by albite and beryl (B).

water came from the cooling, hardening magma. Where solution was more rapid than deposition, cavities were produced. Nuclei of minerals formed in these holes; as passing waters dropped some of their loads, they built these nuclei into the huge crystals that we have described. In other places some of the original dike remained as a lump or sheet in the remade pegmatite.

Although quartz was deposited early in the development of pegmatite dikes, it also remained in solution longer than any other mineral. It therefore was carried farthest, as hot waters worked outward into crevices. Many pegmatite dikes turn into quartz veins which represent the last deposits of the solutions after they left the magma.

Thus we see that a single dike may vary greatly from one part to another. There also may be differences between a dike and its nearest neighbor, since different materials gathered in different parts of one magma. Thus a dike filled from one spot or level might have a large supply of tourmaline or beryl, while another may contain a great deal of mica and apatite.

Though true pegmatites are coarse granites, pegmatitic structure is found in gabbros and nephelite syenites. The minerals in these varieties correspond to those of the rocks in which they were produced.

OCCURRENCE.—Pegmatites are found in many parts of the world. Dikes producing minerals of commercial importance occur in Maine, Connecticut, New Hampshire, North Carolina and the Black Hills of South Dakota, as well as in Brazil, India and Norway.

USES.—Pegmatites produce feldspar, which is used in glazing china; mica, which is important in electrical insulation; topaz and beryl for gems; apatite for fertilizer; fluorite for smelter fluxes and etching acid, and so on. Uraninite, found only in pegmatites, is an important source of radium.

## Syenite
### (PLATE 20)

Syenite is a crystalline rock that resembles granite in appearance but contains little or no quartz. Its dominant mineral is orthoclase, though it commonly contains smaller amounts of plagioclase and some hornblende, pyroxene and biotite. If the rock is coarse-grained, it may show bits of magnetite. All these supplementary minerals combined, however, never equal the amount of the orthoclase. For this reason pink, yellow and gray are the commonest colors of syenite. The texture usually is evenly granular, though the orthoclase may form thin flat blocks that are longer than wide. These blocks show roughly parallel arrangement, which probably was developed by movements of the magma during crystallization.

The specific gravity, like that of granite, depends upon the mineral content and ranges from 2.6 to 2.8.

VARIETIES.—Syenite is not a very common rock; it formed either as an independent intrusion or at the edges of great bodies of granite, where quartz became scarce. There are many gradations between syenite and granite, depending upon the amount of quartz that is present. A syenite comparatively rich in quartz is called *syenite-granite;* it really represents an intermediate stage between granite and normal syenite. Other varieties of syenites are recognized, according to the predominant iron-magnesian mineral: *augite syenite, hornblende syenite* and *biotite syenite.*

*Syenite porphyry,* really only a textural phase of syenite, contains large orthoclase phenocrysts in a groundmass of feldspar grains, with little or no quartz. If the groundmass cannot be determined, the large crystals make the rock look like syenite. Hornblende, biotite and pyroxene may be present, either as phenocrysts or in the groundmass. They may occur separately or all three may be associated in one rock, though biotite and hornblende are more commonly found together.

*Orbicular syenite* resembles orbicular granite in structure. It is a rare variety.

OCCURRENCE.—Syenites occur in the White Mountains of New England, on the shore north of Boston, in Arkansas and Montana and in Germany, the Alps and southern Norway.

USES.—Syenite is a durable rock and resists weathering as well as, or even better than, granite. The absence of quartz, with its tiny bubbles of carbon dioxide, makes syenite more heat resistant than granite and should make it more desirable as a building stone. A dark gray syenite with pearly blue reflections, which occurs in southern Norway, is used extensively in northern Europe as an ornamental stone. Syenite is not widely used in America, partly because it lacks the fame of granite and partly because supplies are not generally available.

## Nephelite Syenite
### (PLATE 20)

Nephelite syenite is more than a variety of syenite, for it shows some of the variations that the true syenites present. It is characterized by the presence of nephelite and generally soda-lite, in addition to the feldspars, augite, mica, hornblende and pyroxene, all of which are common in ordinary syenite. The feldspars are principally orthoclase and albite, though micro-cline characterizes some types of this rock. Nephelite forms grains without cleavage, resembling quartz. Sodalite, which typically is bright blue, may help to distinguish nephelite syenite from ordinary syenite. There are many interesting and rare accessory minerals in nephelite syenite and especially in the pegmatite dikes that cut across them.

The colors of nephelite syenite are variable, though gray is common. The texture generally is granular, resembling granite; it may also be porphyritic as well as pegmatitic.

VARIETIES.—Nephelite syenites vary greatly from place to place. Variations in the proportion of the minerals composing them may produce many forms, even in one limited region. Thus each outcrop is characterized by its own association of varieties and its own rare minerals.

OCCURRENCE.—Nephelite syenites occur as small stocks or large dikes and are rare in comparison with granites. Large areas are exposed only in Greenland, Lapland and southern Norway. In North America these rocks occur in Texas, Arkansas, Massachusetts, Ontario and British Columbia, as well as in many other regions.

USES.—Nephelite syenite is of very little importance commercially because of its rarity. It is quarried for building stone, however, in the neighborhood of Magnet Cove, Arkansas.

## Monzonite
### (PLATE 17)

Monzonite is the name of a group of rocks which look like granites. They are distinguished from granites and ordinary syenites by having orthoclase and plagioclase feldspars in almost equal amounts. The orthoclase may appear as irregular plates with other minerals imbedded in them; irregular bronze-colored plates of biotite, also enclosing other minerals, are common. Augite is abundant, but quartz generally is scarce. Dark brown or green hornblende may be abundant. Apatite, pyrite, iron ores and a few others are fairly common accessory minerals. The commonest color of monzonite is dark gray. The name comes from Monzoni, in the Tyrol.

VARIETIES.—Monzonites vary in appearance and structure as well as in mineral content. Since they are intermediate between the granite-syenite group and gabbros, they grade from one into another.

*Quartz monzonite* is a variety that contains quartz in small amounts. Its texture may be either granitic or porphyritic, and it is classed with granite by some authors.

*Granodiorite* contains more plagioclase than orthoclase and as much as 74 per cent of silica. The texture is porphyritic as well as granitic. Since determination of this rock can be made easily with a hand lens, it may be grouped with granite, as it is in one well-known book.

OCCURRENCE.—Monzonites occur in the Rockies of Montana as well as in Scotland, Norway, the Tyrol and many other regions. Quartz monzonites are abundant in the eastern United States, where they generally are called granites.

## Diorite
### (PLATE 17)

Diorites are a family of rocks that look like dark granite. They are chiefly composed of white, gray or even pinkish plagioclase feldspar and one or more iron-magnesium minerals. These are about equal in amount, though plagioclase usually predominates. This, and the fact that there is little orthoclase, separates diorites from syenite, the dark gray or grayish green color being a good clue to the difference. The ferromagnesian minerals consist mainly of dark green or black hornblende, pyroxene (which cannot readily be distinguished from the hornblende) and brown or yellow mica. Some types contain green augite, while many have at least a small amount of quartz. Apatite, iron oxides, garnet, calcite, chlorite and epidote also may be present. The specific gravity ranges from 2.8 to 3.1, being greater than that of granite because of the larger amount of ferromagnesian minerals.

*Diorite porphyry* is characterized by phenocrysts of feldspar and hornblende, pyroxene or biotite in a groundmass composed of the same minerals. If the minerals of the groundmass are not determinable, identification of the rock must be made from the phenocrysts. This variety is not common.

*Quartz diorite* contains an appreciable amount of quartz. If phenocrysts of quartz are present, the rock is *quartz diorite porphyry.*

*Granodiorite,* described as a variety of monzonite, is placed with the diorite "family" by some authors.

*Hornblende diorite,* which is uncommon, has hornblende as the dominant mineral. Generally more than one ferromagnesian mineral is present, however. Thus hornblende-biotite diorite is a more typical combination.

*Orbicular diorite* contains spheroidal structures like those in orbicular granite. In Corsica such a rock, called corsite, has been used as an ornamental stone.

OCCURRENCE.—Diorites form separate intrusions but they very commonly are connected with large masses of granite or gabbro, with which they intergrade. They do not make up great batholiths but are much more likely to be found in sills, dikes and small stocks. They occur throughout the world, especially where old igneous rocks are exposed in mountains. Because of their dark color, diorites are not much used in buildings, though they are strong and very durable.

## Gabbro
### (PLATE 18)

Gabbro is a dark gray, green or black granular rock which looks so much like diorite that it is difficult to tell them apart. Gabbro is composed of pyroxene, hornblende or olivine (separately or all together) and plagioclase. The ferromagnesian minerals equal or exceed the feldspar in amount; in this respect gabbro differs from diorite. Biotite may be present in very small quantities—another way in which gabbro and diorite differ. The plagioclase feldspar usually is labradorite, appearing as grains or elongate blocks on whose faces striations may be seen with a lens. The plagioclase may be either glassy or waxy; with a lens the olivine appears as yellowish or green grains. The texture of gabbro is granitic or, rarely, porphyritic.

OCCURRENCE.—Like granite, gabbro is found in batholiths, but it also forms small stocks, dikes and volcanic necks. It may even make up the central part of a thick basalt flow, which granite never does. Gabbros occur in New York, Maryland, the Lake Superior region, the Rocky Mountains and California. They are widely distributed in Europe. Their masses never are as large as those of granite.

USES.—Though gabbros make good building stone, their dark color keeps them from being widely used. They are employed in the Lake Superior region; other quarries are in the Adirondacks and Vermont. Masses of iron ores are sometimes found in gabbros; they occur in many places, such as New York, Minnesota and Sweden. Nickel and copper ores in gabbro are worked in Norway, Pennsylvania and at Sudbury, Ontario.

## Anorthosite

A rock characterized by feldspars which are rich in calcium, with or without small amounts of pyroxene and magnetite in the form of tiny grains and specks. The rock itself is white to yellowish or brown to dark gray, looking much like quartzite or even marble. Cleavage of the feldspar grains distinguishes anorthosite from quartzite; with a hand lens one may see the twinning striations which characterize plagioclase. Since a knife will not scratch anorthosite, nor acid make it bubble, the rock may be distinguished from marble by these simple tests.

Anorthosite probably came from magmas that also produced such dark rocks as the gabbros. When plagioclase crystals formed they were heavier than the fluid rock about them and so sank to the bottom of the magma. At first heat was great enough to remelt them, but as the magma cooled that no longer happened. The plagioclase and a few associated minerals then crystallized, forming anorthosite.

OCCURRENCE.—Though not as abundant as granite, anorthosite is the commonest igneous rock consisting wholly, or mostly, of one mineral. It occurs in New Hampshire, underlies 1200 square miles of New York and is found along the Lake Superior shore in Minnesota. Large areas of anorthosite are known in Norway and Russia.

## Diabase
### (PLATE 20)

Diabase is a crystalline or even porphyritic igneous rock that is closely related to basalt, described in the next chapter. It always contains plagioclase feldspar and pyroxene (augite); magnetite almost invariably is present; olivine may be present or absent. Diabase differs from dark granite in having feldspar crystals that are long and narrow. These crystals lie in all directions, giving the rock an interlocking radial texture that is specially noticeable in coarse-grained specimens. Since pyroxene, magnetite and olivine crystallized after the feldspar, they fill spaces that remained. Flakes of biotite and small pyrite crystals are common. The specific gravity is 3 to 3.3.

Diabase is gray, black or deep green in color. The green is produced when augite is replaced by hornblende and olivine by serpentine. Since many diabases are ancient basaltic rocks which have had time to partly decompose, green hues are prominent. The common name of *greenstone* is given to very old, altered diabase.

OCCURRENCE.—Diabase is found in dikes, small laccoliths and in sills, some of which are very thick. It also occurs in lava flows that were so massive as to cool slowly. In the East it forms many of the sills and flows of "trap" rock that range from Georgia to Nova Scotia. The Palisades of the Hudson, opposite New York City, are a diabase sill. Diabase flows are found near Marquette, Michigan; they form the copper-bearing lavas of the Keweenaw Peninsula. There are many great diabase flows in the West; some spread under water and so possess pillow structures as well as pahoehoe-flow characters. In all these places the rock grades into dense, dark basalt. The same is true of diabase intrusions of England and Ireland. There also is much diabase in the Deccan Plateau of India.

USES.—Diabase and other "trap" rocks are so tough that they make excellent paving blocks and crushed stone for use in concrete.

## Dolerite
### (PLATE 20)

In Europe dolerite is applied to many of the rocks called diabase in North America as well as to some fine-grained gabbros and diorites and coarse-grained basalts. If the name is used at all, it should be limited to fine-grained, dark, crystalline rocks that contain labradorite and augite, with small amounts of titanium-bearing magnetite (ilmenite) and a few other minerals. The specimen illustrated is porphyritic, with large labradorite crystals, and comes from Massachusetts.

## Trap
### (PLATE 18)

Trap is a quarryman's name for dolerite, diabase, gabbro, diorite and basalt, all of which are dark, heavy igneous rocks which may be hard to distinguish. Near the Atlantic coast the term is used chiefly for diabases and basalts. It comes from the German word *Treppen,* or "steps," which quarrymen gave these rocks because they break into steplike blocks.

## Peridotites

The peridotites are a group of granular rocks which either consist entirely of ferromagnesian minerals or have so little feldspar that it is unimportant. Pyroxene, olivine and hornblende are the principal minerals; biotite, garnet and a few others may be present. The grains generally are large enough to be determined and may be coarse, but porphyritic texture is rare. Dull green to black are the commonest colors. The specific gravity is 3 or more.

*Peridotite,* strictly speaking, is formed almost entirely of pyroxenes and olivine. *Cortlandite* is composed principally of hornblende and olivine.

*Dunite* consists of olivine with almost no other minerals. It is lighter in color than peridotite and cortlandite, ranging from yellow to dark green. In texture it suggests loaf sugar. Dunite occurs in North Carolina, Georgia and the Dun Mountains of New Zealand, from which it got its name.

*Kimberlite* is a porphyritic mica peridotite occurring at Kimberley, South Africa, and in Arkansas. Greatly weathered kimberlite, or residual clay from it, is the "blue ground" from which diamonds are mined. These diamonds apparently were minerals in the original rock, though they once were supposed to have come from carbon in shale through which the kimberlite was intruded.

OCCURRENCE.—Peridotite and its relatives occur as dikes, sills, laccoliths and small stocks. Where they can be traced deeply enough, these intrusions join larger ones of gabbro. This shows that peridotites are intrusive offshoots of gabbro, just as basalts are extrusive offshoots from the same kind of rock.

In addition to the places already mentioned, peridotites are found in New York, Kentucky, South Carolina and several other states. They are sources of nickel and chromium ore and garnets as well as of diamonds.

CHAPTER VII

# Fine-Grained, Glassy and Fragmental Rocks

THIS CHAPTER groups together all the igneous rocks that are not characteristically coarse-grained. In texture they range from phonolite, with its large crystals of sanidine, to volcanic glass and fine-grained ash beds. As we already have said, most of these rocks hardened at or near the earth's surface or even were blown above it in explosive volcanic eruptions.

## DENSE, OR FINE–GRAINED, IGNEOUS ROCKS

This group is composed of rocks in which all, or almost all, the mineral grains are too small to be determined by the unaided eye. The dividing line between these and some of the fine-grained granitoid rocks is not definite and must remain a matter of personal opinion.

Since determination of the mineral constituents of the rocks in this group is difficult, a division can be made on the basis of color: light-colored ones are *felsites* and dark-colored ones are *basalts*. This division corresponds roughly to the two main divisions of the coarse-grained rocks, the felsites being fine-grained rocks which correspond to granites and syenites, while the basalts correspond to gabbros and dolerites.

## Felsite

The felsites are a group of very dense, fine-grained rocks that are either hardened lavas or solidified magmas; all have dull, stony textures. Felsites are composed chiefly of quartz and feldspars, though most of their mineral grains are too small to be identified and commonly cannot be seen with a lens. In fact, the minerals of some felsites cannot be identified even with thin sections and high-powered microscopes. Colors range from light or medium gray to pink, red, brown, yellow, buff, purplish and light green. A few are white to dark red, but no dark green or black felsites are known. Those that are lavas commonly contain flow structures and bands which show plainly on weathered surfaces. The specific gravity ranges from 2.4 to 2.65.

Some felsites are so dark that they look like the lightest types of basalt. Examine freshly broken pieces of such rock with a lens; if they show many tiny chips and flakes whose edges are white or translucent, they probably are felsite. If the chips are opaque the rock is a basalt, for the opaque chips indicate the presence of pyroxenes and hornblendes. Unfortunately, many basalts contain plagioclase crystals that are translucent in thin flakes, and such rock looks like felsite.

Felsites are the lava and near-surface equivalents of granite, syenite and other related crystalline rocks. They form small dikes and sills, and in such forms they prove that the magma from which they hardened was intruded into cold rocks not far below the surface. Felsites are more common, however, as lava flows of the fissure type, some of which cover hundreds—even thousands—of square miles. In sheet flows and in volcanic cones they generally are intermingled with breccias and tuffs.

FIELD APPEARANCE.—Felsite, like granite, exhibits jointing which usually divides the rock into small blocks or plates. It also may have columnar structure. In weathering, felsites become brown and rusty and crumble in much the same way as granite. The final change into soil takes place when the feld-spars break down and become clay.

OCCURRENCE.—Intrusive felsites are found among the old rocks east of the Appalachians. Felsite flows occur in Maine, Pennsylvania, Wisconsin and the central to southern Rockies, as well as in the Coast Ranges and South America. They also are common in Europe and other continents, where there have been great volcanic outbursts.

## Felsite Porphyries

Felsite porphyries consist of a felsitic groundmass with a few or many phenocrysts of one or more minerals which may be either scattered or arranged in groups. Some petrographers call these rocks *leucophyres,* a term that means light-colored porphyries.

VARIETIES.—The term felsite porphyry, alone, generally is understood to mean rocks whose phenocrysts are feldspars. In most cases, however, we can divide these porphyries according to their kinds of feldspar and other crystalline minerals that can be identified with a hand lens.

*Rhyolite* generally is characterized by phenocrysts of quartz and a glassy variety of orthoclase feldspar called sanidine in a groundmass of tiny orthoclase crystals and volcanic glass, or obsidian. Small amounts of dark minerals such as hornblende and biotite are present, singly or together; they may also appear as phenocrysts along with the quartz and orthoclase. Colors range from light gray to pink, red and brown. Rhyolite also is called *quartz trachyte,* and *liparite* because it occurs extensively on the Lipari Islands, near Sicily. The name rhyolite comes from the Greek word meaning "to flow" and was given because the rock commonly shows flow structures, formed while it was molten.

Rhyolite (PLATE 20) is lava from a granitic magma which cooled and hardened almost quickly enough to become volcanic glass. Great flows of this rock may be seen in Colorado and are crossed by the Canyon–Norris Basin road in Yellowstone National Park. Rhyolites also occur in Great Britain and are widely, though not extensively, distributed in other parts of Europe.

*Trachyte,* or *trachite,* looks like felsite but contains phenocrysts of sanidine in a groundmass of tiny feldspar crystals. The phenocrysts of orthoclase may range from 0.5 to 2 inches in length. Little or no quartz is present. Hornblende, biotite and pyroxene are among its less important minerals; these also may appear as phenocrysts and, according to their proportions, give rise to varietal forms such as *mica trachyte* or *pyroxene trachyte.*

This rock seems to be the result of eruptions whose lavas would have formed syenite had they hardened underground. It is common in Tertiary and modern volcanic deposits of Europe, the British Isles, Iceland, the Azores, Australia and other regions. It is less abundant in Paleozoic rocks, and in North America is much less common than rhyolite. Good trachytes occur in the Black Hills and mountains of the Pacific coast.

*Phonolite* (PLATE 19) is a greenish gray rock composed mainly of sanidine feldspar, nephelite and pyroxene. The sanidine consists of large platy crystals and smaller rectangular crystals imbedded in the groundmass. The nephelite commonly cannot be seen by the unaided eye; it appears in hexagonal prisms with flat ends. If it is very abundant in the groundmass, the rock represents a transitional stage between phonolite and nephelite syenite. If nephelite is scarce, phonolite resembles trachyte. The pyroxenes may be pale or dark green and are commonly complex. The common accessory minerals are apatite, brown garnet and magnetite.

Phonolite derives its name from Greek words meaning "sound" and "stone," because of its ringing, metallic sound when it is hit with a hammer. Some masses of this rock are divided into tall curved columns with four to seven or even eight sides. These supposedly hardened in the necks of volcanoes, though they may fill necks leading to lava flows.

Phonolite is rare in the United States, occurring at Cripple Creek, Colorado, and in the spectacular Devil's Tower near the Black Hills of South Dakota. Phonolites are somewhat more common in Europe, South America, Great Britain, New Zealand, British East Africa and a few other places.

*Latite* differs from trachyte in having a considerable amount of plagioclase feldspar associated with the orthoclase. It is the extrusive equivalent of monzonite. Latite occurs as lava flows in the Sierra Nevada Mountains of California and is very abundant in Colorado. Light gray latite may be seen at the base of Agassiz Peak in the San Francisco Mountains near Flagstaff, Arizona. It also forms a mesa which extends along U.S. Highway 66 and the railroad for five miles west of Flagstaff.

*Dacite* (PLATE 20) is really an andesite which contains quartz and is sometimes called *quartz andesite*. The groundmass is gray, pale brown, yellow or darker shades and often includes white feldspar, black hornblende and biotite crystals. Dacites occur in dikes and intrusions as well as in lava flows. The core of Eldon Mountain just east of Flagstaff, Arizona, is dacite; and flows of dacite cover the thick cone of latite in the core of the San Francisco Mountains. Dacite is found in about the same regions as andesite.

*Andesites* (PLATE 15) are lavas that are mainly porphyritic, though some are compact in texture. They are rather light-colored if they are crystalline—red, gray or pink—but darker if they contain much glass. On weathering they become dark brown or reddish brown. Porphyritic varieties are composed of plagioclase and ferromagnesian crystals in a finer groundmass of either plagioclase feldspar needles or glass. If such minerals as pyroxene, hornblende or biotite are present in a notable quantity, the names pyroxene andesite, hornblende andesite or biotite andesite are applied. Gold and silver ores occur in andesites in Nevada, California and Borneo. The ores are in veins of quartz deposited in fissures; these veins, however, are of a later origin than the andesites, which have been altered by the ascending hot solutions bearing the valuable metals.

Andesites are found among the igneous rocks of all ages. They are widespread and thick in the western United States, especially near the Pacific coast. Mount Rainier consists mainly of andesite; a stream of andesite lava that came down the southern slope of Mount Shasta during one of its later eruptions entered the channel of the Sacramento River and followed it for 50 miles. Gray andesite occurs on Mount Taylor, a prominent volcano that can be seen from U.S. Highway 66 about halfway between Albuquerque and Gallup, New Mexico. This andesite is much older than the black basalt lava in the same region. Andesites also occur in South America and are abundant in Europe, Japan, New Zealand, Java and the Philippines. They were first described from the Andes, as their name indicates.

## Basalt
### (PLATE 21)

Basalts are a group of dense igneous rocks whose colors range from dark gray to green, purplish and black. Their minerals may be too small for recognition, though some basalts are so coarse that plagioclase, augite and olivine can be seen with a lens. Broken surfaces are fine-grained and dull or velvety, without the horny or greasy luster of many dense felsites. Edges of thin chips generally are opaque. The specific gravity is 2.9 to 3.1.

Under high-powered microscopes thin sections show that basalts are composed of tiny crystals of plagioclase feldspar and pyroxene, with some olivine, magnetite and other minerals. All basalts are rather poor in silica but contain a great deal of lime, magnesium and iron. The iron shows in their dark color, while

[ *117* ]

some lime, dissolved and carried to the surface by water, often appears as a white crust on weathered blocks.

*Porphyritic basalt* is more common than the very fine-grained, compact phases. The phenocrysts commonly are green or yellowish olivine, black augite or plagioclase feldspar in a finely crystalline groundmass. Black hornblende with shining cleavage faces and six-sided crystals of biotite are less plentiful. When fresh, the plagioclase crystals are dark gray with smooth lustrous cleavage faces; they vary from one fourth inch to one or two inches in length. Olivine may occur as lumps or nodules in addition to the usual crystals. These lumps, angular or round, vary in size from a fraction of an inch to three or more inches in diameter. The groundmass is composed of small lath-shaped crystals of feldspar and tiny prisms of augite; these are less perfectly formed than the phenocrysts.

*Quartz basalt,* an unusual variety, is found near Lassen Peak, California, and in other places scattered through the West. It contains small sharp pieces of quartz that may be bits of older rocks broken up and brought to the surface while the lava still was soft.

*Labradorite porphyry* is a basalt porphyry containing phenocrysts of labradorite feldspar.

*Amygdaloidal basalts* are porous, blackish lavas whose holes or "blisters" (amygdules) are filled with other minerals. The commonest of these fillings are quartz, calcite and zeolites. Good amygdaloidal basalts make attractive specimens.

FIELD APPEARANCE.—The jointing of basalt is platy or columnar. In old lava flows basalts commonly show columns with three to six sides; good examples may be seen in Yellowstone National Park, near the Snake River in Idaho and at many other places in the West. Most basalts show flow structure, steam tubes, bubble holes and other characteristics of lava flows.

When they are weathered the tops of basalt columns frequently become rounded or domelike, breaking off in curved layers. Where columns are poorly developed, basalt may weather into oval "spheroids" (PLATE 15) that divide into layers suggesting those of an onion.

In volcanic regions where basalts have been affected by steam or hot water their iron-bearing minerals are changed to red or brown oxides. This change frequently makes it difficult to distinguish an altered basalt from a red felsite.

OCCURRENCE.—Most basalt is true lava that flowed from volcanoes or erupted through cracks. It also forms small sills and dikes that hardened near the surface. Both intrusive and extrusive lavas are found in almost all parts of the world, though some of the widest and thickest flows occur in the northwestern United States and the Deccan Plateau of India. In the latter region almost 200,000 square miles of country have been covered with thousands of feet of lava, most of which is basalt.

USES.—Basalt is crushed and used to surface roads in many parts of the West. Some minerals of commercial value occur in basalts. Native iron and graphite have been found in Greenland; native copper occurs in late Pre-Cambrian, or Keweenawan, basalts of the Lake Superior region. The copper was not in the basalt when it came to the surface but was deposited at a later time by ascending hot-water solutions. Sapphire and other gems have also been found in basalts.

## GLASSY IGNEOUS ROCKS

In this group are the rocks that are composed of glass or slag. Minerals are indistinct or are in the first stages of crystallization as globules or needle-shaped rods that can be seen in thin sections under a microscope.

### Obsidian
(PLATES 1, 2, 22)

Obsidian is natural, or volcanic, glass; its typical portions contain no true crystals. It has the bright luster of ordinary

glass and breaks with good conchoidal fracture. The commonest color is black, but red, gray, brick red and brown obsidians
may be found; the obsidian blade shown on PLATE 1 is brown
with black streaks. The color is due to the presence of countless
tiny dustlike particles; black probably is produced by magnetite and red or brown by oxidized magnetite or hematite. Thin
chips are transparent or translucent. The specific gravity ranges
from 2.3 to 2.7; in the commonest variety it is 2.3 to 2.4. The
hardness (5 to 5.5) is greater than that of window glass, which
is easily scratched by obsidian.

The statement often is made that obsidian is glassy because
it cooled too fast for grains or crystals to form. Rapid cooling
undoubtedly was important, but some deposits of obsidian are
so thick that they could not have cooled very quickly. They
apparently were made by very viscous lavas that were too stiff
to permit crystal growth. Indeed, high viscosity probably was
more important than rapid cooling in the formation of most
volcanic glass.

Though obsidian has no true crystals, it does contain *crys-
tallites,* which represent crystals in the making. They can be
seen only under a strong microscope. Two other structures in
obsidian are shown on PLATE 22 and require description:

*Spherulites* are the result of incipient crystallization. They
are gray, white or red balls, some of which are almost microscopic in size, while others are as large as peas and a few reach
the size of eggs. To the eye they seem to be made up of layers;
a lens shows fiber-shaped crystals of feldspar that radiate from
the center of each ball. They commonly are associated with
grainy gray or red layers and with bubbles produced by steam.

*Lithophysae,* or *stone bubbles,* are closely related to spherulites. They are composed of concentric layers of distinct, fragile
crystals that are attached to each other. Most lithophysae have
central cavities that are lined by tiny but very beautiful crystals
of quartz, feldspar, garnet, tourmaline and other minerals.
These structures vary greatly in size, some being several inches

in diameter. Both lithophysae and spherulites are found in the obsidian of Yellowstone National Park.

VARIETIES.—Obsidian is really the glassy or noncrystalline phase of the coarse-grained rocks. Obsidians corresponding to the various kinds of those rocks are known, and an analysis of the commonest form shows a composition (about two thirds feldspar and one third quartz) which is similar to granite. For general purposes, however, the name obsidian is sufficient.

*Pitchstone* is a variety of obsidian in which 5 or 6 per cent of water is distributed in the form of microscopic bubbles. It is probably these bubbles that give the rock its dull luster, like that of resin or tar. Colors are black, gray, red, brown and green. Thin broken edges are transparent or translucent.

*Perlite* is a glassy rock composed of small balls a good deal like stone bubbles. It generally is gray or blue gray, though a red variety is known. The luster is pearly or waxy. If the balls are separated by a kind of lava cement, they are round; where crowded closely, they form octagons and other angular lumps. They are the result of a special type of shrinking which produced spiral cracks in the cooling glass; these cracks may be seen in microscopic sections. Perlite contains 3 or 4 per cent of water, which is more than that found in true obsidian but less than that in pitchstone. This variety occurs in Yellowstone National Park, Italy, Iceland, Japan and a few other places.

*Pumice* (PLATE 21) is a very porous volcanic glass or "lava froth." Its colors range from white to yellowish, gray or gray brown; a rare variety is dull red. A lens shows silky glass fibers full of tiny pores; these fibers commonly give the rock a silky luster, though they may be dull. In some pumice they are parallel; in others they are tangled together. Because they enclose many empty bubbles or cells, the fibers make pumice so light that it will float on water. Chemically, typical pumice is like obsidian or granite.

Most pumice occurs as a crust on flows of felsite lava or in blocks blown from erupting volcanoes. It is formed when great quantities of steam and other vapors escape through lavas that already are cool enough to be pasty or viscous. Steam, blown through the molten slag of a blast furnace, makes something very much like pumice.

Pumice is found in all parts of the world where there have been violent eruptions. It is specially common on islands in the Pacific, though the sort that is powdered for use in soap, polishes and grinding powders is quarried in the Lipari Islands of Italy. Basaltic pumice is found in Hawaii and a few other regions.

*Pele's Hair* is a special type of basalt pumice formed when drops of lava fly up from the boiling lava lake of Kilauea volcano in Hawaii. The drops stretch out into thin threads, or "hairs," of glass which the wind drifts into tangled masses.

*Scoria* (PLATE 16) looks very much like coarse, somewhat cindery slag. It is stony or glassy, or a mixture of both textures, having colors that range from reddish brown to dark gray or black. It is formed when water and other gases bubble through stiff basalt lavas, leaving holes that are too large and too widely spaced for pumice. Scoria is found in all volcanic regions; in those of the West and Southwest it is much more common than pumice. Very fine examples of scoria may be seen at the Craters of the Moon National Monument, Idaho.

*Basaltic glass,* or *tachylite,* is the glassy phase of basalt. It is black, has a resinous luster and is very brittle. Thin sections are dark brown. The texture may be vesicular or spherulitic; small crystals of feldspar and olivine may be seen by the unaided eye. Weathered tachylites are dark brown or red.

Tachylites commonly occur as bombs and cinders, or scoria, thrown out by volcanoes. These are common in Iceland, near Etna and Stromboli volcanoes (Italy) and in ancient tuffs of Great Britain. Tachylites also occur as lava flows, especially in the Hawaiian Islands; they may be vesicular with very rough surfaces or they may have wavy surfaces. A third type of occurrence is on the edges of basalt lava flows or dikes, where cooling was specially rapid. These layers may be very thin—only a fraction of an inch thick—though small tachylite dikes several inches thick do occur as offshoots from basalt dikes.

*Vitrophyre* is a porphyritic obsidian or pitchstone in which there are small phenocrysts of feldspar or biotite and perhaps of quartz and hornblende as well. The feldspar is glassy, but its cleavage distinguishes it from quartz. These phenocrysts were formed deep underground, while the lava was rising to the surface. They were carried up in the fluid rock and imbedded in glass as it hardened. The predominating phenocryst determines the variety: feldspar vitrophyre, quartz vitrophyre or quartz biotite vitrophyre.

OCCURRENCE.—Obsidian and its varieties are found in most regions where there have been great lava flows. In the United States obsidians are scattered through the West; specially famous localities are Yellowstone National Park, Mono Lake in California, Glass Butte in Oregon and the White Mountains of Utah. They also are found in Mexico, Iceland, Italy, Hungary, Germany, Japan and New Zealand. Pitchstone is found at Silver Cliff and near Georgetown, Colorado; it also occurs in Ireland and near Dresden, Germany.

USES.—Obsidian was used extensively by the Indians. They were skilled in working it and made knives, arrow points and spears out of flakes which they split from large blocks or chipped from scattered boulders. Obsidian was especially prized by the Mound Builders of the Ohio Valley; to secure it they made trips to the region that is now Yellowstone National Park.

### Flow, or Fluxion, Breccias
(PLATE 22)

Flow breccias consist of angular fragments of lava imbedded in other lava. They were produced by very viscous flows that continued to move after their surfaces hardened. Movement broke the hardened rock into chips and folded those chips into the fluid mass beneath. Flow structures commonly were developed, and there may be banding of broken and fluid rock, like that in the specimen of PLATE 22. At its coarsest this type of flow breccia is little more than hardened aa. It may contain almost any sort of lava from basalt to obsidian, though andesite, dacite and rhyolite are commonest, especially in the Western states.

Some small deposits of flow breccia probably were formed when magma moved upward through dikes or partly closed fissures in which some molten rock had solidified. As this hardened material was broken up, its fragments were taken into the fluid or viscous mass and so made breccia.

## FRAGMENTAL IGNEOUS ROCKS

Though we generally think of lava as white-hot, liquid rock that flows from volcanoes, this concept is only partly correct. A great deal of lava that comes out of the earth during violent eruptions is material that solidified in volcanic pipes after earlier outbursts. When new eruptions occur this hardened material is broken and blown out. At the same time drops and lumps of liquid lava are shot forth, hardening as they fly through the air. In some places mixtures of this material have been cemented into stone. In others broken bits of lava are scattered about, very much as they fell.

### Loose Fragments of Lava

*Volcanic dust* consists of very fine particles of lava shot out of volcanoes. They are carried great distances by wind and may remain in the air for a long time. Dust from the Krakatau eruption of 1883 was carried around the world, making a thin deposit in places many thousands of miles from the volcano. The dust also caused colorful and brilliant sunsets.

*Volcanic ash* is not really ash, since it has not been burned. It consists of particles roughly the size of peas or shot, which do look like coarse ashes. They are solid or porous fragments of obsidian. Deposits of such fragments are plentiful in the region of Mount Lassen, in the Craters of the Moon National Monument and among the cinder cones of the Southwest. When partly decomposed, volcanic ash makes very rich soil.

*Lapilli,* or *cinders,* are solid or porous fragments that are larger than ash, reaching the size of English walnuts. They are either angular or are rounded by wear against each other during their violent ascent.

*Volcanic bombs* (PLATE 16) are fragments that range from an inch to several feet in diameter. They include both blocks of solidified lava that were broken and tossed out and lumps of molten material that became round, pear-shaped or irregularly massive during their ascent, hardening as they did so. Some even became twisted. Many bombs are hollow or cellular, a type of structure produced by the expansion of gases that were in them before they solidified.

*Ribbon* and *spindle bombs* began as very fluid lava that stretched and twisted as it hardened. *Bread-crust* bombs get their name from their cracked crusts, which hardened while the interiors still were soft. When expanding gas forced the soft lava to swell, the hardened crust cracked.

Bombs are found near volcanoes, since they are too heavy to be carried far by winds. Specially good ones occur at Sunset Crater, near Flagstaff, Arizona, and at the Craters of the Moon National Monument, Idaho.

## Agglomerate and Volcanic Breccia

These are mixtures of broken rock material that was blown out of volcanoes or great fissures. If most of the large fragments are rounded, the deposit is called agglomerate; if they are not rounded, it is breccia. Both of these so closely resemble the andesite conglomerate of PLATE 24 that they are not illustrated.

The principal materials in both agglomerate and volcanic breccia are bombs, lapilli, ash and fragments of obsidian, scoria and stony lava that were torn loose by subterranean explosions and carried to the surface. There also may be lumps of limestone, sandstone, granite or other rock produced in the same way. Such rocks commonly were rounded by bumping against each other as they came to the surface. Some agglomerates contain waterworn, rounded boulders and cobblestones, but these are not major parts of the deposits. If ash alone fills the spaces between the large pieces, the rock is very soft, but if lime or silica from seeping waters has cemented the fragments, the deposit is hard.

The fragmental, or *pyroclastic* ("fire-broken"), rocks commonly are red, brown or brownish gray, depending partly on the nature of the magma and partly on the stones enclosed by lapilli and ash. Many of the great agglomerates of the West are brown or pinkish brown.

ORIGIN.—Volcanic breccia and agglomerate were produced by explosive eruptions. The power of these has been shown by modern volcanoes such as Stromboli and Pelée. In 1930 Stromboli erupted blocks of rock weighing as much as 30 tons, throwing them to a distance of two miles. In 1929 Pelée's black steam clouds surrounded blocks weighing several hundred tons, which traveled farther than those from Stromboli. In two hours a Japanese eruption broke to pieces and scattered the material of a mountain 2000 feet high, while a Nicaraguan eruption of 1835 blew out 18 cubic miles of rock. The great Tambora eruption of 1815 produced 54 cubic miles of debris, which ranged from fine dust to huge fragments.

In some eruptions steam clouds condense into torrential rains that turn the ash, lapilli and other fragments into mud that slowly flows down slopes. Mudflows gather worn boulders, pebbles and soil, mixing them into agglomerate.

Such deposits grade into *volcanic conglomerates,* of which the andesite conglomerate on PLATE 24 is an example. These rocks formed where fragments that might have made breccia or agglomerate fell into lakes or streams and so were worn and deposited by water. They show crude bedding, and the coarsest materials are separated from the finest. Deposits of this sort are found in valleys of old volcanic regions. If their fragments are much worn, they are hard to distinguish from typical con-glomerate deposited by seasonal floods and rains flowing across plateaus of agglomerate or breccia.

OCCURRENCE.—Agglomerates and volcanic breccia are abun-dant in various parts of the Rocky Mountains as well as in the Coast and Cascade ranges. Perhaps the most imposing deposits are those forming the bulk of the Absaroka Mountains, east of Yellowstone National Park; they may be seen best in cliffs along U.S. Highway 20, west of the Shoshone Dam. These fragmental deposits contain boulders of andesite and basalt five to six feet in diameter. Breccia and agglomerates are inter-bedded with basalt flows, volcanic conglomerates, flood deposits and conglomerates with waterworn boulders that were de-posited in lakes and river beds. The lavas and fragmental material apparently came from a great series of fissures and volcanoes that ran northward and southward through the east-ern part of Yellowstone National Park. A thick deposit of andesite breccia forms the lower cliffs at Tower Falls, in the northeastern part of the park; it contrasts sharply with layers of columnar basalt near the top of the Yellowstone Canyon.

There are small deposits of Paleozoic and early Mesozoic agglomerate in New England. Many North European agglom-erates are so much changed that they can be recognized only by careful petrographic study, but others in Germany, France and Italy are much like deposits in Wyoming and Arizona.

## Tuff
### (PLATES 13, 21)

Tuff is a fine-grained volcanic rock of light weight. It may be either chalky or dense, breaking into small sharp chips. Colors range from white through yellow, gray, pink and light brown to rather dark grayish brown. When moistened, tuffs commonly have a "shaly" odor. Unless they are very compact, they feel rough and produce a gritty dust quite different from the smooth particles of true clay or chalk.

Tuff is volcanic ash or lapilli cemented by minerals deposited from seeping water. The most compact sorts may be mistaken for felsite lavas, but a lens generally will show small angular bits of quartz, feldspar and other minerals or even fragments of rocks. Others look like sediments, for after winds carried them particles of ash settled to the ground or fell upon quiet lakes. In either location they formed thin layers which were built up into thicker strata in which ash and ordinary sediment mingled. Where grains of clay, sand or gravel were plentifully mingled with ash, tuff grades into shale, sandstone or conglomerate. It is these bedded tuffs that contain fossils, often both abundant and good. The most famous of fossil-bearing tuffs in the United States are the Florissant deposits of Colorado, which fill old lake beds in what now are the Rocky Mountains.

*Mudflows,* as has been said, often develop during volcanic eruptions. Heavy rain, commonly accompanying eruptions, mingles with ash in the air and on the ground, forming hot mud. When cold, such muds "set" and form tuff. A hardened flow of this sort is to be seen on the northeast slope of Lassen Peak, California.

OCCURRENCE.—Ancient tuffs have been found in New England, Pennsylvania and the Rocky Mountains. Young ones (chiefly dating from the Cenozoic, or Age of Mammals) are common in the Rockies, the Cascades and the Coast Ranges, where they join with agglomerate in thick stratified deposits of volcanic rock. Tuffs also are common in the British Isles, Europe and other parts of the world where there has been volcanic activity.

WEATHERING.—Because it contains pockets of weak or poorly cemented material, tuff often weathers into pitted surfaces. Where joints divide massive tuff, rain and wind wear the rock into pointed domes or irregular cones whose curved and pitted sides are characteristic.

USES.—Tuff has no significant commercial value. A trachyte tuff, however, is used in Rome and Naples as a building stone, and cliff-dwelling Indians that lived in the Los Frijoles Canyon dug rooms into cliffs of tuff, though they used blocks of sandstone in the walls of buildings at the foot of the cliffs. Ruins of these and the cliff dwellings themselves may be seen in the Bandelier National Monument, about 25 miles northwest of Santa Fe, New Mexico. An interesting story about the life of these Indians is contained in *The Delight Makers* by Adolf F. Bandelier.

## CHAPTER VIII

# Rocks from the Sky

ON THE NIGHT of February 12, 1875, a brilliantly white flashing light appeared in the sky at a height of about 15 miles above northern Missouri. The light came from a meteor which gave off streamers of sparks that formed a train 7 to 12 miles long. There also were violent puffs of smoke that whirled into the space behind the speeding meteor.

This glowing body moved northeastward, while its light turned to yellow, orange and orange scarlet. A few miles from Marengo, Iowa, the solid mass at the center of the meteor exploded with a force that shook the ground, jarred windows and sent a shower of stones into fields near the town of Homestead. The rest of the meteor continued on its course and either fell without being seen or rushed into space and away from the earth. From 3 to 5 minutes after it disappeared observers in Missouri and southern Iowa heard a loud crashing explosion that came from the point where the meteor appeared. Rushing, rumbling noises seemed to follow the meteor, dying out a few minutes after it disappeared to the northward.

This, briefly, is the story of the Homestead meteor, which was seen throughout a region about 400 miles long and 250 miles wide. Its explosion produced a shower of more than 100 stones whose weight ranged from a few ounces to 120 pounds, most of them being covered with a black coating produced by heat and sudden cooling as they fell through the atmosphere. Although they have their own peculiarities, they serve excellently as an introduction to meteorites, which Pliny, the Roman naturalist, described as "stones falling down from the sky." Less realistic observers have regarded them as fallen stars, as masses of sand fused by lightning, as rocks thrown out of volcanoes, as human souls turned to stone in punishment of evil deeds or as gods and goddesses. Meteorites also have furnished the basis for many other ancient miracles and monsters, such as the one recorded by a writer in the twelfth chapter of Revelation.

And there appeared another wonder in heaven; and behold a great red dragon, having seven heads and ten horns, and seven crowns upon his heads.
And his tail drew the third part of the stars of heaven, and did cast them to the earth.

A German, writing in 1492, offered a more exalted interpretation. After watching the fall of a meteorite that still is preserved he announced, "I have heard of the Lord by the hearing of the ear . . . but now mine eyes hath seen Him!"

## METEORS AND METEORITES

Stones, stars, deities in disguise—we call them meteors and meteorites. These two words do not have the same meaning, though we sometimes use them as if they had. According to most definitions (there is some disagreement) a *meteor* is any mass or particle that comes from space and falls through the atmosphere with such speed that its surface becomes hot and glows. On the average, this happens 70 to 80 miles above the earth's surface, and the meteors continue to glow until they disappear at heights of 30 to 60 miles. Since their hottest parts are carried away as sparks, most meteors actually burn up. Their ash is carried far and wide by winds, but it finally settles as microscopic dust that has been discovered on high mountains such as Everest, on ice fields of the Arctic and in mud beneath the open oceans.

A *meteorite* is a fallen meteor. That is, it is a mass of stone, metal or a mixture of both which was so large that it survived breaking and burning and so fell upon the earth's surface in recognizable form. Its weight may range from a fraction of an ounce to many tons—perhaps even many millions of tons.

Some writers use the term *meteoroid* for grains or masses that are traveling through space but are too small to be called planetoids, or bodies that act like tiny planets. When—and if—meteoroids come into our atmosphere they grow hot and turn into meteors, while the largest and most durable become meteorites.

*Fireballs* are nothing more than very bright large meteors which glow with light rivaling that of Venus or the moon. They commonly move in irregular or zigzag paths and go to pieces with a series of loud explosions. Those that are not completely destroyed strike the earth, becoming meteorites.

The speed with which meteors and meteorites fall ranges from less than 25 to as much as 80 miles per second *when they encounter the atmosphere*. Friction with the air, which heats the meteors and makes them glow, reduces this speed enormously. Few meteorites are moving at rates of more than a few hundred feet per second when they actually strike the earth. This explains why small ones are found on the surface, sometimes with broken blades of grass beneath them. Even masses weighing 130 to 170 pounds bury themselves only 4 to 8 feet, and a 437-pound meteorite that fell near Estherville, Iowa, in 1879 drove its way only 14 feet into soil and blue clay.

## FEW METEORITES BECOME HOT

Meteorites not only strike the ground at moderate speeds; they do so at low temperatures. Thus a 75-pound stone which fell at

Forest City, Iowa, drove dry grass into the ground but did not burn it, while another mass fell on a strawstack but did not set it on fire. A stony meteorite that fell at Colby, Wisconsin, on July 4, 1917, was covered with frost when it was picked up fifteen minutes later. Though a mass of metal that came to earth in Arkansas was too hot to be handled comfortably three hours after its fall, it did not fuse grains in the soil. A stone that smashed through a log at Concord, Ohio, did not char the rotten wood.

How can we reconcile these facts with heat which makes meteors glow, which burns their stone or metal and which spreads trains of sparks across several miles of sky?

This heat, as we know, comes from friction. Calculations show that a rapidly falling meteor reaches a temperature, at its surface, of 7000 degrees Fahrenheit. Such heat sets the mass itself aglow, along with the air around it. This, by the way, explains why meteors that seem to be hundreds or even thousands of feet in diameter produce comparatively small meteorites. Most of their volume is hot, glowing air, not incandescent iron or stone.

Let us now consider that stone or iron. It has come from the wastes of outer space, where the temperature seems to be 459 degrees below zero on the Fahrenheit scale. For all we know, the meteor (or meteoroid, if you prefer) has been traveling through this frigid space for millions or even billions of years and is no warmer than its surroundings. Then suddenly it enters the air, through which it plunges in a few seconds. Even in metal masses, which are good conductors, there is little time for heat to penetrate the meteor. It is only after friction slows it down to the speed of other falling bodies that the meteorite-to-be can absorb much heat from its glowing exterior.

At the same time friction removes grains from the mass as they become glowing hot. These grains become the trailing sparks; they also reduce the heat that otherwise might warm the mass from which they come. It is no wonder, then, that very few meteorites are more than pleasantly warm when they fall, while some become cold in a few minutes. Masses like the metal meteorite of Mazapil, Mexico, which remained a "ball of fire" for some time after burying itself in a corral, are very unusual.

Surface heat and friction are responsible for the pits that mark the surface of many meteorites. These pits develop where weak portions of the material burn and are carried away as sparks. Those on the stony meteorite of PLATE 23 are small, but on many metal meteorites the pits are large enough to hold a fist or even a baseball. Some of them end in channels, showing where sparks and hot gases escaped.

Closely related to these channels are the "streamlines" produced as hot gases rushed across a meteorite's surface, streaming backward from its tip. These are shown very plainly by the small metal meteorite of PLATE 23, whose upper end actually was forward as it fell through the atmosphere.

## METEORITES ARE RARE

Although the ancient Hebrews saw meteorites fall, and there are records of 142 falls before 1799, most scientists of 1800 disbelieved in these "stones falling down from the sky." One geologist, indeed, said that even if he saw a meteorite strike the ground he would not believe his eyes.

This was perfectly natural skepticism. For thousands of years ignorance, superstition and imagination had been turning meteorites into gods, monsters and other utterly unbelievable wonders in which science could take no stock. Even people who actually saw meteorites fall told conflicting stories, colored by belief and tradition and sometimes purely imaginary. It was inevitable, therefore, that an astronomer who described a fall of meteorites in 1753 was met by the same disbelief that greeted imaginary tales. In 1769 a priest described another fall, bringing one of the stones to the Royal Academy of Science in Paris.

This time a commission was appointed to investigate, but it reported that the stone was only an ordinary rock fused by a bolt of lightning. The priest must have mistaken this lightning for a falling, glowing stone.

Between 1790 and 1803 four falls of meteorites were seen in Italy, England and France. The last one included several thousand stones; it completely convinced another commission appointed by the French Academy. Yet four years later, when two Yale scientists reported favorably on a shower of stones at Weston, Connecticut, skepticism still was widespread. Even Thomas Jefferson, himself an amateur scientist of repute, is supposed to have rejected this report with the comment: "Gentlemen, I would rather believe that two Yankee professors would lie than that stones fell from heaven!"

Yet stones did fall—and they kept on falling. By 1830 the true nature of meteorites was generally admitted and collections were being made. Today meteorites are eagerly studied for the information they can give us about other parts of the solar system and about some of the things outside it. This information, not their rarity nor the tiny quantities of precious metals and diamonds which they contain, gives meteorites their value.

Meteorites are rare—far more so than most gems. There are three reasons for this scarcity. In the first place, although more than 7,000,000,000 meteors enter the atmosphere each year, all except a few thousand waste away or are burned as they fall through the air. Of the few thousands that survive, not more than 900 are large enough to be recognized even if they could be found.

Most of them, however, cannot be found. About three fourths of the 900 strike the ocean and so disappear forever. Many of the remaining 225 fall on uninhabited regions, where there is no one to find them. Most of those that come to rest in inhabited regions are too small to make much disturbance; they therefore are not seen when they fall and cannot be looked for systematically. Finally, the mineral make-up of many of these meteorites is such that they crumble quickly unless they fall on deserts. There seems to be no doubt that most of the metal meteorites that have fallen upon ordinarily moist land weathered into clay-like compounds within a few years.

Even when meteorites are seen to fall they may be very hard to find. A collector once saw a meteorite reach the ground; he was sure it struck in a block not far from his home. Hurrying to get it, he was assured that it had fallen "just a few blocks away." That was repeated again and again, though when the collector got out of the city the location was "the next farm." Being unusually persistent and experienced, the man kept on till he found the meteorite—20 miles from the place where he had been sure that it came to rest!

On another occasion a man "saw" a meteorite strike about 80 miles south of Washington. He offered to dig it up if properly paid, but scientists at the National Museum were doubtful. A meteor had passed over Washington on the same day and hour; someone had seen it strike the roof of an apartment house. But it had also been seen to fall in Maryland. The late Dr George P. Merrill followed the trail from one town to another for almost 300 miles—yet the meteor was still going. If it ever fell at all, no one could find a trace of it.

No, the meteor that became a meteorite in the next block, or across the river, or in your neighbor's pasture, may not be there at all. It may be dozens of miles away, where only lucky accident will reveal it. It may not be anywhere, except as fine dust that drifted and settled after the meteor burned away or exploded in the atmosphere. And it is not at all surprising that only three or four out of each year's 900 meteorites are found and taken to museums.

## HOW TO KNOW METEORITES

These three or four meteorites are found, as well as others that fell long ago. Often they are picked up by people who do not recognize them. Thus one stony meteorite served for years as a doorstep before a traveling collector noticed what it was. Homesteaders near Haviland, Kansas, used stony-iron meteorites as cornerstones of chicken houses, as weights for haystacks and rain-barrel covers and as anchor stones on dugout roofs. A geologist once kept a stony meteorite in his office, considering it an odd boulder of basalt.

A vastly greater number of people, however, find stones that seem to be meteorites but actually are not. Perhaps the commonest of these are lumps of hematite or other iron minerals that were broken, worn and then dropped by glaciers of the last Ice Age. Since they now lie far from iron deposits, it perhaps is natural for people to think that they dropped from space. Nuggets of native copper and glacial boulders of gabbro, basalt and other dark rocks also have been mistaken for meteorites, as have worn pieces of slag from smelters. Even ironstone concretions that seem to be millions of years old have been mistaken for meteorites which fell while the collectors watched. One such concretion was said to have been hot when it was picked up at ten o'clock on an autumn evening!

The best way to recognize meteorites is to know them by handling authentic specimens. If that is not possible, here are a few general rules that will help:

If you find a metallic mass that does not splinter when it is hammered and that lies far from a slag dump or smelter, you may have a meteorite. Your chances are specially good if the mass has a pitted surface or shows channels burned by hot gases which apparently were streaming backward. Both these features are shown on PLATE 23. They often are absent, however, so that a lack of them does not prove that your find is not a meteorite.

A metallic mass that clearly is natural and that is found to contain nickel *by chemical test* is almost sure to be a meteorite. But don't try to identify the nickel by sight.

Very few stony meteorites are porous. A rock that is porous

is likely to be slag or a boulder of vesicular or scoriaceous lava. "Clinkery" masses are almost sure to be either lava or slag.

Freshly fallen stony meteorites generally are covered with black crusts produced by heat, which caused minerals to melt and fuse. If the stone has lain on the ground a long time, the crust will have become brown and may have been removed by weathering.

If you have a stone that seems to be a meteorite, smooth a small part of its surface on an emery wheel. If you can see grains of metal on the surface, either with your eye alone or with a magnifying glass, the specimen is probably a meteorite. Be sure, however, that you are not deceived by grains of mica or tiny pyrite crystals. If you are doubtful, test the grains with a needle to make sure that they are not brittle. Aside from meteorites, only a few rare varieties of basalt contain grains of metal, so that this test is more reliable than any other which the amateur can use.

The final step, of course, is to have a supposed meteorite examined by some competent authority whose word should be taken as final. A surprising number of collectors are unwilling to do this, and some even accuse specialists of dishonesty in reporting unfavorably on finds. Yet specialists are even more eager to discover new meteorites than are collectors; they will not reject a specimen, and go to the trouble of sending it back if there is a chance that it is genuine. But if there is no such chance, they are bound to give an unfavorable report.

## THE KINDS OF METEORITES

### Stony Meteorites or Aerolites
#### (PLATE 23)

Stony meteorites consist chiefly of the silicate minerals, such as olivine, augite, pyroxene and feldspar, with small amounts of metallic alloys and metal sulphides. Oxidation has changed the metals and metal-bearing compounds. Crystals are few and poor; this generally seems to be the result of very rapid cooling when the meteorites formed—wherever that may have happened. Other meteorites apparently were shattered by sudden changes from heat to intense cold, and about 90 per cent of all stony meteorites consist of cemented volcanic dust and sand and so may be called hard tuffs. Of the crystalline meteorites, some resemble basalts, while others are peridotites. One from Egypt is pyroxenite, a rock which contains little except pyroxene.

Most meteorites that are tuffs contain grains, or *chondrules,* which differ from anything formed on the earth. They seem to have been produced by the cooling and partial crystallization of drops of lava. In spite of this they once were described as corals and one-celled animals and were supposed to prove that life existed on other planets.

The meteorite from Cumberland Falls, Kentucky, is a breccia, or cemented mass of fragments, containing coarse whitish pyroxenite and dark tuff filled with chondrules. It resembles a volcanic breccia and suggests that the meteorite came from a large deposit that was made by an explosive volcanic eruption. This material then was squeezed into a compact mass—probably by sharp folding of the sort described in Chapter XVII. Such changes could not take place on a body smaller than the moon.

Stony meteorites are the least rare of our three groups, making up more than five ninths of all known falls. They include an even larger number of specimens, for stony meteorites commonly explode into small pieces and so come to earth in "showers." The Homestead shower included more than 100 separate stones; the meteorite that passed over Holbrook, Arizona, in 1912, broke with several explosions and came to earth in a shower of 14,000 stones ranging from the size of a pea to 6 inches in diameter. They raised "many puffs of dust . . . over the dry sand of the desert like those produced by bullets or the first drops of rain in a heavy shower." The total weight of these stones was about 480 pounds. The largest stony meteorite known fell at Estacado, Texas, and weighed 639 pounds.

## Iron Meteorites or Siderites
### (PLATE 23)

The average composition of metal meteorites is 90.6 per cent iron, 8.5 per cent nickel and 0.01 to 0.59 per cent chromium, copper, cobalt and a few other substances. Most of these metals are combined in two alloys which generally form thin plates separated by still a third alloy. When such a meteorite is polished and etched with weak acid, these plates make crossed markings known as Widmanstätten figures, from the name of their discoverer. The exact pattern of these figures depends on the size of the plates and the angle at which they are cut. Iron meteorites without Widmanstätten figures have their iron alloys arranged in grains or crystals that produce faint parallel lines in series which cut across each other.

Since iron meteorites resist breaking and burning, they are much larger than those of stone. Four meteorites secured in Greenland by Robert E. Peary total 86,500 pounds and are parts of one original mass, while a single iron meteorite from southwestern Africa weighs about 80,000 pounds and a smaller one from Mexico weighs 60,637 pounds. A metal meteorite found in French West Africa in 1921 is 325 feet long, 146 feet thick and weighs at least 1,000,000 tons. Even if we compare these with whole showers of stony meteorites, the metals are far in the lead.

Iron meteorites also show much deeper pits than do those of stone. This is partly because they do not break to pieces and partly because some of them contain nodules of weak material that burn away quickly. One hole in the meteorite found near Tucson, Arizona, is so large that the mass is an irregular ring.

Since iron meteorites resist breaking, they never fall in showers. The one apparent exception to this rule is the metal meteorite of the Canyon Diablo, or Meteor Crater, district in

Arizona. Here several thousand pieces, varying in weight from part of an ounce to 1000 pounds, have been found within 8 miles of a crater which is 4000 feet wide and 600 feet deep. Its rim consists of upturned shattered beds of limestone and sandstone, on which are scattered blocks weighing hundreds or thousands of tons that plainly were thrown out of the crater. There also are great quantities of powdered sandstone, as well as glassy pumice which was formed by the heat of impact or explosion.

There is little doubt that the crater was produced when a gigantic meteorite, or even several meteorites, struck the almost level plain less than 5000 years ago. Borings and other tests indicate that the main mass still lies under the crater, covered with broken rock and wind-drifted sand. Our concern, however, is with the pieces of nickel iron that have been found on the plain. Their angular shapes, with sharp points and edges, show that they did not fall singly. Instead, they came down in weak, probably cracked masses consisting of iron imbedded in iron sulphide or other material that weathered rapidly. Breaking and weathering, not a "shower," produced the scattered pieces that have been picked up by thousands.

Incidentally, some of these pieces show how rapidly meteorites are destroyed. "Shale balls," once common near Meteor Crater, are nothing more than weathered fragments of meteorites; when they are broken some of them still show small cores of metal. In the dry climate of Arizona such cores may last for years, but when they are taken to moist regions they oxidize very quickly, while the shale balls themselves crumble. A considerable part of the Meteor Crater fall may have been lost by such crumbling.

## Stony-Iron Meteorites or Siderolites
### (PLATE 23)

As their name implies, these meteorites consist of iron alloys and stony minerals such as olivine and some of the pyroxenes. The metals generally form an irregular network whose spaces are filled by the other minerals. In some cases, however, the stony material forms small sharp fragments imbedded in metal. Such structure suggests that the meteorite comes from a mass that was intensely squeezed and broken.

Stony irons are the rarest of meteorites; up to 1925 only 37 had been found, 13 from North America. Of these, about 20 contain iron alloys and olivine and so belong to the variety named *pallasite* after Peter E. Pallas, a naturalist who found a meteorite of this type in Siberia. It weighs 1600 pounds and so compares in size with the metals rather than with the stony falls.

## WHERE DO METEORS COME FROM?

This question has been asked for thousands of years, with answers that reflected the knowledge—or ignorance—of the people who gave them. Since the scientific study of meteorites still is less than 150 years old, present answers are no more than theories which may be wrong. In fact, it is well that we consider two erroneous theories along with three others that receive serious attention today.

The first error is the suggestion that meteorites were thrown out of the earth by ancient and violent eruptions. According to this notion, explosions tossed bombs to such heights that they no longer had to fall back to the earth but were able to revolve around it much as the moon does. Unfortunately, though many meteorites are hard tuff and others resemble peridotites, they seem to have formed under conditions not at all like those on earth. So this theory is ruled out by the meteorites themselves, as well as by other difficulties which we need not consider.

Another theory supposed that meteorites came from the moon's craters, which are vastly larger and deeper than volcanic craters on earth. It seems, however, that the moon's greatest craters are not volcanic; they probably were made by immense meteorites which crashed into the moon's surface much as the

Meteor Crater meteorite crashed into the Arizona plains. Moreover, the paths of meteorites, their speeds and their distribution show that they could not have come from the moon.

A much better theory is the one which says that many meteorites once were parts of comets. There is good evidence that comets are no more than swarms of meteoroids which travel through space in a cluster and shine by light reflected from the sun. When one of these clusters breaks up or is scattered it gets in the way of the earth. Thus one comet broke up between 1852 and 1859; but at the proper times for its return our planet has received showers of meteorites. One of these, apparently, was the unusually hot iron that fell at Mazapil, Mexico, in 1885.

Some meteorites, however, enter the atmosphere at speeds so great that they cannot come from comets. They seem to be isolated wanderers from space or material from the dark nebulous "clouds" that lie between us and distant stars. But, since no one knows what is in those clouds nor where they came from, this does not tell us much.

More than a century ago an Italian astronomer suggested that meteorites were leftover bits of the material used in the formation of planets. This idea was given new emphasis by the planetesimal hypothesis of Chamberlin and Moulton. According to it, the solar system began when vast clouds of hot material were torn from the sun by the attraction of a passing star. Much of this material condensed into solid particles or masses called planetesimals; swarms of planetesimals, in turn, became the centers of planets and satellites. Scattered planetesimals, as well as a great deal of gaseous material, combined with the centers, building them up to their present size. Other swarms of planetesimals formed comets, though isolated masses traveled around the sun alone. Such masses might become meteorites; if so, they would be true remnants, or leftovers, of planet-making material. Yet they by no means would rule out meteorites that once were parts of widespread or disrupted comets.

All this does very well for metal and stony-iron meteorites, which might have formed by the cooling and condensation of substance from the sun. But most stony types are hardened ash; others are peridotite or a breccia of various rocks. How do they fit into the picture?

They suggest that our sun had a family of planets before the present solar system was formed. These ancient planets apparently were dry and small, resembling Mercury or the moon, and the rocks at their surfaces were not like any made on the earth. When the second star approached, the little planets were broken into the bits we now know as stony meteorites. If the star actually sideswiped our sun, as some mathematical astronomers believe, such breakup would be inevitable. And if the shattered planets had nickel-iron cores, like the cores of the earth, they have produced iron meteorites as well as those of stone.

Here are three theories, with four different suggestions for the origin of meteorites. It may be that all these suggestions are good: that some meteorites come from comets, some from space between the stars and some from disrupted planets, while the remainder are lone planetesimals which revolved around the sun until they encountered the earth. At the least these are possibilities to think of as we look at meteorites.

PLATE I
ROCKS USED BY STONE AGE MAN

Novaculite spearhead, Arkansas.
Quartz-gneiss ax, Oraibi, Arizona.

Chert spearhead, Florida.
Obsidian blade, Trinity County,
California.

Quartzite blade or spearhead,
Tennessee.
Jadeite carving, Mexico.

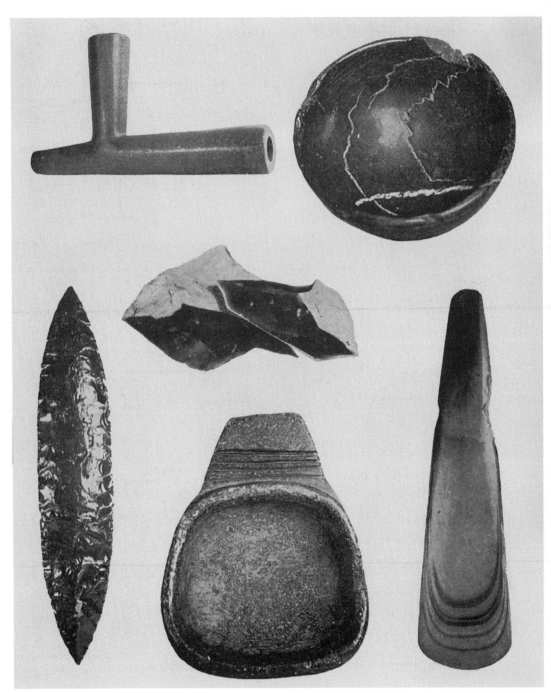

PLATE 2

ROCKS USED BY STONE AGE MAN

Catlinite pipe, Devil's Lake
Agency, North Dakota.
Obsidian blade, northern
California.

Old Stone Age flints showing
patina, Loire Basin, France.
Soapstone dipper, Santa Barbara,
California.

Serpentine bowl with asbestos
veins, Dos Pueblos, California.
Limestone "spatula," Colorado.

PLATE 3
IMPORTANT MINERALS

Amphibole, Calumet Island, Ottawa River, Canada.        Apatite, Renfrew, Ontario.
Galena, Rossie, New York.        Epidote, Prince of Wales Island, Alaska.
Cassiterite, Potosi, Bolivia.        Native copper, Keweenaw Peninsula, Michigan.

PLATE 4

IMPORTANT MINERALS

Aragonite, Tintic mining district,
Utah.
Iceland spar (calcite) showing
double refraction, near Big
Timber, Montana.

Calcite, Guanajuato, Mexico.
Sand-calcite crystals, White River,
Badlands, South Dakota.

Fibrous amphibole or asbestus,
Val Malenco, Italy.
Aragonite rosette, Amarillo,
Texas.
Dolomite crystals, Picher,
Oklahoma.

PLATE 5
IMPORTANT MINERALS

Selenite (gypsum), Rochester, New York.
Gypsum showing transparency.
Barite, Junction Creek, Colorado.

Crystals of selenite, Logan County, Kansas.

"Desert Rose" of selenite, Sahara Desert, Algeria.
Beryl, Portland, Connecticut.
Fluorite showing cleavage planes, West Moreland, New Hampshire.

PLATE 6

IMPORTANT MINERALS

Halite (salt) crystals, Zipaquira,
Colombia.
Crude graphite, Colombo, Ceylon.
Magnetite, Brewster, New York.

Corundum, Transvaal, South
Africa.
Garnet, Salida, Colorado.

Garnets, Monroe, Connecticut.
Franklinite, Franklin, New Jersey.
Clinochlore (a chlorite mineral),
Brewster, New York.

PLATE 7

MICA, HORNBLENDE AND HEMATITE

Mica (muscovite), near Chester,
Delaware.

Hornblende, Kragerø, Norway.

Botryoidal hematite, Cleator
Moor, Cumberland, England.

Fibrous hematite, Ironwood,
Michigan.

Mica (muscovite), South Dakota.

Specular hematite, Vestmanland,
Sweden.

Mica (lepidolite), Varutrask,
North Sweden.

PLATE 8

FELDSPARS, QUARTZ AND VESUVIANITE

Albite, Amelia Courthouse, Virginia.
Microcline, De Kalb, New York.
Microcline and smoky quartz, Varese, Italy.

Microcline, Klein Spitzkopje, South Africa.

Microcline (Amazon Stone), Pike's Peak, Colorado.
Microcline, San Diego County, California.
Vesuvianite, Sanford, Maine.

PLATE 9
IMPORTANT MINERALS

Sulphur crystals, Cianciana,
Sicily.

Marcasite disk in shale, Randolph
County, Illinois.

Serpentine (chrysotile), near
Globe, Arizona.

Pyroxene, St Lawrence County,
New York.

Pyrite showing striations, Bingham Canyon, Utah.

Malachite, Bisbee, Arizona.

Augite (a pyroxene) Ogdensburg,
New York.

PLATE 10
IMPORTANT MINERALS

Rose quartz, Southington, Connecticut.

Spodumene, Huntington, Massachusetts.

Fibrous chrysotile (asbestos), near Globe, Arizona. (U.S. Bureau of Mines.)

Flint nodule from chalk, Isle of Rügen, Baltic Sea.

Chalcedony, Tanitcha Plateaus, Arizona.

Quartz, Arkansas.

Wollastonite, Imperial County, California.

PLATE 11
IMPORTANT MINERALS

Smoky quartz showing striations,
Alexander County, North Carolina.
Smoky quartz with tourmaline inclusions,
Jefferson County, Montana.
Fluorite, or fluorspar, England.

Stibnite, San Benito
County, California.

Sphalerite (zinc blende), Yugoslavia.
Black tourmaline, Crown Point,
New York.
Staurolite (dark) and kyanite (light)
in schist, Switzerland.

PLATE 12
INTRUSIONS
AND
EXTRUSIONS

Little Sundance Hill, in eastern Wyoming, is a laccolith whose cover of strata has not yet been removed. (Darton, U.S.G.S.)

Bear Butte, near Sturgis, South Dakota, is a laccolith whose cover has been eroded till only upturned edges of strata show east and west of the butte. (Darton, U.S.G.S.)

Craters in these cones, built of stiff lava, are more than sixty feet deep. They stand on pahoehoe flows. Craters of the Moon, Idaho. (Russell, U.S.G.S.)

Alesna, or The Bodkin, is a volcanic neck of columnar rock in northern New Mexico. (Dutton, U.S.G.S.)

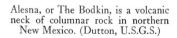

Prehistoric Indians dug houses in this southward-facing cliff of tuff, which contains chips of obsidian. Bandelier National Monument, New Mexico.

PLATE 13

DIKES, GRANITE AND TUFF

Two diabase dikes cross red beds exposed beside Alamillo Creek, New Mexico. (Darton, U.S.G.S.)

A jointed basaltic dike cuts Ordovician limestones on Valcour Island, Lake Champlain. (G. H. Hudson.)

Metamorphic granite between bands of dark mica schist; the granite looks like gray intrusions. Near Worcester, Massachusetts. (Keith, U.S.G.S.)

PLATE 14
LAVAS

Lava, now diabase, flowed out on a sea bottom in Proterozoic times. Glacier National Park, Montana.

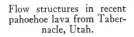

The edge of an aa flow near Lassen Peak, California. Lapilli cover the slopes around the lava. Notice remains of trees killed by eruptions. (Diller, U.S.G.S.)

Flow structures in recent pahoehoe lava from Tabernacle, Utah.

Pahoehoe lava from Kilauea Volcano, Hawaii, hardened in a cascade as it flowed over the edge of older lava. (Mendenhall, U.S.G.S.)

These pillow lavas probably flowed into a lake. Highland Creek, California. (Ransome, U.S.G.S.)

Weathered spheroidal lava near Cascades, Oregon, shows layers, or "shells." (Diller, U.S.G.S.)

PLATE 15
ANDESITE AND OTHER LAVAS

This gray andesite from Storey County, Nevada, contains hornblende crystals.

Ledges of laminated andesite look like sedimentary rock, although they are hardened lavas. Franklin Hill, California. (Hardin, U.S.G.S.)

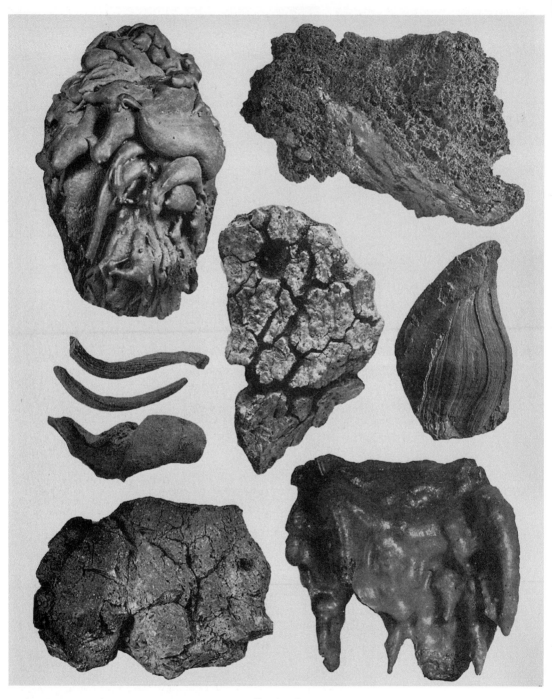

PLATE 16

LAVA AND VOLCANIC BOMBS

Lava drip, Kilauea, Hawaii.

Ribbon and spindle bombs, Craters of the Moon National Monument, Idaho. (Stearns, U.S.G.S.)

Bread-crust bomb, Lipari Islands, Italy.

Bread-crust bomb, Craters of the Moon National Monument, Idaho. (Stearns, U.S.G.S.)

Scoria, or lava slag, Niu-fou Island.

Basaltic bomb, near Burns, Oregon. (Piper, U.S.G.S.)

Stalactites in basaltic lava, Kilauea, Hawaii.

PLATE 17

GRANITE, MONZONITE AND DIORITE

Graphic granite, Auburn, Maine. (Bastin, U.S.G.S.)

Monzonite showing biotite and hornblende, Yosemite
National Park, California. (Calkins, U.S.G.S.)

Granite, Yosemite National Park, California. (Calkins, U.S.G.S.)

Porphyritic granite with feldspar phenocrysts, Yosemite National Park, California. (Calkins, U.S.G.S.)

Graphic granite, Topsham, Maine.

Diorite cut by light aplite, Yosemite National Park,
California. (Calkins, U.S.G.S.)

PLATE 18

GABBRO, GRANITE AND TRAP

Olivine gabbro, Volpersdorf, Silesia.

Hornblende gabbro, Yosemite National Park, California. (Calkins, U.S.G.S.)

Orbicular granite from glacial drift, Quonochontaug, Rhode Island.

Pegmatite dike in granite. Black tourmaline at the margins, Cape Elizabeth, Maine.

Biotite orbicules in granite, Nashua, New Hampshire.

Trap dikes in granite, Norway, Maine.

Devil's Tower, in eastern Wyoming, consists of columns of phonolite. The slope in the foreground is shale. (National Park Service.)

PLATE 19

PHONOLITE AND GRANITE

"Sheet structure" in granite is produced by almost horizontal joints. Quincy, Massachusetts. (Dale, U.S.G.S.)

Needles of the Black Hills, South Dakota, are weathered, jointed granite.

Deeply weathered granite crumbles away from rounded residual boulders and breaks up into sand. Nevada City, California. (Gilbert, U.S.G.S.)

PLATE 20

IGNEOUS ROCKS

Dacite porphyry, Clear Creek, Shasta County,
California.

Rhyolite with spherulites, hills between Cole-
man's and Long valleys, Oregon.

Diabase, Somerville, Massachusetts.

Syenite, Davidson College, North Carolina.

Biotite nephelite syenite, near Little Rock,
Arkansas.

Dolerite with labradorite phenocrysts, Cape
Ann, Massachusetts.

PLATE 21

IGNEOUS ROCKS

Tuff, faulted and metamorphosed, Yosemite
National Park, California. (Calkins, U.S.G.S.)

Pumice, Canary Islands.

Liparite tuff, Douglas       Scoriaceous texture in pahoehoe basalt,
County, Colorado.               Hawaii. (Stearns, U.S.G.S.)

Vesicular basalt, São Miguel, Azores.

Amygdules in basalt, Oahu, Hawaii.

Olivine basalt, Pilot Knob, Colorado.

PLATE 22

LITHOPHYSAE, SPHERULITES AND OBSIDIAN

Lithophysae in obsidian.

Flow structure in obsidian.

Obsidian showing conchoidal fracture and
indistinct flow structure.

Spherulites and steam bubbles in obsidian.

Obsidian showing conchoidal fracture.

Flow breccia in obsidian.

All specimens from Obsidian Cliff, Yellowstone National Park, Wyoming.

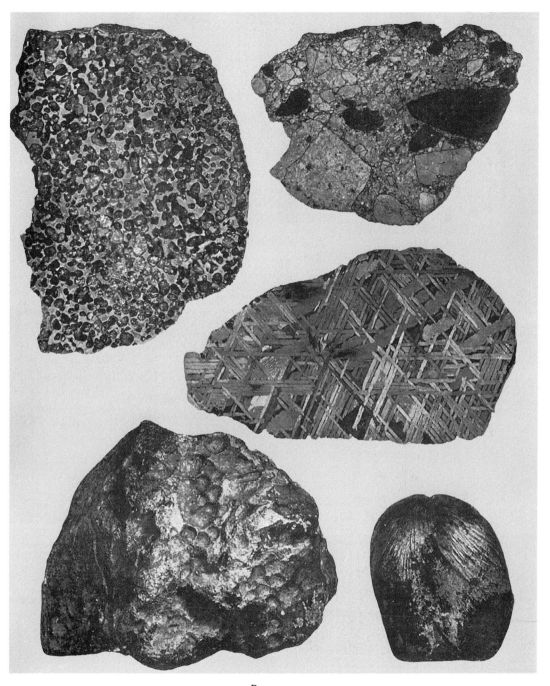

PLATE 23

METEORITES

Polished stony-iron meteorite, Springwater, Saskatchewan.

Brecciated stony meteorite, Cumberland Falls, Kentucky.

Iron meteorite showing Widmanstätten figures, Coopertown, Tennessee.

Stony meteorite showing pits and crust, Barber County, Kansas.

Flight marks, or "streamlines," on iron meteorite, Freda, North Dakota.

Beds of clay, cobbles and river-worn gravel of Cretaceous age in Washington, D.C.

Talus cones gather at the foot of a mountain in Mount Assiniboine Park, British Columbia.

PLATE 24
TALUS AND CONGLOMERATE

"Puddingstone" conglomerate of pebbles and cobbles imbedded in sandstone at Bic, Quebec. (Walcott, U.S.G.S.)

Beds of andesite conglomerate near Highland Creek, California. The fragments were deposited by a river and so do not form agglomerate. (Ransome, U.S.G.S.)

Glacial boulders lie on rock scraped and smoothed by moving ice. Yosemite National Park, California. (National Park Service.)

This jointed granite is being split by a juniper tree that took root in a crack. Sierra Nevada Mountains, California. (Gilbert, U.S.G.S.)

Plate 25

GLACIAL DEPOSITS AND
WEATHERING

These outwash gravels were deposited by a river flowing from an Ice Age glacier. At one time the stream deposited a bed of fine sediment. Near Oconomowoc, Wisconsin. (Alden, U.S.G.S.)

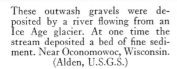

Boulders, pebbles, sand and clay are mixed in this glacial till near Oconomowoc, Wisconsin. Tillite looks like this, except that it is hard. (Alden, U.S.G.S.)

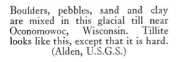

PLATE 26
MUD BRECCIAS
AND
CONGLOMERATE

Floods and storms tore up cracked beds of mud on the bottom of a very shallow sea. Some of the mud formed storm rollers; some became layers of mud breccia among cross-bedded sands that now are quartzite. Proterozoic of Glacier National Park, Montana.

Mud-cracked dolomite in the first stage of becoming breccia. Polygons have been slightly moved and cracks are filled with chips. Proterozoic of Glacier National Park, Montana.

Here worn, rounded pebbles of mud were deposited in coarse sand. Since the pebbles are rounded, the rock may be called conglomerate. Proterozoic of Glacier National Park, Montana.

Concretions in Tertiary clay. Toadstool Park, near Adelia, Sioux County, Nebraska. (Darton, U.S.G.S.)

This weathered, eroded sandstone near Livingston, Montana, shows many cavities. (Walcott, U.S.G.S.)

Canyon de Chelly, Arizona, is eroded in dark red sandstone of Permian age. (Santa Fe Lines.)

PLATE 27
SANDSTONE AND CLAY

Coarse-grained Permian sandstone from Cumberland, England.

PLATE 28
SEDIMENTARY ROCKS

Kaolin clay, Pike County, Arkansas.
Pisolitic bauxite (aluminum ore), Floyd
County, Georgia.
Conglomerate, Custer County, South Dakota.

Argillite, Washington County, New York.
Chert nodules in limestone, Franklin, Tennessee.
Oil shale showing conchoidal fracture, Hartley,
New South Wales.

Oölitic Clinton ore; a hematite deposited in a Silurian sea, from Danville, Pennsylvania.

Stalactites of limonite, Eufala, Alabama.

PLATE 29
IRON ORE AND GYPSUM

Banded gypsum, produced when layers of anhydrite absorbed water, swelled and crumpled.

An open-pit iron mine at Hibbing, Minnesota. The ore, mostly hematite of Huronian age, is mined with steam shovels. (Hibbing Tourist and Information Bureau.)

A small cone of geyserite, or siliceous sinter. The ground is covered with the same material.

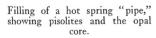

Two pieces of geyserite, showing different forms.

Filling of a hot spring "pipe," showing pisolites and the opal core.

PLATE 30
GEYSER AND HOT SPRINGS
DEPOSITS

Yellowstone National Park,
Wyoming.

Geyserite deposits in the Biscuit Basin. (© J. E. Haynes, St Paul.)

Travertine quarries at Gardiner, Montana, use the deposits of ancient springs.

Liberty Cap, in Yellowstone National Park, Wyoming, is the travertine core of a hot springs deposit. (© J. E. Haynes, St Paul.)

PLATE 31
TUFA AND TRAVERTINE

Travertine from Gardiner, Montana.

Tufa deposited on leaves. Bear Spring, Beaverhead Canyon, Montana.

Orange Spring tufa deposit, Yellowstone National Park, Wyoming. (© J. E. Haynes, St Paul.)

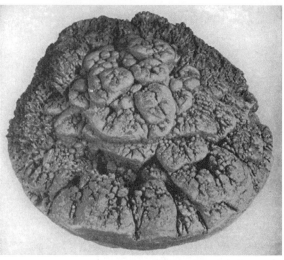

Tufa deposited by a colony of algae in ancient Lake Lahontan, now Black Rock Desert, Nevada.

PLATE 32
TUFA AND KAOLIN CLAY

Stalactites and stalagmites in Carlsbad Caverns, New Mexico. (National Park Service.)

The outer parts of this pegmatite dike have weathered to white kaolin clay, but the center is resistant quartz. Bryson City, North Carolina. (Keith, U.S.G.S.)

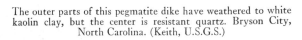

Tufa deposited on grass by a hot spring in Pierce County, Washington.

PLATE 33
ALGAL LIMESTONES
AND DOLOMITES

A Proterozoic algal reef in Glacier National Park, Montana, lies on laminated dolomites and limestones that were bent down under its weight.

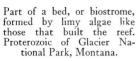

Mottled Ordovician dolomite whose dark parts probably were red coralline algae. Near the Shoshone Dam, west of Cody, Wyoming.

Part of a bed, or biostrome, formed by limy algae like those that built the reef. Proterozoic of Glacier National Park, Montana.

PLATE 34
LIMESTONES

Oölitic limestone, Key West, Florida.

Weathered limestone showing stylolites, Cottonwood District, Utah. (Calkins, U.S.G.S.)

Pisolites, Carlsbad, Bohemia.

Photomicrograph of fine-grained oölitic limestone, Bedford, Indiana. (Loughlin, U.S.G.S.)

Coquina, St Augustine, Florida.

Lithographic limestone showing conchoidal fracture, Yale, Kentucky.

Photos by U. S. Bureau of Mines.

PLATE 35
PEAT AND COAL

Lignite, Montana.

Bituminous coal, Franklin County, Illinois.

Splint coal, Harlan County, Kentucky.

Peat, Manitowoc County, Wisconsin.

Cannel coal, Cannelton, Pennsylvania.

Anthracite, Schuylkill County, Pennsylvania.

Cross-bedded Cretaceous sandstone of Kansas, which probably formed under water.

PLATE 36
CROSS-BEDDING AND UNCONFORMITIES

Tufa is being deposited unconformably on ancient limestones at Turner Falls, Oklahoma.

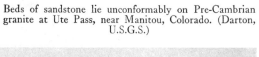

Beds of sandstone lie unconformably on Pre-Cambrian granite at Ute Pass, near Manitou, Colorado. (Darton, U.S.G.S.)

Cross-bedded sandstones in Walnut Canyon, east of Flagstaff, Arizona, probably were Permian dunes.

These modern symmetrical ripple marks were formed by waves in a shallow bay. San Juan Island, Puget Sound, Washington.

Small waves rippled across sand bars, broke up and formed these crossed ripple marks on Ordovician sandstone near Cooksville, Ontario.

PLATE 37
RIPPLE MARKS

Measuring current-made ripples in Proterozoic quartzite, Glacier National Park, Montana. Such marks are steeper on one side than the other.

Changing winds built new ridges across old ones, forming these irregularly crossed ripple marks. Proterozoic of Glacier National Park, Montana.

When these fresh-water muds dried and cracked, their broken edges turned upward. Stratford Hall, Virginia.

Filled burrows of snails in Carboniferous sandstone from Texas.

PLATE 38

MUD CRACKS AND BURROWS

These muds lay flat, while some of the cracks became three inches wide. Small salt crystals show that the mud was salty. Proterozoic argillite, Glacier National Park, Montana.

These hardened, cracked muds also contain casts of salt crystals. Edges of the cracked polygons turn downward. Proterozoic argillite, Glacier National Park, Montana.

PLATE 39
RECORDS IN STRATA

Varve laminae in Eocene oil shale from lake deposits in Garfield County, Colorado. (Bradley, U.S.G.S.)

Pits made by sleet that fell on Proterozoic muds of Glacier National Park, Montana. At the right is a piece of hardened mud that covered and filled sleet prints. Below is a small slab of rain prints found among the sleet-marked layers.

Fillings of channels that developed when currents swept across mud-cracked beds. Proterozoic of Glacier National Park, Montana.

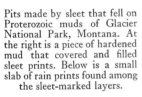

PLATE 40

RECORDS IN STRATA

Dendrites of manganite, Saxony, Germany.

Casts of drag marks, Streetsville, Ontario.

Calcite veins in limestone, near Higate Springs, Vermont. (Walcott, U.S.G.S.)

Stylolites in marble, Knoxville, Tennessee.

Stylolites in dolomite, Lockport, New York.

Landscape marble, Bristol, England.

Casts of salt crystals, southwestern Colorado.

PLATE 41

STRUCTURES IN SEDIMENTS

Geode in rock, Renfrewshire, Scotland.

Septaria, Johnson County, Kansas.

"Cauliflower" chert nodule, near Mercersburg, Pennsylvania. (Stose, U.S.G.S.)

Quartz geode, Warsaw, Illinois.

Clay concretion, Connecticut River, near Deerfield, Massachusetts.

Limestone with sandy laminae, Cottonwood District, Utah. (Calkins, U.S.G.S.)

Concretions in Cretaceous sandstone, near Newcastle, Wyoming.
(Darton, U.S.G.S.)

Cone-in-cone from Stiverdorf, Austria.

PLATE 42
STRUCTURES IN SEDIMENTS

Cone-in-cone in limy shale, near North Girard, Pennsylvania. Many cones cross a bedding plane.

This double sandstone dike in Cretaceous shale has a soft, shaly center. Tehama County, California. (Diller, U.S.G.S.)

Mud balls after a flood in Gallisteo Creek, New Mexico. (Lee, U.S.G.S.)

PLATE 43

FRACTURED AND METAMORPHIC ROCKS

Contorted schist, opposite Peekskill, New York.

Apatite (dark) replacing albite, Keystone, South Dakota.

Slickensides in silver ore, Butte, Montana.

Faults in laminated sandstone, Black Hills, South Dakota.

Parallel joints in argillite, Washington County, New York.

Jaspillite and hematite showing fault breccia, Ishpeming, Michigan.

This granitic vein was closely crumpled as the rock around it became gneiss. West of Helsinki, Finland.

Folded Jurassic chert in the Berkeley Hills, east of San Francisco Bay, California.

PLATE 44
FOLDED ROCKS

These white and red quartz-ites in Glacier National Park, Montana, were raised, broken and crumpled when the Rocky Mountains were built. They now rise above the trail to Sperry Glacier. (Hileman)

The cleavage face of this Ordovician slate cuts across layers and beds, some of which are darker than others. Slatington, Pennsylvania.

Dark, fine-grained schist intruded by granite. Some of the schist now forms inclusions. San Juan Mountains, Colorado. (Howe, U.S.G.S.)

PLATE 45
SCHIST AND SLATE

Slate near Penrhyn, Pennsylvania, shows cleavage and joints developed when Ordovician shale was metamorphosed. (Walcott, U.S.G.S.)

Pressure that produced this slate folded beds of shale, squeezed them and produced cleavage planes that cut across the folded strata. Slatington, Pennsylvania. (Hardin, U.S.G.S.)

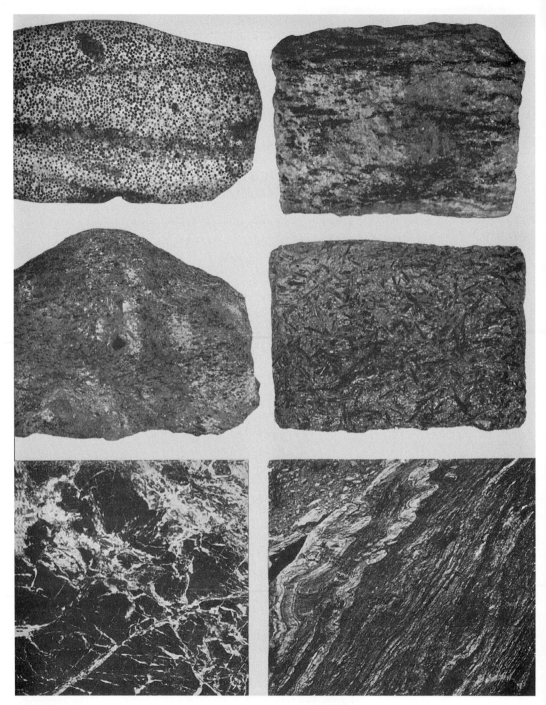

PLATE 46

METAMORPHIC ROCKS

Siliceous oölite, College Center, Pennsylvania.

Mica schist with garnets, Monroe, Connecticut.

Serpentine, or "verd antique marble," Roxbury, Vermont.

Granite gneiss, Eleven Mile Canyon, Colorado.

Tourmaline schist, Keystone, South Dakota.

Folded quartz in granitoid gneiss, near Cranberry, North Carolina. (Keith, U.S.G.S.)

PLATE 47
METAMORPHIC ROCKS

Alum marble, Baltimore, Maryland.                    Talc, Smithfield, Rhode Island.

Marble, near West Rutland, Vermont.          Amphibolite, Mount Blanc, Switzerland.

Brecciated marble, Pyrenees Mountains.          Quartzite, Madison County, Montana

PLATE 48
ORES AND LODESTONE

Native gold in quartz pebble, French Guiana.

Magnetite (an iron ore), Essex County, New York.

Lodestone, a natural magnet, Magnet Cove, Arkansas.

Crystallized gold in rock, Santian River, Oregon.

Chalcopyrite (a copper ore), Chester County, Pennsylvania.

Native silver with calcite gangue, Batopilas, Mexico.

# CHAPTER IX

# New Rocks from Old

So FAR AS WE CAN TELL, the earth's first rocks were formed by the condensation of intensely hot, whirling, gaseous stuff which was torn from the sun by another star as it swung past through the heavens. Experts disagree as to whether this sun-stuff formed a ball which was hard from the beginning or one which was molten and hardened as it cooled. In either case formation of the earth was followed by an era of volcanic activity in which magmas arose, lavas poured out and ashes built volcanoes. Huge meteorites also crashed into the earth's surface, making pits many miles wide, surrounded by mountain ranges. With the eruptions, they gave our planet a surface as rugged as that of the moon.

Though the igneous rocks of that rugged surface were resistant, they soon began to go to pieces. Heat and cold broke them into blocks or curved fragments; gravity pulled those fragments downhill; winds blew the smallest ones onto plains. Rain, gathering in rills and rivers, washed other rock bits into newly formed seas, while water that sank into the ground dissolved mineral grains and took that dissolved stuff to rivers. At the end of their travels both fragments and dissolved materials settled in beds of *sediment,* so extensive that they formed rock. When these rocks were raised into land they also were broken, worn or dissolved and so became sediment that settled in new deposits. This cycle has been repeated countless times, which explains the abundance and variety of sedimentary rocks.

## SEDIMENTARY ROCKS VARY

We have said that sedimentary rocks are those deposited by wind, water, ice or gravity or built up by plants and animals. Most of them consist largely, or even wholly, of material that was worn or dissolved from older rocks. Some were worn and deposited directly, as when winds took sand grains from granite cliffs and piled them into desert dunes which in time became beds of sandstone. Many have longer, more complex stories. Thus clay grains in a bed of shale may have been loosened by frost or chemical solution, taken to valleys by winds and rain water, carried to the sea by rivers and finally washed into place by currents moving through shallow bays. Many limestones consist of material that was dissolved by water seeping underground and was taken to the sea by rivers. There corals, snails and other animals extracted some of the dissolved material, turned it into calcite or aragonite and so produced rock-building sediment. Coal consists of material which plants took from soil (by way of water), as well as carbon and oxygen which they got from the air. When the plants died these substances settled in bogs and slowly became beds of stone.

Though sedimentary rocks differ greatly in their beginnings, most of them agree in three important respects. First, every bit of their material sank, dropped or otherwise moved downward into place, instead of rising from within the earth. Second, sediments have settled in layers, beds or strata, so that sedimentary rocks are stratified. Finally, the processes that have made sediments, carried them and turned them into new rocks are at work today, just as they have been at work for the past 2,000,-000,000 years. We may watch them on hills, in valleys and caves and along the shores of lakes and seas. Since they work constantly and constantly find new materials, they show us sedimentary rocks in all stages of formation, from freshly broken, loose fragments to compact deposits which are hardening into rock. And if what we see is not convincing, we may duplicate many of the natural processes at home or in laboratories, experimenting again and again until we know what happens. On a small scale we turn ourselves into nature and make the things we want to explain. That seldom is possible when we deal with igneous rocks.

In order for sediment to form, rocks must break, crumble, dissolve or wear into bits. The first three of these changes come from *weathering*. Actually, weathering includes a variety of processes which we group as mechanical and chemical. The former breaks rocks without changing their minerals. Chemical weathering, on the other hand, combines minerals or materials in minerals with substances from water and air. In doing so, it forms compounds which swell, crumble or dissolve. Together, these types of weathering produce most of the material that we see in sedimentary rocks other than peat, lignite and coal.

*Freezing* and *thawing* are forms of mechanical weathering that are effective on high mountains and in cold countries where water freezes during winter and melts in summer. During spring and fall there is freezing every night and thawing every day. Thawing lets water run or seep into pores, joints and other cracks; freezing makes it expand one eleventh, with a force of 2000 pounds per square inch. If the temperature keeps on dropping, this force increases, and at 8 degrees below zero Fahrenheit ice pushes against the rocks that surround it with a pressure of 34,000 pounds per square inch. Repeated freezing and thawing, therefore, will break even the most resistant rocks into smaller and smaller fragments. The cliffs of many northern mountains are made up of countless blocks broken and loosened in this manner, while even small pebbles may be split by the force of expanding ice.

Temperature change also seems to cause mechanical weathering, but it is helped by chemical action. When a rock is heated its minerals expand; as it cools they shrink. This happens most often on high mountains and in deserts, where rocks are heated to 100 or 150 degrees Fahrenheit in midafternoon but cool to 40 or 50 degrees at night. In the Sahara Desert, for instance, the temperature may drop 110 to 130 degrees in ten or twelve hours; in Central Asia a rise of 90 degrees has been recorded in the six hours from 7 A.M. to 1 P.M. Since different minerals expand and contract *at different speeds,* these changes set up unbearable stresses in even the strongest rocks.

The strains are unbearable, but we do not know what they alone might accomplish. While mineral grains are expanding and shrinking, air and small amounts of moisture change some of them chemically. These changes produce swelling and weakness, much as iron is weakened when it forms rust. As these effects are combined with those of expansion and contraction, grains of feldspar, quartz and other minerals are loosened. Thus granite may become a crumbling mass of grains, ready to fall apart at a touch (PLATE 19). In dry regions coarse-grained rocks often split into curved slabs or shells that cover mountaintops or fall to the ground around boulders. If these layers or shells result chiefly from changing temperature, they are said to be caused by *exfoliation.* If chemical change is the more important, the process is *conchoidal weathering.* It generally produces the most distinct and the thinnest shells.

*Animals* and *plants* destroy rocks both mechanically and chemically. Burrowing creatures, such as earthworms, ants and ground squirrels, bring loose material to the surface where heat, cold and frost can break it. Earthworms do still more, for they swallow soil to get food that is in it. As the soil goes through their muscular gizzards it is ground into finer and finer grains. It is estimated that an ordinary earthworm population will work over and grind a zone of soil 6 to 12 inches thick in 50 years. That is equivalent to 10,000 or 20,000 feet in a million years—no small contribution to the country's supply of loose, fine-grained sediment.

Plants send roots into soil and cracks that cut boulders or bedrock. Ferns and grasses split off blocks weighing 2 or 3 pounds, while tree roots break stones that weigh many tons. In each case solid stone is turned into fragments which can be moved elsewhere. One tree or grass clump is not important, but those of thousands or millions of years provide great amounts of sediment. The work of one tree is shown on PLATE 25.

So much for mechanical work. When earthworms grind soil grains together they also affect them chemically by means of digestive juices. The simple plants called lichens, which grow on rocks from moist valleys to exposed mountain peaks, produce an acid that dissolves some rock grains and loosens others. Thus the stones become pitted, so that other plants can grow upon them and split them. One group of bacteria, or "germs," is able to make nitric acid that alters minerals in both soil and hard rocks. Like splitting by roots and grinding by earthworms, these processes accomplish little in a year, but in the long epochs of earth history they must have turned much mineral matter into sediment.

*Solution,* the most familiar form of chemical weathering, depends largely on impurities in water. Salt and gypsum are the only minerals that dissolve readily in pure water—but water in the ground is not pure. It contains carbonic acid, acids from decaying animals and plants and other substances which combine with minerals, making them soluble. Limestone yields easily; if pure it disappears, but if it is impure it leaves clay and other substances which are important in many soils. The dissolved calcite is carried away, eventually becoming the rocks described in Chapter XIII. Sandstones whose grains are held together by calcite crumble readily, but those which are cemented by quartz yield very slowly. So do such igneous rocks as granite and diorite, though we shall see that they are attacked by other sorts of chemical weathering.

*Carbonation* both aids solution and works independently. It depends on the remarkable ability of carbon dioxide, the gas that makes charged water "fizz," to combine with minerals, producing new substances. Many rocks contain calcium and iron; these unite with carbon dioxide, forming lime and iron carbonates, which dissolve readily. In igneous rocks carbonated water (all water in the ground is mildly carbonated) turns feldspar into kaolin, quartz and soluble carbonates—a change that also may be brought about by pure water. Such changes allow granites and other massive rocks to crumble, especially when they also are attacked by hydration.

*Hydration* is the union of water molecules with others in minerals. Rusting is the most familiar example: iron combines with oxygen, making iron oxide, which then unites with water in the hydrated iron oxide, called rust. In rocks hydration is most important when it attacks feldspars. It always causes an increase in volume, so that the new compounds, which require more space than the old ones needed, exert pressures which break the rock into fine bits. Near Washington, D.C., in the Sierra Nevada Mountains and elsewhere hydration has turned granite into rock so soft that it can be dug with spades. In spite of this, only about 14 per cent of its mineral matter has been removed by solution.

*Oxidation* chiefly affects iron minerals and, as we have seen, may come before hydration. Acting alone, it turns dark or colorless minerals into others that are red; followed by hydration, it produces yellow, red-brown and brown compounds. These colors often appear as "shells" on rocks whose interiors range from blue gray to green or black. Scratching with a knife will show that the "shells" are softer than the dark cores— another result of the stresses that are caused by the increase in volume that comes with oxidation alone, as well as with hydration.

The great thicknesses of brown and red shales, sandstones and other rocks exposed in various parts of the country at least suggest the importance of oxidation throughout geologic time.

## WEAR, MOVEMENT AND DEPOSITION

While rocks are being broken and decomposed they also are being worn. Air, through which sunshine reaches and heats granite, moves and so becomes winds that are able to pick up mineral grains and drive them against rocks. Flowing water carries pebbles and bits of sand, which hit and wear each other as they go. Other waters pound cobbles together, break blocks from cliffs and roll boulders down mountain valleys. Ice, which pries blocks of stone from cliffs, also grinds them into sand or microscopic clay grains.

Rock wear means movement. For sand to wear bits from cliffs or boulders, it must be lifted, carried and whirled against them. Before pebbles can grind one another down, they must be moved and tumbled by rivers or waves. Even rocks in the beds of glaciers and streams will not be worn much unless other rocks are pushed or rolled across them. Movement of fragments, or *transportation*, is essential to rock wear, just as strains and chemical changes are vital to weathering. It also is necessary if sediments are to gather in beds and formations such as we see among sedimentary rocks.

Since movement cannot last forever, it must lead to *deposition*. Winds, even in the desert, diminish; in doing so, they drop the dust and sand that have polished boulders and battered minerals from cliffs. Where rivers slow down or become overloaded they pile gravel into bars or leave layers of mud on flood plains. Waves heap "shingle" into beaches, while glaciers, which may carry rocks hundreds of miles, finally melt and drop their loads. Indeed, more than half of North America is covered by rocks that were broken, worn and finally dropped by melting Ice Age glaciers.

It is this settling or dropping—deposition—that produces sedimentary rocks. We need not examine its details here, however, for they must be discussed in connection with each sort of sedimentary rock. Instead, let us turn to another question: that of how sediments become stones.

## STONES FROM SEDIMENTS

Weathering, wear and deposition produce rocks, for rocks may be loose material such as gravel, dust or sand. Only rarely, however, do those processes make strata which are hard enough to be called stone. For that there must be still another step; one that will fasten loose grains together and bind them into firm beds. We call this process *consolidation;* when it goes so far as to make true stones we also call it *induration,* from a Latin word which means "to harden." Consolidation is the better term for it includes all stages that lead from loose sediment to stone but induration is useful.

*Cementation* probably is the commonest means by which sediments are consolidated and is the only one that can be seen in operation today. In almost all loose rocks pores are filled or partly filled by water that carries minerals in solution. When they are deposited most of these minerals fasten chips or grains together; when enough grains are fastened the combination makes a solid rock. We can see almost the same process when Portland cement mixed with water, sand and gravel hardens or "sets," to make concrete. The concrete really is a conglomerate; the fact that it generally is mixed with 60 per cent gravel, 30 per cent sand and 10 per cent cement shows how little of the last is needed to make a strong, durable stone.

In nature the commonest materials available for rock cement are lime (calcite), iron carbonate and silica. Calcite is the most abundant and the most soluble; it forms the cement in many ancient rocks as well as in others of recent age. A hard lime-cemented sandstone dredged from the harbor of Marseilles contained coins of England's King Henry V, who reigned until 1422. Modern coral reef limestones are cemented only a short time after they are deposited—yet this is not the rule for all limy deposits, either ancient or modern. Many ancient limestones show that they slid, rolled or were disturbed by waves long after their mud settled, while the limy dolomite beds under the algal reef shown on PLATE 33 remained soft enough to be bent and squeezed when the reef had reached considerable size.

Iron carbonate, when exposed to air, commonly becomes hematite (iron oxide: $Fe_2O_3$), a strong, durable cement. When deposited among sand grains it makes a resistant brown or reddish sandstone, which already has been mentioned. In Florida iron-bearing spring water cements sand into a hard, old-looking sandstone, but bones and Indian arrowheads buried in it show that this sandstone is geologically young.

Silica is the most durable of all cements and the least soluble. When it fastens sand grains together they make very hard, resistant stone, of which quartzite is a familiar example. As we shall see in Chapter XVIII, however, it ranks as a changed, or metamorphic, rock. Beds of volcanic ash have been cemented into tuff by silica that was dissolved from their own grains and was redeposited.

*Pressure* apparently does not harden sediments, though it aids the process of induration. Many ancient muds and sands settled on sea bottoms that sank during thousands or millions of years and arose only to sink again. Strata filled these basins to depths of 3, 5 or even 10 miles, and their weight developed tremendous pressure on beds lying near the bottom. With weights of 50,000 to perhaps 5,000,000 pounds above them, grains of mud were packed together so tightly that only minute pores remained to be filled with cement. Such compaction was specially effective in beds that consisted of tiny sharp fragments.

Some geologists think that pressure also helps turn loose

sediment into stone by enabling crystals to form. The actual work of solution and redeposition is done by water, however, and the crystals lock worn mineral grains together. Where this happens there is a change in minerals, so that hardening grades into metamorphism, discussed in Chapter XVII.

As a matter of fact, very little is known about this or any other process that turns loose sediment into stone. Until much more is discovered we may concentrate on sedimentary rocks themselves, without trying to explain why some become stone in a few years though others remain clay or sand through several geologic ages.

## CHAPTER X

# The Clastic Rocks

IN CHAPTER IX we found that weathering and other processes of erosion produce two main kinds of sediment. One is dissolved by water, acids and gases; its particles are too small to be seen with even the strongest microscope. They are carried away by water, and some of them remain in it until chemical processes make them settle. Others are taken from water by animals and plants; they are built into shells, skeletons, stalks and leaves before they are deposited. Such sediments are called *organic,* but those that settle directly from water are known as *precipitates.*

The second kind of sediment consists of material worn or broken from older rocks. These fragments range from clay grains to boulders in size and may be seen either with the eye alone, with a lens or with a microscope. Even the microscopic pieces make water look muddy or milky when it contains them in large numbers. Because they are fragments from larger rocks, we call them *clastic,* a name taken from the Greek word meaning "broken." When they settle into beds or strata these pieces form *clastic rocks.* Soil, sandstone and clay are examples of rocks produced by these broken, worn sediments.

## CLASTIC SEDIMENTS AND ROCKS VARY

Fragments settle in various ways, forming beds of rock. Some pieces are dropped by winds, some by water, while some merely roll downhill. These variations, however, have little or no connection with the kind of sediment. If we are going to classify the broken pieces themselves, their size gives a much better basis. Here is a system of division worked out by several authorities and based on the materials as well as the results of sedimentation:

| Name of Fragments | Diameter | Hardened (or indurated) Rock |
|---|---|---|
| 1. Boulders | 10 inches to 50 feet | Coarse conglomerate |
| 2. Cobbles | 2½ to 10 inches | Coarse conglomerate |
| 3. Coarse pebbles | 1/6 to 2½ inches | Conglomerate |
| 4. Fine pebbles | 2 to 4 millimeters* | Fine conglomerate |
| 5. Very coarse sand | 1 to 2 mm. | Very coarse sandstone |
| 6. Coarse sand | ½ to 1 mm. | Coarse sandstone |
| 7. Medium sand | ¼ to ½ mm. | Sandstone |
| 8. Fine sand | ⅛ to ¼ mm. | Fine sandstone |
| 9. Very fine sand | 1/16 to ⅛ mm. | Very fine sandstone |
| 10. Silt | 1/256 to 1/16 mm. | Siltstone or shale |
| 11. Clay | Less than 1/256 mm. | Claystone or shale |

*A millimeter is about 1/25 of an inch; 4 millimeters are, therefore, a little less than 1/6 inch. For small measurements millimeters are more easily used than fractions of an inch.

When we classify rocks made of these sediments we generally group those containing the first nine together as *coarse,* leaving the remaining two as *fine.*

Another classification, however, divides clastic rocks according to the agents that deposited them. Thus we have *aeolian* rocks, deposited by wind; *fluvial* rocks, laid down by running water; *glacial* rocks, dropped by melting glaciers, and so on. The chief difficulty with this arrangement is that one agent, such as wind, will deposit sand in some places, black soil in others and loess in still others, while glaciers, rivers and seas show equally great variety. Such a classification is bound to put different rocks together, which does not help when we try to identify them.

Still a third classification groups rocks into three classes. First come those that are loose, or *unconsolidated;* they have been neither packed nor cemented into firm strata. Opposite these stand the hardened, or *indurated,* rocks which have been squeezed or cemented into stone. Between these are the soft, or *semi-indurated,* group—rocks which have been packed or partly cemented but have not become solid stones. Here are common examples of each group:

| *Unconsolidated* | *Semi-indurated* | *Indurated* |
|---|---|---|
| Soil | Earthy Sandstone | Conglomerate |
| Gravel | Clay | Firm Sandstone |
| Sand | Adobe | Hard Shale |

As a general rule, unconsolidated rocks have been formed within the last million years; many of them still are forming today. By contrast, most indurated strata are ancient, dating from geologic ages older than the Tertiary. The rule is only a very rough one: some late glacial conglomerates are indurated, while soft shales and clays are found among sandstones 200,-000,000 to 400,000,000 years old. Still, it is safe to conclude that any thick series of hard clastics or chemically precipitated rocks is of Paleozoic or greater age, while considerable thicknesses of soft or semi-indurated strata are younger than the Paleozoic—perhaps even younger than the Age of Reptiles. Thus the soft clays of the Badlands in the Dakotas and Wyoming were deposited in Tertiary epochs, while gray clay-like shales in eastern Utah and near Mesa Verde were deposited in a Cretaceous sea. But the very hard argillites and quartzites of the Rocky Mountains in Glacier National Park date from a Proterozoic age that ended about 600,000,000 years ago.

In this book we shall divide the clastic rocks according to their fragments, beginning with the coarsest and least worn (that is, the most angular) and going to the finest, which generally are most rounded. In each subgroup the softest kind of rock is described first and the hardest last. Varieties are based on minerals and other characters. If this is not such a precise system as we should like, it merely emphasizes the fact that clastic rocks have formed on the earth, whose changes take place without regard for classifications and definitions.

## Bedrock and Mantle Rock

We sometimes find it convenient to distinguish between *bedrock,* which lies much as it formed, and *mantle rock,* which has been produced by weathering and other kinds of erosion. Bedrock commonly is hard; it extends from the surface to undetermined depths; it may be igneous, sedimentary or one of those changed rocks called metamorphic and described in Chapter XVIII. Mantle rock, however, is sedimentary; in most places it forms a thin veneer on the surface of the land. In fact, the most widely used definition for mantle rock calls it "a layer of loose material such as soil, clay, sand, gravel and broken rock" which lies at the land's surface. Since this layer is thin and patchy, bedrock commonly is exposed in hills, riverbanks, mountains and even on rolling prairies.

Mantle rock belongs to two main types. *Residual mantle rock* is loose material that lies upon bedrock from which it was formed by weathering. In many regions—southern Missouri and central Kentucky, for instance—this residual mantle rock is clay, which remains as limestone is dissolved. In other places it is gravel, formed by the crumbling of granite or conglomerate. On high mountains such as the Sierras and Pikes Peak the mantle rock consists of huge angular blocks split by frost, heat and cold. Except in these regions of very coarse fragments, residual mantle rock and bedrock intergrade through a series of weathered and partly weathered zones.

*Transported mantle rock* has been moved to its present location by wind, water, ice or gravity, and at least part of its fragments have been developed by wear instead of weathering. It usually rests directly upon bedrock, with no transitional weathered zones.

Mantle rock is tremendously important to land plants, since they live on and in its outer portion. It also provides many animals with dwellings. Burrowers, from crickets to gophers and kingfishers, make their homes in the easily dug mantle rock.

Geologically, mantle rock is important in several ways. It provides much of the material that is carried by winds, streams and other "agents of transportation." This material helps to erode and destroy older rocks, but in the long run it is piled up or dropped and so makes new sedimentary formations. Even if it does not move at all, mantle rock is important because it holds back erosion and weathering of the bedrock beneath it.

## Soils

Soil is the upper portion of the mantle rock, on which plants can grow; it is composed of small rock fragments, usually mixed with decaying vegetable or animal matter. The thickness seldom exceeds a few feet and may be only a few inches. Soil fragments have been subjected to the action of air and water, which have altered and removed some of the original materials and have modified others, while dead organisms (chiefly plants) have added new compounds containing nitrogen, phosphorus, potassium, and so on. These compounds also have stores of energy.

All soil is soft, loose and "earthy," but beyond that it has few uniform characters. To a degree unknown in other rocks, soil is in a continual process of change and development. It is being thickened by weathering and deposition; its topmost layers are thinned by erosion and may be destroyed by fires; its character depends upon climate quite as much as it does on the older rocks from which it is made. It also teems with microorganisms such as bacteria, algae, fungi and roundworms, which vary greatly from one soil to another and which, in their turn, change the soil.

*Residual soil* is produced by the weathering of rock, with little or no movement of particles. Under the true soil is *subsoil,* which contains fragments of undecayed rock and very little plant matter. Beneath this is a zone of partly decayed stone or *rotten rock,* and this grades into unweathered bedrock. Colors range from rich brick red to brown and black. Residual soils are abundant in the southern half of the United States and in other warm, moist parts of the world where glaciers of the last Ice Age did not reach.

*Transported soil* is material broken up by weathering or erosion or both, carried short or long distances and deposited where it now lies. Much of this work is done by creeks and rivers, which carry mud and drop it on their flood plains, producing alluvial soil. In northern North America, Europe and Asia vast quantities of soil were ground fine, carried and dropped by glaciers of the Pleistocene or last Ice Age. They form *glacial soil.* Transported soil may be deposited on unweathered rock. Some soil, especially in dry countries, is carried and piled up by wind.

*Volcanic soil* has some characteristics of both transported and residual soils, with other features of their own. Many of the rich volcanic soils in the Northwest are beds of ash that was carried miles through the air and has been weathered since it was deposited. Others are weathered lava beds (largely basalt), with which some decayed plant material now is mixed.

*Loam* is a name often given to dark soils that may be cultivated and that grow good crops. Loam is a mixture of sand and clay, colored yellow to brown or red by iron oxides, plus decayed vegetable matter, which is dark gray or black. Loam feels gritty when rubbed between the fingers, but if the sand grains are removed, it has the feel of clay. Loams of old swamp and lake basins contain so much plant material that they appear black, while those of prairies have much less and are lighter in color. Loam is developed by weathering of, and plant growth upon, soils of various origins, though those that were transported by water and glaciers are specially good loam makers.

## The Pedologist's Classification of Soils

We might give another classification of soils—the one developed by soil science, or *pedology*. Although this classification is based on the present appearance of soils, it considers the climates under which they developed, the importance of plant growth and weathering and original materials. Unfortunately, soil science is young and is making rapid progress, so that the reader will do well to get his information from the latest possible publications. One of these (as this book is written; it will be out of date a few years from now) is *Soils and Men,* the Yearbook for 1938 of the U.S. Department of Agriculture. Pages 948 to 1161 are devoted to soil formation, classification, distribution and to descriptions of the soils of the United States.

## CHAPTER XI

# Coarse-Grained Clastic Rocks

THIS GROUP includes both loose and consolidated rocks which consist largely of fragments as coarse as or coarser than sand. Though many are mixtures, the coarse grains are more conspicuous than the fine ones.

## Talus
### (PLATE 24)

Talus is an accumulation of rock fragments at the base of cliffs, banks or steep slopes. Its fragments range from dust to large angular blocks; most of them are loosened by freezing and thawing of water in cracks or the steady pull of gravity. As they are broken from the cliff or bank they fall, roll or slide until they can go no farther. Large blocks generally reach the foot of the talus pile because they have more momentum than do small chips or fragments. In bouncing or rolling over other stones, they help to break the talus into smaller and smaller pieces.

In high mountains thick deposits of talus accumulate, their blocks of rock being sharp-edged and often very coarse. When ravines, gullies or crevices gather talus and guide it, the fragments pile up over a small area and become a *talus cone*. Cones a thousand feet high, with slopes as steep as 40 degrees, are common among mountains whose tops are cut into peaks, crags and towers. In other ranges fragments fall along the faces of cliffs and so make talus slopes, which also may be formed by the growth of cones lying near each other.

Talus is found throughout the world: at the foot of a bank on a newly cut street as well as among steep mountains. Large cones and slopes develop in deserts, but their true talus is mixed with boulders and smaller waterworn fragments brought from mountains during the rare but violent rains. Both sorts of material may be mingled with wind-blown sand.

## Breccia

Breccia is a cemented mass of rock fragments, most of which are sharp-edged or angular. This character shows that they were not carried far before being deposited. Some breccias, in fact, are cemented talus. They lie among mountains or beside ancient sea cliffs, where fallen blocks are surrounded by cobbles, pebbles and sand and are cemented. A deposit of the latter type is exposed near Taylor's Falls, Minnesota, where coarse blocks of lava are tumbled together, the spaces between them being filled by sandstone containing fossil sea shells.

*Reef breccias* contain angular fragments of corals and limy algae which were broken from reefs and deposited on their slopes. *Cave breccias* contain blocks fallen from cave roofs, cemented by calcite from water that drips upon them. *Bajada breccias* are formed in dry regions, where "cloudbursts" mix boulders, sand, clay and water into a sticky mass that flows into valleys. A bajada breccia in the coastal region of southern California is about 20,000,000 years old; it apparently formed on the eastern slope of a semidesert land of which Catalina Island is a remnant. Some blocks of stone in this breccia are 10 to 12 feet wide.

*Residual breccia* contains fragments produced by weathering and cemented by iron compounds or calcite. Much of the *caliche* forming in Southwestern deserts consists of weathered

[ *163* ]

boulders, chips and pebbles, cemented by calcite. Chert residual breccias are found in southern Illinois and Missouri and the Flint Hills of central Kansas.

## Tectonic Breccias
### (PLATES 43, 47)

These rocks contain fragments that were broken by forces which squeezed, bent or shattered parts of the earth's crust; the fragments then were cemented. Many small deposits are *fault breccias,* produced where earth-breaks (faults) allowed rocks to grind against each other as they moved, breaking off angular chips. *Crush breccias* are much more extensive; they developed during the folding or shifting of brittle rocks or beds that bent at various rates. Many limestones and marbles are so brittle that they were shattered into chips, though their beds were only slightly folded. Where shale and sandstone were bent into mountains, the shale yielded quickly and the sandstone broke. If movement was carried far enough, the sandstone fragments rubbed together until they were rounded; rounded breccias are common in the Alps and some other folded mountains. In level regions such as the central United States, however, movement generally stopped after the rock was broken into chips.

Crush breccias of limestone and marble are found in the Mississippi Valley, Italy, Japan and many other parts of the world. Those which are attractively colored are used as ornamental stone. The Saint Genevieve "marble" of Missouri contains bands of breccia between large blocks of crystalline limestone in which there are petrified snail shells and other fossils.

## Till
### (PLATE 25)

Till is unsorted drift, or the miscellaneous mixture of rock fragments, deposited by melting glaciers. It is also called *boulder clay.* The material consists of angular or partly rounded pieces, many of which are marked by lines or striae made by other rocks that rubbed against them; they range in size from fine clay to boulders many feet in diameter. They may lie just as they were dropped by melting glaciers, or the finer particles may be roughly stratified between boulders, where they were dropped by water from the melting ice. The rock fragments are usually unweathered, and about 75 per cent of them have come from bedrock less than 50 miles away.

Till is mainly uncemented material deposited during the Pleistocene or Ice Age; it is widespread mantle rock in the northern part of the United States, Canada and Europe. It occurs in thick deposits as well as very thin ones and at all elevations from the seashore to high valleys among mountains. In some places it is piled upon bedrock in ridges and hills, making the surface rougher than it otherwise would be; in others till fills valleys in the bedrock but is absent from high spots, thereby decreasing relief.

*Outwash deposits* (PLATE 25) consist of coarse glacial material that was rolled or carried by streams flowing from melting ice fronts and finally deposited. In most cases the individual stones, which range in size from sand grains to small boulders, are rounded by being rolled over and over against other rocks. Remnants of a large outwash deposit, made by a river flowing from the glacial Lake Chicago, may be seen west of Joliet, Illinois. Parts of this deposit are cemented into the rock which we shall call conglomerate. Thousands of tourists see the outwash deposits now forming in the channels of the Yoho and Kicking Horse rivers near Field, British Columbia. Many outwash deposits dating from the late Ice Age lie in the gently sloping valleys of southwestern New York.

## Tillite

Tillite is cemented till. It can be recognized by an almost complete lack of sorting and bedding and generally by the presence of striae on at least a few of the largest pebbles and boulders. In typical tillites the ground-up material (clay) forms a gray or greenish mass in which the larger stones are imbedded. Because cementation takes a long time, most tillites are much older than the last Ice Age. The most ancient, found near the town of Timagami, Ontario, date from early Huronian times —about 950,000,000 years ago. About 350,000,000 years later tillites 870 feet thick formed in Australia, while lesser ones formed in most other parts of the world. A much later tillite, of Permian age, forms the rocks of Squantum Head, near Boston.

## Gravel
### (PLATE 24)

Gravel is a deposit of worn fragments ranging from small pebbles to cobblestones and boulders. Many of the pebbles are quartz, but they include a great variety of hard rocks and even soft shale. Pieces of sandstone, limestone and hard shale generally are flat with rounded edges, for they are pushed along the bottom and worn on one side, then are turned over and worn on the other. Pebbles of granite, quartzite and other very hard rocks are rolled over and over, becoming round or egg-shaped. Pebbles on deserts may be worn into elongate shapes with one, two or three sharp edges.

Gravel is being deposited in lakes, shallow seas, rivers and on land. It also forms beds and channel fillings in formations of Tertiary and even greater age. Its materials may or may not be sorted according to size. Gravel is extensively used in concrete work and in surfacing roads.

## Conglomerate
### (PLATES 24, 28)

Conglomerate is a cemented mixture of rounded pebbles and larger rocks, often with some fine material in addition to the cement. The large pieces may consist of any kind of rock, though such hard, resistant kinds as quartzite and granite are specially common; pebbles may be grains of minerals such as quartz and feldspar. The cementing material also varies greatly: it may consist of sand, clay, limestone, iron oxide or a mixture of these substances. Some conglomerates contain large pieces; some contain small ones; some run the whole range from small to large, while others have both, with nothing be-tween. In these last, large pieces are imbedded in a fine ground-mass, or matrix, much like fruit in an old-style plum pudding. For that reason such conglomerates often are called *pudding-stones* (PLATE 24).

Some of the most widespread conglomerates were deposited along the shores of seas that advanced across continents. Waves broke blocks of rock from the coasts, picked up gravel on low shores and wore the material by tossing it about. They finally dropped it along beaches; as the sea water advanced new beaches of "shingle" were deposited in the same way. When the shingle was cemented it formed beds of conglomerate covering hundreds or thousands of square miles. Since they lie at the bottom of the rock series deposited by an advancing sea, they are called *basal conglomerates*.

Conglomerates that formed on beaches of ancient lakes look much like those deposited by seas but are neither so thick nor so widespread. River conglomerates consist of pebbles rolled along and then dropped by currents, as well as sand, clay and finer cement. Many were deposited as gravel bars and now make "lenses" among cross-bedded sandstones.

Rivers also have deposited conglomerates as they shifted to and fro in channels across deltas that formed in shallow seas. Because the rivers shifted from one bed or channel to another, they were able to deposit their gravel over hundreds of square miles. Some geologists believe that delta conglomerates are the most widespread, thickest and commonest of all. They point out that streams now produce ten times as much gravel per year as seas make and suggest that many conglomerates once thought to be marine probably were made on deltas.

*Stretched conglomerates* are found in very ancient formations, especially where the rocks have been folded into mountain
ranges. The pressures, shearing and pulls developed in this
process frequently distorted conglomerate pebbles, flattening
them into bean-shaped lumps or stretching them into spindle
shapes. These changes generally are accompanied by mineralogical changes in the conglomerate cement. In contrast to
this, conglomerates in mountains that have been pushed, or
thrust, upward (like the Rockies of Glacier National Park
and the Lake Louise region in Alberta) are very slightly
changed.

Stretched conglomerate is the first stage in metamorphosis
which, if continued long enough, would have produced conglomerate gneiss, mentioned in Chapter XVIII.

USES.—Because of their coarse appearance and irregular
character, conglomerates are seldom used for stonework except
in foundations, piers and rough retaining walls. Those in the
Rand district of South Africa contain rich gold deposits. They
seem to consist of "fossil" placers: cemented stream gravels of
quartzite in which grains of gold were scattered millions of
years ago. Some poorly cemented conglomerates also provide
good material for crushed stone.

## Mud Breccias and Conglomerates, "Intraformational Conglomerates"
### (PLATE 26)

In most books on geology the term intraformational conglomerates (which means merely "conglomerates within formations") has been applied to a variety of rocks which resemble
each other in origin more than in appearance. They consist of
thin, generally flat pebbles of sedimentary rock, often mixed
with chips and much smaller pebbles and imbedded in a matrix
of sandstone, shale, limestone or other sediment. Those pieces
differ from the fragments in true breccia or conglomerate in
that they are not derived from ancient formations but from

the breaking up of partially hardened mud layers. These layers generally are little—often only a few months, days or even hours—older than the sediment in which their fragments are redeposited.

VARIETIES.—Many varieties of "intraformational conglomerates" have been described, depending upon their appearance and origin. Some of this complexity is made necessary by the name itself, which ignores the fact that many true conglomerates lie within formations and even within single beds of very different rock. It also ignores the fact that many of the pebbles in "intraformational conglomerates" are as sharply angular as those in many breccias. Finally, it overlooks one of the outstanding features of these rocks: the fact that in most cases their pebbles were only partly hardened mud when they were deposited. Combining this distinction with shapes of pebbles and a few other characters, we have these easily recognizable varieties:

*Mud breccia,* a rock containing thin flat pebbles of onetime mud whose edges are angular or only slightly rounded. These pebbles generally lie in matrix which is coarser than they are; it may range from limestone or dolomite to coarse sandstone. Matrix and pebbles may consist of similar or different material, depending on details of origin.

*Flat-pebble breccia* is mud breccia whose pebbles lie almost flat, or parallel to the bedding planes. In some flat-pebble breccias the pieces of mud moved only a fraction of an inch before they were deposited.

*Edgewise breccia* is mud breccia whose fragments or pebbles lie at various angles. Many of them are curved to match cross laminae, showing that they were soft enough to bend when they settled into their present positions.

By using conglomerate for rocks in this group whose fragments are as much rounded as flat pebbles can be and still retain trace of their original shape, we get *mud, flat-pebble* and *edgewise conglomerates.* These several types may grade into each

[ *169* ]

other in formations where conditions of deposition varied from place to place.

ORIGINS.—We now ask three questions: What broke up the partly hardened muds that became pebbles in mud breccias and conglomerates? What moved them from one place to another? Why do some lie flat in beds while others stand at all angles?

Several geologists have observed that mud layers covering sand flats along seashores become fairly solid during the period of low tide. When the water returns it tears these mud layers loose from the sands, breaks them into pieces and carries them to quiet water where they settle. Edges are sometimes rounded during movement. Sometimes the mud pebbles are covered with silt or mud, forming layers a half inch to several inches thick.

In the North Sea muds are made porous by gases that come from decaying animals and plants. Snails crawling about the flats break the uppermost mud layers into cakes which are floated away by returning tides.

These are processes going on today; they produce flat-pebble breccias or conglomerates. Assar Hadding, who has described many ancient mud breccias of Sweden, seems to accept the work of tides and waves for flat-pebble conglomerates and breccias but thinks that edgewise deposits were made when pebbles fell from shores or when partly hardened muds slid down steep undersea slopes. Several edgewise breccias of the eastern United States and Europe have been described as "subaqueous slides."

Perhaps the clearest evidence on the formation of extensive mud breccias and conglomerates is furnished by the Proterozoic rocks known as the Belt Series, which every visitor to Glacier National Park, Montana, crosses by rail, motor road and trail. Great thicknesses of red and green rock contain mud breccias that were under salty water at some times and lay bare to the sun at others. When they were exposed they dried, hardened and cracked, just as drying muds do today. When water returned it moved the cracked pieces—a little way if the water came gently, much farther when it arrived with a rush, as it seems to have done in rainy seasons. At many times the cracked muds were broken into chips and mixed with sand carried out to sea by the floods.

Thick formations of limestone and dolomite tell a slightly

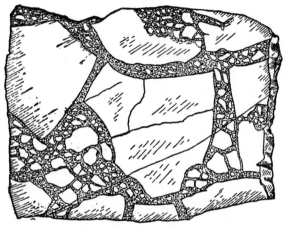

Cracked mud grading into mud breccia. After the mud dried and cracked, waves shifted the broken pieces and filled the cracks with chips. Contrast these angular pieces with the mud conglomerate shown on PLATE 26.

different story. Most of their breccias are edgewise; their pebbles are somewhat rounded and contain several thin layers, or laminae. Apparently the storms that broke them were much more violent than those that swept the green or red mud flats. Beds of dolomite were churned up to depths of five or six inches; sometimes even a foot. When the storms subsided pebbles settled every which way in this churned sediment and also sank between heads of limy algae.

There are mud breccias and conglomerates of several ages, especially Cambrian and Ordovician, in many other parts of the West and the East. Though not all are as clear-cut as those of Glacier National Park, they show that the main factors responsible for their accumulation were the return of water to partly dried mud-cracked flats and storms which swept across shoals whose water was only a few feet deep. Although some of these shoals may have been in lakes, while some of the flats were river flood plains, the majority of both were in widespread shallow seas that covered what now are lands.

## Sand

Sand is a loose, uncemented mass of mineral grains. Some are coarse though others are fine; some are rounded but many are angular. All are produced by erosion of rocks. Quartz is the commonest mineral in these grains, but some sands consist largely of feldspar, others of lime and still others of gypsum. Ordinarily, however, the name sand alone is used for quartz grains, while lime sand, shell sand, greensand (or glauconite) and so on are used for other varieties.

Some sands are produced directly by weathering of old hard rocks (PLATE 19). Others are carried about and sorted by winds, rivers, lake or sea waters, glaciers and even by gravity, which pulls sand downhill into a special sort of talus. Wind piles it into ridges and hills known as dunes, which are found near the shores of lakes and seas as well as on dry sandy plains or deserts. *Dune* or *blown sands* generally have smaller, more angular grains than do the sands of rivers or beaches, while *desert sands* are finely pitted like bits of frosted glass. This frosting, however, can be seen only with a microscope or a very good lens.

Dunes occur along the south and east shores of Lake Michigan; in northwestern Nebraska they form the "sand hills" that are extensively used as grazing land. The Great Sand Dunes of Colorado, a national monument, lie against the Sangre de Cristo Mountains. Some of these dunes are 1000 feet high. In south-central New Mexico are the famous White Sands, also a national monument. They are formed of almost pure crystals or grains of gypsum that are picked up by the wind from an "alkali" lake in the Tularosa basin, east of the foot of San Andreas Mountains.

USES.—Quartz sand, like gravel, is much used in the construction of buildings and surfacing highways. Several kinds of sand are used to make molds in foundries, for molding steel, iron, brass, copper and aluminum. Sand is also used to prevent the slipping of the drive wheels of locomotives and in filtering municipal water supplies as well as in the manufacture of glass. The sands for many of these purposes, however, are derived from sandstones and are not loose, unconsolidated material.

## Sandstone
### (PLATES 27, 36)

Sandstone is a rock consisting of sand grains held together by cement. Since quartz is the commonest sand, the term sandstone without qualification is understood to mean a quartz sandstone. Minerals such as feldspar, magnetite, garnet and mica may be present in varying quantities; if any one contributes largely to the sand grains, a qualifying word is used and we have such combinations as micaceous sandstone. Organic materials, such as fragments of shells or corals, form shell or coral sandstones.

Grains forming sandstone vary considerably in size, producing rocks that grade on one hand into conglomerates and on the other into shales. In general, large grains are more rounded than small ones. When a piece of sandstone breaks, the fracture chiefly follows the cement, so that the sand grains stand out on the broken surface almost like grains of sugar.

Sandstones differ in their cement almost as much as in texture. Silica is a common cement and so is lime; dolomite and clay are less common. Most brown, red and yellow sandstones are held together by hematite or limonite, the principal oxides of iron. Some sandstones, such as the St Peter "glass sands" of the Mississippi Valley, contain very little cement.

The color of sandstone is determined by the color of the grains and the cement. It ranges from white to gray, yellow, buff, brown, red or green. The last color may be due to either glauconite or chlorite, the latter apparently being commonest in very old rocks.

All sandstones are porous, and the degree of their porosity also depends largely on their cement. If there is a great deal of it, the pores are so largely filled that only 5 or 6 per cent of empty space may remain. If there is little cement, 25 to 30 per cent of the rock may consist of pores.

VARIETIES.—Varietal names for sandstone depend upon the kind of sand or cementing material as well as upon texture, origin and quarrying properties.

*Calcareous sandstone* is cemented by calcite, which weathers rapidly and allows the stone to crumble back into sand. Even before crumbling it is soft and easily scratched with a knife or a stick. Colors range from white to brown.

*Ferruginous sandstone* is characterized by having hematite or limonite as its cement. Colors are gray, brown, yellow or brick red. These rocks are fairly strong and durable, though where the cement is deposited irregularly they weather into ridges, pits and even large holes. Under soil, their cement dissolves rapidly, allowing these sandstones to crumble.

*Siliceous sandstone* has silica as the cement, deposited around the sand grains, often giving them crystal form. These sandstones are very hard and durable; they also grade into quartzites, metamorphic rocks described in Chapter XVIII. Colors range from white to red, green or even dull purple.

*Shaly sandstone* has sand mixed with clay particles which form part of the cement. It generally is yellowish brown to gray or greenish gray in color and is softer than siliceous sandstone. Shaly sandstone often gives a "clay" odor when it is dampened or breathed upon.

*Micaceous sandstone* contains, in addition to quartz grains, abundant flakes of white mica or muscovite. They lie on bedding surfaces, or planes, making the stone split easily and giving the split surfaces a silvery appearance. Mica is specially common in shaly sandstones; it made the soft wet rock very plastic, so that it preserved ripple marks, rain prints and the trails of animals walking or crawling across it. The micaceous Chemung (Devonian) sandstones of New York and Pennsylvania are rich in such traces as are very ancient sandstones of the northern Rockies.

*Grit* is a hard, very densely cemented sandstone whose grains are almost large enough to make it a conglomerate. Grit once was much used for millstones. A formation of massive sandstones, conglomerates and shales of Carboniferous age, in England, provided so many millstones that it is known as the Millstone Grit. It is thought to represent both delta and marine deposits and reaches a thickness of 5000 feet.

*Flagstone* is a thinly bedded sandstone which generally contains grains of mica as well as quartz, feldspar and some clay. It breaks easily into flat beds only a few inches thick and can be quarried in large slabs. Before concrete became common, flagstones were used widely for sidewalks and floors. To the geologist or fossil collector they are interesting because many of them contain trails, burrows, rain prints and small ripple marks.

*Freestone* is thick-bedded sandstone that is firmly but not strongly cemented. This permits it to be worked freely and well in almost any direction—hence the quarryman's name.

*Aeolian sandstone* is the consolidated sand of dunes. It usually shows excellent cross-bedding or cross-lamination, the individual layers being steeply tilted, thin, narrow and not much curved. Because of this they commonly meet in wedge-shaped ends. This is only a general rule, however, and there is no absolutely sure way to tell an aeolian sandstone from one whose cross-bedding was developed under water.

One of the oldest formations that has been suspected of containing dunes is the Ordovician St Peter sandstone, exposed at Minnehaha Falls, Minnesota, Starved Rock in Illinois and many other places. In some spots it even seems possible to make out soil beds developed in swamps between dunes. These later were covered by an advancing sea, which piled marine sands

[ *175* ]

on the swamps and reworked many dunes into beaches, bars and shoals under bays.

The much younger Coconino sandstone (Permian) of the Grand Canyon region (PLATE 36) contains beds which almost certainly were dunes, as well as others of doubtful origin. The dune deposits show best in Walnut Canyon, a few miles east of Flagstaff, Arizona. Here they form the steep lower parts of cliffs where Indians made their winter homes 800 or more years ago.

*Green sandstone* contains grains of glauconite which give the rock a greenish color. When such a rock is poorly cemented it may be called *greensand* or (incorrectly) *greensand-marl*. Material of this sort occurs in the Cretaceous of New Jersey.

OCCURRENCE.—Sandstone is very widespread, both geologically and geographically. It has been deposited in every geologic period from early Pre-Cambrian time to the present. Sandstone is so generally distributed throughout the world that specific localities need not be mentioned.

USES.—Sandstone can be quarried in regular blocks or slabs and can be easily shaped for building purposes. It also can be carved into "trim," an early Carboniferous sandstone of northeastern Ohio being one of the most widely used for this purpose in the United States.

Very pure sandstones, especially those that also are very soft, are employed in the manufacture of glass. Because of its lack of impurities the St Peter sandstone in Illinois and Missouri is used extensively for plate glass and optical glass. Other sandstones used for glass are those of Lower Silurian age in Maryland and Pennsylvania and early Devonian (Oriskany) "sands" which are exposed in the Appalachian region from Virginia to the Gaspé Peninsula of Canada. In Huntingdon and Mifflin counties of central Pennsylvania the Oriskany sandstone is 130 to 170 feet thick; it originally was quartzite but through weathering has disintegrated into easily crumbled sandstone. In West Virginia the Oriskany sandstone is 185 to 210 feet thick. Like the Pennsylvania deposits, it is quarried, crushed, washed and dried before melting. The St Peter sandstone of Ottawa, Illinois, can be dug with a shovel, but for quantity production the sand grains are loosened by hydraulic "giants" and pumped out of the pits, after which they are dried and screened. Since the St Peter sandstone of north-central Illinois is 120 to 200 feet thick and in places contains more than 99 per cent silica, it is not surprising that this state leads the country in glass sand production. West Virginia ranks second, Pennsylvania third and New Jersey fourth; the New Jersey glass sands (of Tertiary age) are unconsolidated. Marine sands of Eocene age are used by the glass factories of Los Angeles.

Because sandstone usually is very porous it holds ground water, especially if a fine-grained or impervious shale above the sandstone keeps water from escaping upward. In such circumstances water will seep downgrade through sandstone for hundreds of miles; when brought to the surface by deep wells it provides for the needs of factories and towns and even irrigates farms. Petroleum and natural gas also are contained in sandstones, especially those that have been arched upward. Again an impervious covering is necessary to keep the petroleum or gas from escaping.

## Arkose

Arkose is sandstone whose mineral composition is essentially like that of the granite of granitic rock from which its materials came. Arkose may consist of little except feldspar or it may contain mica along with feldspar and quartz; when firmly cemented it may look very much like granite. The decided angularity of the grains shows that they were deposited soon after weathering loosened them from granites and were not carried far. Where grains are large, arkose grades into breccia and where they are worn, it intergrades with coarse sandstone or conglomerate.

Arkose forms both on land and sea, especially in or near

deserts. If gravel beds now gathering on the slopes of the San Bernardino and other granite mountains of the California deserts are cemented they will become arkose; arkose also is forming where floods carry gravel into the Gulf of California. A red arkose in Mushroom Park (part of the Garden of the Gods, near Colorado Springs) apparently was piled up by rivers which carried iron-stained grains and angular pebbles of quartz, feldspar and granite into a semiarid valley during Permian times, shortly after the Coal Age ended. This sediment came from the reddish granites which now form the Rockies west of Manitou. There are many beds of semiarid valley arkose in the Triassic "red beds" of New England, New Jersey, New York and Pennsylvania, as well as in the Old Red Sandstone of Great Britain, some of whose beds are famous for their fossil fish.

## Greywacke or Graywacke

A gray, blackish or brown rock which is the equivalent of arkose but is made from fragments of older rocks which abounded in the dark iron-magnesian minerals. This does not prevent them from containing quartz, feldspar and even granite or felsite pebbles, but they also include fragments of shale, slate and basalt, as well as hornblende, biotite, magnetite, tourmaline, garnet, etc. The amount of cement usually is small; though generally shaly, it may be limy or siliceous. Greywackes grade into fine-grained conglomerates, with which they compare in origin.

Some books limit the name greywacke to gray or blackish rocks; others include fine-grained deposits containing so much feldspar that they look like felsites. If the latter course is followed, it may be well to distinguish *felsite greywackes* and *ferromagnesian greywackes* as varieties. Greywackes are common in Paleozoic rocks throughout the world, though in North America they often are called merely impure sandstones.

CHAPTER XII

# Fine-Grained Clastic Rocks

Fine-GRAINED clastic rocks include all those which are composed of silt grains or clay grains. The particles are 1/16 millimeter or less in diameter; that is 1/400 of an inch. Such particles are produced by both mechanical and chemical weathering, but they are rounded or have their angles reduced by mechanical wear, through abrasion, grinding or impact.

Some fine-grained clastics have been deposited by glaciers and wind; others are dropped by streams as floods ebb; many have settled in lakes, bays and shallow seas. Others formed essentially where they now lie, by the weathering of older formations which now are the bedrock. Origins may differ greatly, even among the fine-grained clastics of one kind, such as silt or clay.

## Silt

Silt is a soft rock composed of particles which generally range from 1/256 to 1/16 millimeter in diameter. These particles may consist of any kind of rock-making materials, though the commonest minerals—quartz and feldspar—generally predominate. Carbonates, sulphates and organic matter may also be present. The fine particles are produced mainly by abrasion, grinding and impact, though some are small grains of resistant minerals which have survived physical or chemical weathering of older rocks.

Very coarse silt may feel slightly gritty but generally it cannot be told from clay, with which it intergrades. Silt may also grade into very fine sand. Since silts and clays are very much alike, their deposition is discussed under clays.

*Siltstone* is a hardened, or indurated, silt and is usually regarded as shale unless its grains are perceptibly gritty.

## Mud

Mud is a loose, soft rock composed of the fine grains of many minerals. On land any wet soil with little or no sand is called mud. Marine muds chiefly consist of mineral "flour" brought into the sea by rivers and deposited in moderately deep water. Similar muds are deposited on low plains when rivers flood them after storms or in spring. Wet mud always is less plastic than clay and when heated it crumbles into lumps or dust. This is the easiest way to distinguish mud from impure clay.

Muds of several colors cover large parts of the ocean bottoms. Red muds are specially well developed near the mouths of large rivers such as the Amazon, Orinoco and Yellow; blue and gray muds are deposited near land, in water ranging from shallow to deep. Green muds are colored by glauconite, with little or no quartz; they cover about 1,000,000 square miles of ocean bottom at depths of 600 to 7600 feet. Such deposits are seldom seen, however, except by oceanographers.

## Mudstone

Strictly speaking, mudstone is a rock composed of indurated mud. Actually the name is used for soft to hard rocks which contain both mud and clay or silt. Some books apply it loosely to true mudstones, which crumble quickly when they are exposed to weathering, and to coarse dark varieties of shale as well. The name, therefore, does not have much value.

# FINE-GRAINED CLASTIC ROCKS

## Loess

Loess is a very fine-grained claylike or earthy deposit consisting largely of dust. It is very uniform in appearance, rarely shows stratification and feels gritty when rubbed between the fingers. A microscope shows it to consist chiefly of tiny quartz grains mixed with clay and other minerals, plus limy cement. This sometimes amounts to 30 per cent of the whole rock, giving a quick but short effervescence in vinegar or dilute hydrochloric acid. Though it is not hard, loess has vertical cleavage and weathers or erodes into very steep banks that stand with little crumbling. In these banks may be found concretions of impure calcite or iron oxide which commonly assume odd shapes and may contain fossils of land snails and leaves. Loess also contains many small tubes left by decay of roots.

Most of the great loess deposits of North America and Europe date from the end of the last Ice Age, when melting glaciers spread vast sheets of bare till over the country. Winds swept across those till sheets, picked up clouds of fine sediment, carried it for many miles and finally allowed it to settle. Although the separate dust storms probably were no greater than some that swept the western United States during the 1930s, they were more frequent and continued through centuries. As a result they built up deposits of loess that are 10 to 300 feet in thickness. Near Předmost, in Moravia, loess covered the village of Stone Age men who trapped mammoths in pitfalls, ate their meat and apparently piled the animals' bones around their tents to keep out the dust-laden wind.

Chinese loess deposits are 1000 to 2000 feet thick; they form high cliffs in which farmers dig cave houses and barns. Dust in this Chinese loess has come—and is still coming—from the dry, windy interior of Asia, where dust storms often darken the sky for days.

Many creek banks and road cuts in the Middle West expose deposits of loess that formed during interglacial epochs of the last Ice Age, when ice melted as it did a few thousand years ago and climates were even warmer than they are today.

## Adobe

Adobe is a very fine-grained rock that is as coherent as many shales yet crumbles rather readily. It has the harsh feeling of loess; its colors range from pinkish white to deep buff, grayish brown or even chocolate brown. Adobe consists of fine material produced by rock decay on arid mountains, washed into valleys by rain or carried by wind and finally deposited by water. It is found in arid regions, especially in the Southwest and Mexico, where it often is mixed with water and molded into big flat bricks which then are dried in the sun. Many missions and other buildings, hundreds of years old, are built of adobe bricks and finished with adobe plaster. When irrigated, adobe makes very rich soil, even though it contains little decayed plant matter.

## Clay

Clay is a soft rock composed of particles which are less than 1/256 millimeter in diameter. It contains a mixture of crystals, tiny lumps and scales of mineral matter held together by what one writer calls "films of solidified water acting as glue." Crystals are kaolin or other clay minerals, while the lumps consist of quartz and feldspar with varying amounts of organic matter. The scales are mainly mica, chlorite and talc; they make up 12 to almost 30 per cent of the rock's weight.

"Dry" clay—that is, clay whose water is in such tiny particles that it seems to be solid—forms an earthy, lusterless mass; when dampened or breathed upon, it gives a characteristic odor. Like pure kaolin, it sticks to the tongue and when rubbed to a powder between the fingers it takes on a soft, greasy feel. When wet it absorbs additional water, which clings to the scaly mineral grains, allows them to slip over each other and so makes the clay plastic. Still more water turns it into a creamy mixture that trickles into cracks and runs down slopes with surprising speed.

# FINE–GRAINED CLASTIC ROCKS

Some clays are white or cream-colored, but they generally are stained gray, black, buff or red by carbon and iron oxides.

VARIETIES.—Clays are divided into many varieties, according to their origin, nature and uses. *Boulder clay,* for example, is the fine material in glacial till. It is composed of particles produced by abrasion and grinding and perhaps of minor amounts of material from the original soil which covered the land before the glaciers came. Its mineral content depends upon the kind of rocks over which the glaciers that deposited it traveled. In parts of the Rockies and northern Canada boulder clay consists largely of pulverized feldspar from granitic rocks with a mixture of coarser quartz grains. From Illinois to Ohio and New York most boulder clays are pulverized limestone and shale. In most places the clay is mixed with sand, pebbles and boulders, but some deposits contain so little coarse material that the boulder clay can be used to make brick and tile.

*Brick clay* contains quartz sand, iron oxides, calcite and compounds of magnesium, with as little as 14 per cent of kaolin. Brick clay usually is bluish gray in color, but firing turns its iron oxides into hematite, producing yellow, brown or red colors. The iron, magnesia and lime make the clay fuse at relatively low temperatures. Even in ordinary brick kilns the clay will fuse, or flux, giving the finished brick a very hard, glazed surface. Some brick clay is glacial but much is marine.

*Fire clay* is a mixture of kaolin clay and sand, with or without iron oxides. Fluxing minerals are absent or occur in very small quantities. Bricks made from this clay are white or pale buff and endure great heat without crumbling. For this reason they are used to line fireplaces, forges, blast furnaces, etc. Much fire clay lies beneath coal seams and represents the soil on which coal plants grew. Many of these ancient "clays" really are very hard shale and must be ground up before they can be mixed with water and molded into bricks.

*Potter's clay* is an impure clay containing very fine grains of quartz sand and other minerals. Earthenware and stoneware, types of coarse but strong pottery, are made from it. Most potter's clay was deposited in seas.

*Residual clay* is the result of both physical and chemical weathering of rocks, the latter being the more important. The clay is mixed with silt particles, weathered crystals and pebbles or even large fragments remaining from the original rock; none of this material is sorted. The colors of residual clays vary according to their minerals and the climates of the regions in which they develop. Those of warm, damp regions with good underground drainage are red, brown or yellow because the iron compounds in them are oxidized and often combined with water, producing hematite and limonite. In cool regions with good drainage iron is removed, producing the gray or white clays that are the *podzols* of soil science. Dry regions generally have brown, gray or buff-colored clays and silts, in which iron is not greatly oxidized. The gray *sierozem* soils of many semi-deserts in the West, which support sparse growths of grass, sagebrush and rabbit brush or saltbush, include much residual clay.

*Laterite* is a residual clay developed in humid tropical or subtropical regions that have good underground drainage. It is red to brown in color and is covered by a thin layer of organic material. It is produced by the decay of granite or granitic rocks. The process removes a great deal of material but leaves quartz sand mixed with a claylike substance and red oxides of iron. When laterite dries it becomes very hard and stony. Many red rocks of the western United States, Europe and Asia may be ancient laterites, produced when climates were warm and moist and deposited by rivers as they spread over flood plains or deltas. Modern laterites of the tropics are moderately productive soils that support a great variety of plants, though in general only small patches are cleared by native inhabitants.

*Bauxite* (pronounced boze'ite) is a variety of clay that consists of earthy layers or masses, or concretionary balls (pisolites), which are one fourth to one inch in diameter. Pure bauxite is white, but iron oxides stain most deposits yellow, brown or red; those containing large amounts of iron really are laterite. Though the hardness varies, the rock generally is soft. It contains 50 to 65 per cent of alumina, as well as water, silica, iron oxide and titanium oxide. Most bauxite lies at the surface of the ground but some fills old cavities or depressions in ancient land surfaces which now are covered by later rocks. Most deposits are less than 10 feet thick, but that at Baux, France (from which the rock takes its name), reach the unusual thickness of 30 feet. A surprising feature is the occurrence of bauxite deposits at about 900 feet above sea level, few being found above 950 or below 850 feet. In Carter County, Tennessee, however, bauxite lies at a height of 2200 feet.

This Tennessee deposit, like the greater bauxite beds of Arkansas and many others, was produced by the weathering of ancient rock. In Tennessee the ancient rock was shale; in Arkansas it was syenite; in Georgia it was dolomite; in Germany and Ireland it was basalt. The Arkansas deposits, which lie south and southwest of Little Rock, were formed during the Eocene Age, more than 45,000,000 years ago. At that time the land consisted of syenite hills surrounded by shaly and sandy rocks. Chemical weathering destroyed the hills, spreading a layer of bauxite over the whole surface. On the sedimentary lowlands this bauxite contained a great deal of iron and silica, but where it overlapped the relics of the hills the deposit was of high grade. Following the period of weathering which produced the bauxite, sea water returned and deposited a new formation whose rocks must now be stripped to reach the bauxite. Where stripping is too expensive, the mines are driven underground.

Bauxite deposits are found as far west as New Mexico and northward to Virginia; others are known in all continents except Antarctica. France is the principal producer. Bauxite is used chiefly as an ore of aluminum, though considerable quantities are made into chemicals (alum, aluminum sulphate, etc.) and abrasives.

*Kaolin,* or *china clay* (PLATES 28, 32), is an almost pure clay which is white to light buff in color, contains no iron oxides and remains white when it is burned. According to some authors the term kaolin should be applied only to residual deposits produced by the chemical decomposition of igneous rocks containing a great deal of feldspar. In most cases this decomposition is the result of weathering and extends downward to depths of 20, 50 or even 120 feet. In other cases vapors, presumably charged with fluorine and carbonic acid, escaped through crevices in the solidified rock and decomposed it. The feldspar was "weathered" into fine kaolin and quartz, with which may be mixed scales of mica and particles of other minerals that were present in the original rock. Since most residual kaolin deposits are derived from pegmatite dikes, they are long in proportion to their width, which ranges from 5 to 300 feet. North Carolina and Pennsylvania are the most important producers of residual kaolin, though deposits have been worked in Connecticut, Maryland, Virginia and Washington. Deposits in Alabama and Missouri are of minor importance.

*Sedimentary kaolin* consists of material produced by the weathering of highly feldspathic igneous rocks; it is found in the Cretaceous of Georgia and South Carolina and, to a lesser extent, in the Eocene of Florida. During some 200,000,000 years the igneous rocks of what now is the Piedmont were deeply weathered. When the Cretaceous or Chalk Age began the land was tilted and streams became active, carrying the weathered kaolin and other sediments into bays or lakes where it was deposited. These sedimentary kaolins commonly contain quartz, mica and other impurities which must be removed by washing before the clay is used. They are more plastic than the residual clays and are used as "filler" for paper, cloth and window shades, as coating of wallpaper and in the manufacture of rubber, oilcloth, paint, soaps and toilet and tooth powders.

Both residual and sedimentary kaolin is used in the manufacture of high-grade porcelain; it requires careful grinding and mixing. American supplies are inadequate, and about 125,000 tons are imported annually. Most of this supply comes from Cornwall, England. Since it is brought across the Atlantic as ballast, its price at American ports is low. Thus when American lump kaolin sold for $16 to $18 per ton at the mines, English clay could be bought for $13 to $21 at seaports.

Many ancient sediments contain so much kaolin that they may be classed as sedimentary kaolins. Among these are underclays of the Coal Age, which settled in sinking basins just before coal was deposited. Some of these are used as fire clays.

*Bentonite,* a clay that contains the mineral montmorillonite, is an ancient volcanic ash that has undergone chemical change. As has been said, it is highly plastic when wet; small amounts can be mixed with kaolin clays to increase their plasticity. About half the bentonite produced in the United States is used in drilling oil wells; it also is used to filter oil and remove coloring matter from it. Small amounts are mixed with molding sand and used as filler in paper. There are important deposits of bentonite in Wyoming, southern California and South Dakota.

*Red clay* is deposited in oceans, at depths of 13,000 to 24,000 feet. It contains decomposed volcanic ash and pumice; particles of obsidian and tiny mineral grains are common, as is iron dust from meteorites. These materials accumulate so slowly that they have not yet covered the bones and teeth of ancient extinct fish and whales. Red clay covers 51,500,000 square miles of ocean bottom, of which more than 40,000,000 are under the Pacific.

ANTIQUITY.—Though clays are common in rocks of late ages, they are found throughout the geologic series as far back as the late Cambrian. Most clays of greater age than that have been transformed into shale—as, indeed, have many younger ones. Thin clay "partings," however, are plentiful among limestones of Silurian and Ordovician age.

## Catlinite or Pipestone
### (PLATE 2)

Catlinite, the famous "pipestone" of Sioux and other Plains Indians, is a partly indurated clay that is very fine-grained and compact. When freshly quarried it is so soft that it can easily be cut with a knife; primitive tribesmen worked it with stone knives and hand drills. It hardens on drying. Colors range from pale gray to pink, yellowish red and deep red. Light colors grade into dark ones, and there commonly are light mottlings. The rock is distinctly bedded, but bedding does not show in ordinary pieces.

Catlinite is a very ancient marine clay lying between beds of Cambrian quartzite. The Indians secured it from quarries near the present town of Pipestone, Minnesota, where the clay beds are about 18 inches thick. Only about 4 inches, however, are suitable for making pipes. Catlinite also is found in other parts of Minnesota, Wisconsin and eastern South Dakota; it grades into red shale of no value for pipe making.

Though pipestone was discovered and mined by Indians, white men began to manufacture pipes from it many years ago. During the two years ending in 1866 the Northwestern Fur Company made about 2000 pipes and traded them to tribes of the upper Missouri country. By 1890 whites were using saws and lathes to shape the clay into trinkets as well as pipes, providing about 99 per cent of all those that were sold. Even old pipes, used and treasured by Indians, therefore may be of white manufacture.

## Shale
### (PLATE 39)

Shale consists of indurated or partly indurated clay, silt, mud or a mixture of these substances. Though most shales are thinly bedded or laminated, there are conspicuous exceptions to this rule. Some shales are so soft that they can be cut with a knife;

when they dry they crumble readily. Other shales are moderately hard and some, which contain much silica, are harder than most limestones. Whether soft or hard, shales generally split readily between beds and layers. Gray is their commonest color, but black, green, brick red, brown, purplish and even buff are common. Those containing much carbon are called *carbonaceous,* those with abundant calcite are *calcareous,* and so on. *Bituminous,* or *oil,* shale is described in Chapter XV.

Since shales have not been changed much since they were deposited, they preserve many of their original characters and markings as well as great numbers of fossils. One of the oldest richly fossiliferous formations consists of very hard, carbonaceous shale of Middle Cambrian age near Field, British Columbia; it contains plants, jellyfish, worms, lamp shells and other remains. Corals, moss animals and leaves are preserved in many shales. The same is true of ripple marks, mud cracks, rain prints and tracks made by animals ranging from worms to dinosaurs. They are specially distinct in shales which contain much mica and so were highly plastic when they were deposited.

USES.—Some soft shales are ground and used as clay for brick or tile making. Others are mixed with limestone in the manufacture of cement. Oil is extracted from some shales that contain a great deal of organic matter, and a few calcareous shales are used as fertilizer. Shales occur in rocks of virtually all geologic ages in nearly all parts of the world.

## Argillite
### (PLATE 28)

Argillite is a rock that is much harder and more dense than shale, which it resembles in origin, minerals and general appearance. Its cement generally is silica or one of the compounds of iron and silica; since most argillites are slightly metamorphosed (see Chapter XVII), some of their mineral grains are recrystallized and enlarged. Tiny flakes of mica are developed in addition to those originally in the rock, though the latter may be abundant.

Although some argillites grade into slates and others into shaly quartzites, they preserve varves, ripple marks, mud cracks and other structures as well as shale preserves them. This is specially true of the green, brown and red argillites of Pre-Cambrian age which are exposed in the Rockies of Glacier National Park, Montana, and whose markings are described in Chapter XVI.

CHAPTER XIII

# Rocks from Solutions

Thus far we have described only sediments made from
worn, broken fragments which range from mud grains to
boulders. Great thicknesses of sedimentary rock, however, consist of material that once was dissolved. When it came out of
solution it formed rocks, which may or may not have been
chemically changed since their deposition.

## SUSPENSIONS, SOLUTIONS AND PRECIPITATION

To understand the origin of these rocks we must distinguish
between *suspensions* and *solutions* and must make sure what
*precipitation* means.

When a lump of clay is put into water it softens and crumbles
into mud. When we stir the water the grains of clay are scattered, making a dull or milky *suspension*. Let this stand a while
and grains will begin to settle, making layers of clastic sediment.
Even grains that do not settle quickly show when light shines
on the water, much as dust will show in a beam of sunlight that
enters a darkened room. They prove that the grains are really
fragments—pieces of the minerals that make clay.

Now put a lump of salt into water. Though it does not soften,
the lump grows smaller while the water begins to taste salty.

The mineral is being *dissolved,* which means that it is going off into the water, molecule by molecule. There are no fragments, for they cannot be seen and they do not turn the water milky. Yet the lump of salt, if it is not too large, completely disappears.

Thus we see two differences between suspensions and solutions. Suspensions contain fragments or grains that can be seen and so make water muddy. Solutions contain molecules, which cannot be seen and which leave the water clear even though they may change its color or taste.

A third difference appears when we let a suspension and a solution stand in tightly corked bottles. Clay grains in the former begin to settle, though the finest ones sink so slowly that they may keep the water milky for months. Nothing settles from the solution, however. To get a precipitate we must cool the water, let it evaporate, allow some substances to escape or add others which make new compounds. If we allow salty water to evaporate, a ring of salt settles; when we heat well water in a teakettle, driving out carbon dioxide, a "scale" of calcite is precipitated. Living plants or decaying plants and animals also cause precipitation that produces layers of rock.

## CLASSIFICATION

A famous geologist used to tell students that the earth was not made to fit definitions. Then he proceeded to give definitions that must be repeated, and repeated exactly, by all who hoped to get passing grades and escape professorial ridicule. Similarly, we may say that rocks were not made to be classified and then divide precipitated sediments into four main groups:

1. *Saline residues,* which are rocks formed by the evaporation of salt water, causing direct precipitation without chemical change. Most of them form near arid regions, and neither plants nor animals are important in their deposition. Salt, gypsum and anhydrite compose this group, which also includes many potash deposits.
2. *Siliceous rocks,* which contain large amounts of silica, generally

in the form of quartz, chalcedony or opal. They form on land and in the sea, with or without chemical changes; some are deposited in previously formed rocks. With them we group, for convenience, siliceous rocks which consist of the "shells" and skeletons of animals and plants. These are radiolarite, diatomite and modern oozes formed by Radiolaria and diatoms.

3. *Iron-bearing sedimentary rocks,* which contain large amounts of iron compounds and often much silica. Plants played an important part in forming many of them.

4. *Carbonate rocks,* whose most important minerals are calcite and dolomite. Some formed as direct precipitates; others were precipitated by plants; many consist largely of shells or other animal remains and so are not true precipitates.

This chapter describes the first three of these groups. The fourth, which has many special characters, will be described in Chapter XIV.

## SALINE RESIDUES

### Gypsum
### (PLATE 29)

Gypsum is a fine-grained or compact rock that can be scratched with a fingernail, its hardness being only 2. It may contain only the white mineral gypsum, but clay, iron oxides, marl and bitumen generally are present, producing colors that range from light gray to yellow or brick red.

The commonest form of gypsum is a massive rock without distinct layers, though thick deposits commonly consist of layers that differ in amounts and kinds of impurities and, therefore, in color. Gypsum also may be *foliated,* or platy; it shows the rhombic cleavage of the mineral plainly and may have fine fibrous structure. In some deposits foliated gypsum contains cavities, into which project the ends of crystals. Fibrous gypsum generally is found in thin layers or lenses which lie between beds of shale or sandstone. All forms of gypsum are readily dissolved by water, so that beds exposed at the surface have a worn or crumbly appearance.

*Alabaster* is a very compact, finely granular, white or lightly tinted variety of gypsum. Since it is easily cut and carved, alabaster is extensively used for small statues, vases and other ornaments. Its solubility prevents its use as an outdoor ornamental stone. It is not the usual alabaster of the ancients, which was either a cave limestone deposited by water or a kind of travertine built up by springs. Gypsum alabaster is quarried extensively in Great Britain and Italy; it commonly is found in nodular beds and balls or cakes, the Italian deposits being worked by underground mines. The rock is heated to make it resemble marble or stained pink to produce "stone coral." Very coarse alabaster, often called "plaster stone," is used to make plaster of Paris.

*Gypsum sand* is formed in desert dry lakes, where water with gypsum in solution comes to the surface and evaporates. Evaporation produces selenite crystals and irregular grains which the wind drifts into dunes. The most famous of these are the White Sands in southern New Mexico; a large part of these dunes now form the White Sands National Monument.

*Gypsite,* also called *gypsum dirt,* is a sandy or earthy variety of gypsum that forms a surface deposit in Kansas, Wyoming and other Western states. In spite of its impure appearance, it contains a large proportion of the mineral gypsum. Apparently some gypsite deposits were formed in the soil, others in shallow lakes that were fed by springs whose water contained gypsum dissolved from older beds or from other rocks.

A few small gypsum deposits are found around volcanic vents or fumaroles, where sulphurous gases have escaped and combined with the minerals in rocks, especially limestone. Still smaller deposits may have been produced by the oxidation of pyrite and combination of the oxidized compound with calcite.

Most gypsum, however, is sedimentary, forming lenses or widespread beds among other stratified rocks; these deposits

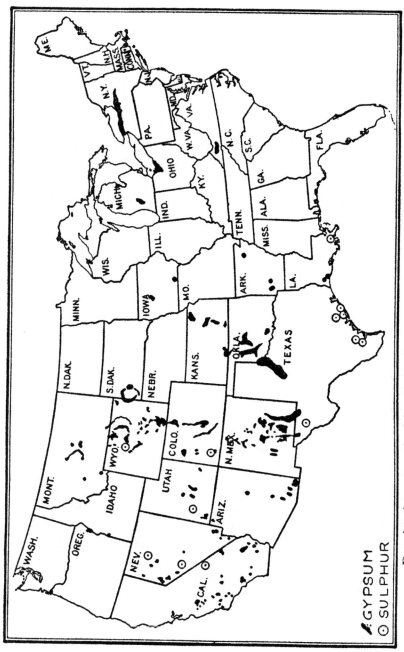

GYPSUM
SULPHUR

Deposits of gypsum and sulphur in the United States. Deeply buried gypsum beds probably are more widespread than this map indicates.

range from a few inches to more than a thousand feet in thickness. Gypsum can be precipitated by chemical reactions, and some geologists believe that many gypsum beds were made when this mineral replaced calcite in limestone. Others think that the greatest gypsum deposits settled in salt lakes or lagoons that were partly cut off from the sea.

Let us picture the deposition of gypsum beds in Ontario, Michigan, New York and Pennsylvania. In late Silurian times, about 350,000,000 years ago, our continent emerged from shallow seas that had covered about one third of its area. Climates turned dry and probably were warm, producing a bare desert. In the center of this desert a remnant of the sea remained, filling shallow lagoons and getting occasional supplies of salt water from the ocean. This water then evaporated, forcing salt and gypsum to settle. We can form some idea of the time involved from the fact that 14,000 feet of normal sea water must evaporate to make 10 feet of gypsum. Since gypsum near Syracuse, New York, is 60 feet thick, it required the evaporation of 84,000 feet of water. Yet even this is a small amount in contrast to the water that must have disappeared to produce gypsum formations 200 to 300 feet thick in the southwestern United States.

We must not suppose, of course, that 84,000 feet of water filled a lagoon at one time. Gypsum lagoons may have been as shallow as Great Salt Lake is today. As water evaporated, tides and storm waves brought more, thus replenishing the supply, which once more evaporated. This continued for century after century, till the gypsum deposit was formed.

All this assumes that the rocks accumulated as gypsum. In many places, however, they were anhydrite and became gypsum only when water combined with their principal mineral. Combination caused expansion; if the surrounding rocks did not yield readily, the newly made gypsum was forced to crumple. Banded, crumpled gypsum of this sort is to be seen at Hillsborough, New Brunswick and other localities. Deeply buried gypsum, on the other hand, may be compressed until it loses its water and so turns into anhydrite.

OCCURRENCE.—Sedimentary gypsum is found from Nova Scotia to Arizona, especially in rocks of Silurian, Permian and Triassic age; it is almost as widespread on other continents. Although small amounts are used as alabaster and in cheap jewelry, the chief use of gypsum is in plaster of Paris, whose name comes from the fact that gypsum early was quarried, ground and burned at Montmartre, near Paris, France. Heat drives water out of the gypsum; when water is added, the plaster replaces its lost molecules, becomes warm for a time and hardens, or "sets."

In this country great quantities of gypsum have been mined in New York, Virginia, Ohio, Iowa, Alabama and Arkansas. Oklahoma also has enormous deposits and is sometimes known as the "gypsum state." There are thick gypsum beds near the famous Carlsbad Caverns, New Mexico, and some of the cave rooms have been produced by solution of gypsum. Near the Black Hills, and in many parts of the Southwest, gypsum beds lie between "red beds" of shale and shaly sandstone which are supposed to be desert deposits.

## Anhydrite

Anhydrite is a fine to coarsely granular rock, coarse varieties showing the seemingly cubic cleavage of the mineral. Thin pieces may be translucent; broken surfaces have a splintery fracture and a satiny or pearly luster. The color generally is white, but anhydrite may be tinted red, bluish, gray or brown by iron oxide, clay or carbon. Anhydrite can be distinguished from gypsum, with which it is closely associated, by its hardness of 3 to 3.5; it can be easily scratched by a knife but not by a fingernail.

Chemically, anhydrite differs from gypsum in having no

water; on exposure to the air it usually takes up water and changes into gypsum. This change also may take place where water seeps into the ground till it reaches beds of anhydrite.

Since anhydrite is precipitated from warm solutions, some geologists believe that it was produced by the evaporation of sea water in lagoons surrounded by hot deserts; thin deposits may represent salt lakes. As with gypsum lagoons, those in which anhydrite settled must have received occasional supplies of sea water, so that evaporation could continue through many thousands of years. A deep well in western Texas penetrates 1200 feet of anhydrite whose banded layers, supposed to represent seasonal deposits, which formed during a period of 150,000 to 300,000 years. At the rate of 1400 feet of normal sea water to one foot of rock, this means the evaporation of 1,680,000 feet of water from that special lagoon, or 5.6 to 11.2 feet per year. These figures, however, are much too low. Not only does normal sea water deposit less anhydrite than gypsum; anhydrite is less bulky and so accumulates more slowly. Indeed, it seems that 2240 feet of ordinary sea water must evaporate in order to deposit 12 inches of anhydrite, which means that 2,688,000 feet of water were needed to produce the deposits found in that Texas well.

Both anhydrite and gypsum mean that water did not evaporate completely; enough of it remained in the lagoons to hold the ordinary salt and a few other dissolved minerals. When more of these accumulated than the water could hold, salt beds also were formed. Thus beds of rock salt commonly (though not invariably) lie above thick formations of gypsum and anhydrite.

Since anhydrite is closely associated with gypsum, it has essentially the same occurrence. Its lack of combined water, however, keeps it from being used commercially.

## Rock Salt

Rock salt is stratified, often massively bedded rock formed of common salt, whose mineral name is *halite*. The grain is fine, medium or coarse; the color is white unless it is modified by red or yellowish iron oxides, gray clay or black carbon. Other properties are those of the mineral itself.

Beds of salt were precipitated in salt lakes or in lagoons like those in which gypsum and anhydrite settled—often, in fact, in the same lagoons. Salt beds in New York are as much as 80 feet thick; at Ithaca the salt-bearing Salina formation (more than 2000 feet underground) contains seven beds of salt whose total thickness is 250 feet. At Syracuse salt deposits are 318 feet thick, and near Detroit they total more than 600 feet. This Silurian "salt basin," whose area exceeds 100,000 square miles, contains about 185,000,000 tons of rock salt. To form it, an average of at least 8000 feet of sea water were evaporated over the area; translated into the engineer's acre-feet, this gives the amazingly large figure of 512,000,000,000. As with gypsum and anhydrite, however, the waters over those 100,000 square miles did not evaporate completely; had they done so, dissolved compounds of magnesium and potash also would have been deposited. Since they were not, we again conclude that the salt water was replenished from the ocean as it evaporated. Some salt also may have come from rocks in the land adjoining the salt basin, especially if those rocks were newly formed, with their pores still filled by water from the sea in which the beds had formed.

According to one theory some of the great rock-salt deposits were formed in deserts, where salt was brought to the surface by either ascent of water and evaporation or by erosion. If the desert was without drainage to the ocean, the salt would gather in a salty lake like the Great Salt Lake of Utah. It seems doubtful, however, that this would produce such thick deposits as those of New York and Michigan.

A salt basin about 20,000 square miles in extent lies in southwestern Kansas, western Oklahoma and northern Texas; in some places the thickness of its rock-salt beds exceeds 400 feet. They are early Permian in age. Rock-salt beds in other parts of the world range from Permian to Pliocene; some in the Salt Range of India may be as old as the Cambrian.

In Louisiana and Texas, as well as in Mexico, Germany and other countries, there are underground ridges or domes of salt. These generally are less than two miles across, with very steep sides; some of them appear to have been pushed through the surrounding strata for several thousand feet. Those of Europe plainly were produced by earth movements which broke rocks, squeezed them and forced the plastic salt into its present form. The American salt domes are nearly circular in ground plan, have almost flat tops and generally are covered with "caps" of gypsum, anhydrite and limestone. Despite the skepticism of some geologists, it seems clear that the salt in these domes is sedimentary and has been forced upward through the overlying rock. The means by which this was done, however, are unknown.

Thick deposits of rock salt which lie near the surface are mined much as coal is mined. There are salt mines in New York and Kansas; one Rumanian mine has been worked since the time of the Romans, while another in Nevada was opened by Indians about 3000 years ago. When white archaeologists explored this mine they found stone hammers, sandals and even corncobs which apparently were the remains of prehistoric lunches.

Deeply buried salt beds are worked in a different way. Holes are bored into the salt; several pipes, one inside another, are put down through the holes, one being driven to the top of the salt and the others to the bottom. When water is forced down the shortest pipe it dissolves salt, after which the brine can be pumped to the surface through one of the other pipes.

## SILICEOUS ROCKS

### Flint
(PLATES 2, 10)

True flint is a very compact rock which consists chiefly or wholly of silica, though calcite and dolomite may be present in very small amounts. There also are organic impurities that produce dark brown, gray or black colors. The siliceous portion of flint may consist of chalcedony alone or of a mixture of quartz and chalcedony, the grain being so fine that it cannot be seen without a high-power microscope. The rock is very brittle and breaks with good conchoidal fracture, the edges of chips being yellowish or translucent. The luster is waxy or dull glassy, the hardness is 7 and the specific gravity is 2.6—slightly less than that of crystalline quartz.

Flint forms irregular nodules (PLATE 10), concretions, veins or even layers. When weathered, the surface of flint first becomes bright and smooth, then it turns into a dull crust which resembles porcelain and is called the patina (PLATE 2). Some flints contain remains of sponges, one-celled animals known as radiolarians and one-celled plants (diatoms). It seems probable, however, that most of the silica in flint was deposited inorganically. In some cases it formed nodules and other masses, shaped as they are today; in others it was again dissolved and redeposited in cracks and cavities or as concretions replacing other rock.

Flint is found among the rocks of every geologic age throughout the world. It is commonest, however, in the Cretaceous chalk formations of western Europe.

### Chert
(PLATES 1, 28, 41, 43, 44)

Chert resembles flint but is coarser and much less uniform in texture. Organic impurities produce colors ranging from light gray to black, though iron oxides and other minerals produce light brown, yellow, dull orange and red varieties. Fracture is less definitely conchoidal than in flint, and the luster is dull or waxy. Broken edges are only slightly translucent.

*Jasper* is red or reddish brown chert, the coloring matter being iron oxide. In some places jasper contains relatively coarse quartz grains and considerable amounts of hematite.

*Jaspillite* (PLATE 43) is jasper interbedded with layers of hematite and considerably squeezed and crumpled by mountain building. In some cases the rock is a metamorphosed jasper. This rock is abundant in the iron "ranges" near Lake Superior, where it is considerably metamorphosed.

*Jasperoid* is the common name for a light gray chert, mottled with brown and yellow, which is found in southwestern Missouri and adjoining regions, where it is associated with zinc and lead ores. Its grain is coarser than that of ordinary chert, and it cements the original broken chert into a hard breccia.

*Novaculite* (PLATE 1) is an extremely fine-grained chert which has been metamorphosed by intense folding. It is white or pale gray, semitranslucent and composed of fine-grained chalcedony. Novaculite is found in Arkansas and is used for high-grade whetstones and hones.

Chert occurs as nodules, concretions and branching masses or veins, but it also forms extensive beds which make up thick formations. Nodules and branching masses like those shown on PLATE 28 are commonest in limestones, especially of early Carboniferous age. Nodules at one level commonly are united or they may join nodules above and below; when this takes place throughout beds several feet thick, the chert forms a complicated network. Most nodules are less than a foot in length, but a few are 10 to 12 feet long and 2 to 4 feet thick. Some contain irregular pieces of limestone, while others are hollow and are lined with quartz crystals.

Chert also forms stratified deposits which range from thin layers to beds 30 inches or more in thickness. Perhaps the best known of these accumulations are the Pre-Cambrian (mainly Huronian) jaspers and jaspillites of the Lake Superior country, which contain a great deal of iron, and the Franciscan cherts of California. The latter probably formed during Jurassic times; they are thinly bedded, brittle rocks seen in Golden Gate Park, San Francisco, in the Berkeley Hills and in other parts of the Coast Ranges. An exposure of broken, crumpled Franciscan chert is shown on PLATE 44.

The origin of chert, like that of flint, is not well known. It once was thought that many nodules consisted of silica from sponges and other invertebrates, deposited in cavities after the surrounding rock hardened. It now seems that most nodules began as lumps of jellylike silica which settled on the sea bottom and partly hardened while the limy muds that covered them were soft. This is shown by the fact that limestone fills the crevices in chert nodules that shrank and cracked as they hardened.

Some geologists believe that silica in the Franciscan cherts came from submarine springs that bubbled up from buried magmas. It is possible that silica in the Lake Superior region came from great lava flows, but recent workers believe that it was brought to the sea by streams which flowed from high granitic lands. At least it is plain that the great chert formations were deposited in broad shallow seas, where dissolved silica could spread far and wide before it settled on the bottom in regular beds or layers.

OCCURRENCE.—Chert and its varieties probably are found in the strata of every geologic period in all parts of the world. In California, Idaho and Newfoundland chert makes up formations 60 to 2000 or more feet in thickness; even nodules, concretions and small layers scattered through limestones and dolomites reach significant proportions. One limestone formation in the Mississippi Valley is 3500 to 4000 feet thick and contains a total of 800 to 1000 feet of chert, while other limestones have been described as "filled" with it.

Uses.—Like flint, chert was much used by old-time Indians and other Stone Age people for arrowheads, spearheads, axes, scrapers and knives. Before the invention of matches it was used to "strike fire" from steel. Today neither common chert nor flint has much commercial value and both are nuisances to quarrymen who produce limestone for industrial purposes and fertilizers.

## Radiolarite

This is a special form of chert or jasper which consists chiefly of the cemented hard parts of one-celled animals called Radiolaria. These hard parts consist of opal and number as many as one million per cubic inch. Colors range from buff to deep red or green and are produced by impurities. Radiolarites occur in the Franciscan series, the Lower Carboniferous of Great Britain and Germany and the Jurassic of the Austrian Alps. Most of these deposits are thin, but a radiolarite formation in Australia is 9000 feet thick. It dates from late Devonian or early Carboniferous times and formed under shallow marine water.

*Radiolarian ooze* is forming at depths of 14,000 to 26,850 feet in the Pacific and Indian oceans, where it covers about 2,290,000 square miles. Radiolarian "tests" form 60 to 70 per cent of the ooze, other constituents being bits of pumice, feldspar, augite, hornblende, shark teeth and nodules of manganese. There is an average of 4 per cent of calcite. Radiolarian ooze forms where other sediment is scarce. At present that condition is met only in oceans, but radiolarites like those of Australia prove that the ooze formed in shallows during some past ages.

## Diatomite or Diatomaceous Earth

This is a soft, chalky-looking rock of very light weight. It consists chiefly of opal "shells" of diatoms, one-celled plants which generally are regarded as algae. Diatomite is white, buff, pinkish or light brown and frequently has a faint clay odor when wet. It is distinguished from clay and shale by its gritty feel. Most deposits are firm and rigid and commonly form very thick beds. Diatomites are Jurassic to late Tertiary in age; those of Maryland, Southern Atlantic States and Alabama are mined for use in paints, cosmetics, polishes, etc. Beds of diatomaceous earth also occur in Missouri, Nevada and California. Some are marine, while others are layers in swampy places that represent the fillings of lakes. Deposits also occur in Germany and other parts of Europe.

*Diatom ooze* is a modern deposit found chiefly under cold oceans south of the Antarctic Circle, at depths of 2400 to 8800 feet. It contains considerable amounts of mineral matter and animal remains as well as diatom "shells." Countless billions of these also settle in shallow water but are hidden by coarser sediments. At Copalis Beach, Washington, a single heavy rain killed so many diatoms that their "shells" formed a continuous ridge along 20 miles of shore, with a thickness of 4 to 6 inches.

## Geyserite or Siliceous Sinter
### (PLATE 30)

This brittle rock consists of a variety of opal in which there are 9 to 13 per cent water. The deposits generally are associated with hot springs and geysers, which bring dissolved silica to the surface. There is little difference between geyserite and spring sinter, though the former commonly is fibrous and is more porous than the latter. Geyserite forms layers and cones as well as irregular masses like those shown on PLATE 30 and others not much larger than peas. No deposits are widespread, and most of those now forming are limited to volcanic regions such as Yellowstone National Park, where water that seeps far into the ground is heated by buried lava. Sinter produced by cool springs is rare and small in amount.

Some geyserite is produced by deposition of silica as waters cool and evaporate, but more is produced through the activity of simple algae living in the hot springs or on wet surfaces where geyser spray falls. These little plants precipitate silica upon their threadlike bodies in the form of gelatin whose color is white in the hottest waters, green in the coolest and yellow, red, pink or chocolate brown in those of intermediate temperatures. When the algae die this material loses its bright colors, takes on a texture suggesting cheese and then begins to harden.

Deposits of sinter and geyserite from extinct springs are found in many parts of the West but are not common in Eastern states where there has been little volcanic activity for a very long time. Limy hot spring deposits (tufa and travertine) are described in Chapter XIV.

## Hot Spring "Pipes"
### (PLATE 30)

The water of hot springs or geysers comes to the surface through cracks or "pipes" in the ground. Very hot water doubtless keeps these clear, but as the water cools it deposits geyserite in irregular layers or pisolitic lumps. Still later, layers of opal or chalcedony are deposited. These may completely fill the pipe or they may leave a narrow tube which is lined with a smooth layer or with quartz crystals that point inward. The section shown on PLATE 30 was cut across a completely filled pipe from which water ceased to flow. Such deposits are fairly common in regions of hot spring and geyser activity such as Iceland, New Zealand, Yellowstone National Park and some parts of California.

## IRON–BEARING SEDIMENTS
### Hematite or Red Iron Ore
#### (FRONTISPIECE, PLATES 7, 29, 43)

As a rock, hematite is fine-grained and compact to loose, earthy and even fibrous. Where crystalline it is dark gray; massive sorts are red to brown, as is the botryoidal or "kidney" variety. Some deposits of hematite are virtually pure, showing all characters of the mineral; others contain clay, sand or silica and grade into red ocher, shale and iron-bearing sandstone.

VARIETIES.—Sedimentary deposits of hematite belong to four general varieties, one of which has two types. Metamorphic hematites are described in Chapter XVIII along with other metamorphic iron-bearing rocks.

*Kidney hematite* and *pencil ore* once were plentiful in the mines of Cumberland, England, though they also have been found in the United States. They form lumps and porous masses which are very hard and have fibrous structure; the character of kidney hematite is shown on PLATE 7. Miners usually rub the surfaces of kidney ores with stove polish to produce attractive specimens. Small lumps must be ranked as minerals rather than rocks.

*Red ocher* is soft, earthy, lusterless hematite that commonly contains much clay. Unusually pure deposits may be ground, baked and used in making red paint, though hard rocks of the Clinton type more often are used for this purpose.

*Clinton ore* (PLATE 29) is a type of sedimentary hematite which gets its name because it is commonest in the Silurian Clinton formation of the eastern United States. The most widespread type is a red or brown oölite in which the hematite forms round or polygonal grains as small as fine sand or as large as peas. Under a lens they show concentric layers like those in the grains of lime oölites. These grains may form the entire rock or they may be imbedded in marl or clay. In hard deposits they are cemented by both calcite and hematite.

*Fossil hematite,* also called Clinton fossil ore, contains layers of shells and other once-limy fossils that were replaced, or petrified, by iron oxide. Most of the fossils are broken or crushed and are cemented by a mixture of hematite and calcite.

Some geologists think that the hematite of the Clinton ores was dissolved from overlying rocks and deposited in place of oölitic limestone. The general opinion, however, is that the

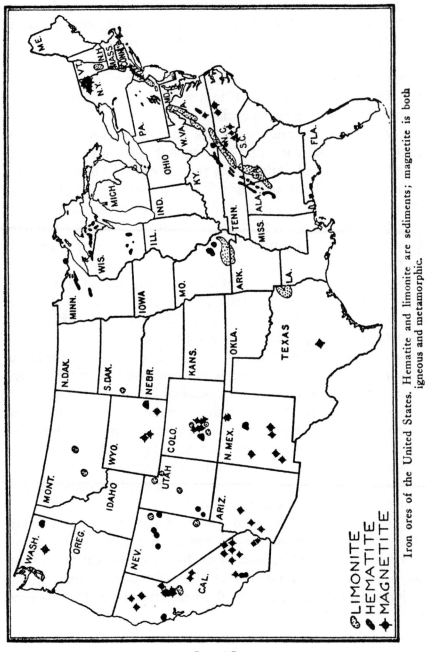

Iron ores of the United States. Hematite and limonite are sediments; magnetite is both igneous and metamorphic.

hematite was precipitated in shallow salt waters of long narrow lagoons and bays. When there were many small grains of mineral matter on the sea bottom, oölites formed around them. When the sea floor was covered with small fossils the hematite replaced them and also formed cement between them.

*Lake Superior iron ores* include earthy to hard rocks which contain large amounts of hematite as well as limonite, jasper, chert and other material. They have had a complex history; at one stage some of them were metamorphic, though others have not been greatly changed. Because all were sediments at the outset, we may give their story here.

It began with a series of shallow seas that covered parts of Minnesota, Wisconsin, Michigan and Ontario during Keewatin and Huronian times. Streams carried great amounts of dissolved iron and silica to those seas from near-by lands that probably were warm and humid. Most of the silica settled in jellylike layers, though much was deposited by algae that grew on the sea bottom. Deposition of iron, however, depended on bacteria. These tiny one-celled plants are abundant in bogs, lakes and quiet shallow seas today, and they cause iron compounds to settle even from water that contains less than two parts of iron per million. Dissolved iron compounds were much more plentiful than that in those ancient seas, so that the deposits, which also contained much silica, became thousands of feet thick.

They were not iron ore, however, nor were they hematite. When they formed, the iron-bearing sediments were carbonate (siderite) and silicate (greenalite), scattered through beds of chert and jasper. As these beds became land some were squeezed, crumpled, broken and changed (PLATE 43), while others merely were lifted. At the same time rain water seeped into the ground, turning the iron compounds into hematite or limonite which, with jasper, became jaspillite. More water acting through millions of years, dissolved most of the silica in the jasper, leaving the hematite and limonite. By this process the proportion of iron to impurities was at least doubled, while the weathered ores sometimes became so soft that they can be dug with steam shovels. PLATE 29 shows one of the great iron mines of Minnesota, where shovels are taking out Huronian hematite for shipment to the steel mills of Illinois and Indiana.

## Limonite
### (FRONTISPIECE, PLATE 29)

Limonite is a brown to yellow rock which may be massive, stalactitic, oölitic or pisolitic or may form residual lumps or pockets of clay. Some limonites were formed by weathering of the Lake Superior iron ores. Beds of limonite in Virginia were produced by replacement of limestone, as seeping water deposited iron oxide with which some water had combined. The pisolite of the frontispiece shows cores and layers of hematite. The outermost layers, however, consist of limonite and so does the cementing material between the pisolitic lumps.

*Residual limonite* is a mixture of clay and lumps of limonite produced by weathering of limestone that contained iron oxides. *Gossan,* however, is impure limonite or rusty, porous quartz formed by the weathering of pyrite or chalcopyrite and quartz. Both residual limonite and gossan have been mined extensively in Virginia.

*Ocher* is a mixture of fine-grained limonite and clay. It is yellow in color and was one of the important paint materials used by Indians and Stone Age men of the Old World.

*Minette ores* of Lorraine and Luxembourg (they have been exhausted in Belgium) are oölitic limonites containing lime, clay, sand, plus small amounts of hematite and other iron compounds. They apparently were formed on the bottom of a Jurassic sea. Other oölitic limonites are mined in Great Britain.

*Bog iron ore,* or *bog limonite,* is a mixture of limonite with sand, clay, decayed plant matter, phosphates and other substances. It is loose and earthy or firm but porous; it also forms hard concretions. When a large amount of clay is present it is called *yellow ocher*. The color generally is brown or brownish black.

Bog iron forms in swamps and shallow lakes, often on clay bottoms. Over it is a layer of decaying plants; between the two, iron oxide is deposited by the water. Deposits are thickest in very shallow waters; few concretions are formed at depths of more than two feet. Many of the commercially important deposits, however, are residual.

Limonites are found from Vermont to Alabama and were important ores during pioneer mining.

### Siderite

Siderite is iron carbonate, $FeCO_3$. As a rock it is crystalline, coarse- to fine-grained and whitish to yellow or pale brown. Weathered surfaces turn dark brown or black when the iron carbonate oxidizes into limonite. Impurities include pyrite, hematite and a few other minerals.

*Clay ironstone* is impure siderite: a mixture of that mineral with clay, sand and limonite. It commonly forms nodules or concretions but also occurs in beds. The color generally is dull brown. When the nodules are dark and kidney-shaped they also are known as *kidney ore*.

*Blackband ore* contains siderite and so much coaly material that it is black. It generally is associated with coal beds, in Carboniferous and younger rocks.

Siderite iron ores seem to have formed under the shallow waters of marshes, lakes, isolated seas and even rivers. The ores are less important in America than are hematite and limonite, but European deposits are of great value, especially in England, France, Germany and Spain. The rock siderite should not be confused with iron meteorites, which often are given the same name though they consist of very different materials.

CHAPTER XIV

# Limestones and Related Rocks

MOST OF THE ROCKS described in this chapter are commonly known as limestones. Though they differ greatly in texture and color, they have three properties in common. First, they consist largely of calcium carbonate, either alone (as calcite and aragonite) or combined with magnesium carbonate in the mineral dolomite. Second, these rocks can be dissolved in hydrochloric acid, though if they contain much dolomite, the acid must be heated or the rock powdered. Third, their hardness never exceeds 4 and generally is about 3, so that they can be scratched easily with a knife.

Two other features of the carbonate rocks also are important. Though some were deposited on land and others in fresh water, the great majority settled in the sea, a fact that is shown by their marine fossils. Moreover, a large part of the calcium carbonate in most limy rocks was taken from solution and deposited by the action of plants and animals. This also is true of some of their magnesium carbonate. In some formations the amount of mineral matter derived from organisms amounts to as much as 98 per cent of the entire rock.

## THE GROUPS OF LIMY ROCKS

We may divide the limy, or carbonate, rocks into four groups, according to their modes of origin:

1. Rocks of clastic, or mechanical, origin. These include edgewise and flat-pebble breccias of dolomite and limestone as well as deposits of sand and pebbles worn from other carbonate formations or from shells, corals, etc.
2. Rocks of inorganic (chemical) origin.
   a. Deposits of calcium carbonate formed by hot springs and waterfalls, in caves and where water evaporates from the ground in dry countries.
   b. Deposits made by chemical changes in lake and sea water. Such rocks often are mixed with those made by organisms and are not easily recognized.
3. Rocks formed partly or wholly of the remains of animals and plants. These remains include shells, the "skeletons" of sponges, corals and one-celled creatures, etc., as well as dome-shaped, branched and jointed structures built by stony seaweeds.
4. Rocks formed partly or wholly of materials that were precipitated because of the living processes of plants, especially small algae and bacteria. These deposits grade into those of Group 3, but they sometimes cannot be told from chemical precipitates.

We need not discuss the rocks of Group 1; except for the fact that they are made of limestone and dolomite, they differ slightly from other clastics but are much thinner and less widespread. The chemical deposits of caves, springs and falls also are small in extent and can be explained when they are described. Those deposits which result from changes in seas and lakes are not well understood. About all we can be sure of is that when carbon dioxide escapes from these bodies of water, calcium carbonate settles to the bottom. This seems to be happening in tropical and subtropical seas and in places where water from great depths has to flow across shallow "banks" like those of the West Indies. It seems doubtful, however, that this process has produced many of the limestones that now are found on land.

One geologist has found that a submarine lava flow which covers 20 square miles and is 100 feet thick can cause the precipitation of a foot of limestone on about 26 square miles of sea bottom just by driving carbon dioxide out of the water. There are many ancient submarine lavas which are more than 100 feet thick, and their eruptions may have produced the unfossiliferous limestones that cover some of these flows. Again, however, it is clear that this process was local and did not produce great thicknesses of limestone nor formations of great extent. This limitation applies with equal force to dolomitic deposits and so emphasizes a fact we already have stated: that most limy rocks were made by plants and animals.

## PLANTS AND ANIMALS FORM ROCKS

We now come to organisms as makers of carbonate sediments. We have seen that calcium carbonate from ancient rocks is dissolved in the waters of rivers, lakes and seas. We also know that an enormous variety of plants and animals are able to take this material out of solution and turn it into shells or other hard parts. At the same time most of them use a small amount of magnesium carbonate, some typical proportions being:

| Organism | Calcium Carbonate | Magnesium Carbonate |
|---|---|---|
| Foraminifera | 77.02–90.11% | 1.79–11.22% |
| Limy sponges | 71.14–84.96% | 4.61–14.10% |
| Reef corals | 97.57–99.95% | 0.09– 1.11% |
| Starfish and crinoids | 83.13–91.55% | 7.79–14.31% |
| Snails, clams, oysters | 96.84–99.95% | 0.00– 1.78% |
| Limy algae | 73.63–99.21% | 10.93–25.17% |

Since a great many limestones contain 80 to 98 per cent of calcite and 1.5 to 20 per cent of dolomite (which is half magnesium and half calcium carbonate), they differ little from the chemical make-up shown by these hard parts of organisms.

We need not list all the animals and plants whose remains form, or help form, carbonate rocks. The plants belong only to one main group, or phylum, but limy animals are found in nine phyla, all of which live abundantly in salty and brackish water and have done so for hundreds of millions of years. It is not surprising, therefore, that they have made formations which are thousands of feet thick and cover thousands of square miles.

When we look at the rocks in these formations we see that they began in two general ways. One group consists largely of shells or other limy hard parts which have been washed together by waves or currents or which have drifted into layers on the sea bottom. In such deposits the larger remains often are worn or broken into chips; they also may lie in ridges or heaps into which currents washed them. If the ridges are made of curved shells like those of brachiopods or mussels, all may lie in one direction or position, "nested" together like saucers or spoons. Some rocks, such as the Chalk of England and France and the Globigerina ooze of modern oceans, consist of little except tiny shells of one-celled animals called Foraminifera. They drifted in water even when they were alive, and their shells must have kept on drifting after the animals died. Many beds contain grains of lime sand worn from shells and corals.

Rocks formed without drifting lack these features. Many shells may be broken but few are worn. The *matrix,* or minerals covering the fossils and filling spaces between them, generally is fine-grained and shows thin even layers, though it may also contain small fragments. If the fossils include corals, moss animals (bryozoans) and other attached bottom-dwellers, some may stand as they grew. Careful search is almost sure to reveal fossils that still stand upright as well as others that spread out on what once were muddy or stony bottoms.

[ *215* ]

## BIOSTROMES ARE BEDS

Beds formed without drifting grade into those built upon the sea bottom by algae, corals, oysters and other organisms. Many books and articles call such beds "reefs"; actually they are strata or "banks" that once covered hundreds—even thousands—of square miles. In Iowa strata built by spongelike stromatoporoids are 5 to 8 feet thick and have areas of 150 to 350 square miles. Some algal beds in the Rocky Mountains are 50 to 150 feet thick and covered 1000 to 2500 square miles before streams and glaciers cut the region into valleys and peaks. Thick banks of shells related to oysters are found near the city of Fort Worth and in other parts of central Texas.

Three features help us recognize such strata, which have been named *biostromes,* from the Greek words for "life" and "stone." First, they contain fossils that show even less wear and breakage than do those of most strata deposited "in place." Second, these fossils belong to only a few kinds yet they form as much as nine tenths of the rock and are crowded closely together. Many of them, in fact, grew upon other shells, corals, algae or whatever other organisms built the banks and still preserve their attachment. Finally, the "banks" do not vary greatly in thickness. They are quite as uniform as other strata and commonly are much stronger. Thus the great algal biostromes of Glacier National Park make prominent gray ridges on cliffs that were cut by Ice Age glaciers.

Rocks of this sort formed in many ancient seas because they were wide, shallow and free from sand or coarse mud. They provided places in which animals and algae could live, finding plenty of sunlight, food and dissolved lime. Those seas also had few strong tidal currents such as those that carry dead remains away from shell banks forming near many shores today. Those currents, or "tidal scour," explain why modern oyster or mussel beds do not form biostromes as did those of Cretaceous and older seas.

Biostromes are not common in lake beds. Notable exceptions are banks of limy algae in the Green River deposits of Wyoming, Colorado and Utah. These are thinly bedded shales that settled in large lakes during early Tertiary times. In many of their bays limy algae lived. At some places they formed domes or biscuit-shaped colonies that grew directly on the bottom. In other places the algae covered logs that drifted into shallows. The logs are now siliceous petrified wood, while the algae are limestone with structure so perfect that their cells may be seen when thin sections are put under a microscope.

## REEFS ARE RIDGES OR MOUNDS

Reefs are ridges or mounds of stone built by animals and plants. In modern seas the commonest of reef-building organisms are corals and limy algae; off the northeastern coast of Australia they are building a series of reefs 1350 miles long and 150 to 350 miles wide. At the atoll of Funafuti, where reef rock is more than 1100 feet thick, the most abundant organisms are red algae called Lithothamnion. Another algal group (Halimeda) is second, one-celled animals (Foraminifera) are third and corals are fourth. Some ancient reefs consist chiefly of corals, others of animals that seem to have been sponges and still others contain only limy algae. Spaces between the coral, sponge or algal masses are filled by cemented sand and mud that were worn by waves as well as by broken fossils.

Biostromes are essentially uniform from top to bottom and edge to edge; reefs, however, are not. In many of them we may distinguish three different regions. The first of these is the *reef core,* a central ridge or dome built by animals and plants packed closely together and generally attached to each other. In many cases it is a solid mass without distinct strata, in which the structure of the organisms is indistinct or lost. The *fore-reef* consists of sediment that settled on the slopes of the reef. This sediment contains inorganic fragments and precipitated grains as well as bits worn from the reef-building organisms. The fore-reef is distinctly stratified; its beds slant, or *dip,* away from the reef core as they are deposited. Some, whose dip was specially steep, slid before they hardened and so produced crumpled or broken beds that resemble edgewise breccias.

A distinct *reef top* is found in reefs that grew close to the surface, where the water was not much stirred by waves. Fossils of the reef top are distinct and not much crowded; some are widely spread or branched, and their structure is well preserved. Spaces between them are filled by bits of shells and other material.

The surface on which a reef formed may be a mud flat, a shoal or even a submerged mountain. Many fossil reefs rest on beds of limestone or dolomite. If it was hard before the reef formed, such a base shows no peculiarities—but sometimes the mud was soft and remained so for many years. As the reefs became large and heavy they pressed the muds downward and squeezed them. Squeezed muds, now gray dolomite and limestone, lie beneath and beside the algal reef shown on PLATE 33.

## PLANTS MAKE SEDIMENT SETTLE

Coral reefs are built by animals and plants that take lime from the sea water and use it to strengthen their bodies. Shell, crinoid and several other kinds of biostromes have a similar origin.

Many carbonate sediments settle, however, merely because algae live in sea water. Like trees and grasses, these algae make their own food. To do so, they combine carbon dioxide with water and energy from sunlight, making sugar and starch. Removal of carbon dioxide from water allows calcite to settle, either upon the sea bottom or on jelly that surrounds the plants. Deposits of this type apparently built the biostrome and reef

[ *218* ]

of PLATE 33, and they are settling near the Bahamas today. They also have produced irregular layers and mottled lime-stones or dolomites that are found in many formations. Only a few of these layers have been examined for traces of algal origin, and the collector who can find good specimens should keep them. He also should make notes and photographs show-ing what the beds are like, for such records may bring new in-formation to light.

It also seems that bacteria, which are one-celled plants, can cause the precipitation of very fine-grained lime muds, like those that have become lithographic stone. As many as 600,-000,000 bacteria live in a single cubic inch of the lime mud near Andros Island, in the Bahamas, and some authors believe that these "germs" use enough carbon dioxide to make that mud settle. Other authors disagree, saying that the muds are precip-itated chemically and merely make pleasant surroundings for the plants. The problem is a difficult one and may not be solved for many years.

## Limestone
### (PLATE 34)

Limestone is any rock that contains more than 50 per cent of calcium carbonate, generally in the form of calcite ($CaCO_3$). Impurities, which may amount to almost 50 per cent of the rock, consist of clay, sand, dolomite, carbon and iron oxides.

In this broad sense limestone includes all the dominantly calcareous, or limy, rocks described on the following pages. In general practice, however, these deposits are treated as if they were distinct kinds, and that plan is followed here. Lime-stone, on the other hand, is used to designate rocks that are fine-grained to aphanitic in texture, the latter term meaning that their grains are too small to be seen without a strong lens. Though many limestones are crystalline, their grains never are as large as those in ordinary granite. Both fine-grained and crystalline varieties generally are compact, though many limestones are porous or even "spongy." Pores are specially abundant in limestones which consist chiefly of fossils, with too little fine-grained or aphanitic material to fill the spaces between them.

Limestones are white or cream-colored when pure, but they are usually colored gray to black by carbon or stained buff, yellow, red or brown by iron oxides. Accessory minerals are pyrite, marcasite and quartz, the last appearing as small crystals that commonly fill cavities. Because of their large amounts of calcium carbonate, limestones effervesce in cold dilute hydrochloric acid. They are dissolved slowly by ordinary water and rapidly by water containing carbon dioxide—the "charged water" of soda fountains. Limestone has a hardness of 3 when it is formed principally of calcium carbonate, but impurities may make it slightly harder; it can, however, be readily scratched by a knife.

Since limestone has been formed in several ways and contains numerous impurities, many variations are found. These include shaly or argillaceous limestone, sandy or arenaceous limestone, lime conglomerate, bituminous limestone and glauconitic limestone. Such varieties are so easily recognized that they need not be described.

FIELD APPEARANCE.—Beds of limestone vary greatly in thickness, though on the average they are thinner than those of sandstone and seldom show cross-bedding. They are commonly interbedded with shale, which weathers more readily than the limestone, causing the bedding planes to be clearly demarked. The beds themselves may be formed of thin layers or laminae which often show more clearly on weathered faces than they do in freshly broken rocks.

Limestone breaks with sharp angular edges, often producing a jagged surface in a cliff. The jagged edges may also be a result of closely spaced joints, which are very characteristic of limestone. Major vertical joints, however, may divide limestone into smooth-faced columns and blocks which suggest the blocks in a crumbling masonry wall. Vertical joints tend to produce precipitous cliffs and ledges that stand out clearly for long distances.

Weathering often develops a thin white coating on pure limestone; impure deposits become buff, tan or brown, especially if they contain iron compounds. Pebbles of limestone that are gray and compact at the center but buff and porous at the surface are common. Beds that contain layers of different character develop differently colored bands, while those whose layers or laminae are unequally resistant take on the rough appearance of the sandy limestone of PLATE 41. Other beds develop pits and channels like those of the weathered block shown on PLATE 34.

When a pure limestone is exposed over a considerable area its surface generally becomes covered with a thin layer of soil that may be washed away from ridges or knolls. Solution makes channels along joints; here residual soil collects and a few plants grow. Pits and holes develop at weak spots, while such insoluble matter as sand, clay and chert produces knobs and small ridges.

We have said that charged water of soda fountains dissolves limestone very quickly. Rain water that has dissolved carbon dioxide from the air and acids from decaying plants also is a strong solvent. Working downward through joints, it makes funnel-shaped depressions called sinks, as well as caves and tunnels through which underground streams begin to flow. These erosional features are typical of limestone areas, especially in moist climates.

VARIETIES.—Here we may place several forms of limestone whose structure, mineral make-up or origin separates them from ordinary limestones.

*Lithographic stone* (PLATE 34) is very uniform, fine-grained and generally is almost pure calcite. It breaks with a conchoidal fracture, is regularly bedded and shows no distinct layers, though it may have bands of slightly different colors. The common tints are cream, very light yellow and bluish gray, and some stones are pinkish. The hardness is about 3. Commercial lithographic stone contains no fossils or calcite veins and very few joints. Some deposits, however, contain all these and are broken or even brecciated.

The best lithographic limestone comes from the region of Solenhofen, in southern Germany, where it has been quarried for approximately a century. Slabs 3 to 6 inches thick are as much as 40 by 60 inches in width and length. The rocks are of Jurassic age and were deposited in lagoons surrounded by coral islands much like atolls of the modern South Seas. Fossil king crabs, insects, jellyfish and even birds have been found in beds between the high-grade lithographic limestones. A deposit of blue-gray lithographic limestone 3 feet in thickness is quarried at Brandenburg, Kentucky; the stones are used mainly in the South and Southwest. Very fine-grained lithographic limestones occur in the Devonian of north-central Iowa, but most of the beds are too much broken and contain too many calcite veins to make the rock commercially valuable. Since zinc and aluminum plates are being used for much lithographic printing, there is less demand for stones than there was twenty-five or thirty years ago, when they were widely used to print pictures and maps.

*Crystalline limestone* is limestone whose calcium carbonate has become crystalline calcite, generally by action of water which seeped down from the surface and through tiny pores in the rock. On its way the water both dissolved calcite and deposited it in the form of crystals. Although crystalline limestone commonly takes a high polish and is sold as marble, it differs from true marble in leaving well-preserved fossils and distinct beds, with no sign of "flowing" under great pressure. A great deal of crystalline limestone is quarried in Missouri and other states and is cut for interior decoration.

*Mottled limestone* also may be cut, polished and sold as marble. The rock is a mixture of lumps or branching structures of one color in a groundmass, or matrix, of another. In some cases the lumps are calcite while the matrix is dolomite or dolomitic limestone, though this order may be reversed. The colors are caused by different impurities, but the lumpy or branching bodies commonly are either poorly fossilized red algae or (less commonly) filled burrows of bottom-dwelling animals. Recent studies suggest that algae are specially important in developing mottled limestones, though some contain petrified corals and other animal remains.

*Shell limestone* contains fossil shells in such abundance that they make up most of the deposit. Such a rock will be porous and crumbly if the cement is weak and small in amount but compact and hard if spaces between the shells are well filled with shell fragments, clay grains and limy cement. In such compact shell limestones the fossils show best after the rock has weathered enough to remove some of the cementing material and the shaly layers that commonly cover beds.

*Coral limestone* is essentially like shell limestone except that it contains a mixture of corals, algae and shells. Many of these are waterworn, while their cementing material consists largely of grains worn or dissolved from the fossils. In some modern "coral" limestones algae form 42 per cent of the rock. In Michigan and Iowa beds which were formed by stromatoporoids (odd animals that probably were sponges) also are called coral limestones.

*Encrinal limestone* resembles coral limestone in origin, but its most important materials are the broken columns of crinoids —the relatives of the starfish that grew on jointed stalks. The button-shaped or bead-shaped sections break like calcite crystals; they are imbedded in a matrix of fossil fragments, compact or crystalline calcite and impurities such as hematite and clay. With the crinoid columns there generally are a few shells, and in some formations there are fragments of other echinoderms, such as blastoids. Encrinal limestone thus compares with coral limestone except that much of it seems to have formed where crinoids grew in "banks" on the sea floor. When they died they fell and broke into bits and their fragments settled into the mud or were covered when more mud sank to the bottom.

Encrinal limestone occurs in the Devonian of western New York and in the lower Carboniferous of the Mississippi Valley.

*Coquina* (PLATE 34) is a rather weak, brittle, porous and light-colored limestone composed of shells and shell fragments cemented by a little noncrystalline calcite. The most familiar coquina is that formed during relatively recent times on the Florida coast, but the name fits similar limestones of other regions and greater age. Coquina grades into porous shell limestone, which sometimes is so soft that it can be cut with a saw.

OCCURRENCE.—Limestone is the most common and most important of the carbonate rocks. It occurs in all geologic ages from the Pre-Cambrian to the Recent, though limestones of the later periods are less firm than the beds formed during the Paleozoic Era. Limestone is widely distributed, occurring in every state in the Union, in many parts of Canada and on other continents. Great numbers of islands consist of coral limestone which still is being built up by the remains of algae and corals.

USES.—Limestone has more varied uses than any other rock. As a building stone it is employed in both outer and inner walls as well as in floors and foundations. Monuments are carved from it or faced with it; bridges and a variety of other structures are made of it. When crushed, limestone is used in the manufacture of Portland cement and is mixed with crushed rock to make concrete or with asphalt to make pavements. It is used to "sweeten" fields whose soil has become acid and is employed in such varied processes as the refining of sugar and copper, the reduction of aluminum ore and the manufacture of paper, glass, soap and sulphuric acid. Large amounts of limestone now are being turned into rock wool for insulation.

Indiana, Missouri, Minnesota and Wisconsin are the chief producers of limestone for building purposes, Indiana leading with 66 per cent of the 1936 production in this country. Much

# LIMESTONES AND RELATED ROCKS

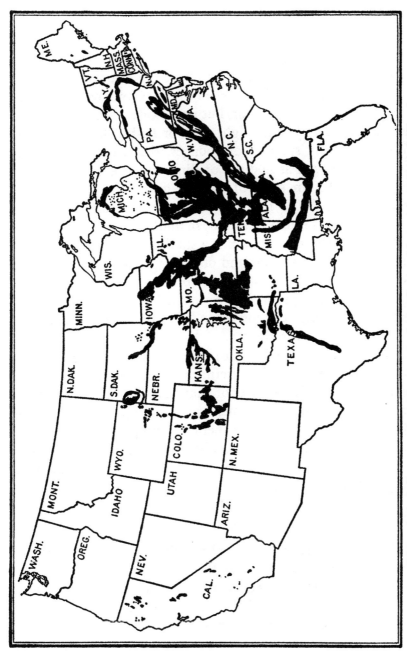

The principal limestone formations east of the Rocky Mountains and in California.
(*Burchard*, U.S.G.S.)

Indiana limestone, however, is oölitic and is described under the heading of oölite.

## Chalk

Chalk is a soft limestone made up of the microscopic shells of one-celled animals, the *Foraminifera*. Commonly chalk is nearly pure and white in color, but iron oxide, carbon and other minerals may stain it buff, light gray or flesh color. Other impurities are glassy spicules of sponges, shells of diatoms and radiolarians, as well as nodules of flint, which are abundant in even pure chalk. In spite of its fine grain, the rock is very porous and will absorb 10 to 20 per cent of its weight in water.

Though it looks much like an ooze that now forms under seas 2400 to 17,500 feet deep, chalk is a shallow-water deposit. This is shown by the sea urchins and other large marine fossils in it as well as by bones of reptiles and other land-dwelling vertebrates. Much chalk probably was formed in shallow, clear and rather warm water, near low islands from which streams carried little or no mud to the sea.

Chalk is found in England, France, Kansas, Texas and many other parts of the world. It sometimes is used for building stone, though most chalk is too soft for that purpose. It is burned for lime, mixed with clay in cement manufacture and spread on fields of acid soil to prepare them for crops such as alfalfa. Chalk also is used in paint, as polish for glass, in tooth powder and as blackboard "chalk," though much of the last is prepared from gypsum.

## Oölite
### (PLATE 34)

Oölitic limestone, generally called oölite, is formed of round grains of calcite which look like fish eggs. This resemblance accounts for the rock's Greek name, which means "eggstone." The grains range up to 2 millimeters in diameter; many consist of layers around a central particle of calcite, sand, clay or shell. Other grains show radial structure somewhat like that of the spherulites found in obsidian. Typical oölites are cemented by pure or impure calcite, which in some cases contains broken fossils or particles of clay. In other formations, however, the cement consists largely of dolomite or even quartz.

Oölites may develop in fresh or salt water, those of the latter being most abundant, but some also form on land. On the coast of Florida, near the Great Salt Lake and beside the Red Sea wind picks up oölite grains and piles them along the shore. There are similar wind-blown oölites in Carboniferous formations of Kentucky, Illinois and Kansas and in the Jurassic of Great Britain. The last show the cross-bedding that is characteristic of dunes and contain fossil eggs which were laid by turtles that scooped out nest holes in the sand well above high-water line. Between these shore deposits are other oölites which show the regular bedding of deposition in quiet, though doubtless shallow, water.

Small deposits of oölite are now forming in pools such as those in the Carlsbad Caverns of New Mexico. Drops of water which fall into these pools allow carbon dioxide to evaporate, so that calcium carbonate settles. Movement of the water seems to roll the particles so that they form round or oval grains.

Oölites also are accumulating on coral beaches of the Bahama Islands and along the east coast of Florida. Most ancient oölites occur in marine formations whose ages range from Pre-Cambrian to Pleistocene. In Great Britain the principal oölites are Carboniferous and Jurassic; the Portland Stone, of which many public buildings in London are constructed, is an oölitic "freestone" whose beds have a total thickness of about 20 feet.

The most famous oölites in the United States are the Indiana or "Bedford" limestones of early Carboniferous age. A section of this limestone, considerably magnified, is reproduced on PLATE 34. It shows small broken fossils as well as oval oölites that formed around dark grains. These limestones form massive beds whose total thickness is 20 to 70 feet. They are found in more than 70 square miles of south-central Indiana, and apparently identical rocks are quarried at Bowling Green, in southwestern Kentucky. A million to a million and a half tons of Indiana oölite are sold every year and are used in buildings from the Atlantic to the Pacific coast.

## Pisolite
### (PLATE 34)

Ordinary pisolite, or pisolitic limestone, contains round or oval grains more than 2 millimeters in diameter. They commonly are as large as peas, or larger, so that the rock is sometimes called "peastone"—which is what its technical name means. Except for size of grains, pisolites are essentially like oölites and apparently were developed in the same ways. Some pisolitic limestones contain little except round balls of calcium carbonate cemented together, with irregular cavities between; others have a matrix of compact, shaly or very fine-grained oölitic limestone. Cambrian pisolites which many tourists see as they hike or ride across Ptarmigan Pass, east of Lake Louise, Alberta, have a shaly matrix that weathers more rapidly than the limestone balls. In some beds these balls are so small that the rock is coarse oölite; in others they grade into biscuit-shaped or egg-shaped lumps that seem to have been formed by algae.

Permian oölites that may be of algal origin form thick beds near the Carlsbad Caverns, New Mexico; excellent specimens may be found along the valley road leading to the cavern entrance. At Carlsbad, Bohemia, pisolite is forming in water from hot springs. As the pressure and temperature are reduced when water comes to the surface, calcium carbonate is deposited in layers around grains of sand or granite. Some of these layers show clearly in the specimen that is illustrated on PLATE 34.

Since comparatively little is known about the origins of both oölites and pisolites, collectors who find good exposures of them will do well to secure specimens, take photographs of the beds and make notes on their occurrence. Such records are not hard to make, and if enough of them are secured, they may add much to our knowledge of a common but puzzling group of rocks.

## Marl

Marl is calcareous clay: a loose, soft, earthy mixture which contains 25 to 75 per cent of calcium carbonate, the remainder being true clay and other impurities. The color generally is whitish, though yellow, green, blue-gray and blackish shades are given by iron oxides or carbon from decayed plant material. Marl generally effervesces in cold dilute hydrochloric acid and weathers readily into coarse soil. When sand is present in significant amounts, the mixture is called *sand marl;* dolomite produces *dolomite marl,* while shells and shell fragments characterize *shell marl.* In the Southeast, however, the name shell marl is used for almost any soft rock that contains an abundance of fossil shells. *Greensand marl,* plentiful in New Jersey, is not marl at all but a sandy deposit of glauconite.

True marl is found in small lake deposits throughout the country but especially in the Northern states, where glaciers left basins that became lakes and later were filled by marl, mud and decayed plants. Lake marls are excellent sources of fossil shells which represent water animals of the last 10,000 to 20,000 years.

## Tufa
### (PLATES 32, 36)

Tufa, also called calc-sinter, is a porous or "spongy" limestone formed by the deposition of calcium carbonate in desert lakes, in shallow bays, around springs and even in streams—especially at or near waterfalls. Colors commonly are white or cream, though impurities may produce shades of brown, red or green. The most familiar deposits of tufa are formed around hot springs whose waters have a great deal of calcium carbonate in solution. When the pressure which forced the water to the surface is released, the water itself evaporates, cools and loses carbon dioxide. This allows calcium carbonate to settle, becoming the mineral aragonite. Aragonite, however, is not stable; water seeping or trickling through the newly formed tufa turns the mineral into the stronger, more durable calcite. As more and more calcite is formed the rock becomes travertine.

North America's most famous and attractive tufa deposits are the terraces of Mammoth Hot Springs in Yellowstone National Park. They are yellow, orange or brick red while the algae in the hot springs remain alive, but when water ceases flowing and the algae die, the tufa becomes white and crumbles. The Liberty Cap is the travertine core of a vanished hot spring whose terraces have been worn away. Another very large hot spring is depositing tufa at Thermopolis, Wyoming.

Thick deposits of tufa formed along the shores and on islands of a salt lake (Lake Lahontan) which filled a basin in northwestern Nevada during the last Ice Age. The tufa forms beds, domes, balls and "toadstools" as much as 6 feet in diameter as well as towers 50 or 60 feet high. The average thickness is less than 20 feet. An island in Pyramid Lake, which is a small remnant of Lahontan, is composed entirely of tufa. Though evaporation undoubtedly caused some precipitation of calcite, most of the deposits seem to have been built up by algae. Similar masses of tufa appear in Mono Lake, California.

Tufas also occur around cold springs, especially in the limestone regions of North America and Europe. In England tufa was employed as early as the twelfth century in the construction of castles; because of its lightness it was much used for vaulting ceilings. Fresh deposits of tufa are very soft and easily cut or crumbled, especially while still moist; when dry they may become hard, though they remain light and porous.

### Travertine and Onyx
(FRONTISPIECE, PLATE 31)

Travertine is little more than a hard compact variety of tufa whose aragonite has become calcite. The rock is banded and contains irregular holes. There is travertine in most places where there have been great hot springs; motorists cross large deposits near the town of Mammoth Hot Springs in Yellowstone National Park. Travertine is quarried near Gardiner, Montana; the rock is white, cream, yellow, pink and red, takes a fine polish and is superior to the famous travertine from quarries northeast of Rome, Italy. Other deposits are worked in Florida and Colorado.

Travertine is used chiefly for walls and interior decorations in railway stations, theaters and other public buildings. Though porous, it is durable; the Romans used it in many outside walls that are standing today, after almost 2000 years.

*Onyx* (FRONTISPIECE) is a banded or mottled variety of travertine deposited by cold springs, by water seeping through cracks and in caves. Onyx is translucent and is colored by iron and other metallic oxides. It takes a high polish and is used for ornamental stonework of many sorts. Kentucky, Utah, Arizona and California contain important deposits, but most of the onyx used in the United States is imported from Lower California, Mexico—whence the name "Mexican onyx."

## Cave Deposits
### (PLATE 32)

In limestone caves water which trickles down walls or drips from ceilings builds up layers, masses and "icicles" of calcite which, as rocks, are only varieties of onyx. Most of these deposits show concentric layers or bands, without distinct crystals. Colors range from white to dark brown, depending on impurities. The name *stalactite* is applied to a deposit that hangs downward from a ledge or cave roof; *stalagmite* to one that is built up from the floor. Some caves have been entirely filled by these structures.

## Tepetate and Caliche

*Tepetate* is a limy deposit made in dry countries where rivers suddenly cover their flood plains or spread out over alluvial fans. The lime is dissolved near the heads of the streams, generally in limestone mountains. When the water evaporates calcite is left as a white crust or as cement between fragments of rock and sand grains.

*Caliche* also is found in dry regions such as deserts and semideserts of the Southwest. It ranges from limy clay to hard stone; in many places it is a conglomerate or breccia of pebbles in resistant white cement. This cement consists of calcite and other minerals which are carried upward by water that rises by capillary action. As the water evaporates, the minerals are deposited at or near the surface. Some caliche is so massive and so regularly bedded that it has been mistaken for ancient marine limestone. Deposits in western Texas and Arizona have been crushed for concrete work and road surfacing.

## Dolomite
### (PLATE 33)

The rock called dolomite looks like limestone and often goes by that name. It actually is a mixture of the mineral dolomite, calcite and impurities, with the dolomite forming more than half the rock; generally more than four fifths. In practice, any magnesian-lime rock that does not effervesce in cold dilute acid is called dolomite. Dolomites are fine- to medium-grained, finely crystalline, shaly, compact or porous. They are white when pure, but shades of cream, gray and brown are common. Iron oxide often produces hues of yellow, brown and red.

Since most dolomite contains calcite, the rock may grade into *dolomitic limestone,* which is 20 to perhaps 45 per cent dolomite and effervesces weakly. A lower percentage of the mineral dolomite is regarded as an impurity in limestone. Dolomites also grade into shale, sandstone and even fine conglomerates.

ORIGIN.—Though dolomite is common in formations of all ages throughout the world, not a great deal is known about its origin. Some beds seem to have been deposited chemically in salt lakes, while many apparently were precipitated in shallow seas. Organisms such as algae contain large amounts of magnesium carbonate, an essential part of the mineral dolomite, and it is quite possible that algal banks and reefs were dolomitic when they formed. A thick buff dolomite exposed in western canyons of the Bighorn Mountains of Wyoming, in the Wind River Canyon and near Shoshone Dam, on the Cody road to Yellowstone National Park, consists of broken, "decayed" coralline algae that contained large amounts of magnesium carbonate when they grew during late Ordovician times.

Many dolomites plainly are the results of a change that turned shells, corals, bryozoans and lime muds from calcium carbonate into dolomite. This process, called *dolomitization,* involved a combination of magnesium and calcium carbonates; it has taken place on land and in the sea, by the action of ground water, hot water and sea water containing magnesium compounds. During this alteration there was a decrease in the volume of the rock, dolomite occupying 12.1 per cent less space than limestone. This decrease may account for some cavities that are found in dolomites such as those of the Chicago region and near-by parts of Indiana and Illinois.

OCCURRENCE.—Dolomites, like limestones, are widely distributed geographically; geologically, they are most common in Paleozoic and Proterozoic rocks. In Europe the term dolomite often is used as part of formation names and so may apply to rocks that are limestones or even shales.

USES.—Dolomite has much the same uses as limestone and other uses determined by its magnesium content. Thus it is burned at a temperature of 1500 degrees centigrade to produce refractory or heat-resistant material for use in steel furnaces and kilns. Dolomite also is used to make basic magnesium carbonate, which is mixed with 10 to 15 per cent of asbestos fiber to make insulating blocks, pipe coverings and cement. The process develops by-products which are used in face powder, paint, rubber goods, drugs, silver polish, agricultural lime, etc.

## CHAPTER XV

# Rocks Once Living

THOUGH THE ROCKS to be described in this chapter contain mineral matter, their great bulk consists of substance which actually has been alive. It was roots, leaves and spores of plants; it was the flesh of animals, which either became sediment directly or did so after being eaten and then excreted by still other animals. This matter of original deposition *versus* deposition after excretion determines the chemical make-up of the rocks. Remains which settled as they died made carbonaceous deposits, while those which passed through the bodies of animals and settled as excreta are phosphatic.

Rocks in the carbonaceous group consist largely, but not wholly, of plant material that partly decomposed under water. The processes of decay were carried out by bacteria, which removed oxygen from the dead leaves, stems and other structures, thus increasing the proportion of carbon in what remained. The result, under one set of conditions, was rocks of the *coal series;* under another, and with different materials at the outset, *petroleum deposits* were produced. In the former there is a continuous sequence from slightly unchanged plants to hard coal, and with this we shall begin.

## THE COAL SERIES

### Peat
(PLATE 35)

Peat is the first stage in the coal series; even it shows two substages. One is a very soft spongy rock which is yellow or dull brown in color and consists of partly decayed plant material. The other is a compact brown or black structureless mass that, when wet, resembles dark clay. The first type makes up the upper part of a peat deposit in which decay has not completely destroyed the grasses, rushes, mosses and other plants. Below this lies the black claylike sediment in which plant materials are almost completely decomposed. This sediment forms much of the dark deposit in bogs and swamps and may be as much as 90 per cent water, so that it shrinks greatly when dried.

In Ireland two other kinds of peat are recognized: *hill peat,* found in mountainous areas, and *bottom peat,* found in rivers, brooks and lakes. Impurities such as sand and clay are present, especially in the structureless claylike peat.

OCCURRENCE.—Peat occurs in many parts of the world, in coastal salt marshes and especially in northern countries where Ice Age glaciers left depressions which now are swamps. According to recent estimates Canada possesses 30,000,000 acres of peat, the United States 20,000,000 acres and Ireland 2,858,150 acres, while continental Europe has about 212,700 square miles. Although peat is plentiful in the North, American deposits of commercial value are located in the Middle and South Atlantic and Gulf states, in many areas east of the Missouri and north of the Ohio rivers and in a narrow belt along the Pacific coast.

USES.—In Europe (especially Ireland) peat is used extensively for fuel. It is either cut and dried as it comes from the bog and is pressed into compact blocks or made into still more compact briquettes. It also can be burned in gas producers. A ton of machine-pressed peat has the heating value of 1.3 tons of wood or 0.7 tons of average soft coal.

Fibrous forms of peat are used in the manufacture of paper and cloth and are pressed into structural materials resembling wood. In the United States peat is used as a fertilizer; for this purpose the fine material, rich in nitrogen, is employed. Fibrous varieties also furnish bedding for stock and packing material, while screenings are utilized for filtering, deodorizing and disinfecting purposes. Peat also can be used in the manufacture of ethyl alcohol.

## Lignite or Brown Coal
### (PLATE 35)

Lignite, also called brown coal, is a soft yellowish, chocolate brown or black rock which splits readily along the bedding, producing thin slabs. In texture lignite is firm, compact to earthy and fragile; in some specimens the grain of wood or intermingled vegetable fibers, as well as bits of resin, lie in an amorphous groundmass. The luster is bright, dull or pitchy; the streak is yellow brown; the hardness ranges from 1 to 2.5 and the specific gravity from 0.7 to 1.5.

The carbon content of lignite varies from 55 to 75 per cent; the rock burns readily with a smoky yellow flame and strong odor. When mined, lignite contains a great deal of moisture, but it becomes powdery on drying and has such a strong tendency toward spontaneous combustion that it must be stored with care. In general it is a satisfactory coal only if it can be bought very cheaply.

OCCURRENCE.—Thick deposits of lignite underlie parts of the Great Plains from Texas to the Yukon Territory; they are Cretaceous and Tertiary in age. Tertiary lignites of Germany form beds as much as 300 feet thick, representing an enormous accumulation of decayed plant material. They are distilled to produce gasoline.

## Subbituminous Coal or Black Lignite

This is a black coaly rock with a dull waxy to glossy luster. It is more dense than true lignite, is banded and shows little woody texture; some kinds consist largely of spores and so grade into cannel coal. Subbituminous coal is poorly jointed, the joints paralleling bedding planes; some varieties crumble when they dry. In spite of this these coals make excellent, clean fuel which burns readily. When relatively free from sulphur they are used in the production of gas.

OCCURRENCE.—Subbituminous coal occurs mainly in Cretaceous and Tertiary formations of the western Great Plains, though beds are found from the Gulf States to Alaska. The largest fields are in Montana, Wyoming, New Mexico and Alberta. One bed in Montana is 28 feet thick; at the town of Colstrip it is mined with electrically operated shovels, each of which can load a 50-ton car in about 6 minutes. At the present rate of production Montana has enough subbituminous coal to last about 9500 years.

## Bituminous, or Soft, Coal
### (PLATE 35)

This is a compact brittle rock that ranges from grayish black to deep black in color and is distinctly banded, or laminated. As the photographs show, some layers are shiny while others are dull. The former, called *glance* or *vitrain*, consist of flattened tree trunks and limbs whose cell walls are preserved in a crumpled state, though all soft parts of the tree have vanished. Only hard woody portions remain; their pores are impregnated with compounds formed by decay of the soft parts of the wood. These compounds later were reduced to carbon, which is black and lustrous. The dull layers, called *matt, dull coal* or *durain*, consist of tiny fragments of plant material mixed with resistant fragments and clay. There also are layers of soft powdery material (*mineral charcoal*, or *fusain*,

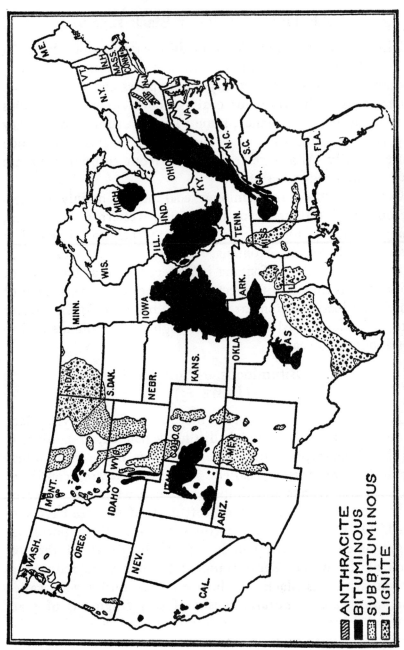

ANTHRACITE
BITUMINOUS
SUBBITUMINOUS
LIGNITE

Coal deposits of the United States. (*Campbell, U.S.G.S.*)

also deceptively called "mother of coal") which may be the result of forest fires that raged while the coal was forming.

Bituminous coal is well jointed and breaks into angular blocks. Aside from clay grains, sulphur and pyrite are common impurities; the hardness generally is between 1 and 2. Besides its ash, soft coal generally contains 60 to 86 per cent of carbon and 14 to 40 per cent of volatile matter that may be driven off as gas, tar, etc., by heating. Varying amounts of volatile material distinguish three varieties of coal which are of great commercial importance:

*Coking coal* hardens into a porous, burnable clinker when it is heated—some coals fall to powder instead. Good coking coal contains 20 to 30 per cent of volatile material.

*Low-volatile bituminous,* or "smokeless," coal contains 14 to 22 per cent of volatile matter and is used in furnaces, steam engines and stoves, especially in cities that have (and enforce) strict smoke ordinances. These coals have the highest heating value per pound of any and therefore are specially desirable as fuels for ships.

*Steam* or *domestic coal* constitutes the great bulk of soft coals that do not have the special qualities of coking or "smokeless" coals but are satisfactory for heating purposes. Some yield a large amount of ash and are very smoky.

Two other varieties are so distinct from ordinary soft coal that they deserve description:

*Splint coal* (PLATE 35) is blocky or massive, with a grayish, rather satiny appearance and coarsely granular fracture surface. It contains much matt or dull matter in which there generally are great numbers of spore covers from ancient plants. Its glance layers are relatively thin.

*Bone* is a laminated deposit of coaly material containing waterworn branches and thin layers of sand. It probably was deposited when sea water overflowed coal swamps, killing the plants and bringing in coarse sediment.

OCCURRENCE.—Bituminous coal occurs in beds or strata a

few inches to several feet in thickness. In North America it is found in "fields" from Nova Scotia to Georgia, through the Middle West, in the Rocky Mountain states and in those of the Pacific coast. Most of these are shown on the map. The oldest of our coals are Carboniferous; the youngest, Tertiary. There also are great coal fields in Europe, Asia, Africa, Australia and Antarctica. South America has less coal than North America, but there are large fields in Brazil and Argentina.

## Cannel Coal
### (PLATE 35)

Cannel is variously regarded as a variety of subbituminous coal or as bituminous coal that formed in special parts of coal swamps. It is a very dense, lusterless rock that looks much like dull tar and does contain much bitumen. It is deep black and breaks with a conchoidal fracture. Cannel contains a large proportion of hydrogen and so burns with a bright flame that explains its name, which means candle coal. Unlike other rocks in this series, it is made up of spores, pollen grains and remains of fully decayed plants. Cannel coal seems to have accumulated in clear water of deep pools or bayous among the swamps. It therefore forms lens-shaped patches instead of widespread beds or "seams." It is found in comparatively small quantities in many parts of the world.

Cannel coal is higher in heat value than are the common coals and burns easily. It therefore has long been in demand as fuel for grate fires. Because of this, almost all known deposits of cannel have been mined, except those that are very high in ash. When distilled, cannel coals give high yields of oil, tar and gas.

*Boghead coal* differs from cannel in being brown and in consisting largely of algal material, with spores in minor quantity. Boghead deposits apparently formed in fresh-water lakes or brackish lagoons, where algae much like modern "water scums" grew in great abundance. Boghead coal is found in Carboniferous and Permian deposits of Kentucky, Alaska, Russia, France, Scotland and other regions, but is not abundant.

## Jet

Jet resembles cannel coal but is harder and is characterized by bright glassy luster, deep black color and great toughness. Instead of crumbling when dry, it is so firm that it can be sawed, carved and polished. Microscopic sections show the structure of wood, chiefly that of the araucarian pine, which has relatives that are living today. Jet probably is pine wood that drifted to sea, sank and was buried in mud that turned to shale. Shales covering jet commonly contain marine fossils, drops of bitumen and pyrite crystals.

OCCURRENCE.—Jet is found in small quantities among rocks of Mesozoic and later ages in North America, Great Britain, Germany, Spain and other parts of the world. It is made into jewelry, ornaments and buttons; obsidian, glass and stained minerals sometimes are used as substitutes.

## Anthracite
### (PLATE 35)

Hard coal, or anthracite, is a compact, dense, brittle rock whose color is steely or jet black. It has a glassy or almost metallic luster, uneven or conchoidal fracture and a hardness of 2 or more. Joints are well developed, and bedding may be observed in all except small pieces. Anthracite contains 86 to 99 per cent of carbon, 1 to 14 per cent of volatile material and a small amount of clay and other ashy impurities. It burns slowly with a pale blue flame and much less smoke than is given off by soft coal.

Hard coal occurs in regions where rocks have been folded, heated and squeezed; small quantities of it also are found where soft coal or lignite was heated by igneous intrusions. Technically, therefore, anthracite is a metamorphic rock.

OCCURRENCE.—Anthracite has been mined extensively in

Pennsylvania and Wales, but much larger deposits are found in China and Russia. Anthracite fields as great as those of Pennsylvania and Wales occur in Indo-China and the Union of South Africa; those of France and Belgium are small and comparatively unimportant.

## The Origin of Coal

We have seen that some members of the coal series were deposited in brackish lagoons and fresh-water lakes. The majority, however, began as plant material that settled on the bottoms of bogs and swamps, where it partly decayed and turned into peat. The process is taking place today in the Dismal Swamp of North Carolina and Virginia as well as in countless shallow Northern lakes. Under the peat is a layer of soil filled with roots, called *underclay*. Beds like it, but generally harder, are found beneath coal seams. Some of them contain very large roots that extend from tree stumps which evidently were surrounded by layers of coal-making material, just as peat now settles around cypress stumps in the Dismal Swamp.

After peat is covered by mud or sand, decay continues by the action of bacteria. These one-celled plants change the dead leaves and stems, taking out the oxygen which they need to sustain life. In this stage both bacterial and chemical action turn the peat into new chemical compounds that are believed to be suspended in water as tiny particles of jelly. The jelly is what we call lignite.

Beyond the lignite stage change comes from heat and pressure, not decay. The weight of rocks overlying a soft-coal bed compressed it, driving out water and gas and leaving a higher and higher proportion of carbon. Where mountain building involved coal beds, pressure became so intense that it drove off most of the volatile matter and so produced anthracite. This sequence is shown clearly in Pennsylvania, where both soft coal and anthracite are abundant. In regions that are not mountainous the coal is soft and contains much volatile matter. As one nears the mountains it becomes harder, and in the intensely folded Appalachians it is brittle, high-grade anthracite.

Coal beds lie between sandstones, shales, limestones and other stratified rocks. Some of these formed under fresh water; others contain fossils, such as lamp shells and corals, which plainly are marine. They show that peat bogs were flooded by salt water from time to time, as the land sank beneath the sea. In Nova Scotia there were 29 such sinkings; after each one the basin was filled with sediment until it became a bog, so that 29 coal beds formed. The meaning of a much smaller series of alternating strata is shown by this table, which is to be read upward from the bottom:

| Rock | Fossils | Events |
|---|---|---|
| Limestone | Lamp shells, corals | Still greater sinking, which turned the bay into a clear sea. |
| Shale | Lamp shells | Water in the bay became less sandy. |
| Sandstone | Worm burrows, plants | The bog sank and became a salt-water bay; waves washed sand from the shore and piled it up in bars. |
| Coal | Coal plants | The lake partly filled, becoming a bog where plants grew and peat began to form. |
| Shale | Coal plants, fresh-water shells | The bog sank, becoming a lake; mud settled on the bottom. Plants drifted in but were too few to make peat. |
| Coal | Coal plants | The valley sank, becoming a bog where forests grew and peat formed. |
| Cross-bedded sandstone | Petrified logs, fresh-water shells | A river often flooded a wide valley, leaving stranded logs and deposits of sand. |

Plant remains doubtless have settled in bogs through at least 500,000,000 years, but not till the latter part of the Devonian period (about 350,000,000 years ago) did land plants become so large and abundant that they could form deposits of peat. Most of these were thin, and since peat shrinks nearly 94 per cent when it changes to coal, they made very tiny coal seams. Only one Devonian coal seam is thick enough to be mined; it lies on Bear Island in the Arctic Ocean, where the climate is now very cold.

In the Carboniferous Age conditions changed. Trees, vines, shrubs, reeds and other plants grew on the banks and in shallows of bogs that covered thousands of square miles. Their remains formed the largest and best deposits of coal in the world, especially in North America and Europe. Peat, which became coal, also formed in bogs during the Permian, Triassic, Jurassic, Cretaceous and even Tertiary ages. Comparatively small deposits are forming today, for the world has only a few large swamps suitable for peat deposition.

## THE PETROLEUM, OR BITUMINOUS, DEPOSITS
### Petroleum or Crude Oil

Though petroleum hardly can be called a rock, it is found in rocks and contains material which can make moderately solid deposits. In its natural state petroleum is a dark, thick, oily substance which consists of compounds of carbon, hydrogen, oxygen and nitrogen and commonly sulphur in what one authority calls "bewildering variety." The oils of various regions differ in the kinds and proportions of these compounds which they contain. Thus petroleum from the Appalachian oil field contains considerable paraffin; that of Illinois, Indiana and Ohio is high in sulphur compounds; oils of the Gulf States and Oklahoma include uncombined sulphur. Nitrogen compounds are specially abundant in California oils and paraffin is scarce. In spite of these differences, however, there is a general similarity among petroleums that allows them to be known by one name.

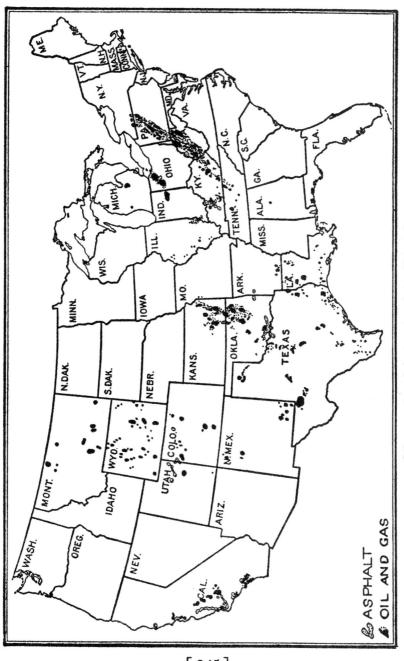

Oil, gas and asphalt deposits of the United States.

*Natural gas* occurs with petroleum and comes from the same original material. The nonburning gas, helium, is found in some gas fields of Texas and Utah; other regions produce carbon dioxide, which can be condensed into "dry ice." Another type of gas can be cooled, condensed and made into a very rich gasoline that must be mixed with low-grade refinery gasoline for use in automobiles.

ORIGIN.—Several chemists have thought that petroleum and natural gas were formed from inorganic substances. It is true that volcanic gases and igneous rocks contain some compounds like those in crude oil, but they are not plentiful enough to explain great oil fields. Moreover, there is no evidence that petroleum has been heated greatly, though such heating would be necessary if it were made from inorganic materials.

Much crude oil is found in marine rocks, where it is associated with salt, sulphur and gypsum. Such oil was produced by the decay of dead plants and animals. Plants were the more important; they probably ranged from large seaweeds to one-celled algae. When they died their remains accumulated near the shores of shallow bays or landlocked seas, forming dark layers containing fatty oil. This material was covered with mud. As the process was repeated, it built a formation of dark shale or limestone that was the "mother rock" of both petroleum and natural gas.

Thus far the story is fairly clear, but little is known of the next steps. The organic material began to change—apparently before the mud hardened. Changes continued for a long time, finally producing both oil and gas. Still later, these substances began to work their way through pores in the strata, gathering in "reservoirs." Many of these reservoirs are sandstones or other porous rocks that are bent into upward folds and are covered with impervious beds. Gas, being lightest, has risen to the tops of the porous arches but is kept from escaping by the compact beds above. Oil lies at lower levels and on the flanks of the folds. In most oil fields salt water lies still lower than oil. This salt water is some of the original sea water that was trapped in the muds when they settled, millions of years ago.

This gathering of oil into reservoirs makes it useful to man. Vast quantities of petroleum are scattered through sedimentary rocks but in quantities too small for extraction. Thus a 35-foot

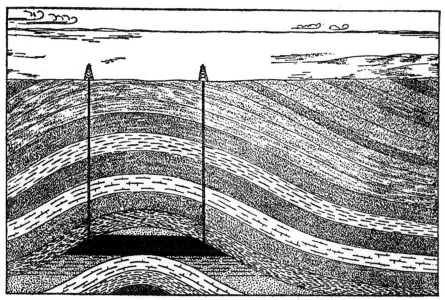

Diagram of an "oil dome." Petroleum has gathered in the part of a sandstone formation marked by black. Gas lies above the oil, and salt water (horizontal lines) is below it.

formation of dolomite near Chicago contains about 7,700,000 barrels of oil per square mile, but it is so scattered that not a barrel can be pumped. Only where oil and gas are concentrated in porous "pools" can they be taken out through wells.

OCCURRENCE.—Petroleum and natural gas are widespread, though they are most plentiful in the Northern Hemisphere. The United States produces more than half the world's supply of oil, and Mexico also is an important producer. There are large oil fields in southeastern Europe and Asia Minor; the oil reserves of Mesopotamia are immense. Burma and large islands of the Dutch East Indies also have important oil fields. Africa and Australia, however, lack significant deposits.

## Asphalt

Natural asphalt is a viscous or hard black rock that varies considerably in composition but resembles petroleum. Asphalt commonly fills pores in sandstone, limestone and dolomite. Rocks that contain large amounts of it can be crushed, spread and rolled into pavements. Asphalt also comes to the surface in pools and "lakes," such as the famous Pitch Lake of Trinidad and the Bermudez Lake of Venezuela. Asphalt pools in Los Angeles trapped countless Ice Age animals that came to them to drink.

Artificial asphalt is produced by distilling crude oil, and natural deposits generally are thought to be formed by evaporation and the action of sulphur compounds. Some authorities, however, believe that asphalt formed directly from plant material by a process different from that which produced petroleum.

## Vein Bitumens

These are a group of viscous or solid rocks whose color ranges from brown to black. They generally have a pitchy odor, burn with a smoky flame and can be dissolved in turpentine, ether or naphtha. They occur as veins, chiefly in sedimentary rocks. The following are some important varieties:

*Uintaite,* or *gilsonite,* is a brilliant black bituminous rock with conchoidal fracture and hardness of 2 to 2.5. It dissolves completely in warm oil of turpentine. Uintaite is found as veins in Tertiary formations of northeastern Utah and western Colorado, some of the veins being 18 feet wide. A similar bituminous rock, occurring in Trinidad and the island of Barbados, is called *manjak.* Both uintaite and manjak are used in low-grade varnishes, as coating for masonry and the bottoms of steel ships, as roofing pitch, insulation for electric wires and as a rubber substitute in garden hose. Uintaite also is employed in the manufacture of phonograph records.

*Ozokerite* also is called *mineral wax* or *native paraffin*. It is a waxy yellowish brown to green substance which is transparent when pure and feels greasy. It occurs in fissures among crushed shales, sandstones and limestones along the line of the Denver, Rio Grande and Western Railway in Utah and in Galicia (once part of Poland), where the body of an Ice Age rhinoceros was found in one ozokerite deposit. When purified, the material is used in candles and ointments and as an adulterant of beeswax.

## Oil Shale
### (PLATES 28, 39)

Oil shale contains a large proportion of bituminous material which can be changed by distillation. When this is done it yields oil, tar and a few other substances, one of which may be ammonia.

Oil shales are either lake or marine deposits, many being finely and regularly laminated. Marine oil shales contain hydrocarbons that came from algae and animals such as fish, whose remains are very abundant. Lake deposits contain algal material in abundance. Thus the Green River oil shales of Wyoming, Colorado and Utah (PLATE 39) are lake deposits and most of their bituminous material is algal, though some beds contain great numbers of fossil fish whose flesh must have produced a substantial amount of oil. Although oil shales are being used in Europe, those of North America are now merely a reserve source, to be used when the supplies of petroleum are exhausted. Deposits range from Carboniferous to Tertiary in age and are found in North America, Scotland, Central Europe, Australia, New Zealand and Brazil.

## PHOSPHATE DEPOSITS

### Guano

Guano is a surface deposit of excrement, chiefly that of birds. It belongs to two general types: soluble and leached. The former is a recent deposit, generally occupying dry or sheltered places; it contains phosphoric acid and compounds of nitrogen. Leached guano has had its soluble materials removed by rain or sea water and so contains little nitrogen.

Leached guanos are found on bird islands of the southern Pacific and the West Indies, while vast amounts of soluble guano were secured from Peru before the supply was exhausted. It is said that the Inca Indians valued guano-producing birds so highly that they imposed the death penalty on anyone who disturbed them. Bat guano has been found in caves of Kentucky, Texas and New Mexico, the Carlsbad Caverns being the most famous of these.

### Phosphorite or Phosphate Rock

Phosphorite is a rock composed of calcium phosphate, calcite, iron oxide, clay and other materials. Phosphorite may be earthy, fibrous, semicrystalline, oölitic, concretionary, compact or even spongy in texture. Gray is the usual color, but black, brick red, buff and white phosphate rocks are found. The simplest test of their nature is to dissolve a powdered piece in nitric acid, filter off the undissolved stuff and add a solution of ammonium molybdate until a yellow precipitate shows the presence of phosphorus. Such a test will be of great value to the quarry owner who suspects that his rock will make phosphate fertilizer.

ORIGIN.—Phosphate rocks originate directly or indirectly from organisms, either from bones and shells which contain a great deal of phosphorus or from guano. In the phosphate deposits of South Carolina the bones of animals are associated

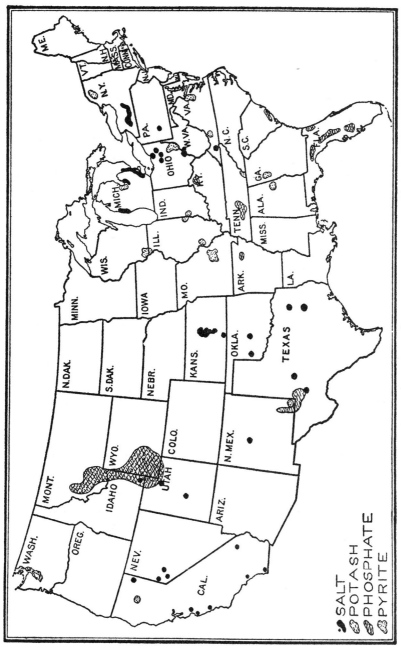

Deposits of salt, phosphate, potash and pyrite in the United States.

SALT
POTASH
PHOSPHATE
PYRITE

with the deposits; in the extensive deposits of Utah, Montana, Wyoming and Idaho calcium phosphate seems to have been precipitated directly from the sea water, which was probably enriched by phosphorus from decaying organisms. Secondary deposits of phosphate result from rain water carrying away the soluble phosphates from guano; as the phosphate-charged waters seep down through joints and cracks they come in contact with limestone, producing calcium phosphate, which is then deposited along joints or in cavities. When beds of limestone containing such deposits weather, residual nodules of phosphate rock may remain, since they are less soluble than calcite.

Phosphorites occur in formations from Cambrian to Recent in age and are being formed today on sea floors where concretions surround the dead bodies of fish. Deposits range from 1/16 inch to 8 inches in thickness, many being less than an inch. They are interbedded with shale and impure limestone and may grade laterally into sandstone. Such conditions indicate deposition in shallow water.

OCCURRENCE.—Florida and Tennessee produced 97.7 per cent of the phosphates mined in the United States during 1936. The deposits of the former are Tertiary in age, while those of the latter are Ordovician. Kentucky, South Carolina and Arkansas produce some phosphate. Probably the largest deposits of phosphate rock occur in Utah, Wyoming, Idaho and Montana and are of Carboniferous age. Since these deposits have scarcely been worked, they represent a reserve that could supply the world for many years. There are minor phosphorite deposits in Russia, Morocco, Tunis and Algiers.

USES.—Phosphate rock is used mainly as a fertilizer, either ground and spread on the soil or treated with sulphuric acid to form acid phosphates. Phosphates are also used for making phosphorus and phosphate chemicals and in the manufacture of refractory bricks and stock foods.

CHAPTER XVI

# Records in Strata

T HE AIM AND END of all geologic work," wrote a scientist in 1882, "is not merely to tell us what rocks are like, but to
enable us when we look at a rock to say how and where it was
formed. When we can do this . . . we learn to look upon rocks
as the pages of a volume, in which is written an account of what
was going on while they were being formed."

We have read some parts of this account: how lavas record
ancient eruptions, granites tell of vanished mountains and till
records the melting of ancient glaciers. We have seen that fossils distinguish land or fresh-water deposits and that gravel,
sand and fine mud settle in different regions offshore. Yet, so far
as sedimentary rocks are concerned, we have only scratched the
surface. Countless beds show how seas covered sinking lands,
how currents scoured channels and how winds, waves, floods,
seasons and other factors affected the deposition of rocks. These
are the records we now shall examine. We also shall consider a
few other structures showing changes that took place in rocks
after they were deposited.

### Unconformities
(PLATE 36)

When a sea advances and drops sediment, when glaciers
spread drift over hard bedrock or when rivers leave mud on

once dry plains, the result is an unconformity. At its simplest, this structure is a surface that represents a break in a sequence of formations. It is a plane of erosion or nondeposition between two groups of rocks.

To understand just what this means, let us look at the picture showing rocks above Montmorency Falls, Quebec. The dark lower rock once was granite that hardened early in Pre-Cambrian times. It then was pushed upward, folded into mountains

A nonconformity near Montmorency Falls, Quebec. Limestone lies on crumpled, worn gneiss.

and worn down; weathering caused its grains to crumble and streams carried them away. At last, near the middle of the Ordovician Age, a sea covered this worn land, depositing beds of limestone. The surface between the granitic rock and the limestone is an unconformity—a break which, at that place, is the only record of many million years.

Another drawing shows an unconformity whose "time interval" is not nearly so great. Here a bed of brown dolomite hardened and was gently lifted into low land, which was weathered and slightly eroded. Then the water returned, so that corals and other limy animals grew upon the weathered dolomite and built irregular layers of limestone. Here the unconformity shows only a slight emergence from the sea, with no mountain building. Its "time value," or the period which it represents, may be only a few hundred years.

These are extremes; they also represent two of the three main

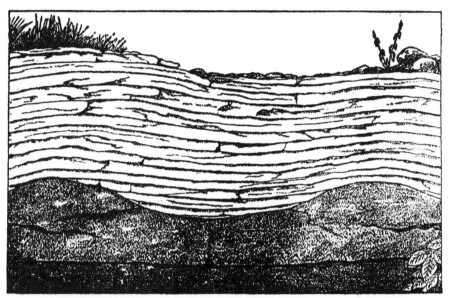

A disconformity in northern Iowa. Except that the upper rocks bend downward into the worn channels of the bed below, the strata show little difference in position.

types of break between rock series. It is worth our while to define these types to make sure of their meanings.

A *nonconformity* is the sort of break seen near Montmorency Falls; another, at Ute Pass, Colorado, is shown on PLATE 36. In the latter region very ancient (Pre-Cambrian) granites were raised, eroded and then depressed, so that beds of sand settled on their surface. Several hundred million years passed between intrusion of the granite and deposition of the sandstone that now covers it. Some nonconformities, of course, are not so great. They represent periods during which rocks were raised, broken and tilted but were not so intensely crumpled as those near Montmorency Falls.

A *disconformity* is a break without perceptible tilting, so that sedimentary rocks above and below the eroded surface are almost parallel. Like the Iowa example, a disconformity means moderate uplift without folding or breaking; in some places sea bottoms merely became shoals that were scoured by waves and currents. Generally, too, such breaks represent periods much shorter than those involved in nonconformities.

A *diastem* is a break in deposition of sediment, accompanied by little or no erosion. Diastems are commonest in the deposits of seas whose waters became so shallow that nothing could be deposited and little or nothing could be worn away. Over some of these shallows the water was quiet and clear, with almost no sediment; in others small waves and currents kept mud from settling, even though it may have been fairly plentiful. Diastems grade into deposits consisting of extremely thin laminae, like those in argillites near Swiftcurrent Pass in Glacier National Park, Montana, where laminae number as many as 390 in a single inch of rock.

Streams also produce unconformities by digging and filling channels, by spreading muds over flood plains and by building alluvial fans and deltas. A river that flowed over an old lake bed west of Green River, Wyoming, made an unconformity which is seen by thousands of summer tourists on U.S. Highway 30. Another ancient river produced an unconformable deposit of red rock now exposed on Beartooth Butte, near the Red Lodge–Cook road into Yellowstone National Park.

In general, we may say that the greater the breaking and crumpling of rocks below an unconformity, the greater was their rise and the longer the time required to wear them down. If two or more unconformities are found in one place (as they are in the Grand Canyon of Arizona), we can compare the amount of disturbance and the probable length of each upheaval. In the Grand Canyon, for instance, it is plain that the unconformity at the top of the Inner Gorge represents a much longer time than the one somewhat higher. It also represents a period of greater uplift and mountain building, for the rocks below it are intensely broken, squeezed and changed. Those

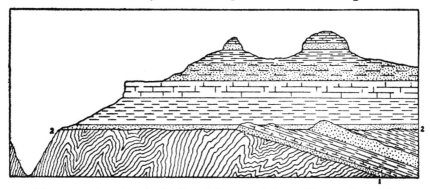

Two nonconformities in the Grand Canyon, Arizona. Very ancient rocks were crumpled and changed into gneiss and schist; then they were worn down to the surface marked 1–1, which was almost horizontal. New beds of rock were deposited, were broken and tilted into mountains and were worn to the surface 2–2, which also cuts across gneiss and schist.

below the second unconformity are broken but are not crumpled nor greatly changed.

## Strata or Beds

As we said in Chapter IX, most sedimentary rocks are divided into beds, or strata, which suggest the courses of brick in a wall. Unless earth movements have overturned or otherwise displaced them, the oldest stratum in a series lies at the bottom, younger ones above it and the youngest at the top.

Some books define a stratum as "a layer of rock which is divided along bedding planes from the rocks above and below it, this division being caused by a break in deposition or a change in the nature of sediments deposited." In this sense a stratum may be a paper-thin layer of shale or an algal biostrome fifty feet in thickness, as well as almost anything between. Other books (mostly European) use stratum for "all continuous layers composed of one kind of material"; in this sense the term corresponds to *formation,* so that we sometimes read about the Chalk "stratum" at Dover or the lithographic limestone "stratum" of Solenhofen, which is divided into many beds.

In America stratum and bed are used with little or no distinction. They mean either one layer or several similar layers of rock which are separated from deposits above and below by bedding planes and often by weak or shaly "partings." Such strata generally range from 2 inches to 2 or 3 feet in thickness; those more than 4 feet thick are relatively rare. Among carbonate rocks strata more than 3 feet thick are likely to be biostromes of algae or animal remains and may contain good fossils. A very thick bed of limestone or dolomite that is not a biostrome may be even more interesting, for very little is known about the way in which such strata form.

*Laminae* and *layers* are divisions of strata. Laminae are the thinner of the two, their number ranging from 3 to 50, 100 or even 400 in one inch of rock. They differ in color, texture and mineral make-up; some cling together, though others separate easily. They are commonest in shales and shaly limestones, in which they make the rock *fissile,* or "splittable." This character, however, also has other causes.

Layers may be merely laminae a half inch or more in thickness, but they also may be groups of laminae that cling together but break away from other groups. Both layers and laminae in shale are likely to be uniform in color, grain and thickness, but those of dolomites and limestones may be mottled, irregular and even nodular, containing two or more kinds and colors of sediment. Some layers also are rough and very irregular.

*Inclined strata* are found where sediment settled on slopes, forming beds of rock that slanted, or *dipped.* No one knows just how steep these original dips can be. In experiments sand has been made to settle in layers at angles of 33 to 40 degrees, though clay did not settle on 30-degree slopes unless it could stick to material already deposited. In the St Francis Mountains of southeastern Missouri ancient hills have been uplifted; sandstones and limestones on their slopes dip as much as 25 or 30 degrees. Strata on the slopes of ancient reefs in Chicago dip as much as 41 degrees, and deposits near modern reefs in the South Seas are inclined 10 to 40 degrees.

This evidence seems clear—but is it? Suppose several beds of mud settle on a steep slope. At the foot of the slope the mud is squeezed and packed more rapidly than it is at higher levels. As a result slopes will become steeper and steeper until they become much more abrupt than those in which the mud actually settles. This process of "differential compaction" probably has been important in producing most of the steep dips mentioned in the preceding paragraph.

*Subaqueous slides* are produced when sediment settles on steep underwater slopes and slips before it hardens. Such slipping produces crumpling of laminae and beds, along with breaking and general mix-up which may make the rock look like edgewise breccia. Slides of this sort are found in several Paleozoic formations of the East, and they also are conspicuous in later deposits of California, Nevada, Utah and other Western states.

CAUSES OF STRATIFICATION.—Though slide deposits are interesting, they are much less important than stratification itself, which marks virtually all sediments. Every bedding plane must be the record of a change that stopped deposition, altered its rate or brought a new kind of sediment. In spite of this we know very little about the changes that produced the breaks between strata. Here are some of the most likely causes:

1. Filling up of a sea or lake basin, so that little or no sediment could settle. The surface of any deposit already formed was washed by currents and waves. When the water deepened and new sediment settled, it formed a separate layer. This cause also explains much stratification in reefs and biostromes. When corals, sponges and algae reached the surface of the water they stopped growing. When the water deepened they began again—but made a new stratum.

2. Storms, floods or currents often carried mud into normally quiet, clear water. The mud halted plant growth in biostromes and made partings on deposits of limestone.

3. Long periods of drought might cut off supplies of sediment, so that the surface of a bed would partly harden and form a bedding plane when sedimentation began again.

4. Any change that suddenly provided a distinctly new kind of sediment would start the formation of a new bed.

5. On land, moist periods would slow down the accumulation of wind-blown dust and sand, letting older beds settle and become compact before new ones could form.

6. Floods in coal swamps spread thin partings of shale over beds of peat which someday would become beds of coal.

Though laminae and layers are thinner than strata, their causes are somewhat better known. We can say definitely, for instance, that a certain dark lamina containing carbon was produced by algae that grew on the sea bottom. Some layers of sand and pebbles plainly were spread out on the bottoms of bays by streams flowing at flood season. Other sandy laminae lie in limestones which seem too pure to have been deposited near the mouths of rivers. Apparently the sands were blown out to sea, where they settled on lime mud. Many layers were produced when shells and other animal remains settled or drifted to the bottoms of seas or lakes. Thus flat shells form layers between limestone or shale, while crinoid stems make up limy layers in other sediment.

### Rhythms and Varves
(PLATE 39)

Both laminae and layers may be deposited in regularly alternating, *rhythmic* series. In many sedimentary rocks we find such regular alternation: dark laminae and light ones, thick layers and thin, through dozens or hundreds of feet. Laminated anhydrites in Texas are 1000 feet thick; 1737 laminations were counted in 13 feet. In the Proterozoic argillites of Glacier

National Park gray and green or gray and brown laminae alternate through about 2000 feet and contain as many as 56 laminae to the inch.

The chief cause of these rhythms is changes in season. Throughout many parts of the world spring and early summer are times of high water, while late summer and autumn are periods of low water. The high waters carry much mud, sand and even gravel, depositing them in relatively thick layers; low waters carry only fine mud and make thin layers. Rhythms of this sort are common in clastic strata of all ages and, where they are coupled with other characters such as plant growth, they afford traces of changing seasons. Each pair of layers is called a *varve,* a term that may be applied to any deposit formed in one year, regardless of its special kind. Most of the varves that have been described, however, consist of two layers or laminae representing the two principal seasons.

Dry and wet seasons have produced conspicuously rhythmic varves. In Glacier National Park thin laminae of red argillite alternate with layers of sand, coarse pebbles and edgewise or flat-pebble breccia. This coarse material apparently represents the onset of rains in semidesert country, when quantities of material were washed into a very shallow sea whose muds were torn up and redeposited by the rushing water. The rainy season ended suddenly; then came weeks of increasing drought when only red mud was deposited. At last the weather became so dry that the shallow water evaporated, leaving mud banks to dry and crack in the sun while salt crystallized in tiny pools. With the return of rains the mud banks were flooded and a new sandy layer was formed.

We have mentioned the varves of glacial lakes. In spring and summer ice melts rapidly; since melting releases a great deal of sand and rock flour, it produces a thick deposit. There is little melting in fall and almost none in winter, so that those seasons are marked by a lamina that is fine-grained and thin—merely the finest mud that settled in the quiet water under the ice. The thick summer lamina grades into the winter deposit above it, just as warm weather grades into cold. The winter lamina, however, is sharply separated from the coarse one begun by the next spring's thaw.

Varves of ancient glacial lakes have been found, but the best-known lake varves indicate warm and cool seasons of about 6,500,000 years. These laminae are in the Green River shales of Wyoming, Utah and Colorado. A piece of this shale is shown on PLATE 39.

A different sort of varve is forming in deep, stagnant parts of Lake Zurich, Switzerland. There a light-colored lamina of limy material settles during summer and a dark one is composed largely of algae that live—and die—during fall and winter. The complete varve is about one fifth of an inch thick.

There plainly are many causes for varves, and the collector who gathers varved rocks may have a detective's job on his hands when he tries to explain them. He also will find many rhythmic deposits which are too thick and too complicated to be varves and whose meaning is unknown. Even many rhythmic laminae may not be seasonal; they probably represent storms, short droughts and so on.

## Cross-Bedding
(PLATES 26, 36)

In cross-bedded deposits the rock layers are tipped or inclined at various angles. Many of the inclined layers form one stratum; it is cut by a tilted or horizontal surface and a new stratum of differently tilted layers begins.

Cross-bedding is commonest in sandstone, though it also is found in limestone and some sandy shales. It was caused by currents that heaped up ridges and then dropped sand or other particles on their sheltered sides, making inclined layers. When the strength or direction of the current changed, the steepness and direction of the sloping layers shifted. Most cross-bedded strata probably were deposited in the shallow waters of seas, lakes, and rivers, but many were formed on land and in deltas. Delta cross-beds are more uniform in direction and form fewer wedges than do those of shore or inland dunes.

*Cross-lamination* is merely cross-bedding on a very small scale. It generally is made by rippling wavelets and weak currents, both of which, however, may affect muds and sands that were greatly disturbed not long before. Thus there is cross-lamination among the beds of mud breccia, sand and storm rollers shown on PLATE 26.

## Ripple Marks
(PLATE 37)

Ripple marks are ridges and troughs that look like waves in rock. They may be formed on sea and lake bottoms, stream beds, beaches and bars, dunes or even on dusty fields. There are two requirements for their formation: sediments whose grains do not stick together tightly and force which can move those grains about. Ripple marks therefore are commonest on sand and under water; even there mud, marl and other "sticky" sediments do not often form ripple marks. Where a layer of sand lies on one of wet mud the sand may form ripples, but the marks stop abruptly at its base. Dry mud, of course, is another matter; when it is broken into dust it forms narrow, sharp-edged ripple marks of unusual perfection.

*Wind ripple marks* are those built by wind blowing steadily in one direction. It thus forms a current which piles dust or sand grains into ridges, rolls other grains up the ridge slopes and tumbles these grains over the top. Wind-made ripple marks thus slope gradually on the sides up which grains are rolled and steeply on the lee sides where they drop. They never are high in proportion to their width, while their dimension from one ridge to the next (the *wave length*) generally ranges from one half inch to 3 or 4 inches. As a rule the gradual, or windward, side of each ridge is slightly convex and the trough between the ridges is rather flat and is wide in proportion to the wave length.

[ *263* ]

Wind ripples are common on beaches, dunes and piles of dust that have drifted from dry, plowed fields. Specially fine ones are seen by visitors to the White Sands National Monument in New Mexico, the Colorado Desert of southwestern California and the Great Sand Dunes of Colorado. Few wind ripples, however, have been found in ancient sand deposits.

*Water-current ripple marks* are higher than wind-made marks of the same length, and the troughs between them are rather angular instead of flat. Most of the ridges have a gradual slope facing the current and a steep one away from it; the former commonly is not convex.

Though many water-current marks are no larger than those made by the wind, most of those found in hardened rocks are higher, wider and steeper. Though ripple marks less than 5 inches from crest to crest have been found in deep water, most of them probably were made by moderate currents at depths of 20 feet or less. Several formations, however, contain ridges 8 to 20 feet in wave length and 2 to 7 feet high, some of which have slopes that are equally steep. These *giant ripples* probably were made by currents in water more than 20 feet deep—in some cases several hundred feet. Giant ripples that are uniform in wave length and that can be traced over several square miles almost certainly were made by currents in wide marine bays.

Water-current ripples are commonest in clastic rocks, especially sandstones. Giant ripples, however, have been found in limestones, for example, near Cincinnati. In some places the crests of the ripples consist largely of broken shells and other animal remains which were piled upon the sticky lime mud.

*Wave,* or *symmetrical, ripple marks* have both slopes steep and concave, while the troughs between them are concave or flat-bottomed. Marks of this sort seldom are very large; the majority have wave lengths of less than 4 inches. As their name indicates, symmetrical ripples are made by waves in water whose depth ranges from a few inches to several hundred feet. In general, large ripples mean large waves and deep water, but small ones may form in either deep or shallow water. It seems probable, however, that the great majority of ripple marks less than 6 inches in wave length formed in water that was not more than 20 to 50 feet deep.

Symmetrical ripples are found abundantly in sandstones and

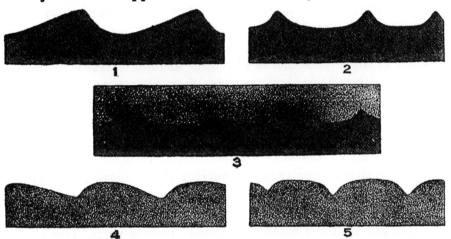

Ripple marks and negatives. 1 is a section of current marks, showing the troughs and ridges that are steep on one side; 2 is a section of symmetrical wave marks. In 3 a bed of wave ripple marks is covered by later sediment. 4 and 5 are negatives, or molds, of current and wave marks, turned upside down.

sandy shales but less commonly in dolomites. Since sediments that contain a great deal of mica in small grains are highly plastic and hold their shapes well, almost perfectly preserved ripples often are found in micaceous rocks. This is specially true in Glacier National Park, where micaceous sandstones, quartzites, shales and argillites are several thousand feet thick. Some strata contain symmetrical ripples a half inch in wave length, while others are much larger. There also is a great variety of cross and compound ripple marks, as well as narrow ridges with wide flat troughs, which are best developed in dolomite. Devonian sandstones in southwestern New York and Mississippian sandstones of Ohio also are famous for their ripple marks.

*Cross,* or *interference, ripple marks* are symmetrical ripples

[ *265* ]

that cross each other, making square, oblong or irregular patterns. Some ridges are sharp, some are rounded and others are flat; depressions between the flat-topped ridges are saucer-shaped and have been called "tadpole nests."

Some cross ripples develop in ponds, around sand bars, among the piling of piers, etc., when waves break up into two sets of oscillations that cross one another. Most cross ripples, however, are formed when the wind changes, so that waves begin to make new marks at angles to those already formed. Where both sets of ridges are sharp they show that the wind has changed quickly; where one set is rounded we may assume that there was a period of calm during which grains in the ridges shifted or slumped. In some beds all the ridges are planed off or flattened by cross waves or currents. Since these features and other details are preserved in ancient ripple marks, they give an excellent idea of conditions in seas that vanished ages ago.

*Compound ripple marks* are produced where waves pile ridges across others made by currents, or *vice versa*. The term also may be used for small wave ripples formed in the troughs between large ones. Such compound ripple marks often make very attractive specimens, but only the simpler types are well understood.

Ripple marks are laid bare when tides go out, when shallow lakes evaporate and when streams lower after floods. Though exposed ripples are stiffened by water that fills pores in layers of sediment as well as by mud grains and flakes of mica, they seldom last long. Really good ripple marks in stone generally mean that the bed was covered by new sediment within a few days. Marks that were not covered promptly show traces of wear by waves, currents or both. Many even are crossed by mud cracks that opened as the sediment dried.

Ripple marks do not tell whether ancient rocks formed in fresh or salt water. They may tell, however, which side of a loose slab is the upper one. Current marks usually have troughs that are wider and less angular than the ridges, and wave ripples always do so unless they have been worn. If the depressions in a slab are narrower and sharper than its high places, it is a deposit that covered a ripple-marked bed. Its ridges and depressions are molds of those made by waves or currents and appear on its under surface.

## Current, Drag and Swash Marks
### (PLATES 39, 40)

*Current marks* are irregular ridges and channels made on shoals or exposed flats. When water drains from flood plains or tidal flats it often gathers in rills or currents that scour channels. Some of these channels are flexuous though others branch in plantlike shapes; the latter, or the sand and mud filling them, often are mistaken for fossil seaweeds. Other channels are several feet deep and two or three rods long. When filled with cross-laminated sandstone they look much like petrified logs.

*Drag marks* were made when currents or retreating waves dragged shells and pebbles across muddy beaches or flats. There they dug grooves or came to rest and allowed water to dig current channels in their lee. Very commonly, the mud became soft shale, but the pits and grooves were filled by sand which continued to accumulate until it made a bed of sandstone. When such a bed weathers we find the groove fillings on its under side.

Much like these are grooves dug by floating icebergs, trees, seaweeds and by the tentacles of some marine animals. Many of these markings have been found in Devonian sandstones of New York and Carboniferous beds of Texas and Oklahoma, but not much has been learned about them. Other marks were made by seaweeds, etc., that grew fast to the bottom but were whipped about by currents. Still another type of mark was produced when the water of receding waves flowed around kelp or other seaweeds stranded on the shore. There are excellent examples of such markings at Point Lobos, California.

*Swash* is the thin sheet of water that glides up a gently sloping beach after a wave breaks upon it. It carries grains of sand, mica and other particles which it drops in a thin wavy ridge, the *swash mark*. Since many waves break, there are many of these marks, which form a branching network. Such networks are found in ancient near-shore sandstones of New York, southern Ontario and other regions.

## Trails and Burrows
### (PLATE 38)

Trails are made by animals that walk or crawl upon wet, soft rocks such as sand, mud and clay, which later harden into stone. Burrows are made by animals that dig or bore into the soft sediments. Trails lie along bedding planes or surfaces and are filled by strata lying above them somewhat as men fill molds with concrete, plaster or metal. Burrows may follow bedding planes but usually cut across them; many are vertical. They also are filled by sediment, but the fillings are upright or flattened "pencils" of stone.

Trails and separate footprints of mammals, birds, reptiles and amphibians have been found; they were made in wet sediments beside streams, pools, lakes or (rarely) seashores. Trails of trilobites, snails, mussels, crabs and other marine animals were made under shallow water or on exposed mud and sand flats; such markings are not common in deposits of lakes and streams. Burrows were made by these same animals and by worms or wormlike creatures. They are found in rocks of all ages from Recent to Proterozoic. Because both trails and burrows are fossils, not rocks, we cannot describe them carefully here. They are worth collecting, however, for they tell a great deal about conditions and life on ancient bottoms and sand flats.

## Mud Cracks
(PLATE 38)

When mud is exposed to the air it dries, shrinks and breaks up into sections or *polygons* much like the columns of shrunken lava, though not so tall. The cracks between polygons generally remain open until water again covers the hardened mud and fills them with new sediment. Both gaps and fillings are found in old rocks in which they go by the name of *mud cracks,* though *sun cracks* and *drying cracks* also are used.

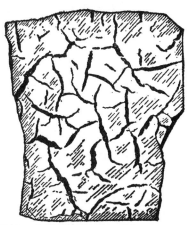

Incomplete mud cracks from Glacier National Park. At the right are actual cracks in a bed of argillite. At the left is a slab of quartzite showing crack fillings, which stand out as ridges on the under side of the bed.

Some mud cracks are very small, while others are long and wide, dividing the beds into polygons as much as sixty inches across. In general, large polygons mean that a thick layer of mud dried, while small ones mean a thin layer.

Many muds shrink so easily that the cracks did not grow long enough to join and make polygons. Drawings show outlines of some common *incomplete* mud cracks. In other strata small cracks cut across laminae at the top of mud layers that already have broken into large polygons divided by wide cracks. In the ancient muds of Glacier National Park these wide cracks cut

[ *269* ]

through the varves of several years, though the narrow ones cut only one or two varves.

In some strata cracks were filled before sediment covered the dried, broken surface. In others the filling is part of the rock overlying the cracked stratum or is cemented to it. When beds split and weather, the lower one goes to pieces or breaks away, leaving the upper as a negative on which the crack fillings stand out as ridges.

Muds of ponds, streams and fresh-water lakes generally curl upward when they shrink into polygons, but those of salt lakes and seas lie flat or turn downward at their edges, the saltiest muds turning downward most sharply. Though there are exceptions to the second half of this rule, it holds good in most cases. Careful search of mud-cracked beds whose polygons are flat or bend downward generally reveals casts of salt crystals (PLATES 38, 40) or marine fossils, both of which mean salty water.

Marine fossils also prove that the beds were deposited in a sea, but if such fossils are lacking, there is a chance that the rocks settled on the bottom of a salt lake. Only careful geologic work will show which of these alternatives is right.

Mud cracks are common in clastic formations of all ages in many parts of the world. There are few places, however, where they are so abundant, varied and attractive as they are in the Proterozoic argillites of Glacier National Park. Fine slabs are to be seen in bridges, in retaining walls and along almost every trail. Mud cracks formed by drying are plentiful in shaly lake limestones of Eocene age along the Lincoln Highway (U.S. 30), east of Green River, Wyoming. They are not common in marine limestones, though a zone of very good ones appears in thinly bedded Devonian limestones of north-central Iowa.

## Rain, Hail and Sleet Prints
### (PLATE 39)

When raindrops fall on wet mud or muddy sand they make round shallow pits surrounded by low ridges. If there are many drops, they overlap, making pits that run together and are indistinct. Hail prints are larger, deeper and have higher ridges; most of them also are oval and are deepest on the sides toward which the hailstones are driven by wind. Sleet prints are small, but they also show the oblique direction which matches the direction in which wind drove them. Ridges seldom are formed.

Like mud cracks and ripple marks, these imprints make negatives when they are covered with sediment. In such negatives the pits become knobs and the rims circular depressions. Marks of all these types are common in the sediments of ancient flood plains, dried ponds and sea shoals which periodically were left bare of water. Rain prints are most common, for rain is commoner than sleet or hail. Moreover, gas bubbles which worked their way to the surface of mud and muddy sand sometimes made pits that cannot be told from rain prints, though they do not resemble hail prints.

## Salt Crystals
### '(PLATES 38, 40)

When fresh-water mud dries it breaks into polygons whose surface may be pitted by rain or hail prints but otherwise is likely to be smooth. As salty mud dries, its surface generally is covered with crystals of precipitated salt. Some of these crystals are so small that they make no impression on the sediment, but others are one fourth to three fourths inch thick. Many are cubes, but a large number have their faces hollowed out till each crystal is a hopper-shaped "skeleton" with only the outlines of a cube. Cubical and skeleton crystals have persisted while the beds of sandy silt in which they lay were covered with other sediment. When the crystals finally did dissolve, silt replaced them grain by grain. On PLATE 38 we see small "fossil" crystals in argillite. Others are found in sandstone and even in shaly limestone or dolomite.

Salt crystals mean salty mud, either of seas or salt lakes. Where the beds are not mud-cracked, crystals probably formed in pools that did not quite dry out. As the water evaporated, however, it became supersaturated, so that the salt precipitated. If mud, silt or sand settled in such water it would cover the crystals and preserve them in specially fine condition. Many of the finest "fossil" crystals are found in beds that show few or no mud cracks.

### Mud Balls and Storm Rollers
(PLATE 42)

Mud balls may consist of mud that is torn from banks and rolled about by currents in streams or shallow bays. Pebbles, sand grains, shells and other things stick to each lump of mud as it rolls along; it may even pick up thin laminae of mud and so grow like a snowball. Ancient balls of this type seem to mean high water, floods or even violent seasonal storms which swept across shallow lakes and sea shoals. They are found in cross-bedded, current-marked rocks of many ages from Proterozoic to Recent. Dark red ones of the "snowball" type may be seen in white or pink quartzites of Glacier National Park, where some argillites show channels made as the mud balls rolled across them. *Adobe balls* are mud balls produced when rains turn weak streams of dry regions into raging torrents that tear lumps of adobe from their banks. These balls also become coated with pebbles.

*Storm rollers* are mud balls that seem to have been torn from submerged muds by storm waves and rolled into shallow water. Such balls have been found on the sandy shoals off Cape May, New Jersey, after storms; the mud seemingly could not have come from the shore. Twisted lumps of hardened mud are common in red shaly sandstones of Silurian age in the lower Niagara Gorge; some of them lie at the ends of channels along which they rolled toward shore.

Many things that have been called storm rollers, especially in central New York, are hardened lumps of very plastic mud that slumped, twisted and even broke soon after they were deposited. Many of these masses have been placed around the parking ground downstream from Taughannock Falls, near the western shore of Cayuga Lake.

*Pudding balls* are formed by water rushing down Western arroyos and gullies after hard rains. Apparently the water picks up so much mud that the lower part of each stream becomes a pasty mixture that rolls over and over instead of flowing. In doing so it makes balls which range from an inch to 15 inches in diameter and are studded with pebbles much as a pudding is studded with fruit. Piles of these balls may be found in channels when the streams run dry. A collector who is caught among badlands of South Dakota or Wyoming during a rain may get many of these balls as well as others of the adobe-ball type.

## Concretions
### (PLATES 41, 42)

Concretions are lumps or masses of mineral matter which generally are harder and more resistant than the sediments around them. They are ball-shaped, oval, flattened and rootlike; some suggest beads fastened together; others branch or even resemble the toy animals made from balls of wood fastened together. Some concretions have pebbles or fossils at their centers, but the great majority do not.

At least fifteen minerals form the cement in concretions, calcite, silica, hematite, limonite, siderite and pyrite being most abundant. Calcite cements the "claystone" concretions of shale and loess; hematite and limonite form the "ironstones" of many sandstones, glacial drift, clays and some limestones, while silica concretions are most plentiful in limestones and sandstones. Siderite is common in clay ironstones, and pyrite concretions are most abundant in dark shales, limestones and coal beds.

The largest concretions are found in sandstone: those of the Tertiary Wilcox formation, in Texas, are as much as 30 feet long. Loglike sandstone concretions of Cretaceous (Laramie) age are 100 feet in length, and concretions 12 feet in diameter are found in the Dakota sandstone of Kansas. Chert and flint concretions generally are a few inches in diameter, though chert concretions 5 feet long have been described. Most claystones are only a few inches long, but those found in Ice Age clays of New Jersey and southern New England have attractive and often beautiful shapes.

Still more attractive, though rare, are *variscite nodules* of Nevada and Utah, one of which is shown on the FRONTISPIECE. It formed in limestone, beginning as a nodule of phosphate. This material apparently was replaced by a jellylike compound of aluminum, phosphorus, iron and water that formed the bright green mineral called variscite. As the jelly hardened it shrank and cracked, and the cracks were filled by other minerals whose colors range from blue gray to yellow. The variscite and sometimes another green mineral called wardite are cut for gem stones.

ORIGINS.—We may divide concretions into two general groups: those that formed at the same time as the sediments around them and those that developed later, generally after those sediments hardened. To the former belong lumps of calcite, pyrite and other minerals that are dredged from the sea bottom today. Many ancient formations also contain concretions of iron oxide, calcite, claystone and chert or flint which evidently began as lumps of stiff jellylike material that formed on sea floors. Some of them apparently were rolled over and over, picking up shells as they went. As the jelly hardened, the shells were petrified. Other gelatinous lumps apparently gathered around leaves or sticks in swampy lakes. The limy concretions called coal balls, which contain perfectly preserved fossils, apparently consist of material which seeped into coal beds when they sank under shallow seas.

Perhaps the largest number of concretions have been formed by water seeping through shale, sandstone and limestone. In some places they dissolved minerals and carried them away; in others they deposited this material in the form of concretions. Some of these minerals filled cavities in the rock; others replaced it molecule by molecule; some merely were deposited in older rocks, where they sometimes pushed the original material aside. No one has satisfactorily explained any of these modes of formation, nor do we know why many concretions took on complicated symmetrical shapes.

### Septaria
(PLATE 41)

Septaria are concretions crossed by networks of cracks in which minerals have been deposited from solution. Most septaria are claystones. Calcite is the commonest mineral filling their cracks; it may be clear and crystalline or amorphous and iron-stained, or both in a single septarium. Crystals of barite, selenite, pyrite and a few other minerals are found in the veins, especially in septaria from Cretaceous shales of Nebraska. Weathered specimens look much like fossil turtles, and that is their common name.

The veins in septaria generally are less than 2 inches wide, enlarging toward the center. This may mean that the outer part of the concretion expanded, cracking the center and pulling it apart; it also may mean that the center shrank greatly after the outer layers hardened. So much mineral matter may have been deposited in cracks that they spread more and more widely and at last broke through to the surface. Septaria whose cracks are filled by quartz may have had the rest of their material dissolved, leaving only the veins as an angular framework.

OCCURRENCE.—Septaria are common in both Paleozoic and

Mesozoic rocks; specially fine ones occur in Cretaceous formations of the West, Devonian beds of New York, Pennsylvania and Ohio and late Carboniferous rocks of the Mississippi Valley.

## Geodes
### (PLATE 41)

A geode is a nodule or irregular ball of rock containing a hole partly filled with crystals, minerals in layers, or both. Quartz is the commonest of these minerals, calcite is second in abundance, while dolomite and even selenite and sphalerite occur. Many geodes formed when seeping water deposited material from solution on the walls of cavities in bedrock; geodes of this sort often are larger than others. Some began with deposition inside shells or other fossils; when enough material was deposited it broke the shell, spread it and filled the cracks as well as the cavity. Such geodes look like small septaria. Many geodes have been filled, becoming solid nodules of minerals; such nodules provide many of our finest banded, or concentric, agates. Lacking cavities, however, they no longer are geodes.

*Rattlestones* generally are geodes from which a central part has been loosened, so that it rattles when shaken. Ironstone concretions also may have cores of uncemented sand which can be shaken. The sand probably was freed by solution of cement that once held it firm.

Geodes are specially common in early Carboniferous limestones of the Mississippi and Ohio valleys but are found in many other formations.

## Stylolites
### (PLATE 40)

We generally see stylolites as jagged, irregular lines that run through strata of limestone, dolomite or marble, though they also have been found in sandstone and shale. They were first noticed in 1751 by a German who compared them with petrified wood. In 1828 another German described them as fossils, naming them *Stylolites sulcatus*.

Actually stylolites are vertically ridged and fluted columns, cones and domes separated by jagged, uneven surfaces. If there are large biscuit-shaped fossils in the rock, stylolites are almost sure to cut into them. Upon each surface, and especially at the ends of columns, there is a layer of clay or sand which represents insoluble material that is scattered through the rock. This insoluble cap, as well as the occurrence of stylolites, suggests that they were made by a combination of solution and pressure in rocks which were not yet hard. Helped by water and the weight of overlying strata, particles of rock began to dissolve one another, pushing the insoluble material upward or downward. Since solution was not uniform, it made the irregular columns and cones. Once one of these began, solution carried it through even such things as corals, which were much harder than the rock in which they lay.

## Cone-in-Cone
### (PLATE 42)

This structure generally consists of a "nest" of concentric cones, though it may contain only one set piled one above another. Shapes and sizes vary greatly, some cones being only a half inch high though others are as much as 80 inches. Most cone-in-cone is dominantly calcareous, though as much as 60 per cent of the material may be clay; gypsum cone-in-cone has been found in Kansas and siderite in Oklahoma.

The cones themselves are ribbed, fluted, striated or covered by triangular ridges or "scales"; depressions covering the cones are crossed by sharp parallel ridges. Generally they seem to have been formed by pressure which forced soft material upward through weak places. Solution of calcite above and around new cones allowed them to work their way into older ones above without splitting them, the dissolved mineral being precipitated in near-by cavities and joints. In some beds the pressure was developed as a concretion formed; in others it was developed during uplift of the land or the building of mountains a few miles away. Near the Belt Mountains of Montana series of saucer-shaped "cones" were developed under concretions. Near Glacier Park columns of clay were squeezed upward through clay, producing rosettes of small and very attractive cone-in-cone.

## Dendrites
(PLATE 40)

Dendrites often are mistaken for petrified moss or other plants. They are dark branching deposits, commonly pyrolusite, precipitated upon layers or fracture faces of limestone, dolomite and even chert. Some dendrites are united by dark bands which suggest thin, hardened layers of soil. Dendritic structures of pyrite sometimes are found in shale. Though dendrites are common in many regions, the finest ones are found on thin layers of limestone at Solenhofen, Bavaria. In agates and some cherts, dendrites have been covered with later deposits of silica. Where these were clear they produced *moss agates* of good quality. Specially fine "tree" agates have come from India.

## Landscape Marble
(PLATE 40)

Some "landscape" marbles are true marbles, with tree-shaped coloration produced by chlorite, iron or other impurities. The sort often seen in museums, however, is polished slabs cut from nodules of limestone found in Triassic marls of Devonshire, England. The lower part of each nodule consists of fairly regular dark and light laminae, while those of the upper part are crumpled. Between the two is a pale gray or buff layer crossed by dark treelike markings that sometimes contain pyrite.

According to one theory the dark parts of these nodules once

[ *278* ]

were mud mixed with vegetable matter that decayed and produced gases. As bubbles of the gas moved about, it disturbed the mud and allowed most of the dark material to rise, forming the landscape markings. This explains why the upper layers arch over every "tree," which supposedly pushed them upward. Rather similar, though much less perfect, markings have been found in some American limestones, but little attention has been given to them.

## Sedimentary Dikes
### (PLATE 42)

Many shale and clay formations of the West contain dikes of sandstone, shale, clay or a mixture of these materials; some even consist of volcanic ash or clay and chalcedony. In form they resemble igneous dikes, and they often stand out in walls or ridges as the beds around them are worn away. Many are crossed by both horizontal or vertical joints which make them look like crude masonry walls. In fact, several of the most spectacular sedimentary dikes are supposed to be ruins of prehistoric forts and are so exhibited to tourists.

Sedimentary dikes have at least three different origins, which we may trace in well-known examples. The first may be seen near the town of Rockwall, some 20 miles northeast of Dallas, Texas, where dikes consist of alternating layers of clay and sandstone, the latter now broken into flat blocks. These alternating layers seem to mean that the material settled in wide cracks that opened in a sea bottom when earth movements widened joints. Some persons believe that the clay and sand were squeezed upward from below, but this explanation hardly fits the regular, alternating layers.

Squeezing does explain dikes east of the Black Hills in South Dakota. Here beds of black, firm shale lay upon other beds of wet, plastic sand which hardened very slowly. When the shale cracked and began to settle, the wet sand was squeezed upward through the cracks, where it finally was cemented into sandstone. Similar squeezing produced the dikes shown on PLATE 42. Notice that the center of each dike consists of stone that is much softer than the sides.

The Oligocene clays of the White River Badlands, east of the Black Hills, contain dikes of a third type. They apparently formed during Miocene times, when the clays settled and began to shrink. This opened a great many cracks, which were filled by sand, mud and volcanic ash from beds higher in the series of shrinking strata. Chalcedony often was deposited along the walls of these dikes. Cracks too narrow to take clastic sediment were filled with chalcedony alone. Great numbers of both veins and dikes may be seen near the little town of Scenic, where pieces of chalcedony may be picked up by the thousand. Some are sheets several inches across, which make interesting specimens.

## CHAPTER XVII

# Heat, Movement and Change

Visitors to Glacier National Park see cliffs where diorite forms dark sills 50 to 100 feet in thickness. Above and below these sills are bands of white rock that form ledges on many an ice-carved wall or peak.

Some tourists glance at the ledges and go on. Others notice that the bands of white rock are harder and more brittle than the dolomites above or below them. They also are more massive, and some of them consist of crystalline grains, unlike material in the gray strata. Though the white rock still shows bedding planes and even mud cracks, something has removed some of its materials and remade others. In short, it has become a *metamorphic* rock, and the processes that brought it to its present state are known as *metamorphism*.

## METAMORPHISM ALTERS ROCKS

Metamorphism literally means "a change in form." To the geologist it signifies any alteration in structure, texture or mineral composition, *providing that change notably modifies the original character of a rock*. Ordinary compaction and cementation of sediments, described in Chapter IX, do not meet this requirement. Though some of them really are the first steps in the production of such rocks as slate and the white crystalline beds of Glacier National Park, they are not included in metamorphism.

This is a fortunate restriction. Even when ordinary compaction and cementation are ruled out, metamorphism still includes two—some authorities say three or four—main methods of rock change, involving at least six different agents that operate in varied combinations. They affect igneous rocks, sedimentary rocks and rocks that already have been metamorphosed. Whatever the materials on which they work, these processes always compress or compact them, producing rocks that are physically and chemically more dense than they were before metamorphosis.

We may recognize two principal types of metamorphism: *igneous* and *dynamic*. The former, which often is called contact metamorphism, includes changes caused by direct contact with hot igneous rocks as well as by heat, water, steam and other gases that come from them. Dynamic metamorphism includes the changes caused by earth movements and compression as well as those which are caused by downward pressure and the action of water—providing they go beyond mere compaction and cementation. We shall see, however, that heat and water increase the effects of compression, while squeezing and movement may play their part in contact metamorphism.

Many geologists apply the term "regional" metamorphism to processes that have changed the rocks of great areas such as the Appalachians and northeastern Canada. Actually these processes seem to be no more than a combination of dynamic and igneous metamorphism on a large scale and hardly require a special name.

We also should mention a minor type of metamorphism, generally called *geothermal*. It operates where sediments are bent downward in great basins that sink through millions of years. Such rocks are covered by later deposits that become 4, 6 or even 10 miles thick. Under such coverings the rocks are subjected to enormous pressure, and they also receive a great deal of heat from the deeper parts of the crust. If their minerals are of the right sorts, the combination of heat and pressure causes them to change or recombine.

Some authors use geothermal metamorphism to explain very hard shales and hard coal, or anthracite, though the latter seems to have been produced by folding that crumpled and raised the

Sill and metamorphosed zones in Glacier National Park. Zones of white marble lie below and above a diorite sill along the Continental Divide.

Appalachian Mountains. The best example of geothermal metamorphism is furnished by the potash-salt deposits of Germany. Their original salts were precipitated in a shallow briny sea or lagoon during Permian times; then they sank until they were covered by 20,000 feet of other sedimentary rock. At the same time the temperature of the sinking salt beds rose to about 200 degrees centigrade. Because of this heat, as well as great pressure, the salts recombined, making many new minerals.

## MAGMAS CAUSE IGNEOUS METAMORPHISM

We gave hot igneous rocks as the cause of contact, or igneous, metamorphism; we might almost have specified magmas. Lava flows have little effect on rocks over which they pass, for they soon surround themselves on bottom, top and sides with a coat of nonconducting scoria. (PLATE 21.) This resists the passage of heat so well that lava actually has been known to flow over snowbanks near the top of Mount Etna. There also are places where lava heated soft coal until it became coke, turned limestone into quicklime and "fired" beds of clay until they became hard red rocks resembling brick. All these, however, are too unusual and too limited to be important in metamorphism.

The sills of Glacier National Park were more effective than lavas, yet they changed the older rocks in zones which are only 10 to 20 feet thick. Many sills have done even less, for they were formed by magmas containing few substances that could dissolve minerals or combine with them. Sills also were hampered by the fact that they spread between strata instead of across them. Even laccoliths, which arched beds of rock upward, show this limitation. Dikes, stocks and batholiths, which cut across bedding planes, are much more important metamorphic agents.

The greatest zones of igneous metamorphism surround and cover batholiths, where temperatures near the magma ranged from 870 to 1200 degrees centigrade (1598 to 2192 degrees Fahrenheit). Beyond this intensely heated zone was a much thicker one which was not so hot and in which changes depended chiefly on solutions that came from the cooling igneous rock. Most large magmas were rich in these solutions, and they also exerted great pressure. For a distance of several miles around one batholith limestones were crushed and then cemented into breccia. Near other batholiths the surrounding rocks were squeezed and crumpled, while magma was squeezed out in thin sheets that now alternate with layers and irregular blocks of the surrounding, and therefore older, *country rock* (PLATE 45). When the blocks of country rock were broken loose and imbedded in magma they became inclusions, which are described in Chapter V.

## THE COURSE OF IGNEOUS METAMORPHISM

Let us now trace the course of metamorphism near a dike cutting shales, sandstones and limestones. If the magma contained much water it absorbed some of the rocks around it by a process in which melting and solution combined. The magma also heated rocks which it did not absorb, raising some of them to temperatures of 600 to 800 degrees centigrade: 1112 to 1472 degrees on the Fahrenheit scale. Such heat baked the shale into a very hard variety of argillite, turned sandstone into quartzite and forced calcite grains to become crystalline, altering the limestone to marble. Since the dike's supply of heat was limited, all these changes took place in two thin *contact zones* resembling those above and below the sills in Glacier National Park.

When we consider a batholith we find that heat was not the sole cause of metamorphism, even near great intrusions. Indeed, it was much less important than substances which, though they were part of the magma, went into the country rock.

The most plentiful of these substances was water, both as liquid and as steam. We have just seen that water helped some small magmas rise by dissolving part of the rock which they encountered. Large "wet" magmas contain vastly more water than there was in any dike, and this supply was concentrated when the molten rock crystallized. As we found in the discussion of pegmatite dikes, magmatic water also contained an enormous store of dissolved minerals which it dropped as soon as conditions changed.

Conditions were bound to change. Magmatic water was under tremendous pressure, which forced it out of the batholith and into the country rock. There it penetrated cracks and pores, leaving molecules of quartz or other compounds in spaces that were not too hot. At the same time the water dissolved minerals from the country rock and carried them away. Some of these dissolved substances combined with others; as the water cooled or became saturated, the least soluble of these new compounds also were precipitated. In impure sandstone, for instance, molecules of kaolin, calcite, feldspar and mica recombined, forming crystals of chlorite, epidote and other minerals that turned the rock green, blue gray or even black. In impure limestone, silica joined calcium oxide and other substances, making wollastonite, pyroxene, plagioclase and some types of garnet. When water was accompanied by such gases as chlorine, fluorine and boric acid (as it generally was) they produced tourmaline, vesuvianite and still other minerals characteristic of igneous metamorphism.

When new minerals merely filled cracks and pores that already were present the process is called *injection*—a term also applied to the filling of cavities by almost water-thin magmas that then proceeded to harden. Often, however, water produced cavities by solution before it filled them with other minerals. This was *replacement,* also called *metasomatism.* It generally took place some distance from great intrusions, at temperatures below 570 degrees centigrade, or 1060 degrees Fahrenheit. Replacement of feldspar by apatite is shown on PLATE 43.

Since hot water can travel a long way, rocks were changed in a thick zone surrounding the batholith. Nor were such effects limited to regions of typical igneous intrusion. Almost all gneisses and schists, and many schistose marbles, show the results of replacement even though they are regarded as dynamically metamorphosed rocks.

Many igneously metamorphosed rocks are banded. It once was the fashion to say that the thickest of these bands were produced when formations surrounding great magmas became so hot and so impregnated with water that they flowed. Such flowing movement supposedly allowed minerals to be sorted out in layers as distinct as those of sediments. It now seems that many bands were developed during layer-by-layer replacement of the sort that produced the banded schists and granites shown on PLATE 13, while others are the remains of original beds or bands developed when partly hardened magmas flowed, making imitation gneisses.

## MOVEMENT HAS ALTERED ROCKS

Let us now turn to the dynamic changes that produced the slates of eastern Pennsylvania. In Ordovician times, about 300,-000,000 years ago, these slates were layers of black mud on the bottom of a shallow sea. As epochs passed, the mud hardened by the processes of compaction and cementation described in Chapter IX. At the same time the sea basin sank, allowing vast amounts of new sediment to settle upon the hardening mud. After some 200,000,000 years our slates-to-be were firm shales that lay beneath younger formations 5 to 6 miles in thickness.

As the Paleozoic Era came to an end eastern North America was squeezed by rocks beneath the Atlantic Ocean. They pushed the hardened sea muds upward, shoved them miles toward the west and crumpled them into huge, high folds. In the end those folds formed the Appalachian Mountains, which stretch from eastern Canada into Georgia and Alabama.

We can tell what happened to the shales without much difficulty. They first were bent into low upward and downward arches. Then they were squeezed into sharp folds by pressure so great that it raised the 6 miles of rock above them and crumpled the shales into mountains. Had the process involved nothing more than lifting, it would have demanded 150,543,-360,000 foot-pounds of work to put a single cubic foot of shale where it now could be reached by quarrymen.

Mountain building, however, did not *lift* rocks. It pushed them from one side, which was a very different matter. In

Pennsylvania and some other Eastern states thrusting was so intense and lasted so long that it compressed beds, forced them to break and slip past each other and crowded them into much less space than they once occupied. It also developed considerable heat by friction, just as we can develop heat by pounding iron, rubbing pieces of stone together or squeezing lead in a vise.

Heat developed by friction helped water that was present throughout the rocks to crystallize such minerals as quartz and mica, many of which are flat. Pressure forced many of these crystals and other mineral grains to lie in one general direction, oblique or at right angles to the direction of pressure. Since the beds were folded into various positions at different places, cleavage cut across strata at many angles. This is shown by the quarry, fold and single block of slate on PLATE 45. The surface of that block is a cleavage face, while its stratification appears as light and dark bands that run across the cleavage surface.

## WATERS AIDED DYNAMIC METAMORPHISM

The change from shale into slate was truly dynamic, caused by movement, pressure and the heat which they produced, with only slight action by water that sank into the shifting ground. Such agents also turned sandstone into quartzite, but they did not develop marble nor intensely metamorphosed rocks. To do that another agent was needed: one that was lacking from the slate region of Pennsylvania but plentiful in southern New England. There granite magmas worked their way upward during folding, producing many large batholiths which sent out hot magmatic water that kept on rising through pores in the country rock of large areas. When that water reached beds of limestone it turned them into marble; it also turned slate into schist and changed granite into foliated gneiss. In other places serpentine, soapstone and asbestos rock were produced by water that worked its way through pores of rocks that were being folded and sheared. The metamorphic granites of PLATE 13 and Chapter VI also were developed by magmatic water.

Such changes were brought about by replacement, which we already have discussed. They show that the division between igneous and dynamic metamorphism is not as sharp as it is bound to appear in a book that must go from one subject to another. There is movement, pressure and crumpling during intrusion; solutions from magmas work their way into rocks that are being changed dynamically. Indeed, it is hard to imagine really intense dynamic metamorphism without the help of water and solutions, most of which have come from magmas. As one authority puts it, "dynamic action in perfectly dry rocks probably is ineffective."

At least it is vastly less effective than it was supposed to be twenty years ago.


## METAMORPHISM MAKES FOLIA

Probably the most distinctive feature of dynamically metamorphosed rocks is their structure, which allows them to split into flakes, sheets or slabs. As we found in examining slate, this structure depends chiefly on the parallel arrangement of platy minerals. It is called *foliation,* from the Latin word for leaf. The minerals most effective in producing foliation are mica (especially muscovite and biotite) and the chlorites. These minerals form thin plates with perfect cleavage; when they are arranged in parallel series they allow the rock to split.

The granite gneiss from Colorado (PLATE 46) shows very imperfect foliation. Its quartz was turned into tiny grains, its feldspar was partly crushed and its biotite was "shredded" or squeezed and recrystallized in irregular streamers. Still greater pressure, heat and replacement would have divided this rock into distinct crumpled folia like those of the granitoid gneiss from North Carolina, also shown on PLATE 46. Comparable metamorphism would have turned the slates of PLATE 45 into crumpled schists. Schist made foliate by igneous metamorphism is shown on PLATE 45.

## TIME ALSO WAS IMPORTANT

There remains one important factor in both contact and dynamic metamorphism, at which we have barely hinted. It is *time*—time that often extended beyond human comprehension. A dike or sill might cool in a few years, but a batholith remained hot for hundreds of centuries. The uplift of any major mountain system, such as the Appalachians, involved hundreds of thousands—probably many millions—of years. In several areas of intense metamorphism both intrusion and uplift were repeated, each through long epochs.

All this was important. Even violent forces, acting for a short time, could do no more than metamorphose rocks in a small region or zone. During epochs they could accomplish much more, altering rocks near them thoroughly and affecting others which were miles away. Moderate forces, acting for equally long times, also were able to produce argillites, quartzites and other metamorphic rocks of great thickness and extent. Thus the long periods of geologic time, listed in Chapter IV, become important factors in the alteration of both sedimentary and igneous rocks.

## MOST JOINTS COME FROM EARTH MOVEMENT

In Chapter V we described fractures, called joints, which were produced when magmas cooled, shrank and hardened. Many joints, however, are found in sedimentary and metamorphic rocks. How did they come into existence, and what—if any—is their relationship to the processes of metamorphism?

Suppose we visit a limestone quarry or a gorge worn in brittle shale. Running up and down the quarry wall or obliquely across it are series of joints. Some of them may have formed when lime muds dried and hardened, since these processes also involved shrinking. Most of the joints, however, are too sharp to have come from shrinking alone and are too regular in direction. Some even resemble the cracks produced when a piece of glass is pulled, twisted or intensely squeezed.

All these factors seem to have been involved in the making of joints. The land has risen and sunk many times, rocks straining and bending with every movement, until they finally broke. If such treatment of rocks seems difficult, notice that very little movement can make great numbers of joints. Thus beds of brittle shale which still are horizontal may be crisscrossed by fractures which cut through them as sharply as a knife cuts through cakes of soap.

*Torsion,* or *twisting, joints* were produced when rocks moved upward or downward without folding and without metamorphism. They lie in parallel series which may divide beds into quadrangular blocks that suggest the stones in a wall. Where twisting was intense, however, the joint systems generally are tilted and cut each other obliquely.

*Tension joints* are one result of folding. Where rocks are arched upward they stretch, and unless they are very deeply buried the rocks in those arches finally break. This has happened many times; in weakly cemented beds, such as most sandstones, the fractures separated grains, making irregular joints. In brittle, fine-grained rocks, however, the joints cut directly across beds, making smooth joint faces along which rocks break in walls, columns or blocks when they are exposed to weathering and erosion.

*Compression joints* developed where rocks were intensely folded and squeezed, as they were in dynamic metamorphism. Fractures of this sort are abundant in argillite, slate and phyllite; they also are found in gneiss and some schist. Compression joints generally are inclined and lie in series which divide great masses of rock into blocks, columns or slivers.

## FILLING OF JOINTS MADE VEINS

Joints provide openings along which water can work its way from magmas and so help in contact metamorphism. Ground water also seeps downward through joints, depositing calcite and other minerals. Such *veins* are plentiful in limestone, dolomite and shale, as well as in some moderately metamorphosed rocks. A series of calcite veins filling small joints in limestone is shown on PLATE 40.

Some veins are less resistant than rocks around them, so that they weather into narrow furrows. Others—especially those that are filled with quartz—are more resistant. When a rock cut by such veins is weathered they stand out as ridges or complex networks that suggest coarse honeycombs.

## BREAKING AND MOVEMENT MADE FAULTS

In many places earth movements were too intense to stop with mere fracture, or jointing. Instead rocks were forced upward, downward or sidewise until they moved as well as broke. When movement was greater on one side of the break than the other, it produced a structure known as a *fault*.

Faults have occurred in almost all parts of the country and in almost all kinds of rock. They may be found, therefore, in hills, creek banks, quarry walls and road cuts, as well as in loose boulders of fields and shores. They show best where veins or strata have been displaced, as they are in the block of sandstone shown on PLATE 43. Here several tiny faults are crowded together, their displacement clearly shown by layers of pink, buff and red sandstone.

These *normal faults* are found in regions where there has been neither intrusion nor metamorphism, but they also are common in rocks that have been broken, moved and transformed by magmas. Where there has been dynamic metamorphism, however, rocks were squeezed and folded before being broken. The process is illustrated by diagrams of Glacier National Park. This *thrust fault* is inclined at a low angle and is not so sharp

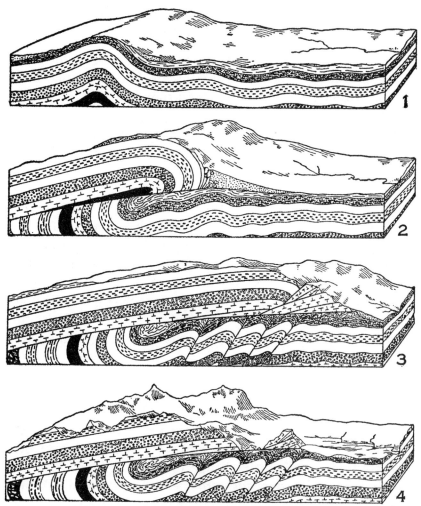

Folding and thrust faulting in Glacier National Park. In 1 the rocks are arching into folds, at the end of the Cretaceous Period. In 2 the strata have folded and broken and are moving eastward along an almost horizontal fault. 3 shows the result of still more movement, with a series of small faults at the front of the moving rock mass; 4 shows the mountains as they are today. Rocks above and below this fault are not greatly metamorphosed.

as the average normal fault. Some thrust faults even follow bedding planes and can be recognized only by changes produced as one rock mass moved against another.

## FAULTING HAS CAUSED METAMORPHISM

Faulting, although it is not an important cause of metamorphism, does change rocks on a small scale. Where normal faults cross sandstones, the moving rocks ground against each other and were heated. With the help of seeping water, pressure and heat sometimes produced a thin "squeeze" of quartzite along the fault plane. In limestone and dolomite the squeeze is likely to be marble.

*Slickensides,* or *slickens,* are much thinner than squeeze zones, being little more than smoothed, scratched surfaces along which moving rock masses rubbed. Rubbing caused friction, which produced heat; heat and water in the rock pores allowed minerals to change or new ones to be deposited. Many slickensides in limestone are covered with quartz, others in marble bear serpentine, while faces of dark diorite are made glossy by green epidote. Even clay may show excellent slickens, with paper-thin zones in which the rock has been altered, with the formation of mica and other minerals.

## FOLDS ARE SIGNIFICANT

We have mentioned folding as one cause of dynamic metamorphism. We sometimes find, however, that rocks have been intensely folded with little change in minerals. This is true of limestones and other deposits in the central Appalachian Mountains and of cherts in the Coast Ranges of California, one example appearing on PLATE 44. Yet the moderately folded rocks of Glacier National Park, shown on the same plate, have been turned into quartzites and argillites which show flat grains of mica and slaty cleavage. Gneiss and schist (PLATES 43, 44 and

46) are much more intensely crumpled. Specimens which show this crumpling often are small enough to go into collections. In addition to being attractive, they help tell the story of dynamically metamorphosed rocks.

CHAPTER XVIII

# Rocks That Have Changed

WE HAVE SEEN that the processes of metamorphism can affect rocks of all sorts. This means that metamorphic rocks include many that once were igneous, others that were sediments and still others that already had been metamorphosed. The changes which these rocks have undergone range from mere hardening, seen in baked clays and in argillite, to transformations in which new series of minerals were produced. Thus common sandstone has become schist with layers of flaky mica, brittle coal has turned into soft graphite and shale has become veined serpentine.

All this seems very complicated—as, indeed, it is. The varieties and gradations of metamorphic rocks are many, each difference recording some special character in the original rock or some feature of the process that changed it. On the other hand, these many variations may be grouped into fewer than a dozen main kinds, or "species." The reason for this is indicated by the following table, which lists a few of the most familiar sedimentary and igneous rocks, with their metamorphic equivalents. Here we see that metamorphism turns rocks which are different into others that are much alike: thus both conglomerate and granite may become gneiss, while shale, tuff, basalt and several other kinds become schist. Varietal groupings also

ORIGINAL, HARDENED AND METAMORPHOSED ROCKS

| LOOSE SEDIMENT | CEMENTED SEDIMENT | SLIGHTLY METAMORPHOSED | METAMORPHOSED | HIGHLY METAMORPHOSED |
|---|---|---|---|---|
| Talus | Breccia | Stretched conglomerate | | |
| Gravel | Conglomerate | Conglomerate quartzite | Gneiss | Schist |
| | | | | |
| Quartz sand | Sandstone | Sandy quartzite | Quartzite | Quartz schist |
| Mud, silt, clay | Shale | Argillite | Slate or phyllite | Schist, serpentine |
| Lime sand, marl, | Limestone | Crystalline limestone | Marble | Talc schist (rare) |
| lime mud, coquina | | | | |
| | Dolomite | Crystalline dolomite | Dolomite marble | Talc schist (rare) |
| | Limonite, siderite | | Magnetite | |
| Peat | Soft coal | | Anthracite | Graphite |

| LOOSE VOLCANIC ROCK | FIRM IGNEOUS ROCK | | METAMORPHOSED | HIGHLY METAMORPHOSED |
|---|---|---|---|---|
| Ash, lapilli | Tuff | | Meta-tuff | Schist |
| | Basalt (fine-grained) | | | Chlorite schist |
| | Peridotite, dunite | | | Talc schist |
| | Rhyolite, trachyte | | | Schist |
| | Gabbro, dolerite | | Greenstone | Schist |
| | Granite, syenite | | Gneiss | Schist |
| | Magnetite | | Magnetite | |

ignore original nature of the rocks. Thus some talc schists once were peridotite, others dunite and still others iron-bearing marl or dolomite.

In general neither museums nor collectors make a systematic attempt to trace the origin of each metamorphic rock. Quartzite, slate, phyllite and marble can be distinguished as modified sediments; so can gneiss which contains traces of pebbles, or schist in which some fossils survive. On the other hand, a gneiss or schist containing phenocrysts is apt to be igneous. When such clues are lacking it is enough to place a specimen in one of the recognized metamorphic species or varieties, without thought of its original nature.

The minerals of metamorphic rocks are much the same as those of the sedimentary and igneous groups. A few, however, are found principally or exclusively in metamorphics: these are kyanite, staurolite, tremolite, grossularite and wollastonite. Grossularite, a garnet containing calcium and aluminum, is found chiefly in metamorphosed limestones. It therefore is in contrast to pyrope, the "precious" garnet, which is found in both peridotite and metamorphosed igneous rocks.

## IMPORTANT METAMORPHIC ROCKS

### Gneiss
#### (PLATES 1, 46)

Gneiss is a banded rock that generally looks like granite. It contains quartz, feldspar and mica in grains large enough to be seen without a lens. Its bands may be straight, wavy or crumpled and of uniform or variable thickness. The feldspars belong to various kinds and are white, gray or red; they usually are shapeless or elongate grains that can be distinguished by their cleavage. Quartz also forms irregular grains but with conchoidal fracture and waxy luster. The mica is biotite, muscovite or a mixture of both; it consists of flakes, narrow strips and irregular pieces most of which lie along the bands. Hornblende is found in some gneisses, garnets in others and epidote in many. Fissility is poorly to well developed, being greatest in gneisses that are distinctly banded and contain much mica.

VARIETIES.—Gneisses differ according to the rocks from which they formed and the minerals in them. Thus we have *granite gneiss, syenite gneiss, hornblende gneiss,* and so on. Some gneisses show pebbles; the one used to make the ax of PLATE I looks much like quartzite, from which it was developed. The name gneiss alone generally means *mica gneiss,* probably formed by metamorphosis of granite containing much mica. Gneiss developed from pegmatite contains slightly changed inclusions of the original rock and very beautiful orthoclase crystals.

ORIGIN.—Much gneiss was produced by metamorphism under great heat and pressure, such as were developed when mountain ranges were built. Other gneiss was developed by hot solutions coming from deeply buried magmas, in the manner already described for metamorphic granites (Chapter VI). The nature of the original rock is doubtful if metamorphism has gone very far. In general sedimentary gneisses are associated with marble, quartzite and sedimentary schist. Igneous gneisses have the chemical make-up of such rocks as granite, syenite or diorite; they do not contain pebbles.

OCCURRENCE.—Gneisses are found in all parts of the world; some of the greatest masses are of Archeozoic age, though younger ones are well known, especially in New England. Gneisses are common in the Rockies, northeastern Canada and the Appalachians; good exposures of gneiss may be seen in Bronx and Central parks, New York. Thick masses of gneiss also form the cores of the Himalayas, mountains of Scandinavia and Scotland and the Harz Mountains of Germany. "Gneiss" itself is a term which the Harz miners long have used for crystalline rock in which mineral veins occur.

## Schist
### (PLATES 13, 43, 45, 46)

The schists are a group of metamorphic rocks that have much finer texture than gneisses, though the two groups intergrade. True schists consist of thin crystalline plates or layers which lie parallel to one another and generally are very much crumpled. These layers (folia) are much more distinct than those of gneiss and can be told from sedimentary layers by the facts that they are not continuous over wide areas and are made up of flat crystal grains, not particles broken or rounded by erosion nor produced by precipitation.

VARIETIES.—Like gneisses, schists fall into two main groups: those derived from sedimentary rocks and those originally igneous. The former are much the more abundant; in some cases they preserve traces of bedding planes and even fossils. As the following descriptions indicate, however, each of the principal varieties of schist contains rocks of both igneous and sedimentary origin.

*Mica schist* (PLATE 46) is the commonest schist and the most abundant of all metamorphic rocks. The purest form is composed of mica and quartz in thin, alternating, wavy folia; when the mica is muscovite, such schist is silvery white or pale gray. Feldspar, hornblende and some carbonaceous material generally are present, coloring the rock gray or blackish. Dark micas give yellowish, brown or greenish tints. Crystals of garnet, epidote and other minerals commonly are present. Mica grains are flat and so abundant that they allow the rock to split easily along the folia, which they cover so thickly that the quartz can be seen only with a lens. Most mica schist is intensely metamorphosed slate or shale, though one variety began as conglomerate and still preserves some of its pebbles. White mica schists were produced by metamorphism of felsite and pale granites.

*Quartz schist* consists of quartz and white mica; it originally was micaceous or feldspathic sandstone or sandstone which contained considerable shale. It grades into highly metamorphosed quartzite.

*Tourmaline schist* (PLATE 46) contains crystals of tourmaline in addition to the usual schist minerals. In the specimen illustrated the tourmaline was deposited by hot solutions from a magma or pegmatite dike, which further metamorphosed the surrounding schist. Other tourmaline schists are metamorphosed igneous or replacement deposits.

*Talc schist* is a variety in which talc is the dominant mineral. Hornblende, magnetite, chlorite and some other minerals may be present. The talc appears in fine scales or foliated masses; quartz may occur as individual grains, lenses or veins. The rock is rather soft, has a greasy feel and has pronounced cleavage; its colors range from white to green or dark gray; a waxy luster is common. Some talc schists are altered igneous material such as peridotite or dunite, while others are undoubtedly of sedimentary origin and represent ferruginous marls or dolomites.

Talc schist does not make great formations but occurs with other metamorphic rocks in eastern Canada, along the Appalachian Mountains from New England to Georgia, in California and Oregon and in Brazil, Germany and other regions. It is an important source of the mineral talc.

*Chlorite schist* contains chlorites as the principal minerals. It generally is yellow green, blue green or very dark green in color and contains crystals of magnetite, hornblende, epidote, calcite, dolomite and other minerals. Quartz is present as lenses and veins. Some chlorite schists are metamorphosed beds of ash or fine-grained lava, but many are altered shales and iron-bearing clays. Chlorite schists are commonly associated with talc schists and form bands or masses among mica schists and gneisses.

OCCURRENCE.—Schists are found in most areas of great dynamic metamorphism, such as the Alps, Scotch Highlands, Scandinavia and both eastern and western North America. They range from Archeozoic to Jurassic in age: the schists of eastern Canada began as sediments in Pre-Cambrian and Paleozoic times, while those in the Mother Lode belt of California were Carboniferous shales, and many schists in the Alps were Jurassic mud deposits. There are excellent exposures of schist in New York, Baltimore, Washington and some other Eastern cities.

## Amphibolites and Hornblende Schists
### (PLATE 47)

The amphibolites are a large group of metamorphic rocks that consist partly or largely of amphibole; augite, chlorite, garnet, feldspar, quartz and mica also are present in varying amounts, the last three being the most easily distinguished. In coarse varieties the amphibole generally occurs as slender prisms or blades which may be more than an inch long. In fine varieties the grain may be so minute that individual minerals cannot be seen, even with a good lens; such rocks look like slates. Colors range from light green and yellow green to dark green or black, the darkest shades being most common. Amphibolites are hard, brittle when highly schistose, and heavy, their specific gravity ranging from 3 to 3.4. Though many amphibolites are schistose, some are massive and very tough.

VARIETIES.—As with most other metamorphic rocks, definitions are not very precise. One scheme divides these rocks into true amphibolites and hornblende or amphibolite schists. Since this division matches the appearance of these rocks, it is the one we shall use.

*Amphibolites,* in this sense, are massive, commonly dark rocks that may contain considerable feldspar. The prisms and grains of feldspar are so interwoven there is no cleavage. Rocks of this sort generally are found in the midst of gneisses and mica schists, most of which apparently were developed from igneous rocks.

*Hornblende,* or *amphibolite, schists* are schistose rocks whose amphibole prisms are arranged in parallel positions, producing cleavage. This cleavage may be further developed by plates of mica, which in some cases are so plentiful that the rock grades into mica schist.

ORIGINS.—Both their occurrence and their minerals show that most amphibolites, and many amphibolite schists, are metamorphosed gabbros, dolerites, diabases and peridotites. Some of the original minerals commonly remain, so that transitional stages between gabbro or diabase and amphibolite are common.

Greywackes, as well as impure limestones which contained sand, clay and iron compounds, commonly were metamorphosed into hornblende and other amphibolite schists. In this process water and carbon dioxide were forced out of the rock, while lime, iron, magnesia and alumina combined with silica, forming amphiboles. Thus hornblende schist sometimes became the final stage in metamorphism of marble.

OCCURRENCE.—Amphibolites and amphibolite schists generally occur as narrow bands or circular or elliptical masses in the midst of gneisses and schists. The former represent sills, dikes and sedimentary deposits; the latter are metamorphosed stocks or bosses. The rocks themselves are widely distributed in northeastern Canada, in the metamorphosed belt which extends from New England to Georgia, in the Lake Superior region and the Sierra Nevada Mountains. They also are found in England, Scotland, the Alps and other parts of Europe.

## Soapstone
(PLATE 2)

Soapstone is a massive dark gray, green or greenish gray rock without cleavage but with a silvery or satiny fracture. It is a mixture of talc and chlorite scales tangled together, with amphibole, serpentine, quartz and other minerals as impurities. Soapstone is very soft and can be sawed or cut into blocks and slabs of almost any size and thickness. These resist both heat and acids and are used for sinks and table tops in chemical laboratories, for electrical switchboards, hearthstones, mantels, etc. Indians and other Stone Age peoples carved soapstone into orna-

[ *303* ]

mental figures as well as into dishes and pots for cooking. Because of this latter use, soapstone is sometimes called *potstone*.

*Steatite* is a compact, massive rock closely resembling soapstone, though it is lighter in color. It is composed mainly of talc which is minutely crystalline to finely granular.

OCCURRENCE.—Soapstone commonly occurs as lenses associated with schists, gneisses and igneous rocks. Deposits are found in regions of dynamic metamorphism in many parts of the world. In the United States the chief deposits of commercial value are in New York, Vermont, California, North Carolina, Georgia, Maryland, New Jersey and Pennsylvania.

## Greenstone

Greenstone is a rock in which chlorite is abundant, producing pale gray green, yellow green or dark green colors. The rock is massive and generally is rather soft, with structure too compact for the mineral grains to be determined. Much greenstone has been made by metamorphism of gabbro and dolerite; if those rocks contained amygdules, little balls or spots of calcite and quartz may be found. Deposits in which shearing and compression have developed folia are called *greenstone schists*. Greenstone is found in New England and the central Appalachians, northern Michigan and Minnesota, England and mountainous parts of Europe.

## Serpentine
### (PLATES 2, 46)

This rock consists of masses of the mineral serpentine mixed with hornblende, olivine, pyroxene, magnetite and other minerals. Serpentine usually is compact, has a waxy luster and a smooth or splintery fracture and can be cut with a knife unless it contains enough silica to make it hard. The color is yellowish green, yellow, brown, olive or green so dark that it is almost black. Some masses are clouded and translucent, but the serpentine most commonly used is crossed by a network of white or

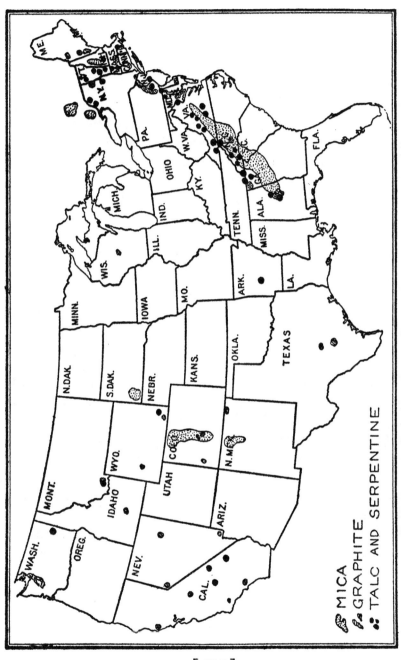

Important deposits of mica, graphite, talc and serpentine. All are products of metamorphism, though graphite also is found in igneous rocks.

MICA
GRAPHITE
TALC AND SERPENTINE

pale green lines in a dark, opaque mass. Smooth surfaces feel greasy, but the rock is distinguished from talc schist and epidote by its greater hardness.

Serpentine was produced when water from magmas changed basalt, peridotite, dunite and similar igneous rocks or when such water metamorphosed hornblende schists that once were sediments. Rock serpentine is found in many parts of eastern Canada and the United States as well as in California, Oregon, England and Europe. It is used as an ornamental stone ("verd antique marble") and one variety contains nickel ore.

## Magnetite
### (PLATES 6, 48)

As a rock, magnetite is dark gray to black, heavy and granular; most of the grains belong to the mineral for which it is named. Impurities consist of dark hematite, pyrite, quartz, calcite, garnet, apatite, augite and olivine, depending upon the origin of the magnetite and the rocks with which it is associated. Some masses, generally rather small, are so strongly magnetic that they act as true magnets or lodestones.

Magnetite is either an igneous or a metamorphic rock. Igneous masses, produced by segregation of magmas, are described in Chapter XIX. Magnetites in Essex and some other counties of New York apparently were deposited by hot waters from gabbro intrusions, which replaced syenites and other rocks. The whole series later was metamorphosed into gneiss, schist and lenses of very granular magnetite. Some magnetite also may be metamorphosed limonite or clay-ironstone.

The most important deposits of metamorphic magnetite in North America lie in New York, New Jersey and Ontario.

## Itabirite or Specular Hematite Rock
### (PLATE 7)

Itabirite consists principally of micaceous, or specular, hematite and quartz. The hematite is bright, steely gray in color and luster and consists of very thin leaves of irregular outline, suggesting small bits of mica. The quartz is in grains or lumps of grains. Except for its luster, the rock suggests a mica schist, as the exceptionally pure specimen of PLATE 7 shows. Magnetite, mica, pyrite, talc, garnet and other metamorphic minerals are common in variable quantities.

Some itabirite deposits grade into micaceous schist. The rock seems to have been formed by metamorphism of sandstones and sandy shales rich in iron. It is found in the Carolinas, eastern Canada, Norway, Sweden and Germany. It underlies extensive areas in Brazil and the African Gold Coast.

## Quartzite
### (PLATES 1, 46, 47)

Most quartzite is metamorphosed sandstone, with which it intergrades so completely that no distinct division can be made. Typically, quartzite is a very firm, hard rock composed of crystals that have been formed by deposition of quartz around sand grains, whose outlines still can be distinguished. The luster is glassy or greasy like that of quartz; the fracture is uneven, splintery or conchoidal. Grains of feldspar, hematite, chlorite, muscovite and other minerals are present as impurities which commonly give the rock a pink, brownish or brick-red color. Some of these impurities were present as cement in the original sandstone, but others were developed during metamorphosis. When muscovite is present in large amounts it causes the development of folia and cleavage, so that the rock grades into quartz or mica schist. Many beds of quartzite in the Appalachian region are divided by layers of mica which allow the rock to split into thin flat slabs.

Some quartzites look much like grainy limestones but may be distinguished by their hardness, which is 7, and lack of effervescence. Hardness also separates them from fine-grained felsites, as do stratification, ripple marks and other sedimentary features.

*Conglomerate quartzite* is a variety developed by metamorphism of conglomerate instead of sandstone. Small grains are crystalline, but pebbles commonly retain their original form.

*Siliceous oölite* (PLATE 46) consists of rounded grains of chalcedony which was deposited around sand grains, forming balls like those of true oölite. There commonly is a matrix of amorphous chalcedony between the grains.

*Buhrstone* is a variety of quartzite filled with odd, long pores. Being very hard and tough, it once was used for millstones, or buhrs. It probably began as limestone filled with small fossils. The calcite was replaced by chalcedony and other quartz while the fossils were dissolved, leaving holes. Most buhrstones are of Tertiary age and occur in Massachusetts, Georgia, South Carolina and France.

ORIGIN.—Metamorphism that produced quartzite generally was less intense than that making gneisses and schists. Indeed, some quartzite has been formed when water deposited quartz around sand grains only a few feet below the surface; blocks of quartzite produced in this manner weather out of the loose Reading sands of England. Most quartzites, however, are ancient rocks which have been deeply buried and then lifted into mountains or hills; pressure and some heat seem to have affected them while quartz was being deposited from underground water. Schistose structure and compression of pebbles also show the effects of great pressure such as is developed during uplift. Some quartzite shows igneous metamorphism; in this case heat and quartz-charged water were the main agents of change.

OCCURRENCE.—Quartzites are common in many parts of the world; most of them are found among early Paleozoic and older sediments. They are very resistant to weathering, making cliffs, towers and ridges.

USES.—Most quartzites are too much shattered by jointing to make good building stones, though such rocks as the Sioux Quartzite of northwestern Iowa and eastern South Dakota are very durable. Crushed quartzite is used in road work and blocks are used in tube mills which grind ores and cement materials.

## Slate
### (PLATE 45)

Slate is a hard, dense and very fine-grained rock that splits into thin layers which cut across bedding planes. This ability to split is called *slaty* cleavage; it distinguishes the rock from argillite, which generally splits only along joints and bedding planes. The commonest minerals in slate are quartz, mica, chlorite and carbonaceous material, none of which forms grains large enough to be seen without a microscope.

Slate is moderately metamorphosed shale, very fine arkose or even tuff. It was formed when rocks were tilted, folded and squeezed during the process of mountain building. The pressure was so great that many of the particles recrystallized and were flattened, often at right angles to the direction of compression. This gave the rock a "grain" that allows it to split easily along the planes of flattening but not across them. Since cleavage planes were made by pressure, they might or might not agree with the original bedding. If the rocks lay flat and were squeezed horizontally, cleavage planes developed at right angles to the beds; if the rocks were tipped or the pressure came obliquely, cleavage oblique to the bedding was produced. In areas of intense folding, such as the slate belt of Pennsylvania, cleavage cuts across bedding at all angles.

*Banded slates* contain beds of different colors, cut by cleavage so that slabs are crossed by color bands representing the strata.

OCCURRENCE.—Most slates are found in regions where shaly formations were folded into mountains. Some are as old as the Keewatin; those of the Alps and California are Jurassic. Most of the American slate deposits that are commercially important lie in Cambrian and Ordovician formations of the Eastern states. Slate is split into slabs for use on roofs and is crushed to give a surface to manufactured roofing. It also is used for black-

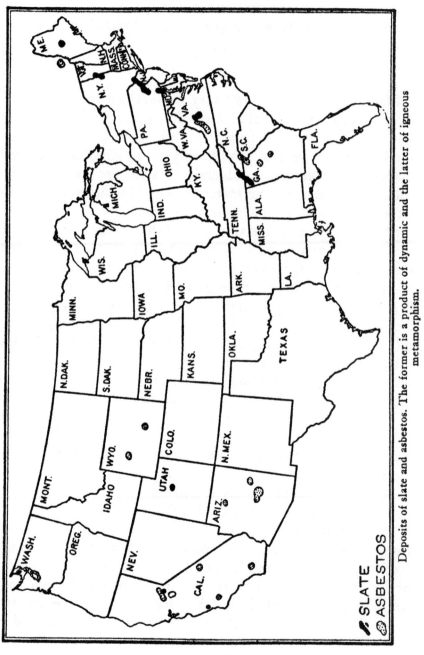

SLATE

ASBESTOS

Deposits of slate and asbestos. The former is a product of dynamic and the latter of igneous metamorphism.

boards, bulletin boards, switchboards, laboratory tables, wainscoting, memorial tablets and breadboards.

## Phyllite

This rock resembles slate in appearance and cleavage. It differs in having been metamorphosed more thoroughly, so that it splits into very thin sheets or leaves that are flat, bent or closely crumpled; these account for the name, which means "leaf stone." It also contains much more mica than does slate, the cleavage sheets being covered with a special form of muscovite that has a silvery surface. Quartz is the second commonest mineral, though it generally cannot be seen clearly; chlorite ranks third in importance. Phyllite is brittle, has a greasy feel, commonly shows satiny luster and is red, yellowish or green in color.

Some phyllites are metamorphosed sediments; others are felsites and tuffs, so intensely compressed and sheared that their feldspars have been turned into mica. Phyllites are commonest in very old rocks in regions where mountains now stand or stood during earlier geologic ages. They are specially abundant in the northern Great Lakes region, the Appalachians and the Alps.

## Hornfels

Hornfels is a very dense, hard rock in which the granules are too small to be seen without a microscope and all trace of original stratification or structure has been destroyed. The fracture is conchoidal and there is no cleavage. Colors range from light gray and pale green to very dark gray, the dark hues being commonest. Such dark rocks look like basalt.

Hornfels was produced by igneous metamorphism of clay, shale, slate, impure limestone and dark igneous rocks, such as biotite and basalt. This metamorphism took place very near the intruding magma. Hornfels therefore is found near hardened intrusions in many parts of the world.

## Marble
(PLATES 40, 47)

Marble is metamorphosed limestone: a granular rock composed of crystalline calcite grains that show excellent cleavage. They reach a half inch in thickness, but the majority are less than one eighth inch thick. In the coarse varieties of marble the fracture surface resembles lump sugar; in the finest it has a soft, rather velvety luster. The hardness is 3, as in calcite; marble is easily scratched by a knife and effervesces strongly in dilute hydrochloric acid. Both characters distinguish it from quartzite, which it may resemble.

Pure marble is white, massive and shows no trace of cleavage. Impurities such as carbon, hematite and other minerals stain the rock gray, buff, yellow, red or black; the color may be uniform but generally is spotted, veined or "marbled." Thin layers within strata generally have been destroyed by metamorphism or are shown only by indistinct, wavy color bands. Such bands help distinguish marble from crystalline limestone, which is only slightly metamorphosed. Some marbles, especially pink varieties from Tennessee, contain well-developed stylolites (PLATE 40), while bands of impurities may produce poor, irregular cleavage.

The lack of cleavage in pure marble is a puzzle, since some marbles are closely associated with schists whose cleavage is well developed. The difference probably depends partly on the purity of the marble, partly on the fact that its grains can turn without flattening and largely upon the ability of calcite molecules to move and adjust themselves to pressure. This allows new crystals to form without any radical change in shape or mineral nature, as happens in schists and slates.

VARIETIES.—From the viewpoint of artists and architects marbles are divided according to color and appearance, with many different names. In general *statuary marbles* are the purest and most massive white kinds, which can be quarried in thick blocks and carved effectively. *Architectural marbles* have uniform texture and color, ranging from white to pink. These rocks can be cut into comparatively thin slabs as well as blocks and are used in columns, walls, floors and steps. *Ornamental marbles* are brightly colored, the colors generally being arranged in patterns by brecciatión or veins.

Geologically, most marbles are either calcitic or dolomitic. *Calcite marble* is the "pure marble" of preceding paragraphs; it was produced by metamorphism of limestone. *Dolomite marble* is metamorphosed dolomite and is a mixture of crystalline dolomite, calcite and other minerals. It is somewhat harder than calcite marble and effervesces very weakly or not at all in dilute hydrochloric acid.

*Brecciated marble* (PLATE 47) is a tectonic breccia whose fragments consist of marble, cemented by variously tinted deposits of calcite that also may be crystalline. It is popular for columns and interior trim. *Cipolino* contains so much mica that it is distinctly foliated. Roman builders used it for temple walls and columns.

As has been said, quarrymen and builders use "marble" as a trade name for almost any limestone or dolomite that can be cut and polished. Thus "madrepore marble" is dark limestone containing fossil corals, while "shell marble" is limestone of various colors whose patterns are produced by fossil shells, crinoids and other remains.

These rocks are noncrystalline and can be ruled out easily, but it is hard to draw a line between true marble and crystalline limestone. In some of the latter, fossils are preserved and there is no trace of squeezing or movement of rock materials. But there also are beds of crystalline rock whose fossils are distorted, whose layers are crumpled or indistinct and whose materials plainly moved as they crystallized. Yet these beds lie between beds of ordinary limestone. Only the evidence of movement allows us to say that these crystalline rocks are marble while the others are not.

ORIGIN.—Marbles of the sort just described probably were crystallized by water that worked its way through beds, with little heat or uplift of the rocks. Others show movement and breaking but few traces of heat.

Small bodies of marble have been produced by contact igneous metamorphism; those of Glacier National Park are examples. Most great marble deposits, however, are in regions of dynamic metamorphism, where rocks were broken and folded. At the same time water bearing dissolved minerals spread out from deeply buried magmas, and these waters may have been responsible for most of the metamorphism. This is specially true of the marbles of New England.

OCCURRENCE.—There are immense deposits of marble in the Pre-Cambrian formations of eastern Canada as well as in Cambrian and Ordovician formations of Vermont, Massachusetts, Georgia, eastern Tennessee, Colorado and other states. Italy and Greece have produced much marble, that of Carrara, Italy, having been used for statuary for about 2000 years. Marble also is found in Germany, Switzerland, Scandinavia and many other parts of the world.

## Lime-Silicate Rocks

There are many gradations between limestones and sandstones or shales. When such intermediate rocks were metamorphosed, carbon dioxide was forced out of the calcite and was replaced by silica, while such gases as fluorine and boracic acid produced other mineral recombinations. When such changes were caused by igneous metamorphism they generally resulted in massive rocks; when dynamic metamorphism was the dominant cause the rocks commonly were well foliated. All contain considerable amounts of silica in various mineral combinations, which explains the term *lime-silicate rocks*.

*Wollastonite rock* is a massive white rock resembling marble but distinguished by its greater hardness. It contains a large proportion of the pyroxene, wollastonite, generally accompanied by diopside (another pyroxene) and hornblende. In North America this rock occurs chiefly in California.

*Garnet rock* consists of garnet grains which may or may not show crystal faces and other minerals, of which calcite is likely to be the most important. There also may be considerable magnetite. The color generally is yellow to reddish brown. Garnet rock occurs in northern New York, New England, Montana, the Alps and other regions.

*Epidote rock,* or *epidosite,* is largely composed of the mineral epidote, with quartz, garnet and other minor minerals in variable amounts. Epidosite is granular to schistose, yellowish green or mottled yellow, green and white in color and commonly is very tough as well as hard. Thin pieces are translucent. Some deposits are metamorphosed sandstones and impure limestones; others once were dark intrusions or lava flows. Variegated deposits are cut for ornamental stones and are polished as low-grade gems. Epidote is found in New England, Brazil, Germany and other regions.

## Jade
### (PLATE 1)

Jade is a name commonly applied to two different sorts of fine-grained metamorphic rocks which are very tough and so can be elaborately carved. During the late Stone Age and the Bronze Age these rocks were made into knives, daggers, hammers and ornaments; many of these have been found in ruins of Swiss lake dwellings. In medieval and modern times the Chinese have been famous for their jade carvings, most of which are made in Peiping.

*Nephrite* sometimes is regarded as the true jade. It consists of compact or fibrous masses of amphibole whose color ranges from green, yellow or gray to white. The specific gravity is about 3 and the hardness about 6. When polished, the rock has a waxy luster and is slightly translucent. Nephrite seems to consist of much-changed serpentine, pyroxene or olivine which first became fibrous amphibole and then was made dense by pressure and earth movement. Much of that used in China comes from quarries in mountains of Turkestan, where it forms veins and pockets in hornblende schists and gneisses. Nephrite also is found in Siberia, New Zealand, Germany and other regions.

*Jadeite* consists of a mineral related to pyroxene; its color generally is pale, though when chromium is present it may be apple or emerald green. Its specific gravity ranges from 3.2 to 3.4, so that it is noticeably heavier than nephrite. It also is somewhat harder but not enough so to interfere with carving.

Some petrographers think that jadeite is a metamorphosed nephelite syenite; others say that it began as a very impure limestone. It is found in Burma, Turkestan, Alaska, British Columbia and Mexico. The Aztecs called it *chalchihuitl*, though they probably applied the same name to turquoise, green microcline and other minerals. Most of the jadeite used by Chinese artists comes from Burma, where boulders that lie in laterite are stained red and so become specially valuable.

## Novaculite and Jaspillite
### (PLATES 1, 43)

Novaculite is a light gray or white rock interbedded with steeply dipping slates and shales in mountains of central Arkansas. The rock has been regarded as metamorphosed chert or siliceous silt; at least some beds are extremely fine-grained sandstone whose fragmental quartz grains are visible under the microscope. Once used by Indians, it now is quarried for high-grade oilstones, though joints and flaws make much of the rock useless. It is a bit surprising to find a modern surgeon sharpening his scalpels on stone that is identical with that in the prehistoric Indian spearhead shown on PLATE 1.

Jaspillite is metamorphosed chert, described with Lake Superior iron ores in Chapter XIII.

## Anthracite
### (PLATE 35)

Anthracite, or metamorphic coal, is described in Chapter XV. It is produced by folding and compression and, on a small scale, by contact metamorphism from dikes, sills or other igneous bodies. Frequently, however, such intrusions produce so much heat that coal becomes a *natural coke.*

CHAPTER XIX

# Ores and Their Origins

METAMORPHISM has changed old rocks into new ones, and in doing so it often made ores. Yet not all ores are metamorphic. Some are igneous, others are sedimentary and still others were produced by weathering. In short, ores have been produced by a variety of processes, some of which have been studied for decades but still are poorly understood.

## WHAT ARE ORES?

Before we go into these matters let us clarify this word *ore*. To many of us it means any rock that contains metal; one widely used dictionary gives that definition. Actually an ore is either a rock or mineral mass from which metal may be extracted with profit. This changes our everyday idea in two ways:

First, it puts emphasis on the fact that metals can be taken out of ores, saying nothing about how they occur in the first place. As a matter of fact, most ores contain metals as parts of minerals which are compounds and which must be crushed, heated and chemically changed before they will yield the metal that is in them. Thus iron ore consists largely of hematite, magnetite, limonite or siderite, while most copper ore contains chalcocite, chalcopyrite, malachite and other compounds that do not look at all like copper and contain such substances as oxygen, sulphur, carbon, water, silica and iron. Lead generally is mined as galena, tin as cassiterite, zinc as sphalerite, and so on. Although copper ores of northern Michigan contain pure copper, gold and silver are the only familiar metals that are more common in the metallic state than in minerals which are compounds.

Second, our revised definition specifies that the metal be extracted with profit. This means that the term *ore* is commercial as well as geological, and its application to a given deposit depends on such factors as cost of mining, refining and transportation as well as on demand and market price of the pure metal. More than one "lean," or low-grade, deposit is an ore because it lies near a railroad, though much richer masses are worthless because they are hundreds of miles from transportation. On the other hand, deposits that were not ore to miners of a half century ago are now ores because cheap, effective means of treatment have been invented. Thus the low-grade porphyry copper deposits of the West became ores after 1900, when a way of concentrating their copper compounds was devised. The increasing use of alloys has turned many once worthless deposits into ores that now have great value.

## ORE DEPOSITS, ORE SHOOTS AND GANGUE

Even with good markets and low costs, however, a mine seldom can use all the material in an ore-bearing body of minerals or rock. This body, called the *ore deposit,* consists of the ore and a variable amount of ore-bearing material that is not worth mining and sometimes is called *protore.* As we have seen, cheapening of production or some other factor may turn the protore into ore.

In veins and dikes ore generally is concentrated into irregularly shaped bodies called *ore shoots.* There is no very good reason why this name should not also be applied to lenses or dikes of ore in great masses of igneous rock, but few authors use it in this way.

Even in an ore shoot there almost always are large amounts of valueless minerals termed *gangue*. In some shoots this material forms lumps or lenses that can be separated and thrown out in mining. In other shoots gangue minerals and those of value are so intimately mixed that they can be separated only by special methods after the ore is crushed. Quartz is the most plentiful gangue mineral, though calcite, barite and fluorite are common. Dolomite, pyroxene, hornblende, feldspars and a variety of other minerals also are found as gangue.

## SOME ORES FORM IN MAGMAS

Let us now consider a rising magma like the one that produced a great mass of anorthosite near Lake Sanford, in the Adirondacks of New York. As it approached the surface that magma began to cool and harden. Plagioclase feldspars crystallized, moving toward the top of the mass; small amounts of pyroxene went with them. The lower part of the magma became a heavy, dark, fluid mass of pyroxene, olivine, magnetite and ilmenite, the last being a compound of iron, oxygen and titanium. Some of this material apparently was forced through cracks in the partly hardened anorthosite, forming gabbro dikes that contain shoots of titanium-bearing magnetite. The heaviest material, however, apparently settled in large irregular bodies of black rock that contains little except magnetite and ilmenite, about 60 per cent of its mass being iron.

Events were somewhat different at Iron Mountain, in eastern Wyoming, where another anorthosite magma hardened in Pre-Cambrian times. Here the magma divided into an outer shell of anorthosite and a central core of fluid magnetite mixed with ilmenite and a few other minerals. When the anorthosite hardened and cracked, the magnetite was forced up in a dike 40 to 300 feet wide and about 6500 feet long, now called Iron

Mountain. Its impurities are biotite, olivine and feldspar. Like the Lake Sanford deposit it will became valuable iron ore when someone learns how to smelt it cheaply and efficiently.

Both these deposits were produced by *magmatic segregation*— by the separation of minerals in a fluid but crystallizing magma. This process took place at temperatures ranging from 600 to 1100 or 1200 degrees Fahrenheit. In some cases it seems clear that heavy minerals sank to the bottom of a magma just because they were heavy, while light ones went to the top. In others such minerals as chalcopyrite and sphalerite separated from the rest of the magma as it cooled. Whatever the exact nature of the process, it generally produced coarse-grained, dark ores that sometimes are porphyritic, the large crystals being those of the ore minerals.

Magmatic segregation produced the now metamorphosed magnetite deposits at Mineville, New York (Chapter XVIII), as well as in Sweden and the Ural Mountains of Russia. It also produced chromium ore in Rhodesia and platinum minerals in Rhodesia and the Transvaal. It seems probable that the ores of Sudbury, Ontario, which yield large amounts of copper and most of the world's supply of nickel, were produced by magmatic differentiation in a sheetlike intrusion about 5000 feet thick, which has been folded into a spoon-shaped structure (*syncline*) 36 miles long and 16 miles wide. The upper part of this intrusion is granite and the lower part gabbro. Most of the ore lies in the gabbro, but some formed where fluid rock worked its way into ancient formations beneath the thick intrusion.

Diamonds in the peridotite of South Africa also were produced by magmatic segregation, though they did not gather into large masses. Since diamonds are not metallic, the rocks that contain them are not ores in spite of their value.

Closely related to ores of segregation are those produced in pegmatite dikes, whose origin is described in Chapter VI. They consolidate at temperatures of 500 to 565 degrees centigrade and under very great pressure. Pegmatite dikes have been worked for tin near Gaffney, South Carolina, and in the Black Hills; for gold at Silver Peak, Nevada; and for molybdenum in Norway and Australia. None of these deposits is of major importance.

## IGNEOUS METAMORPHISM MADE ORES

Near Cornwall, Pennsylvania, a thick sill of diabase spread out between an upper formation of shale and a lower one of shaly limestone. The shale was baked by heat, but water and gas worked through the limestone, dissolving grains of calcite and depositing magnetite, chalcopyrite and other minerals. By 1938 this deposit had yielded more than 30,000,000 tons of magnetite ore, averaging 37.7 per cent iron, as well as considerable amounts of chalcopyrite.

These ores are products of replacement, which is one of the phases of igneous metamorphism described in Chapter XVII. It has been most effective where magmas of the right kind, such as monzonites, quartz monzonites and granodiorites, penetrated limestones and dolomites. These magmas contained and produced solutions which were rich in metallic minerals; the limestones and dolomites quickly dissolved, allowing the solutions to work their way through pores as they were made. Change was further aided by temperatures ranging from 600 to 1200 degrees centigrade. Pressures also were great, for igneous metamorphism took place at depths of more than a half mile.

Copper is the most important metal mined from replacement ores. In Bingham, Utah, America's largest copper mine takes out ore which in part was produced when a magma that became monzonite porphyry intruded quartzites containing lenses of limestone. Metamorphism extended 2000 to 3000 feet away from the intrusion. A second upwelling of solutions filled pores and cracks that had appeared in the uppermost 2000 feet of porphyry. Thus the lowest part of the intrusion "mineralized" and even metamorphosed the upper, forming an ore body 5600

feet long and 3600 feet wide. A similar series of events produced
the rich copper deposits at Bisbee, Arizona, where ores in the
limestone contact zone are more important than those at Bingham. Some of the silver-lead-copper ores of the San Francisco
district, Utah, also were produced by igneous metamorphism, as
were some tungsten ores of California and Nevada and gold ores
near Philipsburg, Montana.

## MANY ORES FORMED IN VEINS

By far the greatest number of ore deposits are found in veins,
which are mineral deposits filling fissures or cracks. Veins often
divide into branches, forming networks like the one shown on
PLATE 40. If a large network is "mineralized," or contains valuable metal-bearing minerals in most of its branches, it is known
as a *lode*. The famous Mother Lode of California is a network
of quartz veins about one mile wide and 120 miles long, richly
mineralized by gold, with unimportant amounts of pyrite,
sphalerite, galena and chalcopyrite.

The veins of PLATE 40 lie in joints which were filled when
other water deposited calcite that had been dissolved from the
surrounding limestone. Most metal-bearing veins, however,
began as open fissures that were filled by aqueous solutions from
magmas. These solutions moved under tremendous pressure,
forcing their way into cracks and even holding the walls apart
while minerals were deposited. If these new minerals did not fill
the cracks, open cavities remained, some of which are lined with
crystals that pointed inward like the crystals lining geodes.
Sometimes, however, the solutions deposited minerals in regular
layers, producing banded veins that resemble agates or deposits
in caves. Solutions also entered fissures and dissolved particles
from the walls, replacing them with minerals which they
carried. Replacement veins are much less regular than those
made by filling and are less sharply separated from the surrounding, or country, rock.

## DEEP-SEATED VEINS

Although metal-bearing veins differ in many ways, we may group them into three general classes. The first of these are the *deep-seated*, or *hypothermal*, veins, which were formed near batholiths or other deep-seated intrusions by solutions whose temperatures ranged from 300 to 575 degrees centigrade.

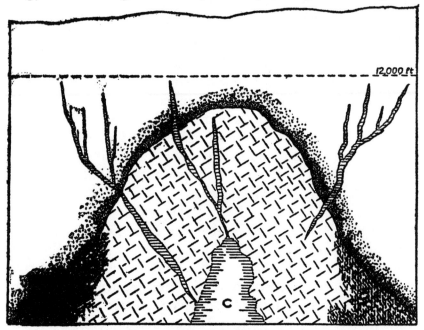

Segregation and deep-seated veins. A batholith whose core (C) is feeding deep-seated dikes and veins. Segregation deposits (S) on the slopes of the batholith may become ores. Dots mark the contact zone, where metamorphism is mostly accomplished by replacement.

Though erosion has brought many of these veins to the surface, they once lay under 12,000 to 15,000—perhaps even 50,000— feet of rock. Some deep-seated veins are continuations of pegmatite dikes, though others grade into zones of contact metamorphism. Their walls show considerable replacement and so are irregular. Lodes are very common.

Though some deep-seated veins are small, others are very large. One in Brazil's great Morro Velho gold mine is almost two miles long, averages 10 to 12 feet in thickness and in 1938 had been mined to a depth of 7526 feet. At this depth the temperature is 127 degrees Fahrenheit. Air cooling reduces the heat and humidity somewhat, allowing miners to work. Gold ore from other deep-seated veins has been mined in the southern Appalachians as well as in Quebec, Ontario and the Black Hills. The Homestake Mine at Lead, South Dakota (pronounced *leed*, for a miner's "lead" of ore), reaches a wide, branching vein that replaced iron-bearing dolomites, apparently more than 600,000,000 years ago. In its first sixty years this mine produced gold worth more than $321,500,000, and it still has large reserves of ore.

The tin ores of Cornwall, England, which have been mined for almost 3000 years, lie in deep-seated veins that came from granite. They cut both the granite and near-by slate and reach 50 feet in width. The tin mineral is cassiterite (PLATE 3); quartz is the principal gangue. The tin ores of Bolivia also contain cassiterite but were deposited by solutions from quartz monzonite. Copper ores of Chile, as well as ores of tungsten, lead, silver and zinc, also are found in deep-seated veins.

## VEINS OF THE INTERMEDIATE ZONE

The second group of ores formed in the *mesothermal*, or *intermediate*, zone, at depths of 4000 to 12,000 feet. Solutions came from deep-seated magmas; temperatures ranged from 175 to 300 degrees centigrade. Fissures filled under these conditions were fairly regular in direction, lacking the lenticular form and irregularity of those at greater depths. Smooth walls and slickensides are common. The ore deposits themselves commonly show irregular banding with some crystals arranged like the teeth of a comb, pointing into the cavities. In limestones, and less commonly in quartzite or igneous rocks, there was replacement in typical irregular veins.

The gold-bearing Mother Lode, west of the Sierra Nevada Mountains, is a series of intermediate veins made by filling; others are found throughout the Rockies from Canada to Mexico. Silver-lead filling and replacement veins of Coeur d'Alene, Idaho, and Leadville, Colorado, belong to this group, as do the cobalt-nickel-silver veins at Cobalt, Ontario. Here diabase sills sent hot solutions both upward and downward into Pre-Cambrian conglomerates and greywackes, forming a series of veins. The copper ores of Butte, Montana, lie in intermediate veins that cut the Butte "granite," really quartz monzonite. The metal-bearing solutions came from deeply buried portions of the batholith after the upper parts had cooled and broken in two series of joints and faults. Batholith and veins cannot be much more than 60,000,000 years old and may be only 50,000,000.

## VEINS OF THE SHALLOW ZONE

*Shallow,* or *epithermal,* vein deposits were made at depths of less than 4000 feet. Indeed, most of them seem to have formed within 1500 feet of the surface, at temperatures ranging from 50 to 200 degrees centigrade. Banding is common and comb structure is more plentiful and much better developed than it is in veins of the intermediate zone. A typical example of both these features is shown in the drawing of gold ore from Arizona.

Most shallow veins are found in Tertiary lavas, especially andesite, latite, trachyte and rhyolite; some apparently are forming today in lavas of Recent geologic age. Since these rocks were broken near the surface, where pressures were slight, they contained many open cracks and cavities in which water deposited minerals in a series of crusts. Lodes developed where cracks were connected, while some of the most shattered rocks allowed breccias to form.

Shallow veins have provided most of the famous gold-silver "bonanzas" of the West, such as the Comstock Lode and deposits at Goldfield and Tonopah, Nevada, and Cripple Creek, Colorado. The Cripple Creek veins, which produced $18,000,000 worth of gold in one year, cut a breccia of phonolite, granite, gneiss and schist in a steep-walled basin that is 2 miles

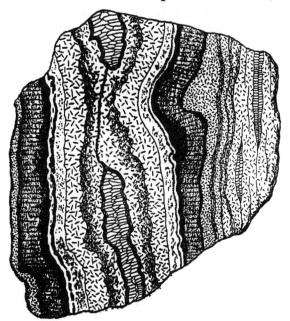

Banded ore from a shallow vein in the Oatman gold district of Arizona. This ore consists of layers of dark brown to green and white quartz, with several bands of comb crystals.

wide and 4 miles long. The ores at Tonopah occur in quartz veins that cut a series of faulted lava flows. The ore minerals are argentite (silver sulphide) and other silver compounds, with some electrum, the natural alloy of gold and silver. The California Mine, on the Comstock Lode, yielded $18,924,850 in 1877.

Lavas of the California Coast Ranges contain many veins of cinnabar which have yielded large amounts of mercury. At present, however, most mercury comes from Spain and Italy. The lead deposits of southeastern Missouri, which are the most important in the world, apparently were produced by waters rising from a deeply buried mass of magma. When these waters reached a formation of dolomite near the surface they replaced grains of dolomite with galena and also filled pores and cracks. Zinc and lead ores of the Tristate District (adjoining parts of Oklahoma, Kansas and Missouri) also were deposited by hot solutions that came close to the surface.

In the Keweenaw Peninsula of Michigan there is a thick series of amygdaloidal, basaltic lava flows, compacted tuffs and coarse conglomerates. Native copper occurs in amygdules, as replacements in the tuff and conglomerate and as sheets or lumps in veins. Although there is no general agreement, the latest studies indicate that this copper was brought up by solutions coming from a gabbro batholith at what now is the western end of Lake Superior. It is probable that this batholith also provided much of the lava into which the copper solutions moved.

## SECONDARY ORE DEPOSITS

The ores which we have discussed developed directly from magmas and so may be called *primary*. Under *secondary* ore deposits we group those that were developed by processes of erosion, weathering and sedimentation. A common practice divides them into ores which are original parts of the rock (*syngenetic*), those left over or *enriched* by weathering, those deposited in older rocks by solution (*epigenetic*) and deposits of heavy metals in river gravels or beach sands (*placers*).

Chapter XIII describes several varieties of iron ore that were produced as original (syngenetic) sediments. They include the Clinton oölitic and fossil hematites which extend from New York to Alabama and reach their greatest development near Birmingham. The oölitic Wabana iron ores of Newfoundland also belong to this group, as do Pre-Cambrian hematites of Brazil and oölitic limonites of Lorraine, in eastern France. The chief iron supply of Great Britain comes from oölitic siderites and other sedimentary ores which average about 30 per cent iron. Copper ores form black shale at Mansfeld, Germany, while sedimentary manganese ores occur in Russia, north of the Black Sea. Important manganese ores of India apparently were sedimentary, though they now form lenses in metamorphic rocks.

Most manganese, however, comes from residual ores produced (or enriched) when manganese-bearing rocks were weathered. This residue is a dark, nodular material which forms pockets in clay or pits in the bedrock.

From Vermont to Alabama weathered limestones contain pockets of residual clay that include lumps and nodules of limonite. These "brown ores" can be mined cheaply, and they often are mixed with local red hematite, especially at Birmingham, Alabama. Georgia and Alabama lead in production, though considerable amounts are mined in Virginia, Tennessee and Missouri. Three important iron deposits of Cuba consist of limonite in residual clay left by weathering of serpentine and hematite associated with igneous rocks.

The Lake Superior iron ores are natural concentrates, rather than residual deposits. They consist chiefly of hematite that was produced when water seeping down from the surface changed siderite and greenalite. Still later, other water removed much of the silica, increasing the proportion of iron in the rock from 25 to about 50 per cent.

Metal minerals in epigenetic ores sometimes were brought from other formations; sometimes they were dissolved from one part of a formation and deposited in another. Thus the "Red Beds" of the Southwest, which are Carboniferous to Triassic in age, contain deposits of copper which came from older formations. At one mine in New Mexico copper minerals filled most of the pores in rock and even replaced a petrified tree trunk 60 feet long. Copper-bearing sandstones are mined in Bolivia, Europe and western Siberia.

At one time the lead and zinc deposits of eastern Missouri, Illinois, Iowa and the Tristate District were thought to be replacements produced by water seeping down from the surface. It now seems that the ore was produced by hot solutions that moved upward from magmas until they reached the shallow zone.

Placer deposits consist of pebbles or sand worn from metal-bearing veins or lodes. The most famous placer deposits contain gold, either as nuggets and flakes or as bits in quartz pebbles like the one shown on PLATE 48. The first gold found in California lay in placer gravels from the Mother Lode, while the largest gold nugget in the world, weighing more than 200 pounds, came from a placer in Victoria, Australia. Platinum comes largely from placers in the Ural Mountains, while 60 per cent of the world's present supply of tin is secured as cassiterite in river gravels of the Malay Peninsula.

"Fossil" placers are interesting as well as important. We have mentioned a Cambrian conglomerate in the Black Hills which contains flakes and small nuggets of gold that apparently were worn from the Homestake lode some 500,000,000 years ago. Other supposed fossil placers are found in the Transvaal, South Africa, where a conglomerate with pebbles about two inches in diameter contains almost microscopic bits of gold and pyrite. Oddly enough, no gold is found in the pebbles, though most of them are quartz. Some geologists believe that both the gold and pyrite were deposited by water seeping downward after the conglomerate hardened while others attribute the origin of these deposits to rising magmatic waters.

This disagreement brings us back to a statement made early in the chapter. The processes that have produced ores are complicated and hard to unravel; although they have been studied for years, there still is no general agreement. For the sake of simplicity, this chapter has ignored most uncertainties and con-

# ORES AND THEIR ORIGIN

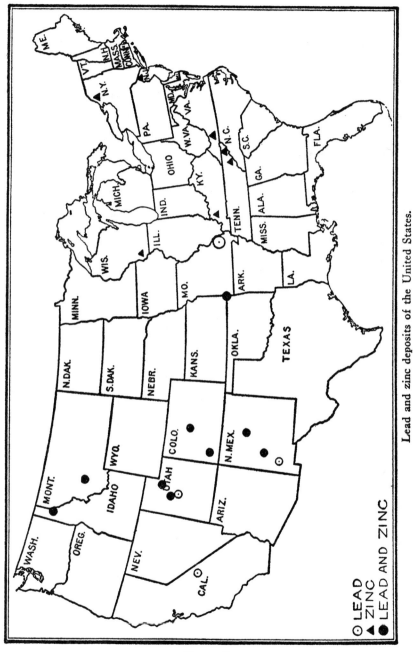

Lead and zinc deposits of the United States.

flicting theories, but the reader who uses other books will find them soon enough. Thus one author says that Michigan's copper was enriched by rain water seeping through the lavas; another is sure that the nickel deposits of Sudbury were made by replacement; a third asserts that the copper ores at Bingham, Utah, were deposited in veins of the intermediate zone.

Still, these differences do not destroy the general picture of ores and ore origins given in this chapter. It shows how closely ores are linked with the formation and changes of rocks and especially the rise of magmas. It also proves a statement made in Chapter I: that we moderns are far more dependent on materials from rocks than were crusaders or cave men.

## CHAPTER XX

# Collect, Travel and Read

LAST YEAR a boy brought us some stones. "Our science teacher says you know about them: what they are and what they mean. Can you tell me how to make a collection of them?"

We spread out his finds and chatted. Granite—a magma that hardened far underground—was raised by mountain building and exposed by epochs of erosion. Sandstone preserved ripple marks made when it was part of a shoal covered by a long-vanished sea. A piece of limestone showed a yellow-brown "shell" produced by oxidation. An oval ball proved to be a concretion worn from beds of marine shale.

From that talk have come two results. One is this book, which is designed to answer students' questions as well as those of adults who want to know what rocks are and mean. The other is a rock collection that grows though the science course closed months ago. That collection fills shelves, shirt boxes and a discarded bookcase. It also occupies its owner's time, takes him outdoors on holidays and has aroused the interest of his parents. Instead of being a "science project," these rocks are now a source of fun for the entire family.

## COLLECTING MUST HAVE A PURPOSE

Most rock collections start as curious stones brought home from a motor trip or hike. To explain them other specimens must be secured—and they, in turn, demand still others. Soon the collector finds that he is making two distinct series. One of these will contain important members of the three main rock groups: igneous, sedimentary and metamorphic. The second will include minerals that are most important as rock builders. These lists suggest the members of each series:

| ROCKS | | |
|---|---|---|
| *Igneous* | *Sedimentary* | *Metamorphic* |
| Granite | Conglomerate | Gneiss |
|   coarse-grained | Sandstone | Slate |
|   fine-grained | Shale | Schist |
| Syenite |   soft | Serpentine or |
| Diorite |   hard |   soapstone |
| Gabbro | Limestone | Quartzite |
| Felsite |   fine-grained | Marble |
| Andesite |   shell or coquina | |
| Basalt | | |
| Obsidian | Dolomite | |
| Scoria | Gypsum | |
| Tuff | Coal | |
| **MINERALS** | | |
| Amphibole | Hematite | Plagioclase |
| Biotite or | Hornblende | Pyrite |
|   muscovite | | Pyroxene |
| Calcite | Kaolin | Quartz |
| Dolomite | Limonite |   crystals |
| Epidote | Magnetite |   massive or crystalline |
| Garnet | Olivine | Serpentine |
| Gypsum (Selenite) | Orthoclase | Tourmaline |

A third series will show characters of hardness, fracture and cleavage, described in Chapter II. This demands the addition of a few minerals that are not in the first rank of rock builders. If the two mineral series are combined, these should be specially marked.

Collectors who are fortunate enough to live among complex mountains, or in a region where glaciers have brought stones of many sorts from many regions, may find a considerable number of these rocks and minerals near their homes. Lacking this, one may gather specimens as he travels. Quarries, road cuts and mine dumps are good places to collect; workmen often pick up attractive minerals which they sell at low prices to tourists. Many a collector has made his rocks and minerals tell a story of vacation trips, with specimens from each scenic area, accompanied by photographs that show how the different rocks occur and what they look like in mountains, seacoasts, canyons and deserts. Such a collection means more than any number of souvenirs and guidebooks and it also "makes sense" of the many rock varieties that are sure to be seen and gathered. Even trips, however, will fail to provide some specimens that are needed. For them one must rely on collectors in other regions or on purchase. In the latter case it is simplest to buy from a large dealer, such as Ward's Natural Science Establishment. When a neatly trimmed "museum" grade specimen of obsidian can be bought for fifty cents and two dozen rock-forming minerals cost only a dollar it does not pay to shop around for bargains.

With the essentials secured, the collector may specialize. For some, specialization means study of all rocks and the securing of a large collection containing every possible sort, or "species." Other collectors prefer to learn a great deal about the rocks near their homes or of regions where they spend their vacations. Some try to get all kinds of volcanic, intrusive, sedimentary or metamorphic rocks. In farming country it is worth while to make a series showing how different rocks break down and become soil. Another may deal with processes described in Chapter XVII, showing how rocks are bent, crumpled and broken by earth movements. Our own special interest is slabs showing the action of waves, currents, winds, storms and other forces whose work is described in Chapter XVI. With them go trails, burrows and tubes of creatures living when the sediments of those slabs were being deposited.

There are two good reasons for specialization. One is that it helps the collector to accomplish something definite, not merely to gather odds and ends. The other is that specialized collections may add something to human knowledge. Rocks may be very ancient, but the science that deals with them is young. Less than thirty years have passed since geologists seriously set out to discover the causes of ripple marks, mud cracks, cross-bedding and details about the origin of limestone. They are learning much, but slowly. Many problems are open to the collector who wants to know, to discover, as well as to get specimens. Once he makes a good start, specialists will help him, sending copies of their articles, exchanging their duplicate specimens for his and suggesting what he should look for to solve his special puzzles.

All this means that collecting is more than just picking up good specimens. When you find a desirable rock label it fully or describe it in a notebook. Tell where it was found, whether it was loose or "in place," and what sort of rocks were around it. If you broke it from a cliff or ledge, make note of the special bed or stratum. Read a few geologic reports, learn how "sections" are measured and described and record them in a loose-leaf notebook. Soon you will learn to notice interesting structures or variations and to secure specimens that show them. Some may be heavy, but what of that? They will give your collection meaning that mere sets of rock species without information simply cannot possess.

## COLLECTING EQUIPMENT IS SIMPLE

Collecting demands things with which rocks can be pried loose, broken, carried and roughly examined out-of-doors. Here are standard pieces of equipment, with a few hints about extras:

*Hammer or Pick.*—For general collecting the best probably is the Plumb Prospecting Pick, which is used by many geologists. Its head is made of nonrusting steel, properly tempered; a special wedge and screw keep it tight at all times. There also are excellent hammers in which the head and handle are made from one piece of metal.

For splitting limestones, shales and other stratified rocks the Plumb Mineral Hammer is better than a pick. Instead of a sharp point it has a flat edge that often does the work of a chisel. The handle, like that of the Plumb pick, is properly balanced.

*Cold Chisels.*—Two: one half or five eighths and seven eighths or one inch wide.

*Wrecking Bar.*—Not essential, but often helpful in moving or splitting large blocks. The 24- or 30-inch length is adequate.

*Knapsack.*—A sturdy canvas knapsack, *not* a rucksack or haversack. A good inexpensive pack is the "Comfort," sold by Abercrombie and Fitch, Madison Avenue and Forty-fifth Street, New York. The medium size measures 14 by 16 by 5½ inches; it will hold rocks, plenty of packing and padding, lunch and incidentals. A similar pack fastened to a pack board is more comfortable, for it prevents rocks from pressing against one's back.

*Notebook.*—One with loose leaves that may be removed and filed. Leaves 5 by 8 inches or a little larger are most convenient.

*Steel Rule.*—A 5- or 6-foot rule is useful for measuring ledges and boulders from which specimens are taken.

*Acid Bottle.*—A glass- or rubber-stoppered bottle with glass rod, for dropping acid on rocks, is convenient but not essential. Fill it with a solution made by mixing one part of commercial hydrochloric acid with one part of water. But pack it where it will not break!

*Knife.*—A knife is useful to pry out delicate minerals and also to test them for hardness.

*Pocket Magnifier.*—The beginner may use one of the inexpensive magnifiers (60¢ to $1.85) with two or three lenses, mounted in black rubber. Lenses of the Bauch and Lomb doublet and Coddington types are better; they cost $3.25 to $4.00. Still better is the Hastings model, magnifying seven, ten or fourteen times and costing about $7.50. In choosing, remember that magnifications larger than ten times reduce the area seen and the distance at which the lens may be held from specimens.

*Paper sacks,* used double, are desirable for samples of gravel, sand, soft clay, soil and volcanic ash. Cloth sacks are more durable and can be used over and over again.

*Wrapping papers* (newspapers will do, though brown kraft paper is more serviceable) and pencils complete the collecting outfit unless one breaks such large blocks that wedges and a sledge become necessary. In much work the wrecking bar and other heavy tools may be left in a car, to be brought out only when there is need for them. The collector who burdens himself with all his equipment all the time is likely to have little energy left with which to hunt specimens.

## TRIMMING SPECIMENS

In the field (which is geologic jargon for "out-of-doors") large slabs or blocks should be collected without too careful trimming, since that may be done in camp or at home. Some specimens cannot be trimmed very much: ripple marks, mud cracks and channel fillings show well only on fairly large slabs. Quartzites, gabbros and other massive rocks, however, may be trimmed down to neat sizes such as 4 by 6, 3 by 4 or 2 by 3 inches. Smaller ones should be made only if a rock is rare or cannot be had in large pieces. For this work field hammers and chisels may be used, though some collectors prefer an engineer's hand hammer weighing 1½ or 2 pounds. End-cutting nippers 8 or 10 inches long also are helpful.

Soft shales and clays may be trimmed to shape with a knife, though they look best if at least one rough surface is preserved.

Those too hard for a knife may be trimmed with chisels or the Plumb chisel-edged hammer. Sand, soil and other loose rocks are collected in paper bags and transferred to cardboard containers or wide-mouthed bottles. The former are cheaper and lighter in weight than are the latter and are somewhat simpler to label.

## SMOOTHING AND SURFACING

Some rocks, when polished, show characters that are not seen on fresh or weathered surfaces. Actual polishing is difficult unless one has a lapidary's equipment, which few collectors own. Here are the steps in a substitute method:

1. Trim the rock down as smooth as possible with chisels, nippers and hammer. If it is not too hard, some irregularities may be removed with a hacksaw.

2. Grind the specimen down by rubbing it over a piece of plate glass on which Number 120 carborundum and a little water have been placed. Add water and carborundum as they are needed and grind till the desired surface is flat.

3. Wash the glass plate or take a new clean one. Using FF carborundum and water, smooth the roughly ground surface until all scratches disappear.

4. Take a new glass used only for this purpose and sprinkle water and Number 600 carborundum on it. Repeat the smoothing process until the rock surface is thoroughly finished.

5. Place the specimen in a box containing sand, making sure that the smoothed surface is horizontal.

6. With a knife or spatula spread a very thin layer of Dupont Household Cement on the smoothed surface. Several china cements will do as well, and so will a solution made by dissolving transparent, colorless celluloid in acetone.

7. Let the cement dry thoroughly in a room free from dust. It will give a polish that brings out details of laminae, oölites, pisolites and organisms such as corals and bryozoans, which form many limestones.

## CABINETS AND TRAYS ARE NEEDED

Rock collections are easily kept. Mold, insect pests and dampness cannot harm stones, no matter how fatal they may be to butterflies or pressed plants. Even dust does no lasting harm, though it is a good deal of a nuisance. The beginning collector who is willing to wash his specimens occasionally may store them in a discarded cupboard or on bookshelves. Small rocks do very well in shirt boxes, which may be had free at any clothing store.

In time, however, any rock collection will outgrow these makeshifts. Then one needs a cabinet with interchangeable drawers, which can be built at home, by a carpenter or in a school workshop.

The drawer is the basis of this cabinet. As shown in the drawing, it consists of a bottom of compo board, plywood or similar material, with plain wood ends and sides. For all except heavy specimens or tools, the bottom may consist of three-ply material and the sides of pine or cypress, a half or five eighths inch thick.

Since sides do not support much weight, there is no need for doweling or dovetailing. Glue and fasten the wood with flat-head screws or nails; attach it to the bottom by the same method. Pulls are not necessary, though holes bored with an inch bit will make them. Be sure that the bottom extends an inch beyond the frame at each side and that the ends are flush. The dimensions given are about maximum; a good all-purpose drawer has over-all measurements of 24 by 24 by 2 inches. Heavy minerals or rocks may demand one four inches deep with inch-thick sides and ends.

The easiest drawer support to install is a strip of half-inch angle iron, screwed to the frame at either end. A wood strip whose cross section is shown in 2 is cheaper, but in using it be sure your cabinet has either a side panel or a series of upright strips. Without one or the other, drawers will slide awry every time you insert them.

The iron or wood supports should be spaced about an inch apart, as indicated in 3. Then, if you want to put a three- or

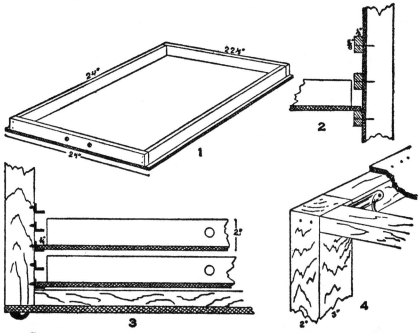

Construction of a simple cabinet. 1 shows a drawer, which may be made two inches or more in depth. 2 illustrates the use of wooden strips on which drawers may slide; 3 shows angle irons. 4 illustrates a simple corner. Metal braces, plus plywood top and bottom, make doweling or dovetailing unnecessary. Sides and back may be left open or covered with plywood.

four-inch object in a two-inch drawer, all you need do is lower it or raise its next neighbor.

Dimensions of the cabinet will match the drawers, with some leeway for sidewise movement and imperfections in your work. This wastes a little space, as does the narrowing of the drawer to clear its supports, but it saves all the tedious nuisance of drawers that seem to be the same size but are not and so do not interchange. Heights also may match needs, though if there is any chance that you will want to make several cabinets and stack them, three feet is a good maximum. Forty inches seems nearly a limit for a framework of two-inch soft wood such as pine, without considerable strengthening.

If one wishes, he may cover the sides, top and back of such a cabinet with plywood and add a plywood door. This improves the appearance and keeps out some dust. Dust may be avoided still more by covering the contents of each drawer with a piece of muslin, cut large enough to allow for high specimens.

Specimens laid in boxes or on shelves become separated from their labels. Numbers help one put them together—but it is better to avoid confusion at the start by putting each specimen in a tray. Trays may be bought at prices ranging from 1½ to 4 cents each, or they may be made from cardboard and gummed tape. Get a heavy, durable card; cut and score it to the proper size; bend up the sides and fasten the corners with pieces of tape that fold over and so stick to the inside as well as the outside of the tray. The steps in making such a tray are shown in the accompanying drawing.

Trays may be of any desired size: 3⅜ by 4¾ by ⅝ inches

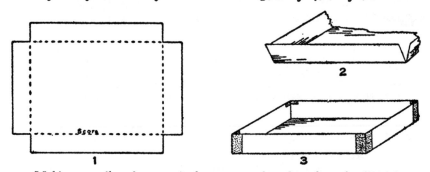

Making a cardboard tray. 1 is the cut, scored card; 2 shows bending of the sides; 3 is the finished tray, fastened and strengthened with gummed tape at the corners.

are good measurements for those holding specimens trimmed to 3 by 4 inches. It is important that a set of trays exactly fill a box or drawer, wasting no space and preventing sliding. It also is well to have different sizes in multiples, so that two small trays fill the space of a large one. A good series is:

Half size:       2⅜ by 3⅜ inches     ⅝ inch deep
Standard size    3⅜ by 4¾ inches     ⅝ inch deep
Double size:     4¾ by 6¾ inches     ⅝ inch deep

## LABELS AND CATALOGUE

Labels may consist of thin Bristol board, heavy bond or ledger paper: those for trays of the sizes just suggested may be 2¼ or 3¼ inches long and 1½ to 2 inches wide. Good sizes frequently may be found among printers' trimmings. Some collectors prefer labels which fill the tray, are bent and have the label material written or typed on the upright portion. These, for our suggested series of trays, will be 3⅛ by 3⅞ and 3⅛ by 6¼ inches, assuring that each label will stand 1½ inches above the bottom of the tray.

Labels may be typed or written, using pen and Higgins' Eternal ink. They should contain specimen number, name, locality and rock series, as in these samples:

| Igneous                52 | Sedimentary            80 |
|---------------------------|---------------------------|
|     Graphic Granite       |     Quartz Conglomerate   |
| Auburn,          Maine    | Near Olean,     New York  |

Other items may be added: geologic age, the name of collector or person from whom the specimen was received, date of collection and references to photographs of rock as it was found:

| Metamorphic                                          315 |
|----------------------------------------------------------|
|                     Dolomite Marble                      |
|                 Proterozoic, Belt Series                 |
|        Garden Wall, Glacier National Park, Montana       |
| B. F. Jones.        July 3, 1939        Photo 87–39       |

If one has more information than this, it should be put in the catalogue. This is kept in a loose-leaf notebook or on cards, the latter being the better. Each specimen is given a number as it is put in the collection; that number is entered in the catalogue, along with a copy of notes made in the field. Here is such a catalogue entry:

216 Mud Breccia                                    Argillite in Quartzite
Proterozoic, Belt Series, Grinnell Formation, Rising Wolf Member. Talus at foot of Pumpelly Pillar, Glacier National Park, Montana. C. L. and M. A. Fenton, July 8, 1934. Negative 114–34.

From large block. Interbedded with rose-red argillaceous quartzites containing symmetrical ripple marks 2.5–3 inches in wave length. Breccias cross-laminated. Quartzite generally white. Mud-cracked argillite in thin layers, somewhat broken.

Negative 114–34 is the one from which the photograph of cross-bedded quartzite and mud breccia on PLATE 26 was printed. There are other negatives that show the talus, the steep glaciated wall above it and bands of quartzite alternating with red argillite. These are not mentioned in the catalogue. They are available, however, and prints from them help give reality and meaning to the piece of rock identified by number 216.

Some collectors use one series of numbers for ores, one for sediments and so on, but this is likely to cause confusion. The simplest plan is to start with 1 and add as the collection grows. If the catalogue is kept on cards, poor specimens may be discarded as better ones are secured, new records being put in place of the old ones. This is specially important to the beginning collector who quite properly will take poor specimens of unusual rocks rather than go without but is sure to get better ones as his collection grows.

## NUMBERING

Numbers, printed or written on gummed paper, may be pasted to specimens with smooth surfaces or fastened to rough ones with drops of very thick glue, china cement or celluloid dissolved in acetone. A more lasting method is to number with enamel. First clean the surface to remove all grease and dust; then make a dot or square of white enamel, just thick enough to give a smooth surface. When this dries make the number in black enamel, using a very fine-tipped camel's-hair brush, practicing on worthless stones until you become skillful.

Temporary numbers may be written on small squares of adhesive tape and fastened to specimens. India or Eternal ink is used; when the number no longer is needed it may be pulled off and thrown away. Among paper or enamel numbers the adhesive tape is a sign that the specimen bearing it has not found a final place in the collection.

## BOOKS, MAGAZINES AND DEALERS *

Although the important rock-forming minerals, and some others, have been described in Chapter III, collectors who gather minerals as well as rocks soon will want additional reference books. One of the best of these is *Getting Acquainted with Minerals,* by G. L. English (McGraw-Hill, 1934), an excellently illustrated volume that contains a short chapter on rocks. *The Book of Minerals,* by A. C. Hawkins (Wiley, 1935), is a small, simply written guide for identification, while *The Story of the Minerals,* by H. P. Whitlock (American Museum of Natural History, New York, 1932), is a still simpler and more readable description of minerals exhibited in a great museum. A rather old book, *Minerals and How to Study Them,* by E. S. Dana (Wiley, 1906), also is useful to beginners, while those who want more advanced information will get it from the fourth edition of Dana's *Textbook of Mineralogy,* revised by W. E. Ford (Wiley, 1932). Collectors who live near New York City will need *Minerals of New York City and Its Environs,* by J. G. Manchester (N.Y. Mineralogical Club, American Museum of Natural History, 1931), a book which contains fine pictures of minerals and localities where they may be found.

Semitechnical books about rocks are few. The *Field Book of*

* *Publisher's Note, Dover Edition*: See the Introduction for a sampling of more recent books and for suggestions on Internet searches.

*Common Rocks and Minerals,* by F. B. Loomis (Putnam, 1923), is devoted primarily to minerals, many of which are illustrated in color; the descriptions of rocks are very brief. A much better, though less attractive, book is the second edition of *Rocks and Rock Minerals,* by L. V. Pirsson, revised by A. Knopf (Wiley, 1926).

Understanding and enjoyment of rocks depend largely on a knowledge of geology such as may be gained from college textbooks. One of the most useful of these for general reading is the third edition of *An Introduction to Geology,* by W. B. Scott (Macmillan, 1932). It has abundant illustrations and gives more attention to rocks as results of geologic changes than do second editions of the *Textbook of Geology,* Part I, by Longwell, Knopf and Flint (Wiley, 1939), and *Elements of Geology,* by W. J. Miller (Van Nostrand, 1939). A popular presentation of geologic principles may be found in *Our Amazing Earth,* by C. L. Fenton (Doubleday, Doran, 1938). A second edition with considerable revision of the chapters on minerals is in preparation.

To many of us rocks mean ores, which are discussed very briefly in this book. Scott devotes twenty-five pages to them, summarizing the treatment in W. Lindgren's excellent but technical *Mineral Deposits,* now in its third edition (McGraw-Hill, 1928). Ores and other valuable rocks also are dealt with in *Economic Geology,* by H. Ries (Wiley, sixth edition, 1932), and *Introductory Economic Geology,* by W. A. Tarr (McGraw-Hill, second edition, 1938). The word "introductory" in the title of this last book is deceptive; it contains 645 pages, with many maps and references.

When the rock hunter travels he will want to carry a few books. The best of these for all-around use are the *Physiography of the Western United States* and *Physiography of the Eastern United States,* by N. M. Fenneman (McGraw-Hill, 1931 and 1938). Describing the land as it is today, Dr Fenneman also tells how it reached its present appearance and what rocks have entered into the make-up of each region. His books demand some acquaintance with geologic technicalities, but they more than pay for the effort which that acquaintance may cost.

For travel in the West one needs appropriate volumes of the *Guidebook of the Western United States,* published by the U.S. Geological Survey and sold by the Superintendent of Documents, Washington, D.C. The six volumes already published are:

*The Northern Pacific Route,* by M. R. Campbell and others. U.S. Geological Survey Bulletin 611, 1916. (Northern Pacific Railway and U.S. Highway 10 from St Paul to Seattle, with a detour to Yellowstone Park.)

*The Overland Route,* W. T. Lee and others. U.S. Geological Survey Bulletin 612, 1916. (Union Pacific Railway and U.S. Highways 30, 40, 91 and 191 from Omaha to San Francisco with a detour to West Yellowstone.)

*The Santa Fe Route,* by N. H. Darton and others. U.S. Geological Survey Bulletin 613, 1916. (Santa Fe Railway and U.S. Highways 50, 85 and 66 from Kansas City to Los Angeles.)

*The Shasta Route and Coast Line,* by J. S. Diller and others. U.S. Geological Survey Bulletin 614, 1916. (Southern Pacific Railway and U.S. Highways 99 and 101 from Seattle to Los Angeles.)

*The Denver and Rio Grande Western Route,* by M. R. Campbell. U.S. Geological Survey Bulletin 707, 1922. (Route of "Rio Grande" and some Rock Island trains; also U.S. Highways 85, 50 and 24; Denver to Salt Lake City.)

*The Southern Pacific Lines,* by N. H. Darton. U.S. Geological Survey Bulletin 845, 1933. (Southern Pacific Railway and U.S. Highways 90, 80 and 99 from New Orleans to Los Angeles.)

There is also a wealth of special bulletins and other accounts published by the federal and state geological surveys. They may be found in most large public and college libraries.

Articles on rocks occasionally appear in the *Nature Maga-*

*zine* (1214 Sixteenth Street, N.W., Washington, D.C.) and in *Natural History* (American Museum of Natural History, New York; they also bulk large in *Desert Magazine* (Palm Desert, California), whose special field is the Southwest. For the serious collector there are both technical and popular magazines. The latter include *Rocks and Minerals* (Peekskill, New York), *The Mineralogist* (329 Southeast 32d Ave., Portland 5, Oregon), *The Lapidary Journal* (Palm Desert, California), and *Mineral Notes and News* (Ridgecrest, California). Many societies issue printed or mimeographed bulletins which contain useful information.

The collector who wants to buy specimens or sell duplicates will find the advertisements of reputable dealers in the magazines already mentioned. Some of these dealers have large and varied stocks; others specialize on the rocks and minerals of their own regions. The latter often offer specimens of exceptional quality which fill gaps in even the largest collection.

# APPENDIX 1

# APPENDIX 1

# Rocks, Fossils, and Ages

We have said that fossils are remains or traces of once living things buried in rocks of the earth's crust. But we did not say that all such rocks contain fossils. Which do and which do not? How can we arrange them in order, and how—by means other than guessing—can we tell their ages?

### ROCKS AND THEIR FOSSILS

Rocks, which vary greatly in hardness and composition, also differ in origin. Origins, in turn, determine our chances of finding fossils in them.

*Igneous Rocks.* The word *igneous* means "fiery"; though rocks of this class did not really burn, all once were intensely hot. They include lavas that came to the surface in eruptions, as well as related deposits that cooled and hardened underground. Most lavas were fluid when they came from cracks or volcanoes and flowed out upon the surface. Subterranean masses were much stiffer; they are termed *magma,* a Greek word for "dough," before cooling. Upon cooling they form granite and similar rocks, which lack the bubbles and traces of flowage that are characteristic of lava.

Igneous rocks that hardened underground contain no fossils, for nothing can live in great heat or far below the surface. Fossils are very rare in lavas, most of which destroyed all plants and animals over which they flowed. Exceptions are the rhinoceros described in Chapter I and tree trunks that left molds in rapidly cooling flows.

Lavas often are blown to pieces and shot into the air, where they cool rapidly. Falling to the ground, they form deposits called agglomerate if the fragments are coarse, and tuff if they are very fine. Both bridge the gap between igneous and sedimentary rocks, since their particles settle upon the earth's surface although they once were hot.

Agglomerate covers many fossil trees, some of which were dead logs at the time of burial. The most famous are in Yellowstone National Park, where as many as eighteen successive forests of redwoods, pines, sycamores, and

* *Publisher's Note, Dover Edition*: The references in Appendix 1 to other chapters are not to chapters in this book. They refer to chapters in *The Fossil Book,* in which Appendix 1 first was published as Chapter II.

[350]

*At the left are two petrified redwoods* (Sequoia) *in tuff, a soft rock composed of volcanic ash. Pliocene, near Calistoga, California. At the right is a mold of a charred pine tree preserved in solidified lava of Recent age. Craters of the Moon National Monument, near Arco, Idaho*

oaks were buried under showers of volcanic rock. Hills west of Vantage, Washington, also contain petrified logs covered by agglomerate and lava flows.

Redwood logs, excellently preserved, are found in light-colored tuff a few miles from Calistoga, California. Ash mixed with mud settled in lakes near Florissant, Colorado, forming light gray shale. It contains enormous numbers of leaves, as well as eleven hundred species of butterflies, crickets, grasshoppers, flies, beetles, and other insects. The butterflies still preserve their original stripes and spots.

Trackways can sometimes be found in ashfalls, or tuff. A famous example is one in East Africa from Laetoli, dated at 3.5 million years. Thousands of tracks of antelope, lions, and even the relatives of modern man are preserved in detail.

**Sedimentary Rocks and Their Fossils.** Though fossils are exceptional in igneous rocks, they are the rule in sedimentary deposits.

Sediment literally means "something that settles"; sedimentary rocks consist of dust, sand, mud, and other materials that settled underwater or on

[*351*]

land. As they did so, they built up deposits called strata or beds, layers, and laminae, depending upon their thickness. Few sedimentary rocks were hot when they accumulated, and many consist largely of shells, corals, plants, and other remains. Coal is a well-known sedimentary rock that is made up almost wholly of plants.

Still, not all sedimentary rocks contain fossils. Most conglomerates, for instance, lack them, for organisms that lived among coarse sands and shifting pebbles were ground to pieces soon after they died. Fine-grained limestones may be equally barren, since they consist of material that once was dissolved in water. Shells and corals are rare in most marine sandstones— corals because they generally don't live amid sand, shells because they were destroyed by acids in beds of sand or by water seeping through the porous rock after it solidified. Where fossils do remain, they often are nothing more then external molds or remains with only coarse detail preserved. Still, in some cases, delicate structures, such as tiny reptile jaws, can be preserved in conglomerates, and exquisite sand dollars with minute detail can be found in ancient sandstones.

In contrast to these barren deposits are others in which fossils are abun-

*Collecting fossil fish from freshwater shale of Triassic age at Princeton, New Jersey*

dant or actually form most of the rock. The Iowa clay shale described in Chapter I contains so many remains that a collector who takes small ones with large may get ten thousand specimens in a day. Slabs of limestone from Missouri are covered with crinoids, while limy shales from the Cincinnati region and southeastern Indiana are crowded with shells. The chalk of England and northern France is little more than a mass of tiny shells through which larger ones are scattered. Other limestones consist of mollusc shells, corals, or the puzzling creatures called stromatoporoids, held together by matrix worn from similar remains. Reefs described in Chapter V consist almost entirely of unworn algal masses.

Even coarse sandstones may enclose bones of large dinosaurs, while fine-grained beds containing clay and mica often abound in tracks and burrows. Other fine-grained sandstones that settled on land are rich in fossil mammals. In the famous Middle Cenozoic Agate bone bed of Nebraska (Chapter XXXIII), fine sandstone merely fills spaces between closely packed skulls and other bones.

*Metamorphic Rocks.*   These are typified by slate, true marble, and contorted crystalline rocks often called granite, though the proper terms are gneiss and schist. Some began as sediments; others were igneous. All have been changed by heat, by steam from buried magmas, or by pressure that bent and squeezed rocks into mountains. The process often went so far that we no longer can tell whether a given deposit began as magma, lava, or sediment.

Intensely metamorphosed rocks contain no fossils; any that may have been present were utterly destroyed. But stromatolites are abundant in some slightly changed marbles, and shells of various kinds have been found in slate, which is mildly metamorphosed shale. Such fossils were flattened and squeezed sidewise or stretched as the rocks were forced into mountain ranges. Though such remains can be recognized, their shapes may be quite different from those the creatures had when alive. Interestingly, the alterations in shape can sometimes be used by structural geologists to understand the direction and intensity of the forces that deformed the original rocks.

### WHERE ARE FOSSILS FOUND?

We now are ready to answer the question of where and how fossils can be found. The first step, of course, is to rule out igneous and metamorphic formations, in which fossils are almost sure to be lacking. Then, unless the collector is interested in special problems such as stromatolites (Chapter V) or animals of ancient rocky shores, he eliminates formations and beds in which remains are likely to be rare and poor. This still leaves him a vast range of formations in which fossils are fairly common to abundant, and good to superb in quality.

About many of these deposits there is no question; experts have combed them again and again and have published reports describing their finds and the best localities for collecting. Other formations are judged to be promising because of their appearance, because they are related to known fossil-bearing deposits, or because specimens found in them appear on curio stands or in museums. Following such leads, the determined collector examines every exposure he can find until he either brings home an array of specimens or proves that they are not to be found.

Here the collector who deals with invertebrates has a great advantage over the one who seeks vertebrate fossils. Although a few beds are filled with teeth and bones, fossil vertebrates are much less common than shells or

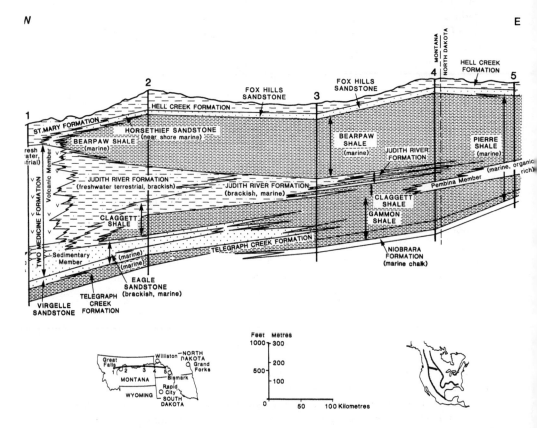

*Diagram of Late Cretaceous formations from northern Montana (left) to South Dakota (right). Location of the section is shown by the line on the map. Shading shows the general extent of Late Cretaceous seas in the west and south of North America*

corals and much harder to identify. Most snails, after all, can be recognized as snails, but a skull or even a skeleton may appear as little more than a light- or dark-colored bump on a rock. In the hands of an unskilled collector it also may be easily destroyed, though many invertebrates (by no means all!) are easily removed from the rocks in which they were fossilized.

## FOSSILS AND FORMATIONS

Every collector soon notices that fossils of certain types are found in particular kinds of rocks. Marsh plants, for example, are most abundant in shales and sandstones between beds of coal. The colonial animals called graptolites (Chapter XXI) are generally found in dark, fine-grained shales that split into thin layers. Both reptile tracks and invertebrate trails characterize fine-grained sandstone, especially where it is interbedded with shale. Corals are found in limy shales and massive limestones, many of which are the remains of ancient reefs.

*Records of Change.* Equally obvious is the fact that fossils are similar throughout some series of strata, although they differ in others. These similarities and differences show what beds should be grouped together and what should be separated, while the fossils themselves may reveal the conditions under which rocks were deposited.

These related aspects of fossils may be observed along the course of the Two Medicine River in Pondera and Glacier counties, Montana. At first we find ledges of gray to buff sandstone whose beds bear traces of shifting currents and waves (cross-bedding), as well as impressions of shells related to some that now live near sandy seashores. Next come greenish-gray clays and soft sandstones with oyster shells and basket clams, which now are found in the brackish water of bays where rivers empty into the sea. Above these are clays and sandstones that contain freshwater mussels and snails, as well as plants and dinosaur bones. Some of the dinosaurs look as if they walked on dry land, but others were web-footed reptiles that probably swam in swampy rivers or lakes. Near its middle, the series is interrupted by a thin deposit containing seashells. Evidently the lowland was submerged under the sea but soon became land again.

These rocks are some 1,750 feet thick, and we follow them for miles. Then we come to dark gray, rather limy shale with petrified shells of molluscs whose nearest relatives now are marine. The shale is capped by more coarse sandstone with oysters, basket clams, and jingle shells, all relatives of molluscs that now inhabit brackish water.

Different fossils, thus, enable us to distinguish several separate units, though some of their strata are almost identical in appearance. We also trace a series of changes in physical conditions. Putting all these facts together in conventional form, we get a composite stratigraphic section, which should be read from bottom to top:

Horsethief Sandstone. Slabby to massive sandstone, brackish-water and marine                                                    360 feet
Bearpaw Shale. Dark gray clay shale with marine fossils that
in several areas grades into sandstones                                 490 feet
Two Medicine Formation. Gray to greenish clay and soft
sandstone, with some red clay and nodular limestone.
Terrestrial and freshwater, with one marine horizon          1,750 feet
Eagle Sandstone. Greenish-gray clay and sandstone with
brackish-water fossils. To the north and west this be-
comes part of the Two Medicine Formation                               200 feet

The formations change from one place to another; witness the fact that the brackish-water Eagle Sandstone gives way to freshwater and terrestrial deposits which add a basal 200 feet to the Two Medicine Formation. Still greater changes appear if we travel southeastward toward the Black Hills of South Dakota. First the lower sandstones and the Two Medicine Formation vanish and the Bearpaw interfingers with a thick formation of shale called the Pierre (pronounced "peer"), which tells of a sea that changed very little while land and salt water repeatedly shifted in what is now western Montana and Alberta. At last, however, the sea shallowed, and sandstone was deposited. Though called the Fox Hills Sandstone, it once was continuous with the Horsethief Sandstone, which caps ridges near the Two Medicine River.

If we take the time—several geologists have done so—we can trace the formations in our section, making sure how they come to an end, intergrade, or overlie one another. We also can trace deposits at the bottom or top of the series to places where they lie upon or are covered by older and younger beds. By repeating this process several times, we expand our first section

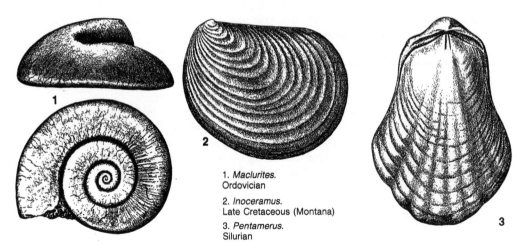

1. *Maclurites.*
Ordovician

2. *Inoceramus.*
Late Cretaceous (Montana)

3. *Pentamerus.*
Silurian

*Three index fossils*

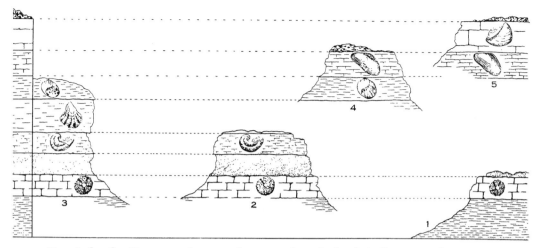

*How index fossils are used to match, or correlate, beds of similar ages. The complete section of these varied strata (1–5) is shown at the left*

into a greater one that shows formations and events in western North America during 35 million years of Late Cretaceous time.

*Index Fossils.* Still, we cannot always trace one deposit to the next or find thick series that overlap like shingles on a roof. When this happens, reliance must be placed upon index fossils.

An index fossil is found in rocks that formed in one limited part of earth history. A certain species of *Inoceramus,* for example, is common in Late Cretaceous shales that extend from Minnesota to Alberta, and formations containing shells of this species settled at about the same time. The snail called *Maclurites* is equally characteristic of certain much older (Ordovician) formations throughout eastern North America. The presence of an attractive coral known as *Pachyphyllum* means that rocks were deposited late in Devonian times, whether they occur in Iowa, Nevada, Arizona, or northern Canada.

A really good index fossil has three outstanding characteristics. First, it is easily recognized, which means that it cannot be confused with fossils that lived at other times. A good index fossil when alive also spread rapidly and widely, becoming common during one small division of time, or epoch, after which it became extinct. Finally, it was easily preserved, leaving a large number of fossils. Rare species may have index value when we find them, but they are much less useful than others that are plentiful.

*Correlation.* To make sure how index fossils are used, let us picture three isolated hills and two quarries. All contain strata in orderly sequence, but no two sequences match. Does this mean that different sediments settled in different places, as they did in Montana, Alberta, and South Dakota? Or do these beds form one continuous series, with the oldest at the bottom and the youngest at the top?

These questions cannot be answered by following strata, for they are hidden or missing in the stretches between our quarries and cliffs. Instead, we

[*357*]

collect fossils from each place and then correlate, or match, them. At the top of Hill 1 we find some sea urchins identical with others collected at the bottom of Hill 2. High up in that hill is an oysterlike shell called *Gryphaea*, which also appears in Quarry 3. A plump snail links Quarry 3 with Hill 4, and a mussel shows that a bed near the crest of the hill is found at the bottom of Quarry 5. By matching strata that contain these index fossils, we arrange our exposures in one continuous series, or section.

Problems in correlation (facies problems) can be caused if certain fossils are found only in one kind of rock. In other words, when alive, these organisms lived in restricted kinds of environments or were preserved only under special circumstances. For example, graptolites are often restricted to black shales, whereas brachiopods are normally preserved in limestones and sandstones. So, when we try to correlate between shales and limestones that may have been deposited at the same time but in different places, we need to find some fossil that occurs in both. Pollen is often such a fossil; it settles from the air into many kinds of environments and thus forms a "time thread" connecting them all.

### DIVIDING EARTH'S HISTORY

This method of correlating rocks by their fossils was first used during the 1790s by an English engineer, William Smith, and two French paleontologists, Georges Cuvier and Alexandre Brongniart. They also used differences between fossils to divide thick series of strata into related groups, formations, and beds. Both approaches appealed to geologists who were trying to escape from an outworn dogma which held that all fossil-bearing rocks had formed during one brief epoch that came soon after creation. Within forty years after Smith announced his ideas, his followers produced a classification of formations and larger units extending from the earliest Cambrian through the "Newer Pliocene." Though terms were defined in a number of ways and many details were lacking, this sequence included deposits from the last three eras of earth history—the only ones in which fossils other than stromatolites and a few single-celled fossils are common and well defined.

As a result of Smith's organization of rocks, the geological time scale was built up. It was not, however, constructed in an orderly fashion. Some units were originally defined by the physical character of the rocks and others by the fossils within them. The Jurassic was first defined by the rocks that occurred in the Jura Mountains, of eastern France and western Switzerland.

*The geologic time scale showing major geologic and biologic events. Snowflake symbols indicate times of major glaciation. FA, first appearance; LA, last appearance. This chart demonstrates the immensity of Precambrian time relative to the short Phanerozoic, the time when fossils were most often preserved. (Modified after Harland and others, 1982)*

## Left chart

| LINEAR SCALE M.y. | EON | ERA | PERIOD | RELATIVE CHANGES OF SEA LEVEL / Events |
|---|---|---|---|---|
| | | | | **RELATIVE CHANGES OF SEA LEVEL** — rising / present-day sea level / falling — 1.0  0.5  0 |
| | | Cz | Cz | Quaternary |
| 100 | | Mesozoic | K | Alpine Orogeny |
| 200 | | Mz | J, Tr | |
| 300 | | | P, C | Gondwana — Variscan Orogeny |
| 400 | Phanerozoic | Paleozoic | D, S, O | Late Ordovician — Caledonian Orogeny |
| 500 | | | € | Assyntic Orogeny |
| 600 | Ph / Pz | Vendian / Sinian | Vend-ian | Late Sinian — Ediacarian metazoan microbiota — Avalonian |
| 700 | Pt 3 | Sinian | Sturtian | |
| 800 | | Z | ? U | |
| 900 | | | | Skillogalee microbiota (primitive algae, prokaryotes, eukaryotes) |
| 1000 | | | | Bitter Springs Formation, Australia — A variety of procaryotes |
| 1100 | | | | Grenvillian |
| 1200 | Proterozoic | Pt 2 Riphean | | Elzevitian |
| 1300 | | | | |
| 1400 | | | | |
| 1500 | | | | Kilarnean |
| 1600 | | ? | | |
| 1700 | | ? | | Oxygenic atmosphere — Hudsonian |
| 1800 | | | | FA of common red beds — LA of banded ironstones — Anoxygenic atmosphere |
| 1900 | | | | Gunflint Iron Fmn, photosynthetic biota (eukaryotes).(?) Fungi, colonial bacteria, blue-green algae.(?) stromatolites in Gunflint Chert U.S.A.& Canada |
| 2000 | | Pt 1 | | Moranian |
| 2100 | | | | Blezardian |
| 2200 | | | | Witwatersrand System, S.Africa (bacteria, cocci, bacilli, algal filaments) |
| 2300 | | | | Huronian |
| 2400 | | | | |

Side arrow: Intracellular specialization ↑

## Right chart

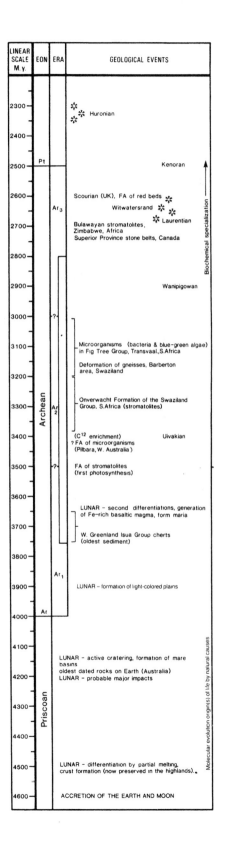

| LINEAR SCALE M.y. | EON | ERA | GEOLOGICAL EVENTS |
|---|---|---|---|
| 2300 | | | Huronian |
| 2400 | | | |
| 2500 | Pt | | Kenoran |
| 2600 | | Ar 3 | Scourian (UK), FA of red beds — Witwatersrand — Laurentian |
| 2700 | | | Bulawayan stromatolites, Zimbabwe, Africa — Superior Province stone belts, Canada |
| 2800 | | | |
| 2900 | | | Wanipigowan |
| 3000 | | ? | |
| 3100 | | | Microorganisms (bacteria & blue-green algae) in Fig Tree Group, Transvaal, S.Africa |
| 3200 | Archean | | Deformation of gneisses, Barberton area, Swaziland |
| 3300 | | Ar 2 | Onverwacht Formation of the Swaziland Group, S.Africa (stromatolites) |
| 3400 | | | (C$^{12}$ enrichment)   Uivakian — ? FA of microorganisms (Pilbara, W. Australia) |
| 3500 | | ? | FA of stromatolites (first photosynthesis) |
| 3600 | | | LUNAR – second differentiations, generation of Fe-rich basaltic magma, form maria |
| 3700 | | | W. Greenland Isua Group cherts (oldest sediment) |
| 3800 | | Ar 1 | |
| 3900 | | | LUNAR – formation of light-colored plains |
| 4000 | | Ar | |
| 4100 | | | LUNAR – active cratering, formation of mare basins |
| 4200 | | | oldest dated rocks on Earth (Australia) — LUNAR – probable major impacts |
| 4300 | Priscoan | | |
| 4400 | | | |
| 4500 | | | LUNAR – differentiation by partial melting, crust formation (now preserved in the highlands). |
| 4600 | | | ACCRETION OF THE EARTH AND MOON |

Side arrows: Biochemical specialization ↑ ; Molecular evolution origin(s) of life by natural causes

The geologic time scale emphasizing the Phanerozoic, the last 590 million years of time, showing major biologic events, sea level, magnetic polarity, and times of major glaciations (indicated by snowflakes). FA, first appearance; LA, last appearance. (Modified after Harland and others, 1982)

| AGE IN M.y. | EON | ERA / ERATHEM | SUB ERA | PERIOD / SYSTEM | EPOCH / SERIES | ESTIMATED EUSTATIC CHANGES IN SEA LEVEL Meters above and below present-day sea level (Rising — Falling) | MAGNETIC POLARITY (Normal / Reversal / Mixed) | GLACIAL PERIODS | ORGANIC REMAINS | GEOLOGICAL & BIOLOGICAL EVENTS |
|---|---|---|---|---|---|---|---|---|---|---|
| 250 | Phanerozoic | Paleozoic | | Permian (P) | Late | | P | ✳ | | LA of trilobites, tabulate corals, orthid brachiopods |
| | | | | | Early | | | | | Proto-Atlantic Ocean finally closed |
| 300 | | | | Carboniferous (C) — Pennsylvanian (Pen) / Mississippian (Mis) | Gzelian / Kasimovian / Moscovian / Bashkirian | | PP | | | FA of winged insects |
| | | | | | Serpukhovian | | | | | FA of pelycosaurs |
| 350 | | | | | Visean | | D-M | ✳ | | FA of cotylosaurs |
| | | | | | Tournaisian | | | | | LA of graptolites |
| | | | | Devonian (D) | Late | | | | | FA of amphibians (labyrinthodonts) |
| 400 | | | | | Middle | | | | | |
| | | | | | Early | | ? | | | FA of ammonoids |
| | | | | Silurian (S) | Pridolian / Ludlovian / Wenlockian / Llandoverian | | O-S | ~~ | | FA of land plants |
| 450 | | | | Ordovician (O) | Ashgillian / Caradocian / Llandeilian / Llanvirnian / Arenigian / Tremadocian | 2nd-order cycles (Supercycles) | ~~ / ? | ✳ ✳ | | |
| 500 | | | | | | | | | | FA of echinoids, bryozoans |
| | | | | Cambrian (€) | Merioneth | | | | | |
| | | | | | St. David's | C-O | | | | FA of vertebrates (jawless fish, graptolites) |
| 550 | | | | | Caerfai | | | | | FA of many invertebrate phyla |
| 590 | Ph | Pz | | | | | | | | FA of exoskeletal material |
| 600 | Proterozoic | Pt₃ | Sirian (Z) | Vendian (V) | Ediacaran | | | ✳ ✳ | | |
| | | | | Sturtian (U) | Varangian | | | | | |
| 1000 | | Pt₂ | Riphean (R) | Yurmatin (Y) | | | | | | FA of eukaryotes (organisms with a nucleus) |
| | | | | Burzyan (B) | | | | | | FA of common red beds |
| 2000 | | Pt₁ | | Huronian (H) | | | | ✳ | | LA of banded ironstones |
| | Pt | | | | | | | ✳ | | |
| | | Ar₃ | | Randian (Ran) | | | | | | |
| 3000 | Archean | Ar₂ | Swazian (Sw) | | | | | | | FA of stromatolites, ? first microorganisms |
| | | Ar₁ | | | | | | | | Oldest sedimentary rocks |
| | Ar | | | Isuan (I) | | | | | | Oldest dated rocks |
| 4000 | Priscoan | | | Hadean (Hd) | | | | | | |
| 5000 | Pr | | | | | | | | | |

| AGE IN M.y. | EON | ERA / ERATHEM | SUB ERA | PERIOD / SYSTEM | EPOCH / SERIES | MARINE — EUROPEAN STANDARD DIVISIONS | NORTH AMERICAN AGE / STAGE | AUSTRALIAN DIVISIONS AGE / STAGE | NEW ZEALAND DIVISIONS EPOCH/SERIES | AGE / STAGE |
|---|---|---|---|---|---|---|---|---|---|---|
| | Phanerozoic (Ph) | Cenozoic (Cz) | Tertiary (TT) | | QUAT. Q / Pleistogene Ptg / Pleistocene / Pie | Pleistocene | Several | Hallian | Werrikooian | Hawera | Castlecliffian |
| | | | | | | | Wheelerian | | | | Nukumarian |
| | | | | | Pliocene Pli L | Villafranchian | Venturian | Yatalan | Wanganui | Mangapanian |
| 5 | | | | | Pliocene E | Ruscinian | Repettian | Kalimnan | | Waipipian |
| | | | | | | Messinian | Delmontian | Cheltenhamian | Taranaki | Opotian |
| | | | | Neogene | Miocene L | Tortonian (Helvetian) | Mohnian | Mitchellian | | Kapitean |
| 10 | | | | | | | | | Southland | Tongaporutuan |
| | | | | | | | | Barnsdalian | | Waiauan |
| | | | | | Miocene M | Langian (Vindobonian) | Luisian | Balcombian | | Lillburnian |
| 15 | | | | | | | Relisian | | | Clifdinian |
| | | | | | | Burdigalian | | Batesfordian | Pareora | Altonian |
| 20 | | | | | Miocene E | | Saucesian | | | |
| | | | | Ng | Aquitanian | | Longfordian | | Otaian |
| 25 | | | | | Mio | | | | | Waitakian |
| | | | | | | | | | | Duntroonian |
| 30 | | | | | Oligocene L | Chattian | Zemorrian | Janjunkian | Landon | |
| 35 | | | | | | | | | | Whaingaroan |
| | | | | | Oligocene E / Oli | Rupelian (Stampian) | | | | |
| 40 | | | | | Eocene L | Bartonian | Refugian | Aldingian | Arnold | Runangan |
| | | | | Paleogene | | | | | | Kaiatan |
| 45 | | | | | Eocene M | Lutetian | Narizian | | | Bortonian |
| | | | | | | | Ulatisian | Johannian | | Porangian |
| 50 | | | | | | | | | Dannevirke | Heretaungan |
| | | | | | | | | | | Mangaorapan |
| | | | | | Eocene E / Eoc | Ypresian | Bulitian | | | Waipawan |
| 55 | | | | | Paleocene L | Thanetian | | Wangerripian | | Teurian |
| 60 | | | | | | | Ynezian | | | |
| | | | | | Paleocene E / Pal | Montian | | | | |
| 65 | | | | Pg | | Danian | | | | |
| 70 | | Mesozoic (Mz) | | | Late (Senonian) | Maastrichtian | Gulfian | | | Haumurian |
| | | | | | | Campanian | | | Raukumara | Piripuan |
| | | | | | | | | | | Teratan |
| | | | | | | Santonian | | | | Mangaotanian |
| | | | | | | Coniacian | | | | Arowhanian |
| | | | | Cretaceous | | Turonian | | | | |
| 100 | | | | | | Cenomanian | | | | Ngaterian |
| | | | | | | Albian | Comanchean | | Clarence | Motuan |
| | | | | | Early | | | | | Urutawan |
| | | | | | | Aptian | | | Taitai | Korangan |
| | | | | | | Barremian | | | | |
| | | | | | Neocomian | Hauterivian | | | | ? |
| | | | | K | | Valanginian | | | | |
| | | | | | | Berriasian | | | | |
| 150 | | | | | Late (Malm) | Tithonian | | | Oteke | Puaroan |
| | | | | | | Kimmeridgian | | | | Ohauan |
| | | | | | | Oxfordian | | | Kawhia | Heterian ? |
| | | | | Jurassic | Middle (Dogger) | Callovian | | | | Temaikan |
| | | | | | | Bathonian | | | | |
| | | | | | | Bajocian | | | | |
| | | | | | | Aalenian | | | | Ururoan |
| | | | | | Early (Lias) | Toarcian | | | Herangi | |
| 200 | | | | | | Pliensbachian | | | | |
| | | | | | | Sinemurian | | | | Aratauran |
| | | | | J | | Hettangian | | | | |
| | | | | | Late | Rhaetian | | | | Otapirian |
| | | | | | | Norian | | | Balfour | Warepan |
| | | | | | | Carnian | | | | Otamitan |
| | | | | Triassic | Middle | Landian | Spathian | | | Oretian |
| | | | | | | Anisian | Smithian | | Gore | Kaihikuan |
| | | | | | | | Dienerian | | | Etalian |
| 248 | | | | Tr | | Scythian | Griesbachian | | | Malakovian |

[362]

| AGE IN M.y. | EON | ERA / ERATHEM | SUB ERA | PERIOD / SYSTEM | EPOCH / SERIES | MARINE | | | NEW ZEALAND DIVISIONS | |
| | | | | | | EUROPEAN STANDARD DIVISIONS | NORTH AMERICAN AGE / STAGE | AUSTRALIAN DIVISIONS AGE / STAGE | EPOCH / SERIES | AGE / STAGE |
|---|---|---|---|---|---|---|---|---|---|---|
| 250 | Phanerozoic | Paleozoic | | Permian | Late | Tartarian / Kazanian / Ufimian | Ochoan / Guadalupian | | D'Urville | Malakovian / Makarewan / Waiitian / Puruhauan |
| | | | | | Early | Kungurian / Artinskian / Sakmarian | Leonardian / Wolfcampian | | Aparima | Braxtonian |
| | | | P | | | Gzelian | Atokan | | | Mangapirian |
| 300 | | | Pennsyl- vanian | Carboniferous | | Kasimovian / Moscovian | Virgilian / Missourian / Desmoinesian | | | Telfordian |
| | | | Pen | | | Bashkirian | Morrowan | | | |
| | | | Missis- sippian | | | Serpukhovian | Springerian | | | |
| 350 | | | Mis | | | Visean | Chesterian / Meramacian / Osagean | | | |
| | | | C | | | Tournaisian | Kinderhookian | | | |
| | | | | Devonian | Late | Famennian / Frasnian | Chautauquan / Senecan | | | |
| | | | | | Middle | Givetian / Eifelian | Erian | | | |
| 400 | | | | | Early | Emsian / Siegenian / Gedinnian | Ulisterian | | | |
| | | | D | | Pridolian | | | | | |
| | | | | Silurian | Ludlovian | 9 named ages | Cayugan | Melbournian | | |
| | | | | | Wenlockian | | | Eildonian | | |
| | | | S | | Llandoverian | | Niagran | Keilorian | | |
| 450 | | | | Ordovician | Ashgillian | 16 named ages | Medinan | Bolindian | | |
| | | | | | Caradocian | | Cincinnatian | Eastonian / Gisbornian | | |
| | | | | | Llandeilian | | | | | |
| | | | | | Llanvirnian | | Champlainian | Darriwilian | | |
| | | | | | Arenigian | | | Yapeenian | | |
| 500 | | | | | Tremadocian | | Canadian | Castlemanian / Chewtonian | | |
| | | | O | | | | | Bendigonian | | |
| | | | | Cambrian | Merioneth | Dolgellian / Maentwrogian | Croixian | Lancefieldian | | |
| | | | | | | Menevian | | | | |
| | | | | | St. Davids | Solvan / Lenian | Albertan | Idamean | | |
| 550 | | | | | | | | Templetonian | | |
| | | | | | Caerfai | Atdabanian | Waucoban | Ordian | | |
| | | | | | | --- ? --- | | | | |
| 590 | Ph | Pz | | € | | Tommotian | | | | |

Major divisions of the geologic time scale during the Phanerozoic showing how different names are used on different continents, and in both marine and terrestrial sequences. The subdivisions are defined by the fossils in rock sequences. Boundaries between divisions are drawn using biologic events such as appearance and disappearance of various organisms. Tying together such subdivisions on different continents is not easy but is done by using both fossils and radiometric dating. (Modified after Harland and others, 1982)

[363]

| TERRESTRIAL LAND MAMMAL AGES | | | | AGE IN M y. |
|---|---|---|---|---|
| EUROPEAN | NORTH AMERICAN | SOUTH AMERICAN | AFRICAN | |
| Oldenburgian Biharian | Rancholabrean Irvingtonian | Lujanian Ensenadan/Uquian | | |
| Villafranchian | Blancan | Chapadmalalan Montehermosan | Rodolfian | |
| Ruscian | Hemphillian | Huayquerian | Lothagamian | 5 |
| Turolian | | | Ngororan | |
| Vallesian | Clarendonian | Chasicoan | | 10 |
| Astaracian | Barstovian | Friasian | Tarnanian | |
| | | | | 15 |
| Orleanian | Hemingfordian | Santacrucian | Rusingan | |
| | | | | 20 |
| Agenian | | Monte Leon | | |
| | Arikarean | Colhuehuapian | | |
| Arvernian | Whitneyan | | | 25 |
| | Orellan | | | |
| | | | Fayumian | 30 |
| Suevian | Chadronian | | | |
| | | Deseadan | | 35 |
| Headonian | Duchesnean | | | |
| | | | | 40 |
| | | Divisaderan | | |
| | Uintan | | | |
| | | | | 45 |
| | Bridgerian | Musterian | | |
| | Wasatchian | | | 50 |
| | Clarkforkian | Casamayoran | | |
| | Tiffanian | Riochican | | 55 |
| | | | | 60 |
| | Torrejonian | | | |
| | | Salamancan (marine) | | 65 |
| | Puercan | | | 70 |
| | Lancian | | | |
| | | | | 100 |
| | | | | 150 |
| | | | | 200 |
| | | | | 248 |

The Eocene, on the other hand, was set up as those rocks in the Paris Basin, of France, that contained a suite of marine molluscs of which 3.5 percent were living species. New definitions were added, and over the next century and a half the geological time scale was standardized and expanded to include many units not in the original.

**AN EARLY DIVISION OF THE TERTIARY PERIOD BY SIR CHARLES LYELL**

| Formation and Epoch | Meaning of Name | Percentage of Species Still Living |
|---|---|---|
| Newer Pliocene | Newer More Recent | 90–95 |
| Older Pliocene | More Recent | 35–50 |
| Miocene | Less Recent | 17 |
| Eocene | Dawn of the Recent | 3.5 |

Today our geological time scale is made up of three kinds of geological units: rock, time-rock, and time units. Rock units are ones that describe the physical (lithologic) characteristics of the rocks themselves; for example, the red beds, the Judith River Formation, or the Strezlecki Group. Time units refer only to the passage of time, and thus the Cenozoic Era is all of the time between 65 million years ago and today. The Cretaceous Period is the time between 130 and 65 million years ago. Time-rock units involve both time and rocks; that is, fossil sequences in rocks. And these time-rock units are what geologists often use when they organize the sedimentary rocks of the world in an orderly succession. The Cenozoic Erathem, then, is the rocks that were deposited during the Cenozoic Era, and it is the fossils that define the boundaries.

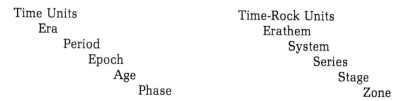

    Time Units                    Time-Rock Units
        Era                           Erathem
           Period                        System
              Epoch                         Series
                 Age                            Stage
                    Phase                          Zone

As you can imagine, time-rock sequences are not always complete in one area. So the Cenozoic Era means all the 65 million years from its beginning to its end; the Cenozoic Erathem, on the other hand, is not so continuous a unit. It is all the rocks and fossils deposited during the last 65 million years, and there may be breaks in this record caused by erosion, nondeposition, or nonrecognition because characteristic fossils are lacking. We must be careful, when thinking and talking about these three units, not to confuse them: time, rocks, and rocks deposited during a specific time as defined by fossils, are all different concepts.

***From Fossils to Changes in the Earth.***   Lyell's divisions did well enough so long as geologists knew more about fossils than they knew about rocks and the earth. In time, however, they discovered that this method of dividing earth history put effects in place of causes. The Cretaceous Period did not begin because certain molluscs and reptiles came into existence, nor did it end because they died out. It was a time when lands were low and seas spread widely, though there were progressive upheavals in the western United States. Similarly, the Pennsylvanian was more than a time of fernlike plants and primitive trees; it was one in which seas often spread and withdrew, turning their basins into swamps where the raw material of coal could settle. The Pleistocene, or Ice Age, on the other hand, was distinguished by high lands, changing climates, and glaciers that repeatedly spread in the Northern Hemisphere. These events are merely reflected by fossils, which adjusted themselves to the world in which they lived.

The number of time divisions has grown as knowledge of earth's history has increased. When Charles Lyell published his *Elements of Geology*, in 1838, he described sixteen epochs and formations distributed among three larger units, the Primary (or Transition), Secondary, and Tertiary. Today we recognize at least nine eras, as many as twenty periods, and a still larger number of epochs. These are listed in the accompanying table of earth history, in which names, events, and dates are correlated with outstanding developments in life.

As the number of periods and epochs increased, groups and formations grew smaller and smaller. Lyell's Cretaceous "group" is now a system; his Lias "formation" has become a series. Modern formations generally are limited to strata that settled during one compact portion of earth history, under essentially uniform conditions, and in one limited region. Many formations, therefore, contain one dominant kind of rock and take names from localities in which they are well developed. Others comprise rocks of two or more kinds, so intimately linked that they plainly belong together. These differences are reflected in names such as Brunswick Shale, Selma Chalk, St. Peter Sandstone, and Green River Formation. The last is a complex sequence of shales, sandstones, limestones, and marls deposited in two large, shallow lakes. Strata as varied as those along the Two Medicine River may be either a formation or a group.

### AGES OF FOSSILS AND ROCKS

So far, we have seen how fossils can be used to set up a relative sequence of rocks. Dinosaurs, we know, occurred after trilobites became extinct and before woolly mammoths and humans arrived on the scene. But fossils themselves cannot give an age in years. It was this relative time scale that formed the basis of the geologic time scale we know today, based on the order of appearance and disappearance of various fossils in rock sequences. By the end of the 1800s, this relative time scale was well refined.

The question of how old in years the fossils were, however, remained unanswered. Soon after the discovery of radioactivity, in 1896, by Henri Becquerel, some geologists realized that it could provide a basis for determining the age of a rock in years. The reason for this was that radioactive processes were found to proceed at a constant rate under the range of temperature, pressure, and chemical conditions on the surface of the earth. A wide variety of dating techniques based on radioactive decay have been developed in this century. Each technique has its particular strength, which makes it possible to date certain types of samples that could otherwise not be dated. The well-known carbon-14 technique is commonly used to date samples of charcoal and plant material found in Late Quaternary sites no older than about forty thousand years. The potassium-argon technique is useful for dating samples no younger than about 1 million years and was used widely to date moon rocks on the order of 4,000 million years old.

Though the range of ages dated by the two techniques are so different, both are based on the same fundamental principle: after a known period of time called the *half-life,* the amount of the original radioactive material remaining in a rock sample is reduced by half because of radioactive decay. If a second period of equal duration passes, half of the remaining half, or one fourth, of the original radioactive material will remain. Thus, by measuring the amount of the radioactive material remaining and determining how much was originally present, it is possible to decide how much has decayed and thus how long it has been since the decay process started in the rock sample.

An analogous situation would be to determine how long it had been since a leaking bucket was filled. If the bucket leaks at a constant, known rate and you find it half full, you can determine how long ago the bucket was filled.

The time when a fast-leaking bucket was last filled can be determined within relatively narrow limits, because a large quantity of water is lost in a short time, making measurement easy. On the other hand, a fast-leaking bucket soon runs dry, and thus it is possible to determine the time of filling only if it is in the relatively recent past. A slow-leaking bucket can date the time of filling further into the past, but the limits of error of the age determination are much greater, because a small change in volume represents a long period of time.

In the same way, carbon 14, with a half-life of only 5,730 years, can give a date with an error of only a few years. But a mass of carbon 14 equal to that of the earth would not have a single original atom of cabon 14 remaining after one million years. In that period, the sample would have decreased, by half, 174.52 times. Or, in other words, there would only be one part in 3,434 followed by forty-nine zeros of the sample left. As such a qauntity of carbon 14 would "only" be about 25 followed by forty-nine zeros atoms, the chance that even a single one would have survived that long is slightly less than one in one hundred. It is for this reason that carbon 14 is useful only for dating events during the past forty thousand years. In geologic terms, that is the very recent past. But, even after that relatively short period, there is only about 1 part in 125 of the original carbon 14 remaining in the sample.

On the other hand, the oldest rocks on the earth and the moon, which have been dated by the potassium-argon method at about 4,000 million years, have about one-eighth the original potassium 40 that was in the sample to begin with, as the half-life of that isotope is 1,400 million years.

The "14" of carbon 14 refers to the total number of particles that form the nucleus of the carbon atom. Carbon 14 is a particular isotope of carbon that happens to be radioactive. Carbon 12, which is another carbon isotope, has twelve particles in the nucleus and is not radioactive. Almost 99 percent of the carbon on earth is carbon 12 and most of the rest is another stable isotope, carbon 13.

Carbon 14 is produced when cosmic rays from outer space bombard nitrogen 14 high up in the atmosphere. Approximately 70 tons of carbon 14 are produced in the earth's atmosphere this way each year. The carbon 14 so prduced is absorbed by plants (and sometimes in turn by animals that eat them). When the animals (or uneaten plants) die and are thus no longer incorporating any more carbon into their systems, half the carbon 14 is lost every 5,730 years. Dates can be determined by analyzing the relative amounts of the two isotopes carbon 12 and carbon 14. The ratio changes, as the carbon 14 decays and the carbon 12 does not.

The annual production of 70 tons of carbon 14 in the earth's atmosphere is an average that is known to have fluctuated over the past few thousand years. It is only one of the factors that leads to an error of measurement in a radioactive-decay age calculation. Therefore, such an age will be expressed with a ± error factor, for example as one date on South American sloth dung of 10,832 ±400 years. In other words, the sloth may have lived as little as 10,432 years ago or as much as 11,232 years ago. Spruce trees in Manitowoc County, Wisconsin, were pushed over by ice of the last great glacier that reached the Mississippi Valley. They died at least 10,668 years ago or as much as 13,668 years ago.

Many other radioactive dating schemes exist and differ from the carbon 14 and potassium-argon techniques primarily in the ways the abundances of the isotopes involved are measured. Among the others is the first one developed, the well-known uranium–thorium–lead series. The basic underlying principle of all these techniques, however, is the same: the constancy of the rate of the decay process.

Some chemical processes proceed at uniform rates under special conditions. Amino acids are the building blocks out of which proteins are constructed and are present in all living cells. In a living organism, the structure of all the amino acids is referred to as left-handed. However, once an organism dies, the amino acids begin to convert to their right-handed, or mirror-image, structure, at a rate dependent on the temperature. Eventually, a 50–50 mixture of left- and right-handed amino acids is reached, and then the ratio remains constant. In situations in which the temperature in the past can be reasonably assumed to have been constant, such as the bottom of the deep sea or inside a cave, it is possible to date samples as old as one million years by this method.

Methods that depend on radioactive bombardment of samples have been developed as well. One of these is thermoluminescence. Trace amounts of radioactive isotopes present in all substances release particles as these isotopes decay. These emissions (alpha, beta, and gamma rays) disrupt the crystalline structure of the surrounding material. If the material is heated, at a certain temperature the flaws in the crystal start to disappear. As this happens, light is released. The more flaws, the more light is released. The amount of light released is therefore a measurement of how much radioactive bombardment the sample has undergone. By also measuring the trace amount of radioactive isotopes in the sample, the time since the crystals were formed can be determined. For a basalt flow, this would be the time the lava cooled. This method is useful for dating samples as old as one million years or as young as a dozen years.

Tree rings provide a method of accurately dating the past few thousand years. A major problem with tree rings is that "annual" rings may not occur each year. Drought, for example, can stop the formation of a distinct pair of rings for a given year. The relative widths of rings reflect the climatic conditions, and the sequence of widths of rings makes it possible to relate the cross sections of various tree. For example, a sequence of five wide bands followed by fourteen narrow ones followed by seven wide ones might occur only once in all of geologic time. If that sequence were found at the outer part of one tree and the inner part of a second, it would be possible to establish that the first was a mature tree when the second was young. By carrying the sequence from the second to the first, the overall sequence of tree-ring relative widths could be extended backward in time. Such tree-ring sequences must obviously be established for restricted areas, as the entire earth does not have the same climatic fluctuations. The best-established tree-ring sequence, or "dendrochronology," is for the bristlecone pine of the Sierra Nevada in California, which goes back about nine thousand years.

An analogous dating process that is worldwide in its scope is "paleomagnetic dating." On a time scale of hundreds of thousands to millions of years, the magnetic field of the earth reverses polarity. That is, after a reversal, the end of a compass needle that now points north would point south. As sediments accumulate, particles rich in nickel and iron become aligned with respect to the magnetic field of the earth. As the sediments harden into rock, the orientation of these particles is 'frozen' so that it is possible to determine the position of the magnetic poles when the hardening occurred, as more fully explained in Chapter III. Similarly, such particles in a lava preserve the orientation of the earth's magnetic field at the time of cooling and solidification, when movement was no longer possible.

Where long vertical unbroken sections of rock are preserved, it is sometimes possible to determine the relative thickness of the magnetically reversed and normal periods. These can be compared with the known sequence of reversed and normal periods that have been dated by such means as the potassium-argon method, mentioned above. Dating of the section in question can then be carried out if a plausible match of the sequences can be made or, as the process is aptly termed, the magnetic "signature" can be recognized.

Still another method of determing age relies upon dark and light layers of clay and silt that settled in lakes of glaciated regions and in some others besides. Each pair of layers, or varve, represents a year; to learn how much time one deposit represents, we count layers and divide by two. Longer series are secured by matching overlapping sections and estimating gaps where they do not overlap. By this method, one authority found that 13,500 years have passed since ice melted from the southern tip of Sweden. Another worker counted 6.5 million varves in deposits of the great Green River lakes of ancient Colorado and Wyoming. Those lakes, therefore, lasted 6.5 million years, an amazingly long time for inland waters whose basins were not very deep.

# APPENDIX 2

# APPENDIX 2

# Continents Have Moved and Climates Have Changed

Today if you stood on the tip of Sandy Hook, in New Jersey, and looked out to the east, you would see nothing but open ocean for as far as the eye could reach. Similarly, you would see only blue-gray water if you were to peer out to the south of the Great Australian Bight. This has not always been so. Were you to step back in time several millions of years, Africa could have been seen from New Jersey, and the great southern continent of Antarctica would have been clearly visible from southern Australia.

#### WEGENER'S CONTINENTAL DRIFT

The idea that continents have moved is not new. It was originally offered to explain the amazing parallelism of coasts on opposite sides of the Atlantic Ocean. Geologists were aware of such an idea by the beginning of the twentieth century. But not many took the idea seriously until Alfred Wegener published a book entitled *The Origin of Continents and Oceans,* first in 1912, with an expanded version in 1915. As support for this idea, Wegener and others, especially the South African geologist Alexander Du Toit, put together a long list of evidence. This list included data from paleontology (in particular, paleobiogeography—the study of the distribution of plants and animals in the past), paleoclimatology (the study of the distribution of ancient climates), the geometrical fit of continents on opposite sides of ocean basins, and structural and general geological studies that investigated sequences of rocks on opposite sides of ocean basins that seemed similar.

Although the evidence given by Du Toit and Wegener was suggestive, neither man could offer a convincing explanation of how the continents themselves could have moved. What was the force that drove continents through the oceans? Geophysicists argued that from what they knew about the physical properties of earth materials, continental drift was not possible.

[*372*]

But the geological and paleontological evidence hinting at continental drift was still there. How was the problem to be resolved? Geologists from many disciplines debated, argued, discussed, and continued to do so for several decades before any convincing solutions to this puzzle were reached.

After a stalemate of nearly thirty years, the debate about continental drift heated up again in the 1950s. This was not because of additional evidence of the kind that Wegener and Du Toit had compiled, but because of data from two other areas of geology: the magnetic properties of rocks and the nature of the ocean floor.

### A GEOLOGICAL ARGUMENT

Many rocks contain particles of iron and nickel. Before the rocks harden, these particles tend to align themselves parallel to the prevailing magnetic field. Therefore, as the rock cools and hardens, a point (the Curie point) is reached, where the particles are no longer able to change orientation as the magnetic field shifts. By determining the "frozen" orientation of these particles, the direction of the magnetic field at the time the rock hardened can be measured. And in this way the former position of the magnetic north and south poles relative to the site where the rock sample was collected can be determined. Such a pole position is called a "paleomagnetic pole."

When a series of paleomagnetic poles of differing ages have been determined for a single landmass, it is possible to draw a "polar wandering curve" through these poles. Such a curve links the paleomagnetic poles in order by age and records the shifting position of the magnetic pole as seen from a single landmass. If the magnetic poles had wandered and there had been no continental drift, the polar wandering curves of all the continents would be the same shape. However, this is not the case, and the different shapes of these polar wandering curves imply that the various continents have moved with respect to one another.

Another kind of evidence bearing on the continental drift controversy was data being gathered on the topography of the ocean floor. Maurice Ewing and Bruce Heezen, working at the Lamont-Doherty Geological laboratories, in Palisades, New York, had plotted information being gathered by ships equipped with sonar devices. This allowed the mapping of the ocean bottom by bouncing sound waves off the seafloor. They discovered enormous mountain chains beneath the oceans, and these seemed to be connected all around the globe. This super chain was more than thirty-five thousand miles in length and, on the average, six hundred miles wide. Ewing and Heezen noted that the ridge in the Atlantic Ocean nicely split the ocean in half, with Europe and Africa on one side and the Americas on the other. They also noted that in the middle of the mountain chain and running the length of it was a central valley, like a rift valley (such as that in East Africa today), which might imply that this area was in a state of tension. This might be interpreted as an area of opening, the original split between the Americas and the Old World of Europe and Africa.

More evidence came to light. There was a high heat flow over the mid-ocean ridges: the ocean bottom was warmer in these areas than on either side of them. There were also frequent earthquakes in these areas. Another, seemingly unrelated, fact was that the ocean basins seemed to have relatively young features. With all the deep-sea drilling up until the early 1960s, the oldest rocks known in the ocean basins were of earliest Cretaceous or very latest Jurassic age. Therefore, the ocean basins that we know today had been in existence for only some 140 million years.

With all this in mind, some geologists suggested that the central mountain ranges, or ridges, in the ocean basins could be looked upon as areas where there was some sort of upwelling of hot material from within the earth. This rising material could explain the high heat flow, the rugged elevated topography of the ridges, and the tensional situation in the rift valley. To explain this, a convection-cell model was proposed. This is best likened to what happens when you boil a thick soup in a saucepan. Heat is applied from the bottom just as it would be if the heat came from deep in the earth. This warms the bottom layers of soup, causing expansion. The bottom layer of soup becomes lighter than the upper layers, moves to the top, and is then forced to move sideways as more hot liquid wells up from below. The path that an individual pea in a thick pea soup would take defines a convection cell. The cell is completed when the soup on top is cooled, contracts, and sinks to the bottom to begin the journey all over again. So geologists explained what might be happening in the earth's crust underneath the mid-ocean ridges and thus offered a general solution to the puzzle that had bedeviled Wegener and Du Toit as they tried to explain how the continents could have been "powered" on their drifting journey across the ocean basins.

In 1962, H. H. Hess, of Princeton University, drew all of the known information together about the ocean basins and convection cells. His paper, which he called "geopoetry," because it was a little short on data, was titled the "History of Ocean Basins." It became known to the everyday geologist as the theory of seafloor spreading. Basically, Hess said that the oceanic mountain ranges were the places where the convection cells of the deeper parts of the earth rose to the surface. Where the convection cell rose, it caused partial melting of solid-rock material, producing lava, which rose, resulting in volcanic eruptions, such as those in Iceland, as well as those that were purely submarine. As the lava solidified, it formed new ocean floor, which was in turn pushed sideways by more upwelling lava—thus the ocean basins grew. As an ocean basin grew, the continents were pushed along as passengers because of what was going on in the ocean basins. The continents did *not* plow through the ocean basins, as Wegener had supposed.

Hess also suggested that in areas where the convection cells went down, the ocean floor descended to depths to become part of the earth's interior once again. Oceanic trenches were the places where this happened. Thus he could explain why none of the present ocean basins were older than Jurassic in age; ocean-basin floors older than Mesozoic had simply been recycled!

### A GEOLOGICAL REVOLUTION

Hess's proposal put geology on the brink of a real scientific revolution—a period when the basic assumptions or working rules are in a state of change. Shortly after Hess's "geopoetry" appeared, a young graduate student, Fred Vine, and a colleague, D. H. Matthews, made another intriguing discovery. They noticed a number of strange patterns (anomalies) in the earth's magnetic field over the Atlantic Ocean basin. They had plotted out a series of magnetized strips on the ocean floor, which they called "zebra stripes." They thought these could be explained by Hess's seafloor spreading theory. They knew that the polarity of the earth's magnetic field had periodically changed in the past—that is, for some reason not fully understood, the north pole became the south pole and the south pole became the north pole. This had happened many times in the past few hundred million years. They suggested that the magnetic patterns, the "zebra stripes," were formed by different parts of the newly generated seafloor being magnetized according to the prevailing magnetic field as the new lava was added along the mid-ocean ridges. When the magnetic field "flip-flopped," as the north and south poles traded places, the next lava produced at the mid-ocean ridge would be magnetized in the opposite direction to the solidified lava slightly farther away from the ridge. Only in the newly formed lava, still above the critical temperature, the Curie point, could the magnetic minerals orient according to a "new" prevailing magnetic field.

Vine and Matthews' brainstorm was the beginning of the most recent scientific revolution in the geological sciences. One of the most important results of this revolution was not that it gave strong support to continental movement, but that it united in one general theory many aspects of geology that had never been related before. Mid-ocean ridges, earthquake activity, heat flow, and location of volcanoes could be explained by a single, comprehensive theory. So, too, could such features as "zebra stripes" detected on horizontal traverses above the ocean floor be related to the pattern of alternating magnetic polarity observed in vertical sequences of rock found in both cores recovered from the ocean floor and in lava flows on land. The outcome was the theory of plate tectonics, which married the theories of continental drift with seafloor spreading, giving us the basic set of rules geologists play by today—until someone comes up with something better!

What is the theory of plate tectonics? The theory, stated simply, suggests

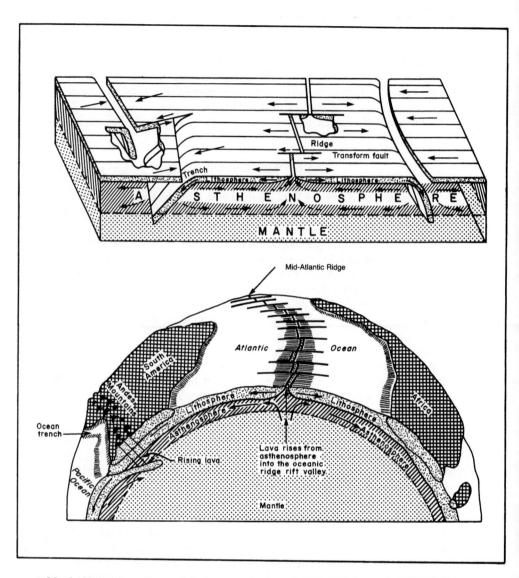

*A block diagram and a model of the earth showing the elements of plate-tectonic theory. Ridges are where lava rises from the deeper layers of the earth to the surface and, once added to the surface, causes expansion of that surface; for example, the Mid-Atlantic Ridge. Trenches are areas where one lithospheric plate dives under another; for example, the trench along the western coast of South America that causes the devastating earthquakes of Chile. Transform faults are areas where crustal plates slide past one another laterally, such as those offsetting the Mid-Atlantic Ridge. It is the relative movement of these crustal (or lithospheric) plates that bring about the drift of continents. (With the permission of P. Wyllie and L. Sykes; drawings modified from their originals)*

[376]

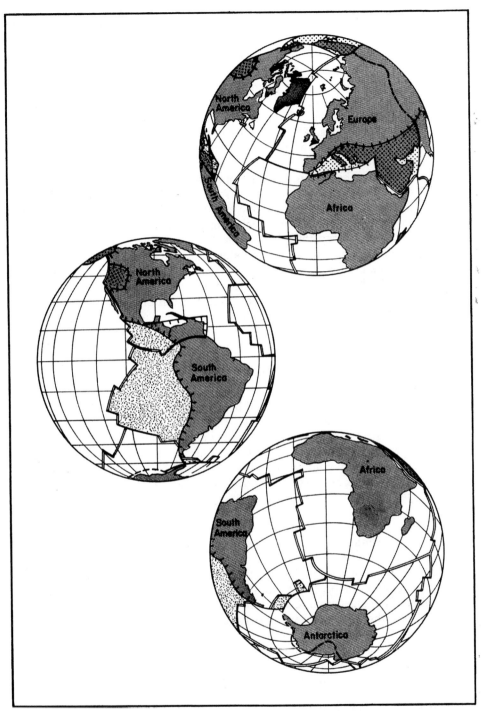

*Three views of the earth showing the several crustal (or lithospheric) plates that exist today. Ridges are indicated by double lines, trenches by hatched lines, and transform faults by solid black lines. All these plates are in constant motion relative to one another. Continents are indicated by gray shading, and other textures are used to outline some of the individual plates. (Modified from F. A. Middlemiss and others, 1971)*

that the upper few miles (up to sixty miles in continental areas) of the earth is divided into a series of thin, rigid plates. This part of the earth's crust is called the lithosphere. These plates meet one another along one of three kinds of boundaries: ridges, trenches, and transform faults. The plates themselves are relatively stable, and earthquake and volcanic activity is mainly confined to their edges. The *ridge,* such as the Mid-Atlantic Ridge, mentioned before, is a place where new material is being added from below, and an area of expansion. Such a boundary is characterized by high heat flow, volcanic activity, shallow to medium-depth earthquakes, and tensional faulting. A *trench,* such as the Marianas Trench, in the southwestern Pacific Ocean, is a boundary along which one crustal plate is moving below another such plate and material is being pushed or pulled into the deeper layers of the earth. Trenches typically have very low heat flow, earthquakes from shallow to deep (which take place all along the descending lithospheric slab as it sinks back into the deeper layers of the earth), and volcanoes above the deeper part of the descending slab. The third kind of boundary, the *transform fault,* is a most unusual kind of fault. It is an area where two plates move past one another laterally and is characterized by shallow earthquakes. It is unusual in that its observed movement is just the opposite of what it appears to be. All of this can be explained by using Hess's seafloor spreading idea—and a Canadian geologist, J. Tuzo Wilson, made a brilliant explanation of this kind of fault in the mid-1960s. Transform faults clearly show up on maps of the ocean basin floor as tremendous offsets of the mid-ocean ridges. They probably resulted in part from tension produced in these massive plates because spreading rates differed along the mid-ocean ridges.

Most geologists today use such a theory as a working model, but not all accept it or totally agree with it. As with science in general, it will stand as a useful idea until something more workable is put forward. Questioning the correctness of it is a necessity of good science and should always be heartily encouraged.

### PAST PATTERNS OF CONTINENTS AND OCEANS

Geophysicists, using the information they have collected over the past twenty years on the location of fossil paleomagneticpoles, have constructed a number of paleogeographic maps for various times in the past. These maps show where the continents we know today have been in times past—relative to one another and relative to latitude and longitude. It is important for us to be aware of such maps as we look at the history of plants and animals, at least during the past 600 million years, when the record of life is good. Then we can see if the distribution of plants and animals supports the reconstructions based on geophysical data or not. If the biological data support the geophysical data, then the reconstructions are probably reasonably good. If, however, there are major contradictions based on different lines of evidence, then it is time to go back to the drawing board, so to speak, and find out whose data are incorrectly interpreted. This check-and-balance system in science leads to a continual reevaluation of observations and allows scientists to continually try to increase understanding of our earth and its inhabitants.

Let's look at some of the past continental distributions based on geophysical information and keep them in mind throughout the rest of the book as various animal and plant groups are explored. This should give a good overall view of what the world was like from both a physical and a biological point of view.

At the beginning of the Paleozoic, in the Cambrian Period, the world was very different from what it is today. As the map for this period illustrates, there was one, very large continent, Gondwana—formed by what are today Africa, South America, Australia, and Antarctica—which was surrounded by a number of smaller islands made up of bits of Asia and Europe. One other, smaller continent consisted of parts of Europe and North America. And then there was an even smaller continent, a fragment of eastern Asia.

As the Cambrian map shows, the continents were constructed of different jigsaw pieces from what they are today. They were also often situated in very different places. Antarctica, for instance, was not over the South Pole. It was instead near the equator, along with North America and Australia. In fact, most of the continental masses in the Cambrian were strung like beads on a string around the equator, and no landmass lay over either the north pole or the south pole. This kind of continental arrangement surely had an effect on the circulation patterns in the oceans and in the atmosphere as well, and thus had an effect on climate.

Because of lithospheric plate movements, by Silurian times, some 420 million years ago, many of the continental fragments had shifted positions. Gondwana had moved into a position over the south pole, bringing such continents as Antarctica, South America, and Africa far south. Australia, North America, parts of China, and Europe, however, were still strung around the equator. Gondwana remained the single large continent, and the few other landmasses were much smaller, all quite isolated from one another. In the Devonian Period, some 390 million years ago, there were essentially two large landmasses, Gondwana still the largest by far, but several parts of North America, Europe, and Asia had merged to form a second continent of significant size, Laurasia.

By the end of the Paleozoic Era, in the Permian Period, some 240 million years ago, all of the major landmasses had merged into one large unit, which Wegener named Pangaea. This, of course, meant that terrestrial animals and plants had the possibility of moving across a single large expanse, if they could tolerate local climatic conditions and cross barriers of inhospitable country. Antarctica was situated at the south pole at this time, and some of

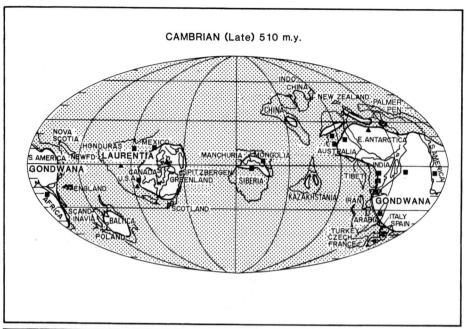

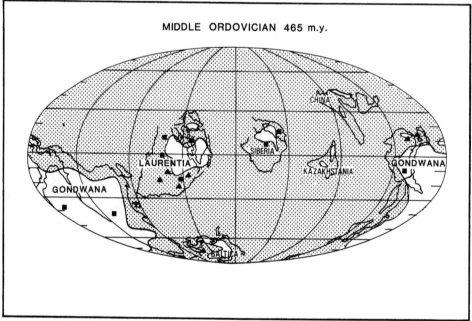

*Paleogeographic maps for the Phanerozoic (Cambrian into the future) of the world showing the location of each of the continents. The symbols on each of the maps show the information used to determine past climates: black squares are evaporites, thick sequences of salts that formed in relatively arid areas; black triangles are reefs, which today are restricted generally to within 30 degrees either side of the equator; black circles are coals that form under humid conditions, generally in temperate or cool-temperate areas. Stippled areas are oceans, white areas are continents, dark hatched areas are ice sheets. Arrows indicate the direction in which certain crustal plates are moving. (The last map in this sequence was modified after a map in* Scientific American, *1970, Vol. 233, no. 4, p. 39)*

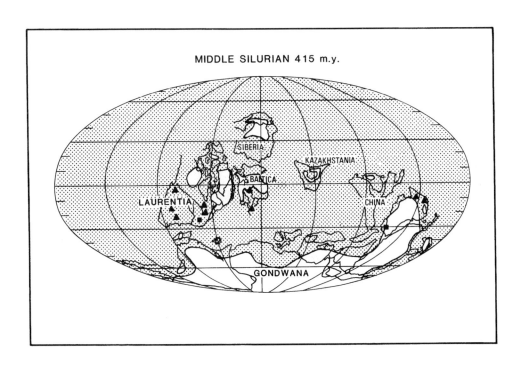

MIDDLE SILURIAN 415 m.y.

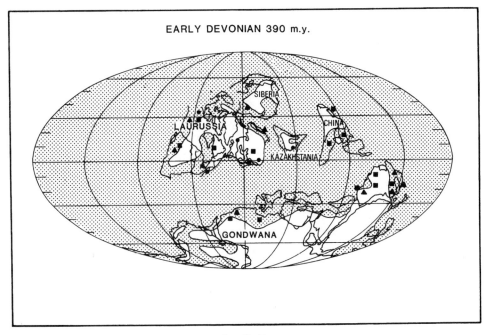

EARLY DEVONIAN 390 m.y.

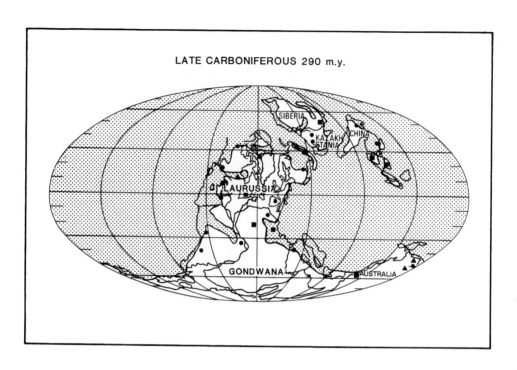

LATE CARBONIFEROUS 290 m.y.

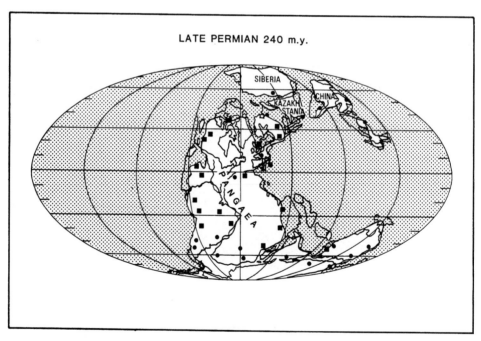

LATE PERMIAN 240 m.y.

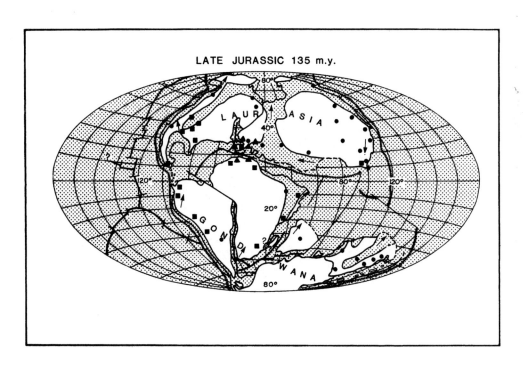

LATE JURASSIC 135 m.y.

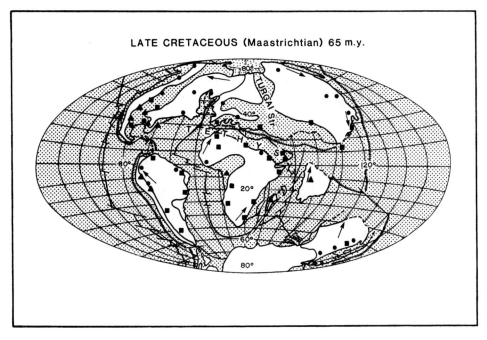

LATE CRETACEOUS (Maastrichtian) 65 m.y.

[383]

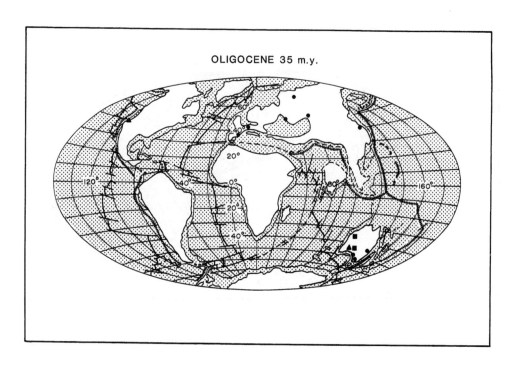

OLIGOCENE 35 m.y.

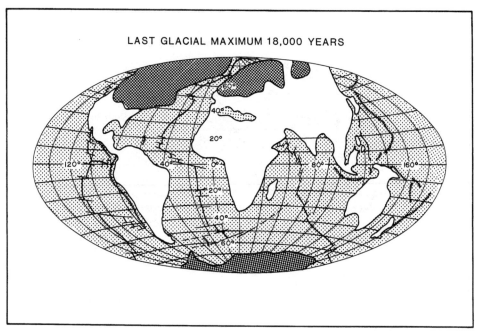

LAST GLACIAL MAXIMUM 18,000 YEARS

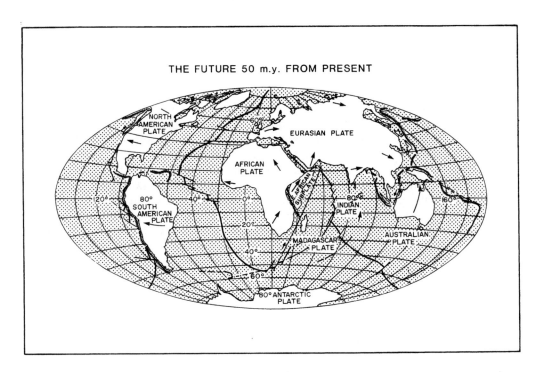

THE FUTURE 50 m.y. FROM PRESENT

what are now northern Europe and Asia were far north of the equator. Other parts of North America and Europe, including Russia, were closer to the equator than they are today. By contrast, South America and Africa were farther south of the equator than today. Australia and New Zealand, still attached to Antarctica, were far south indeed.

During Mesozoic times, the supercontinent, Pangaea, began to break apart. At first, the northern continents of North America and Eurasia broke away from Gondwana. Then Gondwana itself began to splinter, first Africa from Antarctica and South America, and then India broke away. Finally, New Zealand and then Australia began their northerly drift from Antarctica.

By the middle of the Cenozoic Era, the shapes of the modern-day continents were recognizable and in much the same positions they are in today, even though, of course, they were and are still moving. Earthquakes remind us of this movement. Africa and South America are still moving apart; so, too, are North America and Europe. Australia is moving northward, away from Antarctica, and, at the rate of a few centimeters per year, it should collide with Southeast Asia in about 50 million years. East Africa, at the same time, is on its journey away from Africa toward Iran and Asia Minor.

When you look at the paleogeographic maps, then, it is clear that the continents of today are rather ephemeral features. They do not remain constant through time. India and Asia are together today, but 150 million years ago, India neighbored Antarctica and Africa. It has made an incredible journey north across many degrees of latitude to join Asia, and during its collision with that continent threw up the mighty Himalaya Mountains. Australia, once connected directly with the great southern continent of Antarctica, is now on its voyage north to Asia. In the past few million years, as the collision between the crustal plates that bear these continents began, New Guinea has been thrown from the depths of the sea to the clouds forming the towering, snow-covered heights in the midst of the tropics. Continents that we know as solid blocks today have also had a checkered history. Asia today is actually formed of many blocks that in past times had varied associations with many other continents. So one must say that our continents of today are certainly not good reflections of the past. The magnetic properties of minerals in lavas and the past distributions of animals and plants are the clues that can help the geologist put the jigsaw pieces in the right places at the right time.

### CLIMATES OF THE PAST

Besides the actual physical arrangement of continental masses and ocean basins, there are a number of other things that can affect the distribution of animals or plants. One of these factors, of course, is climate. It can serve as a barrier that can hinder or stop movement across an area even if the way is open on other counts.

Climate today, as in the past, is controlled to a great extent by latitude, as well as local topographic relief. Because there is more energy arriving on the earth's surface from the sun at the equator than near the poles, a series of climatic bands exist. The tropical band surrounds the equator, the polar bands straddle the poles, and the temperate band lies somewhere in between. The bands shift positions depending on the time of the year, as the tilt of the earth relative to the sun changes. The positions of these bands and their widths have also changed through geologic time. Their changing positions can now be explained mainly by the moving of the continents. The changing of the widths of the climatic bands, however, has a different explanation.

Several clues are used by paleoclimatologists to estimate what climates were. Tillites, chaotic sediments left behind by melting glaciers, are clues to cold climates. The salt deposits, left behind as evaporites, and reef accumulations hint at the location of the tropical belts. The location of coal deposits hints at moist temperate conditions. The measurement of the ratio of two isotopes of oxygen to one another (oxygen 18 / oxygen 16), as preserved in fossilized organisms, gives some estimate of the actual temperatures of the past. Armed with these tools, despite the problems of an incomplete record, reasonable attempts to sketch the past climate have been made.

Not much is known about climates before 2,500 million years ago, even though sedimentary rocks older than 3,800 million years are present in Greenland and Australia, indicative of the presence then of liquid water. Between 2,500 and 2,300 million years ago, the earth's first known glaciation occurred. We know this because there are large areas covered with tillites and other glacial debris of this age in Canada (the Huronian rocks), South Africa, and perhaps in Western Australia. This ice age was followed by warm and equable (even) climates until another glaciation began about 1,000 million years ago that lasted for 400 million years, ending about 600 million years ago. Many of the tillites left by the glaciers of this ice age are known to occur in very low latitudes; that is, near the equator. (They also occurred near the poles.) All continents except Antarctica have these late Precambrian tillites, and indications are that this was the coldest period that has ever occurred on the surface of the earth.

At the beginning of the Paleozoic, climates were warming, and the glaciers had all disappeared. Even continental fragments that lay at 55 degrees latitude seemed to enjoy warm climates. By the Ordovician Period, however, climates had begun to oscillate rather dramatically, and by the end of the period another glaciation was affecting parts of the world: Africa and, more marginally, North America and Europe. The evolutionary patterns of certain animal groups were markedly affected by this glaciation, as we will see later —both by the temperature drop itself and by the lowering of sea level, and the resulting loss of near-shore marine living space on the continental shelves, as the growing glaciers tied up more and more seawater.

The cold period ended in the Silurian, and warming continued into the Devonian Period. Temperatures were high throughout the Devonian, even though there may have been small glaciers in polar areas of South America. Some evaporites (salt deposits left behind by high evaporation rates in high-temperature conditions) extend to about 40 degrees of paleolatitude, at least 5 degrees farther than they do today. Such arid conditions changed to much more humid ones in the Carboniferous, as is suggested by the massive coal deposits of this age in North America, Europe, and Asia. Such high humidity may have triggered glaciation at the end of the Paleozoic, which had widespread effects. By the end of the Carboniferous and during the first part of the Permian, glaciers affected much of Gondwana, leaving behind their tillites, striated rock pavements grooved by the passage of the mighty glaciers, and oxygen isotope ratios suggestive of low temperatures. By the end of the Paleozoic, however, for some unknown reason, glaciation stopped, and warming began once again. Life, especially near-shore marine organisms, however, had been severely affected by the drastically lowered sea levels, many of them never to recover.

The warmest climates the world has ever experienced were characteristic of parts of the Mesozoic. Between the Middle Triassic and the Late Cretaceous, the thermal maximum of all earth history since life began was reached. It was only during the latest Cretaceous that the long, somewhat intermittant cooling began that eventually climaxed in our present glacial/ interglacial setting. Large-scale temperature drops occurred in the Late Eocene and the Middle Miocene. It was during the last major drop that the bulk of Antarctic ice built up. Ice advances and retreats have characterized the past 2 million years with a cyclicity of about a hundred thousand years. The last major ice advance ended about eighteen thousand years ago, but just what the future holds is not clear. There are a number of yet controversial theories. Man's addition of massive amounts of carbon dioxide to the atmosphere in the past century as a result of industrial activity will most certainly play a role in determining what comes next in the way of climates—but just what role and how quickly the changes will occur is still the big question.

What is clear from such an overview is that today's climate, and arrangement of continents, are not typical of the past. In fact, the glacial climate in which we do live is rather atypical for most of geologic time. More often, temperatures have been higher and climatic belts not so clearly defined on a north-south traverse as today. This is why it is sometimes rather difficult for us, looking back in time, to get an accurate feeling for what the world might have been like for a trilobite, or a dinosaur.

# INDEX

# INDEX

# INDEX

[*391*]

# INDEX

# INDEX

# INDEX

# INDEX

# INDEX

# INDEX